International Political Economy Series

Series Editor
Timothy M. Shaw⬤, University of Massachusetts Boston, Boston, USA;
Emeritus Professor, University of London, London, UK

The global political economy is in flux as a series of cumulative crises impacts its organization and governance. The IPE series has tracked its development in both analysis and structure over the last three decades. It has always had a concentration on the global South. Now the South increasingly challenges the North as the centre of development, also reflected in a growing number of submissions and publications on indebted Eurozone economies in Southern Europe. An indispensable resource for scholars and researchers, the series examines a variety of capitalisms and connections by focusing on emerging economies, companies and sectors, debates and policies. It informs diverse policy communities as the established trans-Atlantic North declines and 'the rest', especially the BRICS, rise. NOW INDEXED ON SCOPUS!

More information about this series at
http://www.palgrave.com/gp/series/13996

Agnes Gagyi

The Political Economy of Middle Class Politics and the Global Crisis in Eastern Europe

The case of Hungary and Romania

Agnes Gagyi
University of Gothenburg
Gothenburg, Sweden

ISSN 2662-2483   ISSN 2662-2491   (electronic)
International Political Economy Series
ISBN 978-3-030-76942-0   ISBN 978-3-030-76943-7   (eBook)
https://doi.org/10.1007/978-3-030-76943-7

Cover credit: © Rob Friedman/iStockphoto.com

This Palgrave Macmillan imprint is published by the registered company Springer Nature Switzerland AG
The registered company address is: Gewerbestrasse 11, 6330 Cham, Switzerland

PREFACE

The middle class seems to occupy a central place in debates about recent global transformations. The global waves of mobilizations that followed the global financial crisis of 2008 have been associated with the revolt of the middle class—its downward mobility in former Western welfare democracies, and its new ambitions and frustrations in what has been increasingly referred as the new global middle classes. Images of middle class-dominated protests and their social media representations have permeated post-2008 political imaginaries, arriving to a dominant understanding of middle class indignation as a progressive force, which links anti-austerity welfare demands to the claim to renew democratic institutions emptied by neoliberalization.

This book speaks to this debate from an East European[1] angle. Here, new middle classprotests have addressed local effects of global transformations in terms of a failure of postsocialist transition promises, and have formulated various proposals for their renewal. In the history of

---

[1] To ease reading, the book follows the practice of contemporary political and public debates to refer to ex-socialist countries of the former Soviet bloc as Eastern Europe. In terms of more exact academic traditions that differentiate between different sub-regions according to various criteria, the book looks at what has been defined as East Central Europe: the ethnically diverse region that has historically been a borderland between competing Hapsburg, Russian and Ottoman powers. Where necessary, I use East Central Europe to make this reference clear.

modern East European middle class politics, this gesture fits into a long-term pattern, where disillusionment with failed promises of catching up with Western standards generates new developmental projects, formulated along new socio-political alliances. Commentators have interpreted this pattern as a historical tendency of East European middle classes to use political tools to maintain and expand their positions, in the lack of an economic base for middle class development similar to Western countries. Instead of a specificity of East European "backwardness", I propose to take this angle as a starting point for a comparative perspective on contemporary middle classprotests.

In post-2008 commentaries, the progressive nature of anti-austerity pro-democracy protests has been associated with middle class indignation over a fast polarization of wealth (the 1% vs. the 99%), which closes opportunities for middle classdevelopment. In Western contexts, this has also been described as the "crisis of democratic capitalism"—an end to postwar development's promise for capitalist growth associated with the expansion of middle class positions, and the resulting annihilation of class tensions locally and (with time) globally. In this framework, previous promises and current indignation over their failure seem to point in the same direction: a resuscitation of a more equal, more democratic growth, favorable to middle classdevelopment. However, looking at the structural conditions of Western middle class growth—held up as a model for other global regions—, instead of a harmonious picture of global development, we see an increasingly polarizing system, where the formation of Western welfare societies is based on the extraction potential of Western capital, and the multiplication of white collar jobs is tied to the monopolization and formalization of knowledge capacities in the service of managing those extraction flows. This book proposes to consider the politics of contemporary middle classprotests in terms of how these contradictions, ingrained in middle class ambitions and associated developmental ideologies, relate to current transformations of structural conditions in different global positions.

In order to place East European cases within that context, in Chapter 1 I propose a framework based on a world-systems approach, which considers social movements as part of local dynamics of global integration. In Chapter 2, I describe East European middle class politics within that framework, as a specific driver of semi-peripheral developmentalist illusions. Comparing the cases of Hungary and Romania, in Chapter 3 I follow how this factor played out throughout respective transformations of successive regimes and their countermovements after 1973, the crisis that marked the decline of the postwar global accumulation cycle. Arriving to post-2008 demonstrations, I point out how expressions of middle class frustrations link into local constellations of new developmental alliances, conditioned by different patterns of late socialist and postsocialist development. This analysis provides a better contextual grasp on how protest movements that have been widely greeted as East European equivalents of Western anti-austerity pro-democracy protests actually connect to the process of postsocialist integration into a hierarchical global system. But its conclusion regarding the progressive potential of these movements is not encouraging. To discuss that potential, the last chapter turns towards new left segments of post-2008 mobilizations.

Whether the new wave of middle class politicization can serve as a base for a renewal of left politics that can challenge the logic of capitalist polarization, and set off the global transformation necessary for a just climate transition, has been intensely debated in post-2008 new left politics internationally. The Hungarian and Romanian new left initiatives I discuss provide an example where left political orientations are reborn on an educated middle class basis, after a long period of repression of left stances in postsocialist contexts. In Chapter 4, I show how middle class activists' own perspectives as well as specificities of local integration constellations are reflected in new left programs, and how activists' work increasingly binds these programs into concrete forms of organization and external alliances. The conclusions I draw do not provide a general solution to the conundrum of middle class emancipative politics. Instead, they serve to emphasize certain contradictions, and then contribute to an empirical orientation among their consequences.

I wrote this book as part of a longer quest for answers which, in my case, started as an East European participant of the alterglobalist movement in the 2000's. Perplexed by the contradictions between local and international forms of alterglobalism, I went on to do a Ph.D. on the local forms and international context of Hungarian and Romanian alterglobalism, both of which I also participated in. In the decade following my defense in 2009, I worked in various activist and research collaborations within the region, participating in what this book describes as the formation of an increasingly interconnected field of new left thought. The collective work within the Working Group for Public Sociology "Helyzet" in Budapest, which aimed to understand Hungarian developments in terms of the country's long-term systemic integration, was particularly formative for my orientation.

In 2015–2016, due to a research fellowship at the New Europe College in Bucharest, I had the opportunity to conduct a research which expanded and changed the understanding of Hungarian and Romanian new leftactivism which I had as a participant. This understanding has been completed by an empirical follow-up of later developments until 2019, as well as by continued debates with activist and researcher friends—many of whom are quoted in this book. In thinking through the issues that this book addresses as common problems of post-2008 left thought, I was also inspired by international discussions with academic colleagues and activist peers, which opened new comparative dimensions, but also strengthened my sense of a need for a greater capacity to translate between East European and global cases of new mobilizations. Conversations facilitated by *LeftEast*, debates within social movement research networks, especially around the journal *Interface*, the long-term discussion on European integration within the Critical Political Economy Research Network, and the global inter-movement debates within the framework of the Transnational Institutes's New Politics program were especially instructive in this regard.

This book is born from these debates as much as it is from individual research. Even if, according to the rhetoric of academic research, it speaks of post-2008 mobilizations and their new left segments as its object of analysis, it is itself a product of the collective effort of self-reflection that these discussions are engaging in. Instead of speaking "of" this effort, this book speaks to it, offering its analysis as a contribution to a collective process of political orientation.

I thank the New Europe College and the Visegrad Fellowship of the Open Society Archives for their support for essential segments of the research process, as well as the Kertész Imre Kolleg for its writing fellowship, without which the book would have never taken shape. I am equally grateful to the editors of the Palgrave International Political Economy series and to the manuscript's reviewers for their support and thoughtful comments.

Tallinn, Estonia   Agnes Gagyi
February 2021

CONTENTS

Social Movements in Eastern Europe: Problems of Understanding Non-Western Contexts

Social movements are a specific social phenomenon to understand. Since they organize with the intention to change existing social structures, their understanding necessarily engages with those intentions. For example, it is usually part of movement politics to question the basic concepts through which their social environment is described. How activists and researchers negotiate such intentions in describing movements is part of the broader struggle over social transformation that movements act within. The phase of global mobilizations that started after 2008 constitutes an increasingly intensive example to such struggles, where movements' claims over social rights, direct democracy, racial justice, climate politics, or various new conservative frameworks deeply influence the ways the present crisis is understood and politicized.

Trying to make sense of movements in non-Western contexts brings in another layer of the same problematic. In the modern history of our world, Western domination through economic, colonial, geopolitical, and military means has been matched by a hierarchical knowledge infrastructure where dominant forms of knowledge are defined by universal models distilled from Western experience, and information about non-Western contexts that is relevant for Western debates. Within social science, the division between sociology, a discipline aimed at Western industrialized societies, and anthropology, developed to understand "primitive" societies, is one classic example (e.g. Stremlin, 2001). If we look at notions

A. Gagyi, *The Political Economy of Middle Class Politics and the Global Crisis in Eastern Europe*, International Political Economy Series, https://doi.org/10.1007/978-3-030-76943-7_1

that are currently used as universal descriptions of key functions of modern societies—like the state, democracy, or the middle class—we find that these are defined according to Western models of historical experience, and then universalized across other global regions. This kind of universalization of Western models poses a knowledge problem both for understanding non-Western contexts, and for contextualizing Western developments within their global connections. As Marxist, black, decolonial, and feminist authors (e.g. Fanon, 1967; Gramsci, 2000; Hennessy, 1993; Mignolo, 2002) have long emphasized, hierarchical knowledge structures, and the hardships they pose for people in dominated positions to recognize and express their own experience, are key issues in any social struggle. This chapter deals with how these problems appear in the understanding of social movements in non-Western contexts like Eastern Europe. To transcend such limitations in the understanding of social movements of the present crisis, the chapter proposes a framework that addresses movements as integral part of global processes.

A TIME–SPACE BIAS IN DOMINANT UNDERSTANDINGS OF SOCIAL MOVEMENTS

Social movements were constitutive in the formation of modern societies, and the topic of social movements has been present in the development of modern social thought since its beginnings—from authors of the French Revolution to Thomas Paine, Tocqueville, Marx, Weber or Durkheim. This tradition of thinking about movements engaged with the political aspect of movement knowledge in a direct way, putting authors' claims next to those of movements. Even in later moments in the development of academic social research, many researchers dealt with movements as inherent aspects of broad questions of social transformation. We can think of E. P. Thompson's (1963) take on the formation of the English working class, Barrington Moore's (1966) or Charles Tilly's (1978) treatment of social conflicts as a main element of modernization, to the understanding of non-industrial societies in terms of their relations with the pressures of global modernization (Wolf, 1982), the study of grassroots movements' role in urbanization (Castells, 1989), or historical sociologies of labor struggle in Transatlantic colonial expansion (Linebaugh & Rediker, 2013).

Social movement studies as a more narrow sub-discipline developed as a relatively late branch in the history of modern Western social sciences, as part of an institutional boom of social science after 1945, particularly in US universities. In this context, the first wave of research that dealt with movements regarded social mobilizations from the perspective of behaviorism, from an interest point of an anti-fascist and anti-communist US political discourse. This line of research looked at movements as the collective behavior of "mass society", where people lose their individual rational sense through a hypnotic effect of the crowd (e.g. Smelser, 1962). By the end of the 1960s, this approach was challenged by a new wave of young academics who were involved in, or sympathetic to the 1968 movement wave. This new cohort of researchers reconceptualized movements as a legitimate element of the hegemonic (Western liberal democratic) ideal of modern society. Here, movements were understood as a rational form of interest advocacy within democratic politics, worthy of systematic study (Goodwin et al., 2001).

As Cox and Fominaya (2013) underline, the way social movement studies built up its own tools since the late 1960s has been codified in a story of origin, which is ritually repeated in social movement studies texts as a way of solidifying and presenting the sub-discipline as an autonomous territory of research. In the narrative of this story, social movement studies as a systematic field of social scientific study is born with the abolition of psychology-based theories of collective behavior, and the recognition of movements as structural, rational, and organizational elements of democratic politics. From there, the first main step of disciplinary evolution is constituted by the theory of resource mobilization (McCarthy & Zald, 1977). This theory held that despite movements often present their claims as directly following from some grievance, in fact the same type of grievances do not necessarily cause the same types of movements—or any mobilization at all—in various cases. Therefore, movements are not to be explained by grievances, but through an investigation of how they are able to construct themselves. More specifically, this approach looked at the kinds of internal and external resources people used when building and sustaining a movement.

In the origin story of social movement studies, this step is followed by further additions to resource mobilization theory. Such were the ideas of opportunity structure and political process, both looking at how a movement is made possible and how it can maneuver within broader constellations of political structures (Eisinger, 1973; McAdam et al., 1996). Further on, the area of cultural and symbolic resources was added to the picture. Building on Erving Goffmann's (1974) ideas on how experience is organized through symbolic frameworks through which we understand situations and activities, David Snow and his colleagues worked out conceptual tools to understand how movements build their own descriptions of social situations, how they formulate their claims, and how they communicate with external actors (Snow et al., 1986). For instance, the concept of frame alignment referred to the process of creating a common understanding of a situation with which all participants of a movement could identify with. Frame bridging referred to a type of frame alignment where movements reach out to external allies— e.g. by claiming that the issue of the civil rights movement is an issue of democracy. This type of attention to the symbolic level of movement building pointed out that movements' own symbolic frameworks, their identity and culture are resources created by the movements themselves.

This new field of social movement studies, which saw movements not as resulting from structural conditions, but as types of social organization that build themselves through the use of external and internal resources, and by creating their own identity and culture, came later to be synthesized in the theory of "dynamics of contention" (McAdam et al., 2001). Here, movements are understood as various versions of the same phenomenon—contention—and the main research question regarding this phenomenon refers to the dynamics through which instances of contention are built. Dynamics here is used as a concept summarizing all aspects of movement building pointed out by previous theories—from resource mobilization to opportunity structures, political process, and movement framing.

To this US-centered narrative, the origin story of social movement research typically adds the idea of "new social movements", developed in European scholarship around the same time. Cox and Fominaya (2013) emphasize that unlike US social movement studies, the European formation of social movement research preserved a stronger and more direct relationship to movements. Still, what became canonized later as the European paradigm of "new social movements" carried important similarities to US social movement research. Like in the United States, the 1968 movement wave brought a number of engaged or sympathetic academics into European social movement research. Here researchers such as Frank Parkin (1968), Alain Touraine (1981), or Ernesto Laclau and Chantal Mouffe (1985) formulated an understanding of their contemporary social movements as different from "old" (labor) movements that were organized around direct material claims. Contrary to the latter, new social movements were understood as based on immaterial cultural and identity values. In assessing that difference, the theory of new social movements relied on social theories which claimed that social development arrived to a new phase of an affluent industrialized society, where material struggles are no more relevant—a phase that Ronald Inglehart summarized under the concept of postmaterialism (1971).

According to the theory of new social movements, in the context of postmaterialist society, new movements are not concerned with expressing direct material interests of their constituents, but rather engage with issues of identity—like in the case of the women's movement, the civil rights movement, or the LGBTQ movement—or with issues of universal values that do not regard movements' constituencies directly—like in the case of environmental, anti-nuclear or anti-war movements. Not surprisingly, new social movement theories put a high emphasis on the self-constitutive nature of movements. Beyond the more practical approach of US theories of movement building, these theories also built on contemporary European theories of social organization. These theories, like the idea of communicative democratic organization in Jürgen Habermas, or the idea of discourse and discursive power in Michel Foucault, defined symbolic processes as key aspects of social organization. New social movements were seen as engaging within these main aspects of postmaterial societies. In left segments of new social movement theorizing, this trend was reinforced by the insight that the classic social democratic alliance between left parties and workers' unions cannot function any more as a foundation for left politics, and identity-based issues—women's rights, green movements, migrants' or youth movements—need to be focused on together with the symbolic problems of bringing them under the same political roof. While social movement theorizing in left segments of the 1968 movement (and their academic afterlife) was explicitly concerned with the issue of capitalism, and was born from within, or in dialogue with social movements (e.g. Negri, 1989; Tronti et al., 1977), in the solidification of the new social movements paradigm this trend was lost, or relegated to other disciplines like philosophy, history, or industrial relations.

To conclude, the main theoretical frameworks of European and US social movement research put the emphasis on the mechanisms of movements' internal constitution, and its short-term cultural and political context. This was based on the insight that economic deprivation or class position alone does not cause movements, completed by the idea that material relations are not a decisive factor of social struggles any more. This standpoint allowed scholars to single out movements as social phenomena that stand on their own, and look at their development in terms of how they constitute themselves and their relations with the outside world. In the development of social movement studies as a discipline, this meant that movements could be defined as a specific field of study, and specific methodological tools could be developed to address the dynamics of movement constitution in various contexts. In McAdam et al. canonic synthesis (2001), the study of these dynamics was defined as the main object of social movement or contention research. For this delimitation of a distinct sub-discipline with a distinct topic, the study of social movements paid the price that historical, structural relations between movements and the larger process of social development were pushed to the background.

One consequence of this move was that historical-structural biases that transpired into social movement research from their historical contexts were left unreflected within the conceptual frameworks and tools the discipline offered for the analysis of movements. In both US and West European contexts, the separation of the systematic study of social movements from long-term historical and economic contexts happened in the era of postwar affluence. This allowed for a so far unseen growth of North American and European middle classes—the structural position that became the basis for the "postmaterialist" movements addressed by US and European social movement scholarship. This context of affluence, and the relative lack of material focus in what came to be canonized as the paradigmatic postwar social movements, can hardly be generalized throughout space or time.

Besides material affluence, other elements of Western postwar welfare democracies also made their way into social movement research as universalized presuppositions about the conditions of movement building. Such was the presupposition that movements operate in the context of democratic political competition, where they can freely gather resources and represent their claims in public space. As Cox and Nilsen (2014) note, this limited and static view of social movements as one institutional level of an otherwise fixed system of political democracy was tied to a US perspective that did not experience revolutions and regime changes within the lifetime of postwar theoreticians. Arguably, this perspective hardly applies to Eastern Europe, Latin America, or the freshly decolonialized states of the Global South during the same decades. Presuppositions regarding movements' relations to the state also implied a relative lack of violent repression and secret police—unlike the contexts of many postwar movements in state socialist, Latin American, or Third World countries, or of the radical wing of the black movement in the United States. A similar element involved the state's capacity for redistribution that could count as a relevant target and potential resource for movements. As Charles Tilly noted in his debate paper *Social movements here and elsewhere, now and then* (1999), resource mobilization theory's definition of social movements is so tightly linked to the context of postwar Western democratic polity and high-capacity redistributive state, that by this definition one would need to say that there are no social movements in post-Soviet Kazakhstan, despite the variety of ongoing social struggles. To Tilly, this proves not the lack of movements in Kazakhstan, but the deficiency of resource mobilization theory and the implicit theories of democratization, democratic politics, and state structure incorporated in it.

Most of the silent presuppositions that social movement studies inherited from their postwar Western contexts were made obsolete by the decades of neoliberalization following the 1970s, and crumbled with the crisis of 2008, even in Western contexts. The wave of new movements that rose after 2008 voiced explicit material requests in Western countries, too, and criticized welfare structures and democratic politics as insufficient, empty, and hypocritical. This new wave of movements significantly transformed both the structures in which knowledge about social movements is produced, and the contents of that knowledge.

The Return of the Question of Global Political Economy After 2008

In the academic infrastructure of social movement studies, the new movement cycle brought a change comparable to that of the 1968 wave. Throughout the last decade, social movement research has been expanding manifestly, under the influx of a new generation of scholars engaged and sympathetic to new movements. This effect was reinforced by the fact that in the aftermath of the 2008 crisis, there has been an increasing overlap between the social situation of protesters threatened by precarization and (especially young) academic researchers threatened by the neoliberalization of universities and lack of future career options (Roth, 2019). Similar to earlier moments when academic and movement interests overlapped, we see a wave of mutual engagement between movement formation and movement research. New initiatives against academic precarity and higher education austerity reforms become part of the broader movement spectrum. Academic forums of social movement research opened themselves toward activists as discussion partners, and a new wave of engaged research in topics discussed by movements became part of academic agendas (Cox & Fominaya, 2009). The new movement context has had a transformative effect on the core paradigms of social movement research, too. Most significantly, it put the issue of economic claims in the focus of social movement studies, bringing with it a whole series of theoretical problems regarding how to understand relations between movements and the political economy of their social contexts.

Since the field of social movement research was earlier constituted through the delimitation of movements from material issues, the new shift of attention to material claims led to a practical explosion of the field's earlier coherence. Instead of a coherent readjustment of existing scientific frameworks, social movement studies' opening toward political economy happened through a wave of uncoordinated experimentation with conceptual tools taken from social scientific traditions outside of social movement studies. Probably the most emphatic trend among these experimentations has been the "bringing back" of the issue of capitalism to social movement studies (Della Porta, 2015; Hetland & Goodwin, 2013). From a situation where social movement theories tended to underemphasize economic conditions despite existing work that dealt with those issues (e.g. Barker & Kennedy, 1996; Crossley, 2003; Sklair, 1997), this trend performed a significant paradigmatic shift, throwing into the center of social movement debates a plethora of disciplinary intersections with neo-Keynesian analysis (Streeck, 2014), world-systems analysis (Silver & Karatasli, 2015), or Marxism (Barker, 2013; Cox & Nilsen, 2014).

Another direction of questions that resulted from the new focus movements' broader contexts was one that looked at the relationship between democracy and capitalism, reacting to new burning questions raised in public and political debates—like the non-democratic nature of austerity reforms, or the rise of the new right. This trend brought about a further erosion of earlier social movement research frameworks. Instead of focusing on dynamics of movement building, discussions over the new movement wave started to look at social movements as elements of broader social dynamics again—along questions like the transformation

of Western democracies under the impact of crisis, new movements' relation to new populisms (Della Porta, 2013; Stavrakakis & Katsambekis,
2013), or movements as possible agents of re-democratization (Della
Porta, 2014, 2020).

A third, related question that came to attention was how movements
in different points of the globe relate to each other—or, in other terms:
how we can grasp the connection between local movements and a global
financial crisis. Here, earlier concepts of movement waves (Cox & Nilsen,
2014; Della Porta & Mattoni, 2014; Shihade et al., 2012), movement
cycles (Tejerina et al., 2013), continuities between different movements
(Castañeda, 2012; Juris, 2012; Polletta, 2012), or the idea of diffusion of movement repertoires from one movement to another (Della
Porta & Tarrow, 2012) have been employed—but they were also questioned, with reevaluations of what a wave, cycle or "family of movements"
(Ancelovici et al., 2016) may mean in the case of movements arising from
different social environments across the globe. The Varieties of Capitalism framework has been used to make sense of local conditions of
movements in terms of variations in the institutional forms of capitalist
economies and their regulation (Beissinger & Sasse, 2014; Biekart &
Fowler, 2013; Bohle & Greskovits, 2012). Due to the renewed interest
in structural connections among different movement locations, contributions of research traditions that conceive of movements as integrated
elements of the development of global capitalism as a whole, like that of
world-systems analysis (eg. Arrighi et al., 1989; Silver, 2003) have also
been gaining attention within these debates (eg. Silver & Karatasli, 2015;
Smith & Wiest, 2012).

Opening toward questions of economy and social structure did
not only bring new perspectives to previous social movement research
paradigms, but also their direct critique. For example, the lack of attention
to the effect of the capitalist economy on movements has been thematized
as a stringing deficit of earlier social movement research (e.g. Hetland &
Goodwin, 2013). In such critiques, contrary to the conventional story
of social movement studies finally reaching objective scientific standards
as a discipline, founding paradigms came to be opened up for inquiry
through a historical analysis of their interactions with broader processes.
As Hayes (2014) or MacSheoin (2016) put it, social movement theoriza-
tion itself came to be understood in its interaction with global structural
change. Social movement researchers increasingly started to see own discipline as embedded within the same context of historical change in which

movements operate (Cox & Fominaya, 2009). For example, Cox and Fominaya (2013) demonstrated that the US focus in social movement studies' origin story hides the continuity of movement studies with critical social theory in the European context, where social movements were more often conceptualized together with general theorizing on politics, the state, or modern society. Cox and Nilsen (2014) analyzed the birth of research mobilization and new social movement paradigms within the context of political-ideological transformation of Western critical thought after Prague 1968, leading to an avoidance of Marxist paradigms. Poulson et al. (2014), Gagyi (2015), and MacSheoin (2016) pointed at biases of social movement research resulting from specifically Western approaches.

The new rapprochement between Western movements and academic research, together with the new focus on social movement studies' own embeddedness in the same contexts that movements operate in, increasingly opened up social movement research to movements' own perspectives. Building on previous work around movements' own knowledge-making, Cox (2017, 2018) argued that the new meanings and solutions produced by social movements are not only there to be analyzed by research, but should be considered as partners for a social dialogue on our common future. The journal *Interface*, founded in 2009 to facilitate movement-research dialogue, dedicated special issues to dialogues with postsocialist and post-colonial movement perspectives (Cox et al., 2017; Navrátil et al., 2015). If the opening toward questions of broader social processes brought an influx of other social scientific perspectives into social movement research, opening toward movements' own knowledge-making made various branches of movements' political thought more visible in academic debates, questioning and transcending previous biases of mainstream social movement research.

For instance, in their introduction to the *Interface* issue *Social movement thinking beyond the core*, Cox et al. (2017) do a sweeping overview of Asian, African, and Latin American movement perspectives after 1945—from the first wave of Third Worldism following the 1955 Bandung Conference to local subaltern groups' struggles against local developmentalist regimes, the IMF riots of the 1980s and 1990s against neoliberal structural adjustment programs, and new movements toward alternative people's economies (like the Landless Workers' Movement in Brazil or the Via Campesina global peasant movement's struggle for food sovereignty), or the World Social Forums that brought the criticism of neoliberal capitalism and the idea of new reproductive economies together

into a global movement in the 2000s. Cox, Nilsen, and Pleyers emphasize the great potential of non-core movement perspectives in informing,
orienting, and even changing, contemporary Western struggles, along the
principle of global dialogue that has been central to the alterglobalization
movement (e.g. Sousa de Santos, 2007), and has been voiced by the same
authors for years (e.g. Cox & Nilsen, 2007, 2014).

THE "CRISIS OF DEMOCRATIC CAPITALISM" NARRATIVE

Despite promising instances of opening toward perspectives outside the
narrower tradition of Western social movement research, the way perspectives from other disciplines or movements appear in new analyses remains
fragmented—reflecting the fact that their introduction into social movement research happened not through a revolution in how movements
are theorized, but rather by the empirical push of economic claims being
raised, once again, by mass movements in the West. The new wave of
experimentations with traditions of social research outside of social movement studies produced parallel uses of various perspectives, adding up to
a state where the research field that produces knowledge on movements is
incapable of reflecting on itself in a coherent way. One consequence of this
situation has been that topics and questions relevant to Western contexts
can still dominate new approaches despite the crisis of earlier social movement research paradigms. In the treatment of post-2008 movements, a
main effect has been a subordination of narratives on the global crisis
and its protest movements to the Western story of the failure of welfare
democracies. In this book, I will use Wolfgang Streeck's (2014) influential
formulation, the "crisis of democratic capitalism" to refer to this narrative,
which by now became dominant in Western interpretations of the crisis.

The narrative of the "crisis of democratic capitalism" implies that
classic democratic institutions and welfare systems of postwar capitalism
have been eroded by neoliberal reforms since the 1970s, and practically emptied by the new austerity wave of crisis management after
2008. The post-2008 movement wave is explained as a reaction to this
process, where instead of earlier institutions of representative democracy,
protesters seek alternative movement channels to express their claims to
reestablish democratic politics and social welfare. In social movement
research, this diagnosis of post-2008 movements was summarized in the
notion of anti-austerity pro-democracy movements (for a summary see
Fominaya, 2017).

The idea of the "crisis of democratic capitalism" is rooted in the presuppositions of dominant postwar Western ideas of modernization and democracy. Here (e.g. Rostow, 1960), modern history was imagined as a linear trend of development, with Western countries at its avantguard, and other global regions following behind (with something that is often imagined as a time lag, or "backwardness"). The development of capitalist economy and democracy was conceived as an interconnected, mutually reinforcing project—exemplified by the Western model of development from bourgeois revolutions to postwar welfare democracies that provide material welfare and democratic participation for virtually all citizens. The narrative of the "crisis of democratic capitalism" builds on these presuppositions, but marks the experience of Western crisis as an unfortunate turn of the same story.

With this turn, "democratic capitalism" becomes eroded by the neoliberal turn of the Thatcher-Reagan era after the crisis of the 1970s, which rolls back the welfare functions of democratic capitalism, and alienates popular constituencies from mainstream (conservative and social democratic) parties. When post-2008 crisis management applies a new wave of austerity to help banks instead of citizens, this erosion of democratic capitalism becomes fully exposed. This development creates a "post-political" situation in Western democracies where, instead of being channeled through existing structures of political representation, social tensions are expressed either through spontaneous mobilizations, or in a new wave of populist politics (Chomsky, 2017; Mouffe, 2014; Stavrakakis & Katsembekis, 2013).

Within this narrative of the "crisis of democratic capitalism", the stake of new movements is often seen in their potential to save or recreate democracy (Della Porta, 2013; Fraser, 2014; Glasius & Pleyers, 2013). Along this line, movements' horizontal organization (exemplified by the Occupy movement), and the new political initiatives that grew out of the post-2008 movement wave (from municipalism to new party politics initiated by movements) have been understood as potential new avenues for re-democratization (Fominaya & Hayes, 2019; Gerbaudo, 2017). These hopes have been contrasted to the perceived threat of right-wing populism, which in the 2010s grew into a significant political trend in former Western welfare democracies too.

The narrative of the "crisis of democratic capitalism" can hardly be reconciled with the experience of other global regions. Globally, the structures of "democratic capitalism" that characterized postwar Western welfare states represent not a universal trend of development, but a conjuncture period of Western core economies within the postwar global cycle of capitalism. This conjuncture was made possible by core capital's high profitability during the boom phase of the postwar global economic cycle, conditioned by US hegemony over European and Japanese industrial development, and the subordination of Third World development to what US State Secretary John Foster Dulles called "the industrialized nature of the Atlantic Community and its dependence upon broad markets and access to raw materials" (McCormick, 1995: 120). In contrast to ideological formulations of the promise of endless growth, like all boom phases of capitalist cycles, the postwar era of core capital's expansion conditioned the bust phase of the same cycle. The narrative of the "crisis of democratic capitalism" acknowledges the end of this phase of Western development, but it maintains this relatively short and globally exceptional experience of postwar Western democracies as the conceptional base from which current developments and potential futures can be imagined.

"Civil Society" and "Democratic Capitalism": Two Dominant Concepts in Understanding East European Movements

While social movement research that works with the tools of Western social movement studies paradigms has also been developing in postsocialist Eastern Europe (Diani & Cisař, 2014), the main frameworks that defined local and international understandings of social movements in the region have been those of civil society and the narrative of "democratic capitalism". Both concepts and their implications are deeply embedded in frameworks of catch-up development that dominated postsocialist projects of global integration. The dynamics of hope and disillusionment that surround these notions bear similarities with the way social movement research's ideas on "postmaterialism" gave space to the narrative of the crisis of "democratic capitalism" in the case of Western movements. However, the historical context of postsocialist catch-up projects also implies several important differences.

"Civil Society" and the "Rectifying Revolution"

While the concept of civil society has a longer history in political thought, its usage linked to East European transition debates crystallized in the late years of socialism, in a dialogue between socialist and Western intellectuals and activists. Bridging between Eastern and Western activists' respective criticisms of state socialist and Western capitalist regimes, civil society was imagined as an autonomous sphere of self-organization outside of the spheres of politics (state) and economy (free market), and defined mostly in relation to moral values (such as truth or human rights). This notion of civil society made a spectacular global career between the 1980s and 2000s, its applications being broadened to social movements and civil society activities in other continents, and particularly the boom of NGOs established as part of structural adjustment programs in the Global South (Gagyi & Ivancheva, 2017; Kaldor, 2003).

In Eastern Europe, the formation of the concept of civil society was linked to a gradual turn in the politics of internal intellectual criticisms of socialist regimes. Instead of reformist or radical critiques coming from left positions, in the period of late socialism critical intellectuals turned toward liberal social theories and an opposition to socialist regimes based on individual rights. Intellectuals like György Konrád (1989), Vaclav Havel (1986), Vaclav Benda (1991) or Adam Michnik (1986) emphasized the importance of individual freedom vis-a-vis the power of the party state through notions such as antipolitics, living in truth, parallel polis, or new evolutionism. Since limitations to freedom were seen as imposed by state power, the market appeared as beneficial to the flourishing of civil society, rather than a potential threat.

Cold War communication structures made these ideas highly visible in Western debates. Connections between new Western and Eastern movements also contributed to the development and dispersion of civil society ideas beyond Eastern Europe (Keane, 1988). Nuclear disarmament, human rights, or environmental protection were issues around which East–West networks of activists strove to develop transnational networks across Cold War divisions. This dialogue helped the generalization of the idea of civil society as that of democratic, autonomous self-organization against bureaucratic power (Bakuniak & Nowak, 1987; Bugajski, 1987; Cohen & Arato, 1992). By the end of the 1980s, civil society was established as a concept of social self-organization that bound liberal critiques of socialist regimes together with Western new social movements' anti-bureaucratic, grassroots values (Ivancheva, 2011). Beyond Eastern dissidents' works published in the West, the concept came to life as a universal notion of political thought in Western debates (e.g. Cohen & Arato, 1992, Murthy, 1999, Outhwaite & Ray, 2005).

This generalization of the idea of civil society happened within the context of a mounting global accumulation crisis, where core capital's efforts to maintain profitability by penetrating non-core regions' developmentalist regimes went hand-in-hand with a global wave of political democratization. Although it was supported by the internal legitimacy crisis of developmentalist regimes, this process of democratization was strongly contained by new forms of dependency, created through external debt and lender organizations' conditions for structural adjustment. As some critiques claimed, political democratization was even instrumental to creating those forms of dependency, as it took down the barriers developmentalist regimes could maintain in the face of external capital (Amin, 1991; Walton & Seddon, 1994). Within these conditions, as a political idea of the era, civil society could sustain moral ideas of democratic self-organizing while disconnecting them from actual political or economic forms of social control. In a context where dominant narratives celebrated the world-historical victory of "democracy" in the Cold War, the fact that the idea of civil society was rooted in East European dissident critiques against socialism served as a legitimacy base for this notion in face of the problematic relations of global democratization processes.

As many have argued (e.g. Axford, 1998; Petras & Veltmeyer, 1997), the global wave of NGO-ization that happened as part of structural adjustment programs, and put the idea of civil society into institutionalized practice, did not necessarily build strength on the side of social self-organization. Rather, it served as an outsourcing of social functions abandoned by neoliberalizing states, and in many cases, it was directly instrumental to building and maintaining neoliberal hegemony (for East European cases, see Mikuš, 2018; Vetta, 2018). However, the same idea soon came to be used also by movements struggling against the effects of global neoliberalization. The idea of global civil society became a territory where the idea of civil society linked to the promotion of NGO-ization became entangled with new claims for creating transnational civic alliances to counteract the effects of global market liberalization (e.g. Anheier et al., 2005). The alterglobalization movement itself followed this way of conceptualizing global social struggle. While its economic politics went against marketization and austerity, this movement internalized mainstream ideas of globalization as a networked, fluid, global form of social organization that bypasses the organizational capacity of states, and formulated its project within this framework, as a global horizontal network of grassroots organizing. However, by the end of the decade, expectations regarding the effectivity of this type of organizing were exhausted, as the movement met the limitations of existing power structures.

In Eastern Europe, the notion of civil society played a specific role in the way the project of postsocialist transition was conceived. If internationally, the end of socialism was celebrated in terms of a Cold War victory that brought about the unilateral dominance of the Western model of democracy and free market (Fukuyama, 1989), for Eastern Europe, the legitimacy of the democratic transition could not be conceived as a mere result of Western victory. It also had to come from local societies' will and capacity for democratization as the local base of the transition. This internal impetus for democratic transition was largely defined through the idea of civil society. Pre-1989 dissidents' claims for civil society organizing were interpreted as expressions of the internal democratic capacity of local societies. Political mobilizations of various ideologies and fates that surrounded the process of the regime change, from Polish Solidarity or the Hungarian Danube movement to the Romanian Revolution in December 1989, were interpreted as instances where local civil society stepped up against socialist dictatorships in the name of democracy (Della Porta, 2014; Kaldor, 2003). A proliferation of civil society organizing, expected to happen as a natural consequence once society's democratic capacity is not repressed by the party state any more, was supposed to provide the final proof and full development of the internal democratic capacity of local societies.

In the process of the regime change, such depictions of civil society as an internal democratizing force came to be tied to a normative conception of regime change as Western-oriented development. Not independently from the real hierarchies of the transition process, East European transitions came to be understood as the region's return to the progressive path of social development pioneered by Western states—an idea illustratively summarized by Jürgen Habermas' (1990) term "rectifying revolution". In perceptions of the region's role in world history, previous Cold War ideas of competing modernities, as well as late socialist dissident ideas of "third way" development, were substituted by development concepts based on the unquestioned superiority of Western models. In this framework, local forms of social organization came to be assessed and evaluated according to their achievements in approaching those models (Melegh, 2006). Within this context, civil society understood as local societies' inner democratic capacity came to be seen as a key measure of the degree to which local societies were capable to catch up with Western models and become a "real" democracy.

In terms of structures of democratic organization, this ideological use of the idea of civil society was underpinned by two main factors. First, the dissident formulation of the civil society idea happened in an environment where dissidents' outreach to larger social segments, and the possibilities to organize broader forms of democratic decision-making where movement ideologues could be effectively controlled by participants, was extremely limited. Not surprisingly, instead of organizational conditions of democracy, dissident ideas of civic self-organization rather emphasized moral and intellectual aspects (Eyal, 2000). After the regime change, when previous dissidents entered political and academic positions, and stepped up as mediators of the transition process, their leadership relied on electoral politics and intellectual-moral legitimacy; it did not involve widespread democratic links with existing forms of civic organization (Lomax, 1997). The lack of structures through which other social groups could be involved in the formation of the civil society idea, and influence it based on their own experience and needs, was one main condition that helped maintain the abstract ideological character of the concept. The main exception from this was the Polish Solidarity movement, which had a large organizational base in the 1980s, and its leaders only separated themselves from worker constituencies after the regime change, when they came to support neoliberal reforms (Ost, 2006). Another main organizational factor in the implementation of the civil society idea was the financial and legal support given to establishing formal NGOs along the normative civil society idea. Like in other global regions in the same period, this kind of support contributed to a growth in the number of NGOs. However, in contrast to the dissident idea of civil society conceived in universal terms, the new sphere of NGOs was limited to organizations with highly qualified personnel, often with intellectual and previous activist backgrounds (Mikuš, 2018; Wedel, 2001).

These contradictions between the universal concept of civil society and the limitations of its actual organizational conditions constituted a lasting problematic in transition debates. In a context where democratization went hand in hand with new forms of external economic dependence, neoliberal reforms, and a devastating transformational crisis, interpreting local reality in terms of a Western-centered development framework implied a Sisyphean struggle with the contradictions of catching-up efforts. Throughout the next decades, together with other aims of the catching-up project, expectations tied to the development of civil society came to be refuted. Yet still, expressions of tensions between expectations and disillusionment were long contained within the hegemony of the catching-up model. Within those pressing contradictions, the idea of civil society survived as a main neuralgical point of postsocialist debates long after the transition (Gagyi & Ivancheva, 2017).

Noticing that the introduction of parliamentary democracy was not paralleled by an upswing of civil society activity in the 1990s, earlier proponents of civil society started to express a growing disillusionment. Some explained local societies' political passivity as a burdensome legacy of socialism (Felkai, 1997; Tismǎneanu, 1999). This idea later came to be canonized as the thesis of civil society "weakness" in postsocialist countries (Howard, 2003). Others pointed out that the project of civil society never belonged to large masses of East European societies, and didn't play an important role in actual mass movements of the transformation. Instead, its local base was typically constituted by a small number of intellectual dissidents whose outreach and impact was overrepresented by Western attention (Judt, 1988; Körösényi, 2000; Lomax, 1997; Tamás, 1994, cf: Bottoni, 2017; Gagyi & Ivancheva, 2017; Kotkin, 2009).

While empirical evidence that contradicted pre-1989 ideals of civil society became part of mainstream knowledge, the disillusionment with normative expectations did not necessarily instigate a reconsideration of the idea itself. While empirical research addressed problems like the tension between democratization and economic austerity (Ekiert & Kubik, 1998; Przeworski, 1991), low political participation (McMahon, 2001; Howard, 2003; Petrova & Tarrow, 2007), or the dependence of postsocialist NGOs from external financial support (Císař, 2010), in most cases such contradictions of postsocialist development continued to be interpreted within the overarching framework of a "rectifying revolution". Problems of postsocialist transition were still dominantly seen as minor errors within a grand process through which East European societies reconnect and catch up with Western models of development after socialism's blind alley. Divergences from this normative linearity of transition were interpreted in terms of particular local insufficiencies. Accumulating empirical evidence for such divergences came to be systematized in typologies of local developmental characteristics.

As we know by now, the decades following 1989 have not brought about a significant upward mobility of the region within world-economic hierarchies (Morys, 2020). Instead, local regimes went through various waves of catch-up efforts and their busts, similar to most other semi-peripheral areas (Böröcz, 2012). Short-term typologies that analyzed versions of postsocialist development in terms of local successes and insufficiencies of the grand project of catching up with the West interpreted these waves by projecting theoretical models from momentary snapshots of a developmentalist competition. These analyses were then often obliged to reconsider their typologies as soon as local catch-up efforts reached a new phase. Hungary, for instance, upheld as the model example of liberal development in the 1990s, turned out to be a pioneer of illiberalism after 2010. Not long after Beissinger and Sasse (2014) concluded that unlike in other countries, in Ukraine the exhaustion of patience regarding the promises of the regime change does not lead to political mobilizations due to the characteristics of Ukrainian political institutions, the Maidan protests broke out. The constant need for such corrections followed not from errors of empirical research, but rather from the efforts to align East European processes with the normative idea of Western-oriented development, which limited accounts of differences from the normative trajectory to local specificities.

In terms of local forms of civil society organization, similar knowledge effects included a protracted selectivity of attention to specific forms of local self-organization that fit normative models, and subsequent diagnoses that strengthened the hegemony of the "weakness" argument. Research on postsocialist civil society and social movements focused on movements and civil society organizations that belonged to types known from Western examples: human rights, environmental, feminist, anti-war, alterglobalist, and anarchist movements and NGOs (Císař & Vrábliková, 2010; Einhorn, 1993; Flam, 2001; Gagyi, 2011; Hicks, 1996; Jehlička et al., 2005; McMahon, 2001; Mikecz, 2017; Navrátil, 2010; Piotrowski, 2017; Vermeersch, 2006). Nationalist movements were addressed within the same frameworks as examples that represented the opposite, negative direction of desired development, or, as "uncivil" society (Kopeczky & Mudde 2003; Kotkin, 2009).

One main consequence of this selective attention was that organizations that promoted social rights instead of moral issues corresponding to a postmaterialist and anti-political understanding of civil society were systematically left out of discussions of civil society (Mikuš, 2018). The idea of civil society as a new development in the region's young democracies also downplayed the histories of social movements that played a key role in the region's modern history, but did not fit the civil society idea—from nationalist, social democratic, or fascist movements to peasants', ethnic or religious mobilizations. Grassroots, informal forms of social self-organization were also relegated to the background, despite the fact that they traditionally constituted an essential part of the region's social integration into the development of modern capitalism. Kinship networks, nepotism, mutual aid, community self-help, or various strategies of labor withdrawal were historically key to grassroots coping strategies with capitalist extraction (Gagyi, 2019), sometimes up to the degree where they modified top-down development strategies (e.g. Creed, 1995; Seleny, 2006).

In debates about postsocialism, anthropologists looking at grassroots levels of the socioeconomic transformation in the region started to emphasize relatively soon that local forms of social self-organization do not fit the models of individualism and the postmaterial focus on civic values that normative models of civil society implied (e.g. Dunn & Hann, 1996). They proposed to consider broader sets of relations, like those based on kinship or residence, and broadened the scope of attention to informal practices. Another critical current emphasized limitations that follow from narrowing down the scope of democratic self-organization to NGOs. In a context where transition crises and strict conditions of NATO and EU accessions diminished earlier systems of social redistribution and benefits, NGOs were described by several commentators as insufficient and democratically uncontrollable channels where basic state welfare structures are outsourced (Howard, 2003; Kalb, 2005).

While these criticisms did not overthrow the dominance of the normative civil society model for years to come, they marked a growing stream of research on the relationship between NGOs and social organization on the ground. Approaches that posed the question of civil society as that of a relational dynamic between top-down and grassroots projects of social organization produced an increasing body of empirical research on the relationship between world-economic integration, postsocialist state formation, and NGOs (Kalb & Halmai, 2011; Mikuš, 2018; Vetta, 2018). They showed that in many cases, NGOs played key roles in establishing the hegemony of neoliberal reforms (Vetta, 2009, 2018), but top-down projects of civil society also came to be embedded in complex relations of dependence and dependent negotiation within local contexts (Mikuš, 2018; Sampson, 1996). Even in movements that fit Western categories, like environmentalism or feminism, researchers pointed out complex and conflictual relations with dominant Western frameworks (e.g. Ghodsee, 2004; Gille, 2007). They showed that NGOs that carried forward social concerns of dissident movements that were abolished by neoliberal governments, worked hard to sustain insufficient channels of social help for the most vulnerable (Mikuš, 2015, 2016; Ivancheva, 2014; Vetta, 2012). Anthropological approaches to nationalist civil society projects in Eastern Europe have addressed these as elements of global integration, instead of cases of exception (Mikuš, 2018; Riley, 2019; Szombati, 2018). Contradicting the idea of complementarity between marketization and democratization, research on the politics of postsocialist labor demonstrated a connection between transitional hierarchies and labor's shift toward right-wing politics (Kalb & Halmai, 2011; Ost, 2006). While not necessarily engaging with debates on civil society or social movements, research on postsocialist labor has continuously explored forms of workers' protest that fell outside of of the normative framework of civil society (e.g. Ost & Crowley, 2001; Kideckel, 2009; Varga, 2011).

By the 2000s, researchers frustrated with the empirical inexactitude of normative civil society models increasingly argued for broadening research frameworks beyond normative limits. In a famous critique against the normative approach to civil society, Kopeczky and Mudde (2003) claimed that postsocialist disillusionment with civil society expectations came from wrong settings by which those expectations were defined, and resulting limitations of empirical measurement. They proposed to open empirical research toward civic organizing beyond pro-democratic models, including political protest and contentious politics that does not fit democratic frameworks. Kubik (2005) similarly argued that instead of reiterating measurements based on fixed, normative definitions of civil society, we should empirically scrutinize how those definitions relate to local social realities. More recently, Ekiert and Foa (2011) and Foa and Ekiert (2017) have challenged the "weakness" thesis by applying a multidimensional approach to measurement instead of only relying on data on formal civil society organizations and opinion polls. Their results question the idea of demobilization after 1989, point out continuities with forms of organization under socialism, and demonstrate a strong intra-regional differentiation which, in their view, questions the conceptual coherence of "postsocialist" civil society in general. Similar empirically oriented research has questioned distinctions between NGOs and informal organizations, as well as between autonomous and donor-driven organizations, pointing out a variety of modes in which East European movements practically deal with questions of funding and advocacy (Jacobsson & Saxonberg, 2013) Applying a bottom-up, contextual approach more similar to postsocialist anthropology, Jacobsson and Korolczuk (2017) proposed a process- and practice-based approach to the empirical study of civil society.

By today, these claims produced something that we might consider a "corrected" version of the civil society idea. Abolishing the normative core of the concept that tied it to the world-historical narrative of universal Western-led development, and the transitional narrative of East European societies catching up with that model, the "corrected" version of the civil society idea sheds more light on the various forms of social and political organizing that happen in the region. Yet, while enhancing the empirical potential of civil society research, this "corrected" version does not substitute the moral-political vision of the old concept with a new theoretical framework. In this sense, the state of the debate resembles that in social movement studies, where the abolition of frameworks based in postwar Western experience did not produce a coordinated alternative theoretical approach to contemporary movements.

From the movements' side, one main stream of criticism against the idea of civil society came from the alterglobalist movement. Taking verve in the early 2000s, East European forms of alterglobalism bore strong continuities with the idea of autonomy and self-organization implied in the dissident idea of civil society, yet also posed severe criticisms against the normative civil society model ingrained in liberal ideologies of the transition, and the NGO model of its institutionalization. While the civil society idea of the transition was conceived as part of a conflict-free development of market economy, parliamentary democracy, and the free association of citizens, alterglobalists explicitly posed the idea of global civic networks as a social power that could stop or mitigate the negative social effects of global marketization. This critical standpoint went hand-in-hand with an appreciation of informal, horizontal, grassroots organization as a primary form of social self-organization, and a critique of grant-dependent NGO forms as being more limited in their systemic critique.

Despite this criticism, other characteristics of local versions of alter-globalism bore more similarity to previous dissident models. In terms of constituency, in Eastern Europe the main constituency of alterglobalism was provided by a new wave of politicization of the highly educated, progressive youth, and contained little connections to subaltern groups or established left parties and unions, which formed an important part of alterglobalist alliances in other regions. Consequently, main forms of organization consisted in combinations of educated subcultural scenes with formal NGOs (Gagyi, 2011; Piotrowski, 2017). On this relatively narrow organizational ground, alterglobalist groups managed to orga-nize some significant actions, yet their potential to involve broader social segments and build political power through broader coalitions remained limited. Forms of representation built out on the base of alterglob-alist movement networks—like Hungary's green party Politics Can Be Different—resembled democratic parties funded by dissidents rather than parties of the pink tide in Latin America. Instead of coalitions with unions and large movement groups, these cases rather involved intellectual and NGO circles making claims regarding universal social interest based on intellectual analysis and moral principles.

Like in the case of civil society, the limited penetration of alterglob-alism into broader social segments has been explained by researchers as a consequence of socialist heritage: a lower propensity to political participation, and the discreditation of left politics (Piotrowski, 2017). Looking at internal characteristics of the movement, I earlier showed that the local diffusion of alterglobalist frameworks was also limited by the way alterglobalist activists conceived their own politics (Gagyi, 2013). Differences between local contexts and the primarily Western models of alterglobalist organization that East European groups were in contact with posed a strong challenge for local activism. External allies paid little attention to organizational specificities or political environments of local action. In face of differences on the ground, local activists had insufficient tools to reinterpret alterglobalist frameworks in ways that would include East European experiences—like that of social disillusionment with left political symbols widely used by alterglobalists elsewhere. Yielding to hegemonic frameworks of Western superiority and East European catch-up efforts, they started to interpret such differences as insufficiencies of local contexts vis-a-vis external models. In this situation, the idea of autonomy, so important in alterglobalism, came to be associated with a stance similar to dissidents' internal emigration, with local alterglobalist activists discrediting their postsocial environments as backward, and focusing instead on their internal circles and foreign connections.

Parallel to the limited diffusion of the alterglobalist critique of neoliberalism, grievances connected to economic aspects of transition—such as unemployment, austerity, the flexibilization of work, or the squeeze on domestic small and middle enterprises—came to be increasingly expressed in nationalist frameworks, reinforced by a growing discontent in face of the symbolic degradation of local societies in face of Western models (Mikuš, 2018; Varga, 2014). Forms of anti-neoliberal nationalism, crystallizing in inter-class coalitions around domestic fractions of capital, proposed alternative visions of catching up through protected national-capitalist development, and condemned local proponents of liberalization as internal agents of foreign capital. In various versions of political communication against billionaire philanthropist George Soros, his support for local liberal NGOs came to be used as an exemplary case of that narrative—paving the way for the anti-NGO attacks of illiberal governments after 2008 (McLaughlin & Trilupaityte, 2013).

"Civil Society" and "Democratic Capitalism" in Post-2008 East European Mobilizations

Like elsewhere, after 2008 East European countries saw a series of mass mobilizations. In discussions around these mobilizations, the crisis of the idea of civil society, together with the crisis of the normative historical narrative of postsocialist development that it implied, came to be integrated with new Western narratives on the "crisis of democratic capitalism". Experiences of austerity, as well as the delegitimation of representative democracy, were present in Eastern Europe too, together with the rise of authoritarian populism. Inspired by their connections with other European movements, East European demonstrators often expressed these concerns in frameworks similar to the narrative of the "crisis of democratic capitalism" (e.g. Della Porta, 2014; Pleyers & Sava, 2015). Yet, while Western and South European movements focused on issues like austerity and wealth polarization, East European movements rather expressed their claims in terms of the stakes of postsocialist transition—the causes and culprits of its failure, and alternative proposals for catch-up development. While for Western movements, the decline of "democratic capitalism" referred to a past experience of welfare capitalism, in Eastern Europe narratives of decline rather referred to a backslide on a developmental slope, the failure of a hope that has never been fulfilled. In this context, the idea of decline as backsliding became a new iteration of assessments of local situations based on the normative idea of transition.

A key contradiction behind protest claims that expressed local grievances in terms of the idea of democratic catch-up development was that while that idea involved a mutually reinforcing process of political democracy and material welfare, in the real process of the transition, the introduction of parliamentary democracy was paralleled by an economic crisis at the scale of the Great Depression of the 1930s, including mass unemployment, austerity, the dismantling of socialist welfare systems, and a decline in life expectancy (Azarova et al., 2017; Berend, 2009; Cockerham, 1997; Dale, 2011; Kornai, 1993). Social grievances following from the economic hardships of the regime change did not find an expression through the channels of representative democracy. Joining European movement narratives that protested a similar situation after 2008 allowed for an expression of these contradictions, but also implied an invisibilization of the differences between the two cases, and re-importing the idea of normative development into expressions of disillusionment.

In the case of Western and Southern Europe, the claims of post-2008 anti-austerity pro-democracy movements were easier to interpret within the framework of the "crisis of democratic capitalism". Movements' own critique of post-crisis austerity and their claims for real democracy corresponded to analyses of the decline of welfare democracies, and the fact that movements raised these points reinforced these diagnoses as describing the main conflict lines of society. While the integration of Southern European countries in the postwar development of European capitalism and democracy bore significant differences from European core countries, Southern European movements' social critiques allowed for maintaining this main line of analysis, complementing it with a critique of neoliberal European integration (Stavrakakis & Katsambekis, 2014; Tietze & Humphrys, 2014).

In Eastern Europe, the same blows of austerity that sparked post-2008 protests in Europe were already at the root of postsocialist democratization. As Aldo Madariaga (2020) demonstrated in a comparative study of East European and Latin American neoliberalization, this type of democratization rather served the insulation of neoliberal reforms from social pressures than actual political inclusion. At the same time, transitional expectations continued to define the vocabulary of post-2008 East European protests just as the idea of "democratic capitalism" defined the anti-neoliberal critique of Western movements. Consequently, movements and their commentators produced ideological constructs that reiterated contradictions of transition narratives in new ways. Issues like economic hardships, corruption, or anti-democratic tendencies were interpreted through dramatic reactualizations of transition stakes. In the context of new illiberal regimes' rapprochement with Russia and China, the war in Ukraine, and US narratives of a new Cold War, these stakes of internal transition were once again linked to geopolitical conflicts (e.g. Krugman 2012; Puddington, 2014).

Such reactualizations of transitional frameworks put serious limitations on interpreting synchronic links between East European and global processes. One main resulting contradiction was manifested in explanations of East European illiberalisms. A series of analyses described East European forms of illiberalism as following from a backslide in postsocialist development (e.g. Cianetti et al., 2018; Greskovits, 2015; Rupnik, 2007). But how do East European cases relate to the simultaneous rise of the new right globally, including the West? When dealing with this question, this stream of analysis tended to pose East European illiberalism as some kind of a prefiguration of Western right populism. In the underlying imagery of Western-led world-historical progress, this idea of prefiguration implied something like a return of the past through a historical loophole left open by Eastern Europe's inadequate postsocialist transformation. Ivan Krastev and Stephen Holmes' recent book *The light that failed: Why the West is losing the fight for democracy* (2020) provides an outstanding example of such an explanation effort, where intricate spatio-temporal metaphors of political "imitation" between East and West substitute an analysis of simultaneous interrelations of Eastern and Western development. Meanwhile, interpretations that started from Western cases of right populism simply included East European cases within narratives based on the "crisis of democratic capitalism" (e.g. "global Trumpism" in Blyth, 2016). In neither case did new similarities between Eastern European and Western processes engender a conceptual reconsideration of East European processes that would allow for understanding them as real elements of a simultaneous global history instead of local anomalies of an ideal development project, or local cases of Western phenomena.

In this context, the transitional idea of civil society has made a comeback which reflected the problems of its history as well as contemporary tensions. The immediate events that sparked this comeback were the new waves of demonstrations expressing discontent with present forms of democracy, and a series of attacks on NGOs by new right regimes. In the first case, protests were interpreted as a promising new wave of democratization in the region that may make up for the inadequacies of earlier democratization (Pleyers & Sava, 2015; Rammelt, 2018). In the case of anti-NGO attacks, on the side of regimes, these were part of a new struggle for hegemony, which included the remobilization of transitional stakes around an alternative narrative of the regime change. Here, the failure of transitional promises was explained as derailment by foreign interests and their local allies. Next to liberal politicians, NGOs—and most prominently: main liberal NGOs funded by George Soros and other Western funds—were portrayed as such local agents. In turn, international commentaries single out attacks on NGO's as main signs of a new battle over the stakes of normative transition. While attacks on NGOs as an element of new hegemony struggles is a worldwide phenomenon (e.g. Christensen & Weinstein, 2013), in the case of Eastern Europe, they continue to be represented in the normative frameworks of Western-oriented development, its backslides, and associated geopolitical spatio-temporal metaphors (e.g. Rupnik, 2018). Meanwhile, movements themselves return to the normative notion of civil society to express new stakes of contemporary crisis politics—like in the case of Bulgarian or Romanian new middle class movements, where class superiority is framed in terms of "civil society" versus the poor defined as uneducated, backward, and socialist (Petrovici & Mireanu, 2021; Poenaru, 2017; Tsoneva, 2019).

This return of transitional frames in the interpretation of post-2008 movements and new attacks on NGOs has invisibilized the questions that earlier research and movements have posed regarding the idea of civil society. Once again, they obscure the fact that civil society—represented in today's debates by NGOs—does not include most of local society. They obscure the insufficiency of NGOs in tackling the negative effects of the transition. In the interpretation of post-2008 movements, they overwrite local movements' realities by blueprints of transitional frameworks, sometimes to the extent where extreme right movements are taken to be main proponents of democracy (Ishchenko, 2015). But most importantly, by defining civil society and movements in terms of moral ideals of the normative transition narrative (and the insufficiencies of their local application), the return of these frames once again hides from view the broader social process of postsocialist transition, together with its connections to the crisis as a global phenomenon.

In order to make sense of how contemporary East European movements relate to other movements within the same global crisis, we need to be able to tackle them as parts of the same global process. How are we to understand post-2008 movements in global regions that fall outside of the Western experience? What do contemporary claims for welfare and democracy mean in regions that did not have welfare democracies? How do we interpret global connections between post-2008 movements, if the story of the crisis of "democratic capitalism" only covers a fraction of these movements' context? How do we understand differences in movements' outcomes that have to do with their embeddedness in social and geopolitical contexts different from those of Western anti-austerity pro-democracy movements—from the Arab Spring to Ukraine's Maidan or Latin American movements (Biekart & Fowler, 2013; Chalcraft, 2016; Ishchenko, 2015)? To answer such questions, we need to be able to think beyond models that project global frameworks of social development from localized, short-term experiences.

UNDERSTANDING SOCIAL MOVEMENTS AS PART OF GLOBAL CAPITALISM

If new movements deal with effects of a global capitalist crisis, traditions that think movements from the perspective of global dynamics of capitalism should provide meaningful help in making sense of the present situation. Such traditions, inspired by Marx's original conceptualization of capitalism as a system made up by the totality of social relations, go back deep into the history of embedded knowledge-making by movements and politically engaged research. Examples reach from Lenin's ([1917] 1963) and Luxemburg's ([1913] 1951) thought on imperialism or Trotsky's ([1930] 2010) idea of uneven and combined development to anti-colonial, post-colonial and decolonial thinkers (e.g. Chakrabarty, 2009; Fanon, 1963; Grosfoguel, 2006), or approaches that looked at global developmental differences in terms of the integrated flows of global capital accumulation, like research on the articulation of modes of production (Rey, 1973) or Latin American dependency theory (Frank, 1979).

A wave of more academic versions of this line of thought was produced with the disillusionment with existing forms of state socialism and the academization of Western Marxism after the decline of 1968 movements. These include research traditions like world-systems analysis, a school that attempted to integrate anti-colonial and dependency critique within a methodological study of global capitalism as a whole (Wallerstein, 1986), global anthropology (Wolf, 1982), which aimed to understand local organizations of everyday life in terms of their embeddedness in the global capitalist process, or neo-Gramscian international political economy (Cox, 1983), which looks at local political regimes as globally embedded regimes of accumulation. Recent discussions on global labor history (Van der Linden, 2008) integrate in the same tradition. Although largely neglected by classic paradigms of social movement studies, this tradition has constantly produced theoretical frameworks for thinking social movements from the perspective of global capitalist dynamics.

In this book, within the broader streams of international political economy, I will rely on the tradition of world-systems research to build a framework for understanding East European post-2008 movements as movements of the global crisis. From Wallerstein's seminal trilogy (1974, 1980, 1989), this tradition spans through decades of debates with other approaches, and new research incorporating the lessons of those debates (for a summary, see Lee, 2010). The main heuristic principle of the world-system approach is that instead of smaller topics or units of research—like the topic of social movements, or the unit of the nation-state—it takes as the basic unit of social analysis the whole scope of social interactions into which any social phenomena is embedded in. While in premodern times we can speak of several world-systems based on such broad units of interactions, for the modern period of global history that basic unit of analysis is defined as the historical development of the capitalist world-system. Classic periodizations put the beginnings of capitalist history to the fifteenth century (Arrighi, 1994; Wallerstein, 1974). Other world-systems authors question this sharp delineation, pointing at continuities with previous accumulation processes reaching back to 5000 years (e.g. Frank & Gills, 1993).

In the world-systems approach, "capitalism" is not understood as a fix system of social relations—like high-level industrialization coupled with free wage labor, characteristic to the English industrial revolution. Capitalism is seen as a dynamic historical process, in which various regimes of economic, social, and political organization are connected within the historical development of a global system of accumulation. For example, in the case of English industrial revolution, this perspective emphasizes not only the relations between enclosures, industrial capital, and free wage labor within England, but also the threads through which these relations are tied to the slave labor of colonial plantations, the free labor of housewives, the financial capital of the previous cycle of accumulation dominated by Dutch financial-entrepreneurial networks, etc.—including the way these relations serve as a base for the further evolution of capitalism as a world-system. This approach builds on Marx's concept of capitalism, but instead of an emphasis on theoretical generalization, it focuses on the substantive historical process through which capitalism as a global process develops.[1]

Researching capitalism as a historical process, the world-systems tradition devised several heuristic insights that are often quoted as elements of a world-systems "theory". One of these is the differentiation between positions of center, semi-periphery, and periphery. These are conceived as positions characterized by systemic functions concentrated in such positions—e.g. in terms of technologies that allow favorable terms of trade in the world market, in terms of types of labor forms, or in terms of states' capacity to regulate world-market interactions to the benefit of local capital. These functional constellations do not denote geographical regions, and may shift, through time, from one region to another. Such shifts have been analyzed, for example, in terms of shifts of global hegemonic positions across cycles of historical capitalism (Arrighi, 1994) or the dynamics of old semi-peripheries raising to new core positions within such shifts (Chase-Dunn, 1988).

Another main heuristic insight of the world-systems perspective is that, since it understands global capitalism as an integrated historical process, social relations and politics are not conceived as intrastate relations. In contrast to approaches which compare the politics and social relations of various states on a one-to-one basis, the world-systems perspective considers local social relations in terms of their integration in the global

---

[1] In one classic debate, some Marxist authors maintained that the world-systems approach is solely focused on global unevenness in trade relations, and does not see the class aspect of capitalist relations (Brenner, 1977). While this criticism came to be reiterated in later arguments of dismissal of the world-systems approach, the tradition of substantive analysis within the world-systems tradition typically does address class relations as pa'rt of the empirical study of capitalist development (Bair et al., 2019).

social process. Throughout the process of capitalist integration, local social positions become positions occupied within the capitalist world-system, and local social relations become systemic relations performed within local societies. For example, in former feudal societies of Eastern Europe, in the era of industrial revolution, landlords become agricultural capitalists exporting goods to Western markets, while peasants become a cheap bounded labor that contributes to the profitability of Western industrial capital through bringing down the costs of calories in Western labor's reproduction. The tensions and increasing repression in the relation between these two local classes do not merely constitute a development in local politics and class relations; they have to do with the new way local economies are embedded in the global capitalist process. As Cardoso and Faletto (1979) put it in *Dependency and development in Latin America*: within local societies, integration into external processes of accumulation appears as internal force. In their struggles, local actors act according to interests and conditions that are defined not only by positions relative to each other, but also relative to their world-systems context. From this perspective, the task of analyzing social positions, alliances, and political projects within one polity becomes the task of articulating their wider relations along the lines of world-systemic integration. This is a task of historically substantive analysis, taking into consideration specific local constellations of systemic integration and their recurrent transformations across the cyclical reorganizations of the global economy.

A specific point the world-system tradition makes regarding the sphere of politics is that—contrary to earlier world-systems centered around empires—the capitalist world-system does not have a political unit that would embrace the whole range of its systemic interactions (Arrighi, 1999; Wallerstein, 1986). Instead, through the historical development of capitalism, political relations came to be formalized in political units of nation-states, which are much smaller than the range of interactions that their internal processes feed into. Peter J. Taylor (1982), in an attempt to draw the lines of a political science based on a world-systems background, differentiated the level of "real" relations that bind processes within political units to world-systemic dynamics from the "ideological" sphere of state politics. This latter sphere is ideological not only in the sense of the Marxist critique of bourgeois politics, namely that tensions embedded in the totality of capitalist social relations are translated to the level of representative politics of the state, where they cannot be solved due to the state's own subordination to capitalist relations (e.g. Clarke, 1991).

It is also ideological in the sense that it politicizes local tensions born from system-wide processes by translating them into political concepts limited to the spatial and temporal range of state politics. In these ideological formulations, local constellations of long-term systemic processes are conceptualized as short-term stakes on the level of local state politics, tuned to the form of temporary political coalitions they are tied to.

A related insight refers to the idea of state sovereignty, a basic condition of democratic politics as conceived in paradigmatic Western models. While classic Marxist approaches on the state have emphasized the embeddedness of state institutions within the totality capitalist relations, world-systems scholars added to this approach an attention to interstate relations as part of global capitalist dynamics. Within long-term processes of global capitalist accumulation, they identified cycles of system-wide regimes of accumulation (Arrighi, 1994). While in their early stage, these cycles build out new, globally interconnected structures of economic, social, political, and military organization that make possible highly profitable forms of accumulation, in the later stages these social and material structures become overburdened through a growing competition within similar strategies of growth, and cannot accommodate a profitable reinvestment of the profits they produce. Boom periods are followed by crises which lead to the destruction of earlier structures of accumulation, followed by a reorganization and new expansion of accumulation capacities. Giovanni Arrighi (1994) characterized the global cycles of modern capitalism as hegemonic cycles, named after the actors that played a dominant role in their organization. Since the early sixteenth century he speaks of four cycles: the Iberian-Genovese cycle, where structures of global capitalist expansion were organized by Spanish and Portugal empires and the North Italian city states that were financing them, the Dutch and the British cycle, and the US hegemonic cycle after 1945.

In the context of this broader, cyclical process, states are understood not as a universal notion of analysis, but as institutions whose form and function changes across different positions within cycles, and across different phases of the cycles. The Westphalian idea of state sovereignty built on the unity of population and territory, which serves as the base of modern Western conceptualizations of the state, developed within the conditions of a European balance of power as part of a global system of capitalist expansion under the Dutch hegemonic cycle. The internal peace of the Westphalian system was complemented by aggressive competition of external colonial expansion outside of Europe, where European powers fought each other outside of the rules of Westphalian principles (Arrighi, 1994). After the French Revolution and the Napoleonic Wars, the former Westphalian system was reorganized under British hegemony. This time, the intra-European interstate order was complemented not by relatively equal relations of extra-European colonial competition and wars by European powers, but the unilateral dominance of the United Kingdom:

> Massive tribute from its Indian empire enabled the United Kingdom to adopt unilaterally a free trade policy that, to varying degrees, "caged" all other members of the interstate system in a world-encompassing division of labor centered on itself. Informally and temporarily, but nonetheless effectively, the nineteenth-century system of juridically sovereign states was factually governed by the United Kingdom on the strength of its world-encompassing networks of power. (Arrighi, 1999: 135)

After World War II., with the liberation of former colonies, the West-phalian principle of state sovereignty was expanded universally. At the same time, however, as Arrighi puts it, "the very idea of a balance of power that operates between, rather than above states and ensures their factual sovereign equality—an idea that had already become a fiction under UK hegemony—was discarded even as fiction" (Arrighi, 1999, 136). The principle of "sovereign equality", upheld in the first paragraph of Article Two of the United Nations, was complemented by special rights of great powers—regional in the case of the USSR, and global in the case of the United States. The hegemony of the US state and capital over the post-1945 global cycle was institutionalized through global military presence, the dollar-based global monetary system, and the global expansion of a new, vertically integrated enterprise structure of US corporations—an institutional system deeper and more expanded than that of nineteenth-century Britain.

To think politics, sovereignty, citizenship, and democracy across this interconnected and hierarchical development of the global state system requires us to go beyond abstract and normative definitions that conceive each state as a sovereign power, whose politics can be defined by internal social and political struggles. Marxist critiques of bourgeois democracy traditionally emphasized that the separation of the "political" from the "economic" obscures the social relations of power intrinsic to capitalist relations, and quarantines these relations from the realm of potential political decisions. The world-systems tradition adds to this critique an emphasis on the global hierarchies of capitalist relations, due to which chances of local social actors to shape their systemic conditions through political means differ across positions within local and global class relations as well as states' positions within global hierarchies. The normative frameworks of state sovereignty that still dominate political and academic debates on democracy and citizenship not only obscure the domestic capitalist relations that underlaid the formation of Western democracies, but also hide the fact that the Westphalian model of state sovereignty was in its essence based on the external conditions of colonial subjugation of non-European societies, the targeted destruction of their own economic capacities, and European powers' wars of competition over those gains—just like the position of the United States as a global promoter of democratization was based on its global economic and military domination. If we put European and later US models of state sovereignty, democratic politics, or interstate diplomacy back into this context, both their descriptive accuracy and their normative implications change.

In line with the above considerations, world-systems scholars do not conceive of social movements as elements of (potentially) democratic relations within state units. Instead, when looking at waves of mobilizations, they consider how movements are embedded within the cyclical dynamics of the whole system (e.g. Arrighi et al., 1989; Chase-Dunn & Kwon, 2012; Silver, 2003; Silver & Karatasli, 2015; Smith & Wiest, 2012). When thinking about how movements understand and challenge tensions produced by global capitalist processes, this approach helps us trace the connections between different movements' agency and their specific positions within a shared process.

When Cox and Nilsen (2014) consider the potential relevance of a Marxist perspective on global capitalism to today's movements, they start from a double critique of recent applications of Marxism in both academic and movement approaches. On the one hand, they say, academic Marxists focus so much on analyzing structures of capitalist domination, that tend to objectify them, obscuring the historical dynamics of the struggles through which structures take shape. On the other hand, anti-capitalist movement discourse and its academic supporters tend to limit themselves to a celebration of anti-capitalist projects without performing the work of analysis that Marxist tools enable. As an alternative, Cox and Nilsen propose a Marxist approach to movements that puts praxis first.

Instead of (objectified) structures or case-by-case celebrations of movement projects, this approach looks at history as shaped by social struggles, and places movements at the center of that process. In this broader sense of history as social struggle, they differentiate between movements from above (whereby capital organizes and reorganizes structures of accumulation) and movements from below (whereby labor resists those structures and promotes projects of its own emancipation) (Cox & Nilsen, 2014: 54).

Starting from the bourgeois revolutions that underpinned the creation of capitalist relations within Europe, Cox and Nilsen retell the story of global capitalist development in terms of an ongoing struggle between movements from above and those from below. Differentiating between the "liberal capitalism" of British hegemony, the "organized capitalism" of the boom phase of the US hegemonic cycle, and the "neoliberal capitalism" built out after the 1970s, Cox and Nilsen conclude that the current impasse of neoliberal restructuring—as they put it: global elites' lack of a Plan B—the global connections between movements built out throughout the alterglobalist movement, and the new post-2008 global movement wave that sealed the political delegitimation of neoliberalism, brought us to a moment in the dynamics of the historical struggle where it is possible for movements to win significant gains. For this, they argue, global coordination across various movement streams, and the building out of alternative, democratically controlled institutions is as much important as an instrumental engagement with the state that avoids both the fetishization of state power by earlier Marxist currents, and its rejection by the horizontalist autonomism of newer movements (Cox & Nilsen, 2014, 177). To create this capacity, Cox and Nilsen propose a process that goes beyond mere structural analysis or mere celebration of movement instances through a dialogical connection between locally rooted experiences of the struggle.

Authors working on the critical political economy of European post-2008 crisis management proposed a similar approach to European movements (Bailey et al., 2017). Like Cox and Nilsen, they criticized diagnoses that focus solely on macroeconomic relations and capital strategies, claiming that this focus works to underestimate, obscure, or even deny the disruptions caused by labor's resistance, and effectively works against our capacity to imagine change. Against this reification of capitalist structures, Bailey and his colleagues propose a perspective that puts disruption by labor first, and investigates capital's reorganizations as a reaction to the constant threat of disruption. Based on this approach, they retell the story of European integration as a series of reorganizations sparked by labor unrest—from the strikes of the 1960s to contemporary anti-neoliberal mobilizations.

While I agree with the direction of thought that brings movements back to the center of the historical dynamics, I propose to pay equal attention to movements' actions and the structural aspects of global accumulation. Instead of putting either perspective as first, I see the main task in grasping the mutual relations between the two. Regarding Bailey and his colleagues' argument, this can be illustrated by the example of historical continuity: while they rightly point out the strikes of the 1960s as a main cause of European capital's reorganization offensive, from the perspective I propose, these strikes on their own turn are contextualized in the forms of Fordist industrialization that built out both labor's conditions of discontent and the strategic positions within production from which strikes could be effectively waged.

Apart from tracing such historical sequences of capital's and labor's movements, the world-systems tradition also provides tools to grasp the ways capitalist contradictions fold out on different spatial and temporal scales in global history. This allows us to consider factors of the struggle that don't necessarily manifest as a direct clash between movements from above and movements from below. For instance, when speaking of the era of bourgeois revolutions, Cox and Nilsen refer to the British example, and show how movements from below that oppose enclosures meet movements from above that solidify the institutions of capitalist relations through bourgeois revolution. For the colonial aspect of the same story, they refer to Linebaugh and Rediker's (2013) study of slave revolts that oppose Transatlantic colonial structures. In these examples, main aspects of capitalist formation can be linked to direct clashes between movements from above and movements from below. However, in the broader history of struggles that shaped the modern world, many other instances do not offer such illustrative coincidences between the scope of movements and the systemic significance of the structures they oppose.

For example, in an analysis of the French bourgeois revolutions, Wallerstein shows how various groups in different positions participate in the process of the French Revolution, and how their positioned grievances, their inter-class relations, and the negotiated and hierarchical outcomes of the revolution were linked to the process of hegemonic struggle between France and Britain for the dominance of global capitalist expansion (Wallerstein, 1989, 80–125). This analysis offers a different focus on movements: while it still treats them as born from and acting upon history, it does not see them in terms of a string of historical struggles where labor opposed capital, but in terms of a more broad, interconnected space of capitalist organization where actors occupy different positions and their contestations come embedded in multiple scales of struggles within the same historical process.

Regarding colonial struggles, another example could be Eric Wolf's (1982) approach on the social transformations engendered by colonial expansion. While Wolf also tells the story of these reorganizations in terms of struggles, instead of a direct clash between transatlantic capital and transatlantic labor exemplified by Rediker and Linebaugh's study, what his account makes visible is a full-scope transformation of local social organization, where the logic of capitalist extraction benefiting European powers comes embedded within local forms of trade, production, culture, and domination. Besides direct clashes between movements from above and movements from below, this approach makes visible multiple threads of transformation that make various forms of systemic integration possible (and inviting) for local actors. It shows the ways in which systemic pressures reappear within local relations, and the avenues through which organizational power contained in earlier forms of social relations comes to be used to the favor of new accumulation channels.

Some aspects of this approach that I have found particularly useful in understanding East European middle class movements, are the question of scale and the question of middle positions within struggles of hegemony. The question of scale implies that the immediate situations movements react to rarely include the whole systemic process that produced those situations. Movements react to, and operate within scales smaller than the evolution of the whole system, and this influences both their thought, aims and tactics, and the ways their power integrates into the dynamics of the whole system. The actors movements directly face do not necessarily represent the full scope of capitalist dynamics that shape actors' life on the long term. Also, the conditions that make movements successful or unsuccessful do not only reside in the scales they come directly into contact with. The question of scale also poses a challenge to assessing the potential of movements (both from above and from below), if this potential is viewed not only in terms of movements' momentary aims and gains, but also in terms of their long-term system-wide effects.

While on an abstract level, capitalist contradictions can be analyzed in terms of the conflict between labor and capital, in the understanding of concrete movement dynamics, movements' relation to systemic dynamics needs to be addressed beyond points of direct confrontation.

One way a world-systems approach can help us deal with middle positions is its emphasis on the structural processes that underpin or weaken hegemony. If we conceptualize historical struggles as clashes between movements from above and from below, the politics of actors in middle positions appear as marginal sub-cases of capital-labor struggles. Cox and Nilsen (2014: 98), following Gramsci's (1978) classical reconceptualization of the Marxist notion of false consciousness, explain such cases as induced by cultural hegemony, while maintaining a clear distinction between movements from above and movements from below. However, looking at instances of movements across capitalist history, the problem of the ambiguity of middle positions seems to reoccur more often, and provides a stronger factor in systemic politics, than what changes between true and false consciousness can explain. The problem becomes even more disturbing when at closer analysis, movements conventionally considered to be emancipative movements from below, prove to serve systemic aims—like in the case of Western social democracy that helped solidify the system of global extraction after WWII, or in the case of non-core development efforts that contributed to the expansion of capitalist relations globally. When thinking about the politics of actors in middle positions, conceiving them in terms of false consciousness or a "mix" of movements from above and below (as Cox and Nilsen describe the results of national developmentalisms, 2014: 128) does not seem to provide orientation points solid enough to inform movement strategizing. A framework to address connections between systemic process and politics of middle positions is needed, which can take moments of systemic integration as seriously (and see them as real) as moments of revolt.

Two additional aspects that a systemic perspective can add to understanding movements beyond direct capital-labor conflicts, including the role of actors in middle positions, are the issues of inter-capitalist struggle and hegemony. A focus on clashes between movements from above and below might reflect basic tensions of capitalist history, but as an empirical perspective, it hides from view the different positions and strategies of capitalist fractions, and their changing inter-class and cross-class coalitions across accumulation cycles. I agree with critiques that claim that a sole focus on struggles between fractions of capital is theoretically and politically detrimental to the capacity to conceive class struggle (e.g. Bailey et al., 2017; Clarke, 1978). Yet without an empirical investigation of inter-capitalist struggles and their outcomes, we may lose key tools of orientation in understanding movements' conditions and possibilities.

In terms of hegemony, the world-systems tradition, similar to neo-Gramscian international political economy, carries further Gramsci's initial emphasis on both the cultural and the structural elements of hegemony. Here, the full scale of hegemonic relations is seen as a broader set of hierarchical relations with differential gains and limitations in various positions. Besides cultural domination and physical force, the stability of hegemonic relations is seen as provided also by forms of material organization that provide certain integration options for most actors, and put limitations on alternative modes of embeddedness within the same structure. Along with changes in political consciousness and movements' organizational power, changes in accumulation structures' accommodating capacity also constitutes an important factor of hegemonic crises. When the same material structures that capital built out in the boom phase of an accumulation cycle become exhausted, the consequent redirection of capitalist strategies results in the crumbling of earlier material structures together with their accommodating capacity. This situation is not only a consequence of struggles between labor and capital, but also of capital's own crisis and reorganization due to system-level contradictions that follow from its own previous strategies.

What happens to middle positions in such structural transformations, and how it affects the politics of middle positions relative to various fractions of capital and labor, is a sensitive point of hegemony. Middle actors' relative structural gains and political loyalty are key to hegemony, yet due to the structural limits on their accommodation and their capacity for organization, they also pose a constant threat. Word-systems scholars have emphasized that semi-peripheries fulfill a key role in stabilizing systemic flows of extraction, yet also pointed at their subsequent antisystemic potential (Chase-Dunn, 1988). In the case of post-2008 movements, the political directions and alliances chosen by middle class constituencies have been addressed as important factors in the politicization of the crisis (Biekart, 2015). To address this significance of middle positions within hegemonic struggles, the focus on struggles between movements from above and from below needs to be widened to a broader scope of interactions between movements and long-term accumulation structures.

Therefore, while I agree that a sole focus on capital's strategies and the structures of domination cannot properly address and inform movements, I maintain that an attention to movements' relation to structure in terms of a broader, contested, and long-term organization of global capitalist relations has a continued potential for movement analysis. It makes possible to see movements relative to different scales, and relate their immediate environments to broader, long-term processes of global development. It brings into view factors in movements' formation that are not directly visible within local or contemporary stakes of the struggle, and makes it possible to think movement outcomes not only in terms of immediate gains, but also in terms of their long-term systemic effects.

Finally, a perspective on long-term structures of accumulation also seems to be unavoidable if we want to seriously assess the potential of anti-capitalist movements. While approaches that emphasize movement agency rightly point out that workers' struggles also shaped capitalist history, it is also a fact that former moments of "winning" did not end the process of capital accumulation. In this context, momentary gains, losses, and the strategies that led to them need to be investigated against large-scale, long-term reorganizations that made it possible for the system to survive. Instead of necessarily leading to a state of "left melancholy" (Brown, 1999), which Bailey and his colleagues warn us against (2017: 4), I see this kind of awareness as a necessary condition for thinking about movements' potential in today's moment of crisis, when the threat of climate catastrophe makes a full transformation of the system the only realist scenario of "winning".

In the following two sections, I illustrate the potential gains of this approach by several insights by world-systems research traditions on labor struggles and antisystemic movements. Then I briefly outline an interpretation of the current crisis based on world-systems research on long-term global cycles, and raise several points on how it can inform our thought about contemporary movements.

Labor Struggles in Global Product Cycles

One illustrative example to tracing connections between movements and long-term systemic processes is Beverly Silver's (2003) study of how transformations in global production are linked to dynamics of labor organization throughout modern history. As Silver points out, labor struggles appear wherever capital builds out major industrial structures, yet their lasting success depends on the point of the global product cycle they appear in. In core positions, where new and profitable technologies appear at the beginning of the cycle, industries are able to simultaneously accommodate labor's demands and keep their profit margins for longer periods. In more peripheral positions where the same technologies arrive in a later point of the product cycle (mobilized, among others, by labor's pressure in core locations), the same type of movements can be less successful, due to the lower profitability of their later position in the system-wide product cycle.

According to changing relations between labor mobilizations and movements of capital, this line of analysis differentiates between three types of labor movements. The first type is that of labor movements struggling to gain labor rights in new industrial surroundings (where manufacturing capital moves into). The second type are movements that seek to maintain labor rights that were once gained but are newly withdrawn due to a fall in profitability (in regions where manufacturing capital moves out from). The third type is constituted by a growing scope of movements that evolve in environments where a large pool of active labor meets a constant scarcity of employment possibilities (in regions that capital bypasses) (Karatasli et al., 2015; Silver & Karatasli, 2015).

Silver and her colleagues' analysis illustrate the limitations of understanding labor movements based on short-term periods and local effects of systemic processes. The conclusion that "old" labor movements are a thing of the past was generalized from the stabilization of the postwar welfare pact in Western core countries. Today, as labor movements and other movements with material claims appear in Western countries again, earlier concepts of relations between socioeconomic structures and movements are brought back in their interpretations. Yet, this move often duplicates the localized, short-term bias of the previous period, as it proposes solutions for present problems based on previous movement agendas formulated in a previous systemic moment. Ideas for reindustrialization, coupled with a unionization that can again maximize Western labor's share in global capital's profits again (like in social democratic new left agendas, or in the idea of just transition based on green jobs through green growth), represent such limitations: they expect the same gains from movement efforts in the crisis phase of the postwar global cycle as could be achieved in the boom phase, when Western powers had the capacity to organize the flows of a growing global economy to Western economies' benefit.

Another effect of the same time–space bias is that labor movements across the globe come to be compared to the paradigmatic success story of the postwar Western welfare pact. In this type of comparison, movements that appeared in the beginning of the innovation cycle, and had a higher chance to achieve a lasting share of profits, will appear as successful. Labor movements of other global regions, which appear in later phases of the same cycle, under conditions of lower profitability, will appear as unsuccessful. This difference between successful and unsuccessful movements will be understood as something that follows from the weakness or lacks of local advocacy outside of core regions. This diagnosis has influenced both the understanding and the internal organization of the global trade union movement, with the tactical consequence that hardships of local organization in more peripheral locations are hoped to be overcome by stronger organization (e.g. Jürgens & Krywdzsinski, 2009). This focus on local characteristics of the labor movement obscures the the spatio-temporal patterns of global cycles of investment that condition both successes and failures. Within these conditions, the success of labor movements does not only depend from local levels of organization, but also from the globally unequal, cyclical conditions of capital's profitability.

Finally, a main contradiction in applying the time–space bias on Western labor movements' postwar successes to a global level consists in the fact that the strategy that aims for increasing local labor's share of capital's global profits has historically set different fractions of global labor against each other. As Wallerstein (1995: 25) points out, the relationship between the trade union movement and capitalism has been laden by a system-level contradiction between legitimacy and profitability. In order to maintain the legitimacy of the system, capital can make concessions to labor—yet these can be only extended to a smaller part of global labor, otherwise they would pose a risk to profitability. In the present crisis of the postwar global cycle, the lack of concessions to labor leads to the delegitimation of the system in former Western welfare democracies, too—but the forms of accommodation Western labor is presently losing have never extended to the whole of global labor. The systemic contradiction between legitimacy and profitability means that since capital's concessions to labor are globally limited, they always constitute an object of political struggle not only between labor and capital, but also within different segments of global labor. In these struggles, labor's claims intersect with various forms of status-based claims, and join alliances to support status-based claims across class divisions. As Silver and Karatasli (2015, 140–141) put it:

> Fundamental to historical capitalism has been the ways in which status-based distinctions are recurrently mobilized (by capitalists, by states and/or by workers themselves) to carve out special protections from the worst ravages of an unregulated labor market--e.g., through higher wages, job security, health, pension and other welfare provisions--for a segment of the world's working class marked for special treatment along lines of gender, race, ethnicity and/or citizenship. Such special protections seek to mitigate the deep tension between profitability and legitimacy--to square the circle, so to speak--by creating legitimating social compacts for some segments of the world working class while maintaining profitability by excluding the majority from those social compacts. However, the successful extension of such benefits to a privileged group becomes an important incentive for working-class mobilizations along status lines by both privileged and by excluded workers--mobilizations aimed, respectively, at defending or overturning racial, ethnic, national and gender hierarchies. As a result, the history of workers' mobilizations has been deeply interconnected with mobilizations along racial, gender, ethnic and citizenship lines. In a nutshell, mobilization based on class and mobilization based on status have been and will continue to be deeply intertwined.

Thus, in conflicts that set different fractions of global labor against each other in their claims for capital's global profits, hierarchies of status play a strong role. These hierarchies are established through the hierarchical distribution of labor created through the global history of capitalism, as well as by the social struggles that contested and shaped their historical forms. What appears at one point of history as the distribution of labor based on gender, ethnicity, citizenship or race, is the result of a historical process that produced those racial, ethnic, or gender categories as categories of labor distribution. Decolonial or feminist authors have long emphasized that categories of racial, ethnic, or gender differences do not simply mean hierarchies of symbolic recognition, but reflect and sustain real hierarchies of global labor distribution—e.g. between skilled and unskilled industrial labor, agrarian labor, slave labor, and housework (e.g. Mies et al., 1988; Mignolo, 2002; Quijano, 2000).

Citizenship, too, is a status-based category that plays a key role in the reproduction and management of global labor distribution. In the case of postwar Western welfare states, citizenship worked as a means of inclusion; yet if we consider the ways these economies related to the rest of the globe, especially their former colonies reorganized under global economic hierarchies of neocolonialism, functioning as sources of cheap resources and migrant labor (e.g. Meillassoux, 1981), we see that the same citizenship also worked as a means of exclusion and selective, hierarchical use of non-local labor by the same economies. Western narratives on the emancipative, inclusive potential of citizenship show another face when we consider citizenship in a global perspective. Until today, the main factors that determine one's position in global hierarchies are citizenship and gender (Shachar, 2009), two status categories of global labor distribution that are defined in terms of "birth".

Status-based identity aspects of global labor struggles provide fertile grounds for cross-class alliances based on promises of exceptional treatment, and for intra-labor conflicts along the lines of such alliances. Examples reach from conflicts within local industrial labor—e.g. in the case of white immigrant and black workers in the buildup of US Fordism—to intra-household conflicts reflecting gender-based labor distribution, or to contemporary political clashes in Western Europe around migrant workers. If welfare state policies relied on status differentiation in defining the scope of allowances to labor (primarily: white, skilled, male local citizens), the industrial policies that strove to maintain Western capital's profitability after the 1970s crisis used status differences to increasingly flexibilize and polarize labor, and move production toward less skilled, cheaper, and less organized labor (like that of migrants with insecure citizenship status, women, or populations of peripheries through outsourcing).

The way a new wave of right-wing populism connects present grievances of previously privileged Western workers with new versions of nationalist and xenophobic ideologies is often pointed out as a cause for concern. But the relation between previous Western privileges and present status-based hierarchies remains a question within left movements and politics, too. In movement agendas that take past frameworks of "democratic capitalism" as a model, ideas for protectionism, reindustrialization and stronger labor rights easily go hand-in-hand with anti-immigration stances, and with claims to stop the erosion of Western economies' dominant global positions (e.g. Gagyi, 2012; Lewis, 2017).

Antisystemic Movements in a World-Systems Perspective

Beyond labor struggles' positions within systemic cycles, or the utilization of status hierarchies to integrate labor's struggles into systemic dynamics, the world-systems perspective also emphasizes the position movements' strategic contexts occupy within the politically fractured space of the interstate system. From the perspective of movement history, one main aspect highlighted by this perspective is the fracturing of antisystemic movements across global positions.

In the world-systems tradition, antisystemic movements are defined as arising from and going against pressures generated by capitalism (Amin et al., 1990). In the history of the capitalist world-system, movements that addressed such pressures in terms of secular politics arose together with the formation of modern states and state politics. Their main currents contested two main aspects of systemic pressures: of capital on labor (socialism and communism) and of the interstate hierarchy of the world economy (national liberation movements). Politically, these movements formulated different vocabularies and narratives, which opposed each other in fierce ideological debates. While on this level of the debate, they appeared as mutually exclusive, a system-level analysis shows that their differences were based in the different strategic environments provided by different systemic positions within the same global process (Amin et al., 1990).

Despite their differences, antisystemic movements shared a common fate in terms of their integration into system-level processes. After more than a century of political institutionalization of antisystemic movements since 1848, all three types of antisystemic movements succeeded in achieving state power. Through that success, however, all three currents found themselves in a position where their power and their capacity to accommodate reproductive needs was conditional to maintaining and fulfilling relations of integration into global structures of capital accumulation. While they took different routes in tackling the contradictions following from that situation, ultimately all regimes arrived to legitimacy crises, and came to be contested by new movements.

To understand the fracturing of antisystemic movements across global positions, it is worth going back to Marx's original interpretation of capital-labor relations. As Arrighi (1990) points out, Marx's prognosis that the development of capitalist relations leads to a worldwide revolution of the proletariat able to change the whole system, was built on the assumption that the positions of active and reserve labor are filled by largely the same masses of workers. In this case, the development of capitalist relations leads to a mutually reinforcing contradiction between two processes. The first is the concentration of active labor in key sectors of production, whose political organization can pose a growing threat to the system. The second is the growing misery of reserve labor, which acts against the legitimation of the system. If it is the same masses of workers that circulate across the two positions, the growing power of active labor and the growing misery of reserve labor adds up into an antisystemic struggle of the proletariat against capitalism as a whole. However, in the historical development of global capitalism, this expectation was not fulfilled (Arrighi maintains that it is valid as a secular long-term trend, but did not happen in the forms of nineteenth and twentieth-century antisystemic movements). Instead of the same masses circulating across the two positions, positions of active and reserve labor were polarized along the hierarchies of the global distribution of labor. This differentiated concentration led to different versions of antisystemic programs in different systemic positions.

Within the international socialist movement, the crisis of the 1870s, which marked the crisis of the global capitalist cycle dominated by British hegemony, together with the wars that followed it, led to different conditions, and thereby different strategies in different contexts. In core states, investments channeled into the military industry contributed to the growth of organized active labor, while in Russia and China the same period was characterized by a drop in labor's profit shares, and a growing misery leading to social tensions. Bernstein's social democratic program reflected contemporary conditions of core countries: the growing social power of organized labor and an existing potential for democratic political representation. Seeing the decreasing power of trade unions, together with the dissatisfaction of masses stricken by misery and unemployment, in the same period, Lenin formulated the Bolshevik program for a vanguard party made up by professional revolutionaries. These different programs born from different conditions arrived to strategic conclusions that contradicted each other. Their difference became institutionalized in the break between the Second and Third International.

If we follow the evolution of these two branches of the socialist movement across the next cycle of global accumulation after 1945, on the side of social democratic movements we see that their claims were largely accommodated and institutionalized within the conditions of core capital's accumulation. In the United States, the Fordist organization of production that has been expanding throughout the war, created vertically integrated, bureaucratically organized structures, which changed the conditions of labor's organization in two ways. First, it decreased the importance of skilled labor (and together with it, the organizational power of skilled workers). Second, it created large interconnected processes in production, which made the profitability of capital invested in the structures of production vulnerable to coordinated actions by semiskilled workers. Wildcat strikes of the 1930s and 1940s made use of this vulnerability, and created a strong wave of workers' organization. After 1945, this power of the labor movement was recognized and contained within a social pact that included trade unions as institutionalized partners in negotiating and maintaining the order of production, and provided a larger share of profits to labor which allowed for the creation of a strong consumer market for capital's goods. The profitability of the system was stabilized by the fast pace of economic expansion outside of the United States (Baran & Sweezy, 1966; Silver, 2003).

The primary field of the expansion of both Fordist production and consumer markets was Europe (Van der Pijl, 2014). Here, too, by the 1960s, the expansion of Fordist production lines and related reorganizations of labor led to waves of wildcat strikes similar to earlier waves in the United States (Silver, 2003). These movements also succeeded in expanding workers' rights and carving out a larger share of profits for workers. However, the accommodation of these claims soon reached the limits posed by the end of the boom phase of the postwar global cycle. By the end of the 1960s, the parallel development of US, European, and Japanese capacities led to increasing competition, resulting in a drop in profitability, and a growing problem of overaccumulation. This situation also meant that the expansion of external markets no longer compensated for the losses of profit shares to local labor in Western welfare democracies. Capital reacted to these pressures by cutting costs, including putting pressure on state's welfare systems, the reorganization of production, and by fleeing to capital markets. For labor, this meant the gradual loss of welfare guarantees, a growing share of non-organized, cheaper (migrant and women's) labor, and the outsourcing of production to non-core regions. The withdrawal of the welfare state, the erosion of labor's positions that guaranteed its earlier shares of profits, and new conflicts between organized labor's previous status and the influx of unorganized cheaper labor into workplaces led to the delegitimation of social democratic politics.

During the same cycle, the original Marxist program of proletarian revolution went through a double reformulation within the communist movement. While Lenin's program substituted the role of workers' organizations with the professional politics of the communist party, Stalin's program of "socialism in one country" meant that the party became the manager of a local catching-up effort within the global economic and military competition. As Arrighi (1990) points out, this program required that the party is able to maintain its power and legitimacy through successful economic development and the eradication of misery within the conditions of global capitalist competition. At the same time, the same development project required a forced centralization of resources that included the violent repression of workers' and peasants' resistance. This process of forced catch-up industrialization was canonized in the Soviet bloc as the realization of the Marxist project. This ideological image of Marxism linked to misery and state violence contributed to the delegitimation of the communist project in the eyes of Western labor, and helped maintain the legitimacy of the Fordist pact.

The creeping overaccumulation crisis of the post-1945 cycle led to the destruction of state socialist developmental models too. With forced industrialization, the social power of industrial labor grew, yet after the first wave of redistribution through the forced centralization of resources, further redistributive gains for labor could only be secured through economic growth. By the end of the 1960s this growth was halted across the Socialist bloc. Along external conditions of global overaccumulation, this was due to the exhaustion of internal cheap resources of agrarian labor. In addition, the oil crisis of the 1970s deepened the contradiction between the need to import high-level technology, and the complementary export pressure to compensate for import costs. Within the resulting limits of redistribution, the social power of industrial labor and socialist bureaucracy, acted as two—often conflicting, but sometimes also allied—sources of tensions. By the 1980s, waves of strikes and other forms of labor resistance swept through state socialist systems, while members of the bureaucracy and socialist intellectuals turned away from reform socialist ideas and openly supported the abolition of state socialism (Silver, 2003).

The third stream of antisystemic movements, national liberation movements struggling against colonial systems, also made their way to state power after 1945. Building on the power of coalitions between local elites and local labor, national liberation movements came to government after the collapse of colonial empires. While the politics of national liberation movement coalitions entailed strong ideals of social justice, these governments, too, needed to accommodate the requirements of world-market integration in order to stay in power. Here, too, this resulted in efforts toward national development within the logic of global capitalist competition (Desai, 2004). In the developmentalist social alliances that sustained the legitimacy of these regimes, concessions to subaltern groups (like subsidized consumption or access to public services) played a stabilizing role in nation-building projects, and buttressed the power of local elites as mediators of their countries' dominated integration into global accumulation flows (Walton & Seddon, 1994). Starting with the Bandung Conference of Afro-Asian countries in 1955, national development regimes of post-colonial and state socialist countries formed international coalitions which promoted the reorganization of the international institutions of the global economy in a way that gives more chance for peripheral and semi-peripheral development. At the same time, development efforts in peripheral positions required strong sacrifices from local labor, and led to violent repressions of local peasants and workers' mobilizations. Running against strong limitations of world-economic integration in the context of neocolonial economic structures (Nkrumah, 1967), national liberation regimes were finally unable to fulfill the promises of eradicating mass misery and alleviating economic dependence from ex-colonial centers. The contradictions of national liberation regimes came to be expressed in local movements of subaltern groups that criticized national liberation governments as managers of neocolonialism (Banerjee, 1984; Cox & Nilsen, 2014).

Mutual criticisms of the regimes built on the three streams of antisystemic movements also contributed to the erosion of their legitimacy. While Western social democrats criticized state socialism for their centralization of power and repressive politics, state socialist, and national liberation regimes criticized social democracy for its alliance with Western capital. Meanwhile, national liberation regimes of the peripheries criticized core and semi-peripheral regimes for not doing enough to eradicate global hierarchies. These criticisms got stronger as efforts by the Non-Aligned Movement and the G77 group of the UN met increasing resistance in international institutions after the 1970s.

World-systems scholars have interpreted the global wave of 1968 movements as a reformulation of antisystemic struggles (Amin et al., 1990) which took verve in face of the delegitimation of regimes based on previous antisystemic movements. As managers of capitalist integration, none of the streams of previous antisystemic movements managed to consolidate local labor's reproduction claims with the requirements of global accumulation. Depending on speakers' positions, the ways social democratic, state socialist, and national liberation regimes struggled with contradictions between world-economic integration and the local social tensions born from that integration were described either as heroic struggles, or as brutal repression. Ultimately this contradiction exploded the frameworks of legitimacy in each type of regime. 1968 movements turned against the long-term trend in antisystemic movements that conceived the strategy of change through gaining state power. The delegitimation of state power, bureaucratic organization, and universalist developmentalist projects, together with a new emphasis on subaltern positions and grassroots, horizontal forms of organization in these movements set a new paradigm that was to influence further antisystemic waves.

The wave of 1968 movements was met by differentiated strategies of repression from the part of systemic powers struggling with an imminent crisis of accumulation. State violence against the Naxalites in India, the crushing of Latin American popular left movements by US-backed military dictatorships, the Soviet Union's invasion of Czechoslovakia in reaction to the Prague Spring, or the police repressions of workers' and students' demonstrations in Europe constituted one aspect of systemic response. Another aspect implied the reorganization of institutional management structures of capitalist accumulation. The reorganization of management structures included the flexibilization and outsourcing of production, a shift of investments toward financial markets, and an institutional push for the liberalization and deregulation of global markets in order to save core capital's profitability, which came to be known as the global politics of neoliberalism (Roy et al., 2006). As Boltanski and Chiapello (2005) point out, on the level of symbolic frameworks of legitimation, a parallel shift integrated anti-state, anti-bureaucratic, and anti-universalist stances of 1968 movements into a new, networked, individualized, and overly flexible image of capitalist production and consumption. Here, a heightened emphasis on individual freedom and responsibility served to confine agency within the avenues established by accumulation's needs, and shift the responsibility to handle contradictory requirements of accumulation and social reproduction to individual agency (something that came to be analyzed in terms of neoliberal governmentality, Foucault, 1988).

By the 1980s, social democracy came to be seen in core countries as an ideology of the past, tied to over-bureaucratized systems that merely protect the interests of a small, privileged group of organized labor. State socialist governments faced anti-bureaucratic dissident movements and workers' mobilizations. Universalist ideologies of national liberation regimes were questioned by new communitarian and religious movements. The structures of power that antisystemic movements once saw as the aim of struggle and as criteria of movements' success, came to be seen as mere tools of repression. This delegitimation of emancipative projects based on state power, symbolically sealed by the collapse of state socialist systems, was used as a source of legitimation by the new politics of neoliberalism, which promised more freedom and less state intervention, while restructuring institutional channels of accumulation to the benefit of capital.

The 1980s and 1990s were marked by a global sweep of neoliberal reforms that opened previous developmentalist regimes of the semi-peripheries and peripheries for the purposes of core capital's own crisis management. In the context of the crisis of the 1970s, and the availability of cheap credits from financial market swelled with petrodollars after 1973, non-core development regimes recurred to loans to alleviate internal contradictions of dependent development under the imminent global crisis. With the Volcker shock, a rise of interest rates by the FED in order to tackle crisis effects in the United States, the debt service of these loans skyrocketed. The result was a global wave of debt crises which sent non-core developmentalist regimes to the ground. This wave of crisis came to be used as a source for further core crisis management through the structural adjustment requirements that were tied to IMF and World Bank packages of crisis loans and debt management. Structural adjustment programs engendered a series privatization, austerity, and liberalization that sent a large part of non-core populations into poverty, as a price for a new expansion of core capital that was celebrated as a new era of growth by Western elites. In the Global South, the effects of structural adjustment came to be contested by a wave of movements that came to be known as "IMF riots" (Walton & Seddon, 1994).

While "IMF riots" primarily protested the loss of earlier guarantees provided by developmentalist regimes, by the 2000s populations expulsed from the formal economy built out new forms of social and economic organization, and these structures became the base of new political claims that aimed at reproductive autonomy (Zibechi, 2010). The "pink tide" of Latin American left governments and the global alterglobalization movement institutionalized in the World Social Forum built on the social and political power of those movements—with the Zapatista revolution in Chiapas, Mexico serving as an influential model example (Pleyers, 2010). The alterglobalization movement maintained the 1968 criticism of state power and top-down universalist developmentalism. As an alternative strategy, it proposed a worldwide horizontal dialogue of grassroots organizations. In this dialogue, the formation of the movement and its agenda was imagined as a process, instead of a fixed starting point or aim (Sousa de Santos, 2007).

The strategy of the alterglobalization movement also internalized contemporary understandings of globalization as a process that decreases nation-states' influence over economic and social processes. In correspondence with its distantiation from state power, the movement saw its potential for change in the horizontal networks of global civil society, which could match the networked and fluid nature of capital's power globally. This strategy of the alterglobalization movement did not prove to be successful. While it succeeded in building out a significant antisystemic movement culture of the era of neoliberal globalization, its global techniques of social forums and summit hopping (mass demonstrations organized at the time and place of main meetings of international organizations) did not manage to create a type of power that could successfully counteract global capital's moves.

By the time the alterglobalization movement seemed exhausted, the 2008 financial crisis sparked a new wave of movements that, in many ways, carried its heritage further. As several researchers pointed out, the horizontal organization and ideology of Occupy-type movements was strongly marked by the alterglobalist tradition, also because of biographical continuities in activists' trajectories (Castañeda, 2012; Gagyi, 2012); Juris, 2012). The alterglobalist critique of neoliberalism was continued and amplified in the discourse of new anti-austerity movements. Organizational innovations in the political formalization of post-2008 movements—from Corbyn or Sanders' movement-based politics to the new wave of Western municipalism exemplified by the model of Barcelona en Comú—also built on the alterglobalist culture of horizontal politics. Alterglobalism's understanding of solidarity economy as a political ground for antisystemic struggle (Sousa de Santos, 2006) came to be applied in new initiatives for reproductive autonomy.

In the politics of Western new left movements, that trend included a new wave of cooperativism, the proliferation of commons, peer-to-peer, and anti-copyright movements, the change finance movement, various initiatives to reformulate expert knowledge in the service of reproduction instead of accumulation, and the incorporation of solidarity economy and degrowth projects in formal political programs of just transition in the face of climate change (Dale, 2019; Gagyi, 2019). The alterglobalist understanding of reproduction also found a strong continuation in a new transnational wave of women's strikes (McGlazer, 2018). This new focus on reproductive autonomy created through participative, democratic forms of non-capitalist economy has been seen by some commentators as pointing toward a holistic response to the crisis of representative democracy within capitalism's crisis (Karitzis, 2017; Wainwright, 2018). Building on the experience of Latin American pink tide governments' efforts, a new Western wave of new experimental models started to address the question of scaling solidarity economy solutions on a state level (e.g. Hanna, 2018).

Despite these continuities and similarities, other aspects of post-2008 movements diverged from the alterglobalist tradition. One main difference in the conditions from where movement claims are voiced is that while in alterglobalist coalitions, anti-capitalist claims by Global South movements were supported by Western allies from a "postmaterialist" position, the perception of the post-2008 global movement wave has been dominated by Western movements which reacted to grievances that directly hit Western constituencies. In this context, despite mutual references between movements of the Arab Spring and Western Occupy-type movements, or between the more recent waves of Black Lives Matter and Hong Kong protests, post-2008 movements did not formulate a common global framework similar to that of alterglobalism. Instead, Western examples came to dominate the interpretation of new movement waves, while broad differences between movements' contexts and characteristics remained largely unreflected. In this situation, the underlying tendency of Western movement frameworks to defend or reclaim systemic privileges that underpinned previous forms of security becomes more significant. Movement claims that require more allowances to one segment of global labor against another, or aim to retain previous privileges of Western welfare within the framework of the "democratic capitalism" narrative, belong to this category.

Another, related difference is movements' view on state power: while the alterglobalization movement dismissed the idea of taking state power, new movements directly engage with the state, both in their claims and in their political strategies. In these efforts, the state's capacity to defend social groups from crisis effects becomes a limited resource, and the object of intra-group struggles. Finally, the way present crisis dynamics are politicized by global movements after 2008 has been characterized by a stronger heterogeneity than in the case of globally coordinated, but socially less broad alterglobalist networks. In terms of relations between street demonstrations and party strategies, or between social claims and status-based claims, we see a heterogeneity of movement strategies within the new left segment of post-2008 movements. Beyond new left versions, new populist and neonationalist versions of post-2008 anti-austerity movements have been less visible in movement research frameworks sympathetic to new left claims, but increasingly present on the streets and in post-2008 politics (e.g. Florea et al., 2018). Movements that frame their claims in terms of welfare and democracy, but simultaneously voice anti-social sentiments (like the middle class movements covered in this book) also fall outside of either alterglobalist or "democratic capitalism" frameworks, but are nonetheless present. Transitions between emancipative and reactionary phases of the same movement constituency have also been addressed by researchers (Ozarow, 2019; Tsoneva, 2019). Finally, several studies point out that even anti-austerity movements that feature similar repertoires and slogans after 2008 represent different social currents, alliances, and interests within the same systemic reorganization (Biekart & Fowler, 2013; Gagyi, 2015; Guzman-Concha, 2012; Poenaru, 2017).

As the issue of climate crisis increasingly penetrates forms of political consciousness, the capacity of current antisystemic movements to perceive different local situations as part of the same global process, and negotiate coordinated forms of action across different global positions and scales, is becoming a key question. From the problem of peripheral industrialization in debates about a just climate transition (e.g. Mathews et al., 2016) to problems of different infrastructural scales—like the relation between community green energy projects and the breakdown of incumbent energy providers whose integrated infrastructures would be necessary for a coordinated transition (Sweeney & Treat, 2017)—the question of a capacity to think and act across global scales arises in all aspects of movement strategizing. The capacity to understand movement positions and strategies in light of a global perception of social and capitalist reorganization is key to building that capacity. In the next section, I review world-systems insights on systemic crises in order to highlight several points that might inform such an orientation within the current crisis.

What is Crisis in a Global Sense?

Interpretations of the 2008 crisis typically point at the liberalization of global finance as the root cause of the problem. Regarding sociopolitical tensions caused by the crisis, movements and critical scholars emphasized neoliberal austerity measures and the polarization of social wealth that preceded the crisis, and was topped by crisis measures that bailed out banks and shifted costs to society (e.g. Fominaya, 2017; Stiglitz, 2009). The narrative of the "crisis of democratic capitalism" connects these phenomena to postwar welfare years as a point of origin, and then follows their development in terms of a process of decline. Cox and Nilsen (2014) discuss the same development in terms of phases of capitalism, the liberal phase of British hegemony being followed by the organized capitalism of postwar years, and then a neoliberal phase after 1970. In the tradition of world-systems research, the same transformations have been investigated in terms of global cycles within the long-term evolution of capitalism. By comparing dynamics of successive cycles and their crisis phases, this tradition offers a horizon of orientation on the contemporary crisis that can go beyond the relatively short-term experience of the decline of Western postwar conditions, and consider today's transformations in terms of the dynamics of the long-term systemic process.

In terms of the social and political implications of crisis phases of hegemonic cycles, the transformation of the structural conditions of hegemony are of key importance. While hegemonic cycles are named by the actors who have the strongest control and benefit the most from the given system of accumulation, hegemony does not only refer to the power these actors exercise through means of ideology and coercion. It also refers to the ways a given system of accumulation is able to accommodate actors in various positions, integrate their interests into the hegemonic interest, and secure a high enough level of collaboration that can underpin the stability of the whole system.

From among the complex political and structural conditions of hegemony in international political economy (Cox, 1983), one important aspect regards how reorganizations of actors' positions relate to the politics of hegemonic crisis. In terms of actors' positions within hegemony, Silver and Slater (1999) differentiate between three types: hegemonic actors, their junior partners, and the dominated. This differentiation only serves to point at types of positions and roles actors fulfill within the hegemonic process; it does not denote concrete groups, as the position of groups during cyclical dynamics can change.

According to this differentiation, hegemonic actors are defined as those who have the most control over, and benefit the most from the given order of accumulation. Their junior partners are actors who, although in less advantageous positions, still benefit enough to have an interest in supporting the system. Their alliance with hegemonic actors in sustaining existing structures of accumulation is key to the formation of a majority interest that can keep dominated actors at bay. The position of dominated actors is defined as one where participation in systemic ways of accumulation is so disadvantageous, that their interests collide with those of the regime. In peak moments of hegemonic power, the collaboration and silence of dominated groups is secured through modes of cultural, coercive, and structural domination (like systemic limits of alternative livelihoods), underpinned by the political power of hegemonic–junior partnerships. This situation, however, changes as soon as established forms of accumulation engender changes in actors' own positions.

Trying to understand the long crisis of the postwar cycle, Arrighi (1994) looks back at previous moments of hegemonic crisis. While other accounts of neoliberal transformation typically emphasize the institutional innovations and new political struggles that led to the transformation of the Bretton Woods system, Arrighi finds that the characteristics of this transformation bear a striking resemblance to earlier moments of systemic crisis. Based on these resemblances, he provides an interpretation of the crisis in terms of a recurrent phase of hegemonic cycles. This take does not imply that the evolution of capitalism would merely proceed through a repetition of the same cycle. Rather, it shows how the ever-growing volume of accumulation and penetration of nature and society that characterizes capitalist history is made possible by cyclical reorganizations of the material, social, and political structures that provide the conditions of accumulation. Elsewhere, Arrighi and Silver (2001) emphasize the ways through which the particular structures of governance, enterprise, or interstate and military relations of different cycles are built on the specific resources and contradictions of previous cycles.

In terms of shared characteristics of hegemonic cycles, Arrighi (1994) points out that in the first phase of the cycle, capital is invested into building out new structures of material circulation (production and commerce), together with the organizational and political infrastructures that serve to maintain and stabilize them. In this early phase, new types of material and organizational structures of accumulation provide a high return on investment, and motivate other actors to follow the example. This leads to the expansion of similar structures of accumulation, and a growing competition over their control and benefits (think the colonial competition of the early modern era, competitive industrialization under British hegemony, or the expansion of Fordist production—and notably: the automotive industry—in the postwar era).

As the cycle arrives in its ripe phase, the same material-organizational structures of accumulation that provided high profitability and encouraged actors to competitively invest into their expansion earlier, become exhausted, and profitability starts to decline. As the profitability of investment in the same structures of accumulation declines, the system faces a growing problem of overaccumulation (Brenner, 2002). Arrighi argues that in all four hegemonic cycles of modern capitalist history, capital's reaction to this situation was a withdrawal from material investments, and a reorientation toward financial markets. The boom of financial markets and their growing dominance over other spheres of the economy, widely discussed in debates over the present crisis as the process of financialization (Epstein, 2005), is seen by Arrighi as a characteristic of global accumulation cycles. While research focusing on the conditions of twentieth-century financialization has emphasized a new, so far unseen level of global interconnectedness through financialization and market liberalization, world-systems research has pointed out that local markets have always been integrated into system-wide flows, and all phases of financialization included a deepening of system-wide connections (Abu-Lughod, 1989; Arrighi, 1994).

In the first phase of the crisis, capital's withdrawal into financial markets, as well as other reorganizations like market liberalization, an increasing penetration of peripheral economies, and an expansion of debt relations, makes it possible for core capital to compensate for declining profitability. Arrighi and Silver (2003) call this the phase of "belle époque", based on how it appears in the eyes of core elites, who experience a new boom of profitability. For most other actors, however, this transformation is highly destructive. The resulting misery and political mobilizations further erode the material and political structures built out in earlier phases.

The phase of financialization brings about the breakup of the social coalitions of the earlier hegemonic order, and a new volatility of political alliance structures. As previous positions occupied in expanding structures of accumulation are destroyed or get scarcer, not only the misery of dominated groups becomes unbearable, but also junior groups experience hardship. Comparing the political dynamics of the four historical cycles, Silver and Slater (1999) conclude that in the case of junior partners of hegemonic elites, this shift in positions brings about political mobilizations where they struggle to keep their earlier benefits. On the ideological level, this change is perceived and expressed as a crisis of morals and worldview, where previous certainties are brought under question, and new competing visions of history, society, and morals are promoted.

As capital's strategies of financialization and intensified extraction bring about an increased centralization of wealth and the immiseration of societies, junior groups' experience of downward mobility and surrounding poverty is contrasted to a spectacular growth of wealth on top levels of the accumulation hierarchy. In this situation, junior groups start to condemn the decline of earlier, more beneficial models of accommodation and wealth redistribution, and criticize new accumulation models as unjust, oligarchic, and nepotistic. Turning away from their earlier elite allies, they often seek political alliances with dominated groups, or with alternative elite blocs.

Silver and Slater point at several instances where political alliances and ideologies of junior groups went through such transformations during previous hegemonic crises. For instance, in the beginning of the 1780s, Dutch Patriots claimed that the earlier stability of the Republic is threatened by "nepotism and oligarchy", and demanded radical democratic reforms to reestablish its earlier glory (Schama, 1989, 148–150, quoted by Silver & Slater, 1999: 164). In the same period, revolutionaries in

Europe and North America also contested new forms of wealth distribution as extremely unequal, and criticized financial speculation for bringing about a crisis of commerce. In the Netherlands, the wealth of Amsterdam as a financial center was contrasted with the experience of deindustrialization due to the crisis of shipbuilding and the contraction of wages. While "merchant-bankers and the wealthy rentiers might never 'had it so good'" (Boxer, 1965, 293–294, quoted by Silver & Slater, 165), workers' conditions were steadily declining. Groups who used to occupy junior positions in industry and commerce were also suffering from decline. Parallel to those economic difficulties, "the attitude of the small burgher – the shopkeeper, guildsman, or arisan – toward the periwigged oligarchs became decidedly more ambivalent" (Schama, 1992: 43–47, quoted by Silver & Slater, 1999: 165–166). Political discontent fueled by deindustrialization and economic polarization was directed at "self-satisfied and short-sighted rentiers and capitalists, who preferred to invest their money abroad rather than in fostering industry and shipping at home and thus relieving unemployment" (Boxer, 1965: 328, quoted by Silver & Slater, 1999: 165). Burghers also complained that interconnections between economic and ruling elites formed tight nepotistic coalitions that secured avenues of still lucrative activities (like long-distance trade and high finance) for themselves. Silver and Slater conclude that the alienation of junior groups from elite allies characterized all declining hegemonic powers during their final flowering as financial centers. As they quote Kevin Phillips:

> Finance cannot nurture a [large middle] class, because only a small elite of any national population – Dutch, British or American – can share in the profits of bourse, merchant bank and countinghouse. Manufacturing, transportation and trade supremacies, by contrast, provide a broader national prosperity in which the ordinary person can man the production lines, mines, mills, wheels, mainsails and nets. Once this stage of economic development yields to the next, with its sharper divisions from capital, skills and education, great middle-class societies lose something vital and unique, just what worriers believe was happening again to the United States in the late twentieth century. (Phillips, 1993:197, quoted by Silver & Slater, 1999: 166)

These symptoms of the last phase of Dutch hegemony may sound very familiar today. The critique of deindustrialization and financialization, linked to the condemnation of wealth polarization and the destruction of economic possibilities in middle positions has become a main tone in the politics of declining European and US core economies, from Occupy's famous formulation of the contradiction between the 1 and the 99% or new social democratic projects to new right populism.

While this destabilization of political support by junior groups might be most visible on the level of formal politics, in phases of crisis, the increased misery of dominated groups and their own mobilization also contributes to the political destabilization of hegemony. The restructuring of earlier hegemonic alliances brings about an era of political turmoil, where various groups and their coalitions—including new alliances between competing fractions of earlier hegemonic, junior, and dominated groups around new economic and political projects—struggle to utilize state infrastructures to protect their benefits and promote their interests. Besides political turmoil, states also face a growing lack of capital resulting from the process of financialization. Interstate competition for financing, together with political instability and increasing clashes between different protectionist projects increases the risk of military conflict—which then serves as a new avenue for profitable investment. This leads to what Arrighi and Silver (1999: 133) call the phase of "systemic chaos". This final, violently destructive phase brings about widespread social, political, and military conflicts, and the final disintegration of the earlier order of global accumulation.

In the case of previous cycles, this phase of destruction was followed by the reorganization of accumulation under the control of a new hegemon. Phases of hegemonic crisis also imply the simultaneous growth of new avenues of accumulation within the crisis of the old hegemony. The expansion of Fordism in early twentieth-century United States can be one example to this process. In terms of subsequent reorganizations of the material-organizational structures of accumulation, the withdrawal of financialized capital from material investment is not only a sign of crisis, but also a vital condition of capital's reorganizing capacity. Becoming liquid through withdrawing into financial markets makes it possible for capital to disengage from exhausted structures of accumulation, and seek out new possibilities for investment into accumulation structures capable of expansion.

Whether the present crisis of the US-dominated cycle is paralleled by a similar capacity for capitalist reorganization is debated. Today, too, the "belle époque" of financialization is followed today by a growing wave of social and political conflicts globally. The decline of earlier Western core economies, a new wave of protectionism challenging globalist capitalist alliances, and related international conflicts are paralleled with the rise of China not only as a new economic power, but also as an active promoter of a differently structured world-market integration (Arrighi, 2007; Tsui et al., 2017). World-systems research has traditionally pointed out two main differences between today's and earlier phases of systemic crisis. The first is the scale of destructive military power (e.g. Arrighi & Silver, 2001), which makes it less likely for new centers of the world economy to achieve a hegemonic position through a series of military conflicts. Instead, the combination of the US' downward mobility and great military power is seen as a combustible mix that can lead to more catastrophic scenarios.

The other main difference researchers point out consists in the different scale of exhaustion of the system's natural resources. As ecosocialists (e.g. Foster, 2000; Salleh, 1997) and a new wave of world-systems based research on "world ecology" (Moore, 2015) have emphasized, natural resources constitute an integral part of the accumulation structures built out by capitalist hegemony. Their integration happens not only through a mere extraction of resources, but also through the complex ways in which models of accumulation create and govern the value, availability, life, and use of those resources. Patel and Moore (2017) summarized these ways as the production of cheap and free resources for accumulation's sake.

The use of women's free labor in housework, their cheaper labor in workplaces, or the free and cheap resources provided by colonial agriculture and slave labor to Western industrialization are such examples. Along the forms of accumulation concentrated in core regions of the world economy—like the trade centers of colonial empires, the industrial technologies that played a dominant role in contemporary economies, or the financial centers of late hegemonies—these "external", free and cheap resources played a key role in systemic cycles of accumulation. The intercontinental triangle of slave trade, the sugar plantations and silver mines of South America, the role of Baltic forests in the formation of the Dutch maritime empire, or the transition to high calories species in agricultural regions subservient to Western industrialization are classic historical examples. More recent conflicts around enclosures of forests, fisheries, or lands of indigenous and peasant communities are part of that longer process through which the production of cheap "external" resources has created the social and ecological conditions of accumulation (Moore, 2015; Wolf, 1982). The use of fossil energy itself—the main source of today's climate crisis—has been analyzed as an outcome of capital's techniques to optimally combine the subordination of labor and nature to the production of surplus value (Malm, 2016).

The production of certain types of cheap resources, and the conditions that enable and control them, have been part of the process through which hegemonic regimes built out new material structures of accumulation. The exhaustion of these resources, too, has played a key role in the exhaustion of accumulation structures in later phases of cycles. How to create new forms of material and institutional extraction that could produce new free and cheap resources has been an essential question of capitalist reorganization in times of hegemonic transition. Looking at today's crisis, researchers question whether the possibility for such a reorganization still exists. Meanwhile, the development of industrial production and consumption in regions like East Asia or Latin America produces a need for raw materials and agricultural land at a volume that can hardly be reached within present conditions of the world economy. This increased search for resources produces new tensions and increasingly violent efforts to transform contemporary economic, social, and political relations to the benefit of competing actors (Andreas & Zhan 2016; Cotula, 2013).

Finally, the climate crisis itself is transforming the structure of existing resources. In this context, capitalist strategies that merely aimed to detract calls for transformation are giving space to a volatility of experimentations with new avenues of investment, and growing conflicts between capitalist alliances favoring different scenarios. A growing social awareness of the crisis, together with resulting political pressure, and the real-time effects of already ongoing catastrophes, put an additional weight on hegemonic forms of accumulation, while new capitalist alliances make efforts to channel new movements' energy into their own projects. Debates around green growth and various versions of Green New Deal are good examples of struggles around those efforts. However, despite new initiatives for capitalist answers to the climate crisis, evidence suggests that responses based on the requirement of profitability are not able to reduce emissions in a way that could ensure survival (Sweeney & Treat, 2017). The conflict between the need to expand the forms of cheap resources, and the need to reduce growth in order to avoid climate catastrophe suggests that both the present systemic chaos, and potential new forms of accumulation would soon lead to new explosions of crisis. In this context, the question of a new hegemonic reorganization seems to be overshadowed by the question whether the verve of the secular process of capitalist development can be halted at the brink of mass extinction.

CONCLUSION

This chapter dealt with the problem of knowledge perspectives that define the ways movements are understood—by academic and public discussions as well as by movement actors themselves. I argued that dominant conceptualizations of contemporary movements have been limited by a time–space bias on Western postwar forms of welfare democracies. While the earlier consensus that defined movements as an institutional level of democratic politics in affluent, democratic capitalist societies crumbled with the new movement wave after 2008, the discourse around new anti-austerity movements preserved effects of the same bias. I summarized these as the narrative of the "crisis of democratic capitalism". Here, present forms of crisis are conceived in terms of a decline of previous forms of democracy and social inclusion in postwar Western societies. This perspective tends to obscure class conflicts within welfare societies, the broader relationships between Western welfare democracies and the rest of the global economy in the same cycle, and the continuity between the boom and bust phases of the postwar global accumulation cycle.

Regarding the understanding of social self-organization and social movements in Eastern Europe after socialism, the chapter showed that its dominant concepts implied an application of Western models to local contexts that relegate the understanding of local processes to a contradictory dynamic of normative development vs. developmental insufficiencies. In the case of the notion of civil society, late socialist dissidents' idea of democratic self-organization came to be applied during the transition as a normative framework which defined local struggles of transition as aiming for liberal democratization, and predicted a future proliferation of civic organization after political democratization. The interpretation of post-2008 movements happened through a reactualization of normative frameworks of catch-up development, combined with the Western narrative of the "crisis of democratic capitalism". This kind of reactualization of the ideological link between democratization and catch-up development, and the temporal framework of "backwardness" that it implies, simultaneously acts as a ground for expressing discontent with the fulfillment of that promise, and detracts understanding postsocialist transformation as a real process in global history.

In order to be able to see contemporary forms of mobilizations across different positions as part of the same global history, the chapter proposed an approach that integrates insights following from world-systems research. This approach agrees with new proposals toward a Marxist interpretation of movements as key actors of history, yet instead of focusing on direct conflicts between movements of capital and labor, it is also sensitive to broader, long-term aspects of the dynamics of that struggle. This view enables us to differentiate between various positions and scales of struggles, and consider their relations in terms of the integrated development of capitalism as a worldwide process.

The kind of orientation this perspective can offer on movements was illustrated by insights on the relation between labor struggles and global investment cycles, and on the positioned differences and cross-cycle dynamics of modern antisystemic movements. Both examples highlighted that instead of momentary conflicts that would correspond to universal concepts of antisystemic struggle, contestations born from systemic pressures are integrated into complex dynamics of systemic contradictions across the system's long-term development. Regarding contemporary movements, the chapter agreed with other commentators in that the new wave of antisystemic movements that started from anti-neoliberal resistance in the Global South, and built out a global network in the alterglobalization movement of the 2000s, has greatly influenced post-2008 movements. However, it also pointed out that other characteristics of new movements fall outside of the alterglobalist agenda. Most importantly, since now Western movements voice local grievances instead of a mere moral solidarity with the exploitation of the South, systemic contradictions between Western social democratic politics and peripheries' interests come to be more apparent. Claims to protect Western economies' global superiority, anti-immigration stances, or support for green capitalism find their ways into new progressive politics, while global differences between movements' conditions and fate are pushed to the background of narratives based on Western paradigmatic cases.

Similar to others who have emphasized the importance of a global dialogue that can enable a common strategizing between movements in different global positions (Cox et al., 2017; Karatasli, 2019), I find that the capacity to imagine our conditions and their mutual relations within the same global process is essential in the current moment. As capital's accumulation crisis integrates with the swift evolution of the climate crisis, movements need to be able to simultaneously consider the differences and mutual connections of their immediate conditions, grasp their relations to long-term structural processes in order to assess their space of maneuver, and make coordinated efforts toward aims that surpass the logic of past hegemonic struggles.

From this perspective, among the insights considered in this chapter, the most relevant to current debates seem to be the following. The first is the idea that the current systemic crisis, together with the process of neoliberalization and financialization that preceded it, are regular aspects of hegemonic crises, and are necessary consequences of previous expansion. This insight stops us from seeing previous Western welfare capitalist models as a universal model of development from which current politics are backsliding from, but which could be reached by more struggle. The insights presented by the chapter suggest that instead of a new significant expansion of capital's accommodation potential, in the current situation new hegemonic efforts can only build on increasing polarization, violence, and catastrophic ecological destruction.

Second, the differentiation between the ideological level of politics and the real process of systemic integration implies that we understand the present proliferation of movement claims toward the state not in terms of their potential fulfillment that only depends on the intensity of struggle, but rather as an aspect of systemic crisis, where social groups who lose their positions in the crumbling structures of previous expansion launch simultaneous claims toward states' narrowing capacity to protect their benefits. Compared to the focus on the politics of the ideological sphere in mainstream discussions, this insight helps to re-balance our orientation by directing attention to strategies that deal with the conditions of struggle in terms of systemic processes.

The third main insight regarded capital's limited capacity to accommodate labor's claims. In a strategy that aims higher shares from capital's profitability, this limitation sets labor's fractions against each other, and provides a ground for cross-class coalitions that promise beneficial treatment for limited groups of labor. Besides pointing at a pro-systemic potential ingrained in the struggle for profit shares, this insight also highlights the hidden aspect of global hierarchies in claims intended as progressive. The heritage of Western social democracy is an important case here, as it continues to inspire a strategic imagination that links labor's reproduction needs to domestic capital's capacity for expansion—a horizon that can put serious limitations on conceiving global solutions to the present crisis.

References

Abu-Lughod, J. L. (1989). *Before European hegemony: The world system AD 1250–1350*. Oxford University Press.

Amin, S. (1991). The issue of democracy in the contemporary Third World. *Socialism and Democracy, 7*(1), 83–104.

Amin, S., Arrighi, G., Frank, A. G., & Wallerstein, I. (1990). *Transforming the revolution*. Monthly Review Press.

Ancelovici, M., Dufour, P., & Nez, H. (Eds.). (2016). *Street politics in the age of austerity: From the indignados to occupy*. Amsterdam University Press.

Andreas, J., & Zhan, S. (2016). Hukou and land: Market reform and rural displacement in China. *The Journal of Peasant Studies, 43*(4), 798–827.

Anheier, H. K., Kaldor, M., & Glasius, M. (Eds.). (2005). *Global civil society 2005/6*. Sage.

Arrighi, G. (1994). *The long twentieth century: Money, power, and the origins of our times*. Verso.

Arrighi, G. (1999). Globalization, state sovereignty, and the "endless" accumulation of capital. In D. A. Smith, D. J. Solinger, & S. Topik (Eds.), *States and sovereignty in the global economy* (pp. 69–89). Psychology Press.

Arrighi, G. (2007). *Adam Smith in Beijing: Lineages of the twenty-first century*. Verso.

Arrighi, G., Hopkins, T. K., & Wallerstein, I. (1989). *Anti-systemic movements*. Verso.

Arrighi, G., & Silver, B. J. (2001). Capitalism and world (dis) order. *Review of International Studies, 27*(5), 257–279.

Arrighi, G. (1990). Marxist century—American century: The making and remaking of the world labor movement. In Amin, S., Arrighi, G., Frank. A. G. & Wallerstein (Eds.), *Transforming the revolution* (pp. 54–95). Monthly Review Press.

Axford, B. (1998). *The global system: Economics, politics and culture*. Polity.

Azarova, A., Irdam, D, Gugushvili, A., Fazekas, M., Scheiring, G., Horvat, P., Stefler, D., Kolesnikova, I., Popov, V., Szelenyi, I., Stuckler, D., Marmot, M., Murphy, M., McKee, M., Bobak, M., & King, L. (2017). The effect of rapid privatisation on mortality in mono-industrial towns in post-Soviet Russia: A retrospective cohort study. *The Lancet Public Health, 2*(5): e231–e238.

Bailey, D. J., Clua-Losada, M., Huke, N., & Ribera-Almandoz, O. (2017). *Beyond defeat and austerity: Disrupting (the critical political economy of) neoliberal Europe*. Routledge.

Bair, J., Harris, K., & Hough, P. A. (2019). Roads from Calabria: The Arrighian approach to agrarian political economy. *Journal of Agrarian Change, 19*(3), 391–406.

Bakuniak, G., & Nowak, K. (1987). The creation of a collective identity in a social movement. *Theory and Society, 16*(3): 401–429.

Banerjee, S. (1984). *India's simmering revolution: The Naxalite uprising.* Zed Books.

Baran, P. A., & Sweezy, P. (1966). *Monopoly capital.* NYU Press.

Barker, C. (2013). *Marxism and social movements.* Brill.

Barker, C., & Kennedy, P. (1996). *To make another world: Studies in protest and collective action.* Ashgate.

Beissinger, M. R., & Sasse, G. (2014). An End to "Patience"? In N. Bermeo & L. Bartels (Eds.), *Mass politics in tough times: Opinions, votes and protest in the Great Recession* (pp. 238–245). Oxford University Press.

Benda, V. (1991). The parallel 'polis.' In G. H. Skilling (Ed.), *Civic Freedom in Central Europe* (pp. 35–41). Palgrave Macmillan.

Berend, I. T. (2009). *From the Soviet bloc to the European Union: The economic and social transformation of Central and Eastern Europe since 1973.* Cambridge University Press.

Biekart, K. (2015). The choice of the new Latin American middle classes: Sharing or self-caring. *The European Journal of Development Research, 27*(2), 238–245.

Biekart, K., & Fowler, A. (2013). Transforming activisms 2010+: Exploring ways and waves. *Development and Change, 44*(3), 527–546.

Blyth, M. (2016). Global Trumpism. *Foreign Affairs, 15,* 2016.

Bohle, D., & Greskovits, B. (2012). *Capitalist diversity on Europe's periphery.* Cornell University Press.

Boltanski, L., & Chiapello, E. (2005). *The new spirit of capitalism.* Verso.

Böröcz, J. (2012). Notes on the geopolitical economy of post-state-socialism. In N. Bandelj & D. J. Solinger (Eds.), *Socialism vanquished, socialism challenged: Eastern Europe and China, 1989–2009* (pp. 103–124). Oxford University Press.

Bottoni, S. (2017). *Long awaited west: Eastern Europe since 1944.* Indiana University Press.

Boxer, C. R. (1965). *Portuguese society in the tropics: The municipal councils of Goa, Macao, Bahia, and Luanda, 1510–1800.* University of Wisconsin Press.

Brenner, R. (1977). The origins of capitalist development: A critique of neo-Smithian Marxism. *New Left Review, 104,* 25–92.

Brenner, R. (2002). *The boom and the bubble: The US in the world economy.* Verso.

Brown, W. (1999). Resisting left melancholy. *boundary 2, 26*(3), 19–27.

Bugajski, J. (1987). *Czechoslovakia, Charter 77's decade of dissent*. Praeger Publishers.

Cardoso, F. H., & Faletto, E. (1979). *Dependency and development in Latin America*. University of California Press.

Castañeda, E. (2012). The indignados of Spain: A precedent to occupy Wall Street. *Social Movement Studies, 11*(3–4), 309–319.

Castells, M. (1989). *The city and the grassroots: A cross-cultural theory of urban social movements*. University of California Press.

Chakrabarty, D. (2009). *Provincializing Europe: Postcolonial thought and historical difference*. Princeton University Press.

Chalcraft, J. (2016). *Popular politics in the making of the modern Middle East*. Cambridge University Press.

Chase-Dunn, C. (1988). Comparing world systems: Toward a theory of semipheral development. *Comparative Civilizations Review, 19*(19), 3.

Chase-Dunn, D., & Kwon, R. (2012). Crises and counter-movements in world evolutionary perspective. *World Society in the Global Economic Crisis. Berlin: LIT Verlag* (pp. 43–70).

Chomsky, N. (2017). *The responsibility of intellectuals*. The New Press.

Christensen, D., & Weinstein, J. M. (2013). Defunding dissent: Restrictions on aid to NGOs. *Journal of Democracy, 24*(2), 77–91.

Cianetti, L., Dawson, J., & Hanley, S. (2018). Rethinking "democratic backsliding" in Central and Eastern Europe–looking beyond Hungary and Poland. *East European Politics, 34*(3), 243–256.

Císař, O. (2010). Externally sponsored contention: The channelling of environmental movement organisations in the Czech Republic after the fall of Communism. *Environmental Politics, 19*(5), 736–755.

Císař, O., & Vráblíková, K. (2010). The Europeanization of social movements in the Czech Republic: The EU and local women's groups. *Communist and Post-Communist Studies, 43*(2), 209–219.

Clarke, S. (1978). Capital, fractions of capital and the state: 'neo-marxist' analysis of the South African state. *Capital & Class, 2*(2), 32–77.

Clarke, S. (1991). State, class struggle, and the reproduction of capital. In S. Clarke (Ed.), *The state debate* (pp. 183–203). Palgrave.

Cockerham, W. C. (1997). The social determinants of the decline of life expectancy in Russia and Eastern Europe: A lifestyle explanation. *Journal of Health and Social Behavior, 1997*, 117–130.

Cohen, J. L., & Arato, A. (1992). *Civil society and political theory*. MIT Press.

Cotula, L. (2013). *The great African land grab?: Agricultural investments and the global food system*. Zed Books.

Cox, L. (2017). The multiple traditions of social movement research: Theorizing intellectual diversity. https://mural.maynoothuniversity.ie/8101/1/LC_FMSH-WP-2017-128.pdf. Accessed 5 February 2021.

Cox, L. (2018). *Why social movements matter*. Rowman and Littlefield.

Cox, L., & Fominaya, C. (2009). Movement knowledge: what do we know, how do we create knowledge and what do we do with it? *Interface: A Journal for and About Social Movements, 1*(1), 1–20.

Cox, L., & Fominaya, C. (2013). European social movements and social theory. A richer narrative? In C. F. Fominaya and L. Cox (Eds.), *Understanding European movements: New social movements, global justice struggles, anti-austerity protest*. Routledge.

Cox, L., & Nilsen, A. G. (2007). Social movements research and the 'movement of movements': Studying resistance to neoliberal globalisation. *Sociology Compass, 1*(2), 424–442.

Cox, L., & Nilsen, A. G. (2014). *We make our own history: Marxism and social movements in the twilight of neoliberalism*. Pluto Press.

Cox, L., Nilsen, A., & Pleyers, G. (2017). Social movement thinking beyond the core: theories and research in post-colonial and postsocialist societies. *Interface: a Journal for and about Social Movements, 9*(2), 1–36.

Cox, R. W. (1983). Gramsci, hegemony and international relations: an essay in method. *Millennium, 12*(2), 162–175.

Creed, G. W. (1995). Agriculture and the domestication of industry in rural Bulgaria. *American Ethnologist, 22*(3), 528–548.

Crossley, N. (2003). Even newer social movements? Anti-corporate protests, capitalist crises and the remoralization of society. *Organization, 10*(2), 287–305.

Dale, G. (Ed.). (2011). *First the transition, then the crash: Eastern Europe in the 2000s*. Pluto.

Dale, G. (2019, October 28). Degrowth and the green new deal. *The Ecologist*. https://theecologist.org/2019/oct/28/degrowth-and-the-green-new-deal. Accessed 5 February 2021.

De Sousa Santos, B. (2007). *Another knowledge is possible*. Verso.

Della Porta, D. (2013). *Can democracy be saved?: Participation, deliberation and social movements*. John Wiley and Sons.

Della Porta, D. (2014). *Mobilizing for democracy: Comparing 1989 and 2011*. Oxford University Press.

Della Porta, D. (2015). *Social movements in times of austerity: Bringing capitalism back into protest analysis*. Wiley.

Della Porta, D. (2020). *How social movements can save democracy – Democratic innovations from below*. Polity.

Della Porta, D., & Mattoni, A. (Eds.). (2014). *Spreading protest: Social movements in times of crisis*. Rowman & Littlefield.

Della Porta, D., & Tarrow, S. (2012). Interactive diffusion: The coevolution of police and protest behavior with an application to transnational contention. *Comparative Political Studies, 45*(1), 119–152.

Desai, R. (2004). From national bourgeoisie to rogues, failures and bullies: 21st century imperialism and the unravelling of the Third World. *Third World Quarterly, 25*(1), 169–185.

Diani, M., & Cisař, O. (2014). *The emergence of a European social movement research field* (pp. 172–195). Routledge.

Dunn, E., & Hann, C. (1996). *Civil society: Challenging western models*. Psychology Press.

Einhorn, B. (1993). *Cinderella goes to market: Gender, citizenship, and women's movements in East Central Europe*. Verso.

Eisinger, P. K. (1973). The conditions of protest behavior in American cities. *American Political Science Review, 67*(1), 11–28.

Ekiert, G., & Foa, R. (2011). Civil society weakness in post-communist Europe: A preliminary assessment. *Carlo Alberto Notebooks, 198*, 1–45.

Ekiert, G., & Kubik, J. (1998). Contentious Politics in new democracies: East Germany, Hungary, Poland, and Slovakia, 1989–93. *World Politics, 50*(4), 547–581.

Epstein, G. A. (Ed.). (2005). *Financialization and the world economy*. Edward Elgar Publishing.

Eyal, G. (2000). Anti-politics and the spirit of capitalism: Dissidents, monetarists, and the Czech transition to capitalism. *Theory and Society, 29*(1), 49–92.

Fanon, F. (1967). *Black skin, white masks*. Grove Press.

Fanon, F. (1963). *The wretched of the Earth*. New York: Grove.

Felkai, G. (1997). Két társadalomelméleti illúzió széttörése a jelenkori magyar közgondolkodáson. *Szociológiai Figyelő, 1*(1), 100–124.

Flam, H. (Ed.). (2001). *Pink, purple, green women's, religious, environmental and gay/lesbian movements in Central Europe Today*. Columbia University Press.

Florea, I., Gagyi, A., & Jacobsson, K. (2018). A field of contention: Evidence from housing struggles in Bucharest and Budapest. *VOLUNTAS: International Journal of Voluntary and Nonprofit Organizations, 29*(4), 712–724.

Foa, R. S., & Ekiert, G. (2017). The weakness of postcommunist civil society reassessed. *European Journal of Political Research, 56*(2), 419–439.

Fominaya, C. F., & Hayes, G. (Eds.). (2019). *Resisting austerity: Collective action in Europe in the wake of the global financial crisis*. Routledge.

Fominaya, C. F. (2017). European anti-austerity and pro-democracy protests in the wake of the global financial crisis. *Social Movement Studies, 16*(1), 1–20.

Foster, J. B. (2000). *Marx's ecology: Materialism and nature*. NYU Press.

Foucault, M. (1988). *Technologies of the self: A seminar with Michel Foucault*. University of Massachusetts Press.

Frank, A. G. (1979). *Dependent accumulation*. NYU Press.

Frank, A. G., & Gills, B. K. (1993). The 5,000-year world system: An interdisciplinary introduction. In A. G. Fank, B. Gills, & B. K. Gills (Eds.), *The world system: Five hundred years or five thousand?* (pp. 3–55). Psychology Press.

Fraser, N. (2014, November 7). *Democracy's crisis*. Presented at Erasmus University Rotterdam, upon Nancy Fraser's receipt of an Honorary Doctorate, Rotterdam.

Fukuyama, F. (1989). The end of history? *The National Interest, 16*, 3–18.

Gagyi, A. (2015). Social movement studies for East Central Europe? . *Intersections East European Journal of Society and Politics, 1*(3), 16–36.

Gagyi, A. (2019, April 10) Solidarity and the commons in Central and Eastern Europe. *Green European Journal*. https://www.greeneuropeanjournal.eu/solidarity-economy-and-the-commons-implications-for-central-and-eastern-europe/. Accessed 5 February 2021.

Gagyi, A. (2011). A civil globalizáció 'univerzális' eszméje a 'periférián'. Magyarországi és romániai globalizációkritikus csoportok. PhD Dissertation. University of Pécs.

Gagyi, A. (2012). Occupy Wall Street? Position-blindness in the new leftist revolution. *Journal of Critical Globalisation Studies, 5*(2012), 143–148.

Gagyi, A. (2013). The shifting meaning of 'Autonomy'in the East European Diffusion of the alterglobalization movement. In L. Cox & C. Fominaya (Eds.), *Understanding European Movements: New social movements, global justice struggles, anti-austerity protest* (pp. 143–157). Routledge.

Gagyi, A., & Ivancheva, M. (2017). The Rise and fall of civil society in East-Central Europe: Transnational discursive and funding hierarchies. In N. McCrea & F. Finnegan (Eds.), *Funding, Power and Community Development* (pp. 55–69). Policy Press.

Gerbaudo, P. (2017). *The mask and the flag: Populism, citizenism, and global protest*. Oxford University Press.

Ghodsee, K. (2004). Feminism-by-design: Emerging capitalisms, cultural feminism, and women's nongovernmental organizations in postsocialist Eastern Europe. *Signs: Journal of Women in Culture and Society, 29*(3), 727–753.

Gille, Z. (2007). *From the cult of waste to the trash heap of history: The politics of waste in socialist and postsocialist Hungary*. Indiana University Press.

Glasius, M., & Pleyers, G. (2013). The global moment of 2011: Democracy, social justice and dignity. *Development and Change, 44*(3), 547–567.

Goffman, E. (1974). *Frame analysis: An essay on the organization of experience*. Harvard University Press.

Goodwin, J., Jasper, J. M., & Polletta, F. (2001). Why emotions matter. *Introduction to passionate politics: Emotions and social movements* (pp. 1–24). University of Chicago Press.

Gramsci, A. (1978). Some aspects of the southern question. In A. Gramsci (Ed.), *Selections from political writings* (pp. 1921–1926). Lawrence and Wishart.

Gramsci, A. (2000). *The Gramsci reader: Selected writings, 1916–1935*. NYU press.

Greskovits, B. (2015). The hollowing and backsliding of democracy in East Central Europe. *Global Policy, 6,* 28–37.

Grosfoguel, R. (2006). World-systems analysis in the context of transmodernity, border thinking, and global coloniality. *Review (Fernand Braudel Center),* 167–187.

Guzman-Concha, C. (2012). The students' rebellion in Chile: Occupy protest or classic social movement? *Social Movement Studies, 11*(3–4), 408–415.

Habermas, J. (1990). What does socialism mean today? The rectifying revolution and the need for new thinking on the left. *New Left Review, 183*(1990), 3.

Halmai, G. (2011). Possessed by the spectre of socialism: Nationalist mobilization in "transitional" Hungary. In D. Kalb, & G. Halmai (Eds.), *Headlines of nation, subtexts of class: Working class populism and the return of the repressed in neoliberal Europe* (pp. 113–141). Berghahn Books.

Hanna, T. (2018). *Our common wealth: The return of public ownership in the United States.* Manchester University Press.

Havel, V. (1986). *Living in truth.* Farber and Farber.

Hayes, G. (2014). Social movement studies, Social Movement Studies and the challenges of parochialism: A rejoinder. *Social Movement Studies, 132*(2014), 243–247.

Hennessy, R. (1993). Women's lives/feminist knowledge: Feminist standpoint as ideology critique. *Hypatia, 8*(1), 14–34.

Hetland, G., & Goodwin, J. (2013). The strange disappearance of capitalism from social movement studies. In *Marxism and social movements* (pp. 82–102). Brill.

Hicks, B. E. (1996). *Environmental politics in Poland: A social movement between regime and opposition.* Columbia University Press.

Howard, M. M. (2003). *The weakness of civil society in post-communist Europe.* Cambridge University Press.

Inglehart, R. (1971). The silent revolution in Europe: Intergenerational change in post-industrial societies. *American Political Science Review, 65*(4), 991–1017.

Ishchenko, V. (2015). Maidan mythologies. *New Left Review, 93*(2015), 151–159.

Ivancheva, M. (2011). The role of dissident-intellectuals in the formation of civil society in (Post-)Communist East-Central Europe. In H. Kouki & E. Romanos (Eds.), *Protest beyond borders: Contentious politics in Europe since 1945* (pp. 251–263). Berghahn.

Ivancheva, M. (2014). Continuity in Rupture: The Paradoxical history of the women's movement in Bulgaria. In Lisiak, N. Smolenski (Eds.). Junior Visiting Fellows Conferences (Vol. 33). Vienna: IWM.

Jacobsson, K., & Korolczuk, E. (Eds.). (2017). *Civil society revisited: Lessons from Poland.* Berghahn Books.

Jacobsson, K., & Saxonberg, S. (Eds.). (2013). *Beyond NGO-ization: The development of social movements in Central and Eastern Europe*. Ashgate Publishing.

Jehlička, P., Sarre, P., & Podoba, J. (2005). The Czech environmental movement's knowledge interests in the 1990s: Compatibility of western influences with pre-1989 perspectives. *Environmental Politics, 14*(1), 64–82.

Judt, T. (1988). The dilemmas of dissidence: The politics of opposition in East-central Europe. *East European Politics and Societies, 2*(2), 185–240.

Jürgens, U., & Krzywdzinski, M. (2009). Work models in the Central Eastern European car industry: Towards the high road? *Industrial Relations Journal, 40*(6), 471–490.

Juris, J. S. (2012). Reflections on #Occupy everywhere: Social media, public space, and emerging logics of aggregation. *American Ethnologist, 39*(2), 259–279.

Kalb, D. (2005). From flows to violence: Politics and knowledge in the debates on globalization and empire. *Anthropological Theory, 5*(2), 176–204.

Kalb, D., & Halmai, G. (Eds.). (2011). *Headlines of nation, subtexts of class: Working class populism and the return of the repressed in neoliberal Europe*. Berghahn.

Kaldor, M. (2003). The idea of global civil society. *International Affairs, 79*(3), 583–593.

Karatasli, S. S. (2019, November 1). The world is in a revolutionary moment – how can the global left be a serious player? *Open Democracy*. https://www.opendemocracy.net/en/oureconomy/the-world-is-in-a-revolutionary-mom ent-how-can-the-global-left-be-a-serious-player/. Accessed 4 February 2021.

Karatasli, S. S., Kumral, S., Scully, B., & Upahyay, S. (2015). Class, crisis, and the 2011 protest wave. Cyclical and secular trends in global labor unrest. In I. Wallerstein, C. Chase-Dunn, & C. Suter (Eds.), *Overcoming global inequalities* (pp. 184–200). Routledge.

Karitzis, A. (2017). *The European left in times of crisis: Lessons from Greece*. TNI.

Keane, J. (1988). *Democracy and civil society: On the predicaments of European socialism, the prospects for democracy, and the problem of controlling social and political power*. Verso.

Kideckel, D. A. (2009). Citizenship discourse, globalization, and protest: A postsocialist-postcolonial comparison. *Anthropology of East Europe Review, 27*(2), 117.

Kornai, J. (1993). Transzformációs Visszaesés. *Közgazdasági Szemle, 15*(1993), 7–8.

Konrad, G. (1989). *Antipolitika. Az autonómia kísértése*. Codex RT.

Kopeczky, P., & Mudde, C. (2003). *Uncivil society? Contentious politics in Post-Communist Europe*. Routledge.

Körösényi, A. (2000). *Értelmiség, politikai gondolkodás és kormányzat*. Osiris

Kotkin, S. (2009). *Uncivil society: 1989 and the implosion of the communist establishment*. Random House.

Krastev, I., & Holmes, S. (2020). *The light that failed: A reckoning*. Penguin.

Krugman, P. (2012, March 15). Why Hungary matters? *The New York Times*. https://krugman.blogs.nytimes.com/2012/03/15/why-hungary-matters/?mcubz=3. Accessed 26 January 2021.

Kubik, J. (2005). How to study civil society: The state of the art and what to do next. *East European Politics and Societies, 19*(1), 105–120.

Laclau, E., & Mouffe, C. (1985). *Hegemony and state socialism: Towards a radical democratic politics*. Verso.

Lee, R. E. (2010). Critiques and developments in worldsystems analysis: An introduction to the special collection. *Journal of Philosophical Economics, 4*(1), 5–18.

Lenin, V. I. ([1917] 1963) Imperialism, the highest stage of capitalism. In Lenin, V. I. (Ed.), *Selected works* (Vol. 1, pp. 667–766). Progress Publishers.

Lewis, H. (2017, July 23). Jeremy Corbyn: "wholesale" EU immigration has destroyed conditions for British workers". *New Statesman*. https://www.newstatesman.com/politics/staggers/2017/07/jeremy-corbyn-wholesale-eu-immigration-has-destroyed-conditions-british. Accessed 15 March 2020.

Linebaugh, P., & Rediker, M. (2013). *The many-headed hydra: Sailors, slaves, commoners, and the hidden history of the revolutionary Atlantic*. Beacon Press.

Lomax, B. (1997). The strange death of 'civil society' in Post-Communist Hungary. *The Journal of Communist Studies and Transition Politics, 13*(1), 41–63.

Luxemburg, R. ([1913] 1953). *The accumulation of capital: A contribution to an economic explanation of imperialism*. Routledge.

MacSheoin, T. (2016). The world according to social movement journals: A preliminary mapping. *Interface, 8*(1), 181–204.

Madariaga, A. (2020). *Neoliberal resilience*. Princeton University Press.

Malm, A. (2016). *Fossil capital: The rise of steam power and the roots of global warming*. Verso.

Mathews, R. D., Barria, S. & Roy, A. (2016). *Up from development: A framework for energy transition in India* (TUED working paper nr. 8). http://unionsforenergydemocracy.org/resources/tued-publications/. Accessed 1 February 2021.

McAdam, D., McCarthy, J. D., & Zald, M. N. (Eds.). (1996). *Comparative perspectives on social movements: Political opportunities, mobilizing structures, and cultural framings* (p. 1). Cambridge University Press.

McAdam, D., Tarrow, S., & Tilly, C. (2001). *Dynamics of contention*. Cambridge University Press.

McCarthy, J. D., & Zald, M. N. (1977). Resource mobilization and social movements: A partial theory. *American Journal of Sociology, 82*(6), 1212–1241.

McCormick, T. J. (1995). *America's half-century: United States foreign policy in the cold war and after*. Johns Hopkins University Press.

McGlazer, R. (2018). Transnational Feminist Strikes and Solidarities: Introduction. *Critical times, 1*(1), 146–148.

McLaughlin, N., & Trilupaityte, S. (2013). The international circulation of attacks and the reputational consequences of local context: George Soros's difficult reputation in Russia, Post-Soviet Lithuania and the United States. *Cultural Sociology, 7*(4), 431–446.

McMahon, Patrice C. (2001). Building civil societies in East Central Europe: The effect of American non-governmental organizations on women's groups. *Democratization, 8*(2), 45–68.

Meillassoux, C. (1981). *Maidens, meal and money*. Cambridge University Press.

Melegh, A. (2006). *On the East-West slope: Globalization, nationalism, racism and discourses on Eastern Europe*. Central European University Press.

Michnik, A. (1986). A new evolutionism. In A. Michnik (Ed.), *Letters from prison and other essays* (p. 22). University of California Press.

Mies, M., Bennholdt-Thomsen, V., & Von Werlhof, C. (1988). *Women: The last colony*. Zed Books.

Mignolo, W. (2002). The geopolitics of knowledge and the colonial difference. *The South Atlantic Quarterly, 101*(1), 57–96.

Mikecz, D. (2017). *A globalizációkritikus mozgalom Magyarországon. Lehetőségstruktúra és mozgalmi innováció*. L'Harmattan.

Mikuš, M. (2015). Indigenizing "civil society" in Serbia What local fund-raising reveals about class and trust. *Focaal, 2015*(71), 43–56.

Mikuš, M. (2016). The justice of neoliberalism: Moral ideology and redistributive politics of public-sector retrenchment in Serbia. *Social Anthropology, 24*(2), 211–227.

Mikuš, M. (2018). *Frontiers of civil society: Government and hegemony in Serbia*. Berghahn Books.

Mireanu, M. (2021). The civic duty to denounce: The Romanian middle class and its demands for security. *Critical Criminology*. https://doi.org/10.1007/s10612-020-09546-w

Moore, B. (1966). *Social origins of dictatorship and democracy. Lord and peasant in the making of the modern world*. Beacon Press.

Moore, J. (2015). *Capitalism in the web of life*. Verso.

Morys, M. (Ed.). (2020). *The economic history of Central, East and South-East Europe: 1800 to the present*. Routledge.

Mouffe, C. (2014, July 11–13). *The crisis of representative democracy and the need for a left-wing populism*. Keynote speech presented at the Populismus series (Aristotle University Research Dissemination Centre) conference. Thessaloniki.

Murthy, V. (1999). Leftist mourning: Civil society and political practice in Hegel and Marx. *Rethinking Marxism, 11*(3), 36–55.

Navrátil, J. (2010). Between the spillover and the spillout: Tracing the evolution of the Czech global justice movement. *Czech Sociological Review, 46*(6), 913–945.

Navrátil, J., Lin, K., & Cox, L. (2015). Movements in post/socialisms. *Interface, 7*(2), 1–8.

Negri, A. (1989). *The politics of subversion: A manifesto for the twenty-first century.* Polity.

Nkrumah, K. (1967). Neo-colonialism: The last stage of imperialism. *Science and Society, 31*(1), 78–81.

Ost, D. (2006). *The defeat of solidarity: Anger and politics in postcommunist Europe.* Cornell University Press.

Ost, D., & Crowley, S. (Eds.). (2001). *Workers after Workers' States: Labor and Politics in Postcommunist Eastern Europe.* Rowman & Littlefield.

Outhwaite, W., & Ray, L. (2005). *Social theory and Postcommunism.* Wiley-Blackwell.

Ozarow, D. (2019). *The mobilization and demobilization of middle-class revolt: Comparative insights from Argentina.* Routledge.

Parkin, F. (1968). *Middle class radicalism: The social bases of the British campaign for nuclear disarmament.* Manchester University Press.

Patel, R., & Moore, J. W. (2017). *A history of the world in seven cheap things: A guide to capitalism, nature, and the future of the planet.* University of California Press.

Petras, J., & Veltmeyer, H. (1997). NGOs and imperialism. *Monthly Review, 49*(7), 10–27.

Petrova, T., & Tarrow, S. (2007). Transactional and participatory activism in the emerging European polity: The puzzle of East-Central Europe. *Comparative Political Studies, 40*(1), 74–94.

Phillips, K. P. (1993). *Boiling point: Democrats, Republicans, and the decline of middle-class prosperity.* HarperPerennial.

Piotrowski, G. (2017). *Alterglobalism in postsocialism: A study of central and Eastern European activists.* Doctoral dissertation.

Pleyers, G. (2010). *Alter-globalization: Becoming actors in a global age.* Polity.

Pleyers, G., & Sava, I. (Eds.). (2015). *Social movements in central and eastern Europe. A renewal of protests and democracy.* Editura Univeresitatii din Bucuresti.

Poenaru, F. (2017). *Locuri comune: Clasă, anticapitalism, stânga.* Tact.

Polletta, F. (2012). *Freedom is an endless meeting: Democracy in American social movements.* University of Chicago Press.

Poulson, S. C., Cory, P. C., & Latasha, R. G. (2014). Isomorphism, institutional parochialism, and the study of social movements. *Social Movement Studies, 13*(2), 222–242.

Przeworski, A. (1991). *Democracy and the market: Political and economic reforms in Eastern Europe and Latin America.* Cambridge University Press.

Puddington, A. (2014, 4 October). Viktor Orbán and the state of Hungarian democracy. *Freedom House.* https://freedomhouse.org/blog/viktor-orban-and-state-hungarian-democracy. Accessed 5 February 2021.

Quijano, A. (2000). Coloniality of power and Eurocentrism in Latin America. *International Sociology, 15*(2), 215–232.

Rammelt, H. (2018). *Activistes protestataires en Hongrie et en Roumanie.* L'Harmattan.

Riley, D. (2019). *The civic foundations of fascism in Europe.* Verso.

Rey, P. P. (1973). *Les alliances de classes: Sur l'articulation des modes de production: Suivi de Matérialisme historique et luttes de classes.* F. Maspero.

Rostow, W. W. (1960). *The stages of growth: A non-communist manifesto.* Cambridge University Press.

Roth, G. (2019). *The educated underclass. Students and the promise of social mobility.* Pluto.

Roy, R. K., Denzau, A. T., & Willett, T. D. (Eds.). (2006). *Neoliberalism: National and regional experiments with global ideas.* Routledge.

Rupnik, J. (2007). Is East-Central Europe backsliding? From democracy fatigue to populist backlash. *Journal of Democracy, 18*(4), 17–25.

Rupnik, J. (2018). Explaining Eastern Europe: The crisis of liberalism. *Journal of Democracy, 29*(3), 24–38.

Salleh, A. (1997). *Ecofeminism as politics: Nature, Marx and the postmodern.* Zed Books and St Martins Press.

Sampson, S. (1996). The social life of projects. In E. Dunn & C. Hann (Eds.), *Civil society: Challenging western models.* Psychology Press.

Schama, S. (1989). *Citizens: A Chronicle of the French Revolution.* Vintage Books.

Seleny, A. (2006). *The political economy of state-society relations in Hungary and Poland: From communism to the European Union.* Cambridge University Press.

Shachar, A. (2009). *The birthright lottery: Citizenship and global inequality.* Harvard University Press.

Shihade, M., Fominaya, C. F., & Cox, L. (2012). The season of revolution: The Arab Spring and European mobilization. *Interface, 4*(1), 1–16.

Silver, B. J. (2003). *Forces of labor: Workers' movements and globalization since 1870.* Cambridge University Press.

Silver, B. J., & Karatasli, S. S. (2015). Historical dynamics of capitalism and labor movements. In D. della Porta & M. Diani (Eds.), *The Oxford Handbook of Social Movements* (pp. 133–145). Oxford University Press.

Silver, B. J., & Slater, E. (1999). The social origins of world hegemonies. In G. Arrighi (Ed.), *Chaos and governance in the modern world system* (pp. 151–216). University of Minnesota Press.

Smelser, N. J. (1962). *Theory of collective behavior*. The Free Press.

Smith, J., & Wiest, D. (2012). *Social movements in the world-system: The politics of crisis and transformation*. Russell Sage Foundation.

Snow, D. A., Rochford Jr, E. B., Worden, S. K., & Benford, R. D. (1986). Frame alignment processes, micromobilization, and movement participation. *American Sociological Review, 51*(4), 464–481.

Sklair, L. (1997). Social movements for global capitalism: The transnational capitalist class in action. *Review of International Political Economy, 4*(3), 514–538.

Sousa Santos, B. (2006). *The rise of the global left: The World Social Forum and beyond*. Zed Books.

Stavrakakis, Y., & Katsambekis, G. (2013). Populism, anti-populism and European democracy: a view from the South. In K. Karadiamanti, A. Georgopoulos, & G. Blionis (Eds.), *Populism, political ecology* (pp. 117–125). Green Institute Greece.

Stavrakakis, Y., & Katsambekis, G. (2014). Left-wing populism in the European periphery: The case of SYRIZA. *Journal of Political Ideologies, 19*(2), 119–142.

Stiglitz, Joseph E. (2009, April). *The financial crisis of 2007/2008 and its macroeconomic consequences* (Initiative for Policy Dialogue Working Paper Series). https://academiccommons.columbia.edu/doi/10.7916/D8Q Z2HSG. Accessed 13 March 2020.

Streeck, W. (2014). *Buying time: The delayed crisis of democratic capitalism*. Verso.

Stremlin, B. (2001). Bounding historical systems: The Wallerstein-Frank debate and the role of knowledge in world history. *Review (fernand Braudel Center), 24*(4), 515–531.

Sweeney, S., & Treat, J. (2017). *Preparing a public pathway: Confronting the investment crisis in renewable energy* (TUED working paper nr. 10). http://unionsforenergydemocracy.org/resources/tued-publications/. Accessed 1 February 2021.

Szombati, K. (2018). *The revolt of the provinces: Anti-gypsyism and right-wing politics in Hungary* (Vol. 23). Berghahn Books.

Tamás, G. M. (1994). A disquisition of civil society. *Social Research, 61*(3), 205–222.

Taylor, P. J. (1982). A materialist framework for political geography. *Transactions of the Institute of British Geographers, 7*(1), 15–34.

Tejerina, B., Perugorría, I., Benski, T., & Langman, L. (2013). From indignation to occupation: A new wave of global mobilization. *Current Sociology, 61*(4), 377–392.

Thompson, E. P. (1963). *The making of the English working class*. Victor Gollancz.

Tietze, T., & Humphrys, E. (2014). Anti-politics" and the Return of the Social: A Reply to Alex Callinicos. *International Socialism, 144*. http://isj.org.uk/anti-politics-and-the-return-of-the-social-a-reply-to-alex-callinicos/. Accessed 5 February 2021.

Tilly, C. (1978). *From mobilization to revolution*. Addison-Wesley.

Tilly, C. (1999, August). *Social movements here and elsewhere, now and then* (Center for research on social organization working paper series). https://deepblue.lib.umich.edu/bitstream/handle/2027.42/51344/580.pdf?sequence=1. Accessed 4 February 2021.

Tismăneanu, V. (Ed.). (1999). *The revolutions of 1989, Rewriting histories*. Routledge.

Touraine, A. (1981). *The voice and the eye: An analysis of social movements*. Cambridge University Press.

Tronti, M., Moulier, Y., Bezza, G., Cavazzini, A., & Carlino, F. (1977). *Ouvriers et capital*. Entremonde.

Trotsky, L. ([1930] 2010). *The permanent revolution and results and prospects*. Red Letter Press.

Tsoneva, J. (2019). *The making of the Bulgarian middle class: Citizens against the people in the 2013 protests*. Doctoral dissertation, Central European University.

Tsui, S., Erebus, W., Lau, K. C., & Tiejun, W. (2017). One belt, one road: China's strategy for a new global financial order. *Monthly Review, 68*(8), 36–45.

Van der Linden, M. (Ed.). (2008). *Workers of the world: Essays toward a global labor history* (Vol. 1). Brill.

Van der Pijl, K. (2014). *The making of an Atlantic ruling class*. Verso.

Varga, M. (2014). Hungary's "anti-capitalist" far-right: Jobbik and the Hungarian Guard. *Nationalities Papers, 42*(5), 791–807.

Vermeersch, P. (2006). *The Romani movement: Minority politics and ethnic mobilization in contemporary Central Europe*. Berghahn.

Vetta, T. (2009). 'Democracy Building' in Serbia: The NGO Effect. *Southeastern Europe, 33*(1), 26–47.

Vetta, T. (2012). NGOs and the state: Clash or class? Circulating elites of "good governance" in Serbia. *Democracy at Large* (pp. 169–190). Palgrave.

Vetta, T. (2018). *Democracy struggles: NGOs and the politics of aid in Serbia* (Vol. 25). Berghahn.

Wainwright, H. (2018). *A new politics from the left*. Wiley.

Wallerstein, I. (1974). *The modern world-system, vol. I: Capitalist agriculture and the origins of the European world-economy in the sixteenth century.* University of California Press.

Wallerstein, I. (1980). *The modern world-system, vol. II: Mercantilism and the consolidation of the European world-economy, 1600–1750.* Academic Press.

Wallerstein, I. (1986). Societal development, or development of the world system? *International Sociology, 1*(1), 3–17.

Wallerstein, I. (1989). *The Modern World-System, vol. III: The Second Great Expansion of the Capitalist World-Economy, 1730–1840's.* Academic Press.

Wallerstein, I. (1995). Response: Declining states, declining rights? *International Labor and Working-Class History, 47*, 24–27.

Walton, J. K., & Seddon, D. (1994). *Free markets and food riots: The politics of global adjustment.* Wiley.

Wedel, J. (2001). *Collision and collusion: The strange case of Western aid to Eastern Europe.* St Martin's Press.

Wolf, E. (1982). *Europe and the people without history.* University of California Press.

Zibechi, R. (2010). *Dispersing power: Social movements as anti-state forces.* AK Press.

Wallerstein, I. (1986). Societal development, or development of the world system? *International Sociology, 1*(1), 3–17.

CHAPTER 2

External Integration as Internal Force: Middle Class Politics and the "Politics of Backwardness" in Eastern Europe

In the context of post-2008 mobilizations, the issue of middle class development and related middle class politics became a central element of political debates. While mutual references between middle class-dominated protests across the world contributed to a sense of a general idea of middle class politics, increasing differences in middle class mobilities dynamized by the reorganization of the global system also fueled different directions of ideological and political alliance-making. In the West, the crisis of the middle class became a widely contested issue, from radicalizing middle class protests to mainstream proposals to save middle class development, and with it, the global leadership of Western democracies. In left segments of the debate, many sought to connect the present disillusionment of Western middle classes to broader antisystemic agendas. These efforts, in turn, raised the problem of a middle class base of new left politics. How do you conceive a pro-labor agenda from the basis of a downwardly mobile middle class? How do middle class capacities and preferences influence the forms of political organization? Can the middle class left transcend its own limitations by a critical conscientization of its own vested interests? From conceptual issues to practical organization, the problem of the middle class came to permeate new left debates. Meanwhile, in Eastern Europe, new middle class movements associated the stakes of middle class career prospects with the fate of historical development defined as catching up with Western standards. Due to the intimate

© The Author(s), under exclusive license to Springer Nature Switzerland AG 2021
A. Gagyi, *The Political Economy of Middle Class Politics and the Global Crisis in Eastern Europe*, International Political Economy Series, https://doi.org/10.1007/978-3-030-76943-7_2

connection between developmental expectations and middle class political consciousness, middle class protests worked everywhere as a prime channel through which the dynamics of global crisis came to be translated to local political vocabularies and alliances. To understand the outcomes of this translation, we need to investigate this channel itself as a part of systemic dynamics.

Chapter 2 discusses how the process of dependent development produces specific traits in East European politics, and how these effects work in the relation between limited middle class development and middle class politics. Then it asks how these characteristics relate to Western middle class formation as the paradigmatic reference point of the idea of the middle class, and to the global reorganization of middle class prospects that fuel new middle class politics of the crisis globally. Finally, the chapter turns toward the question whether the current wave of middle class politicization can become a source of antisystemic politics. Regarding this problem, it highlights one additional issue: how a dependence on knowledge-based positions affects the ways middle class actors can conceive of the relation between general historical projects and their own interests.

Dependent Development and the "Politics of Backwardness"

The fact that semi-peripheries occupy in-between positions within global hierarchies of accumulation does not imply that semi-peripheral societies and economies would be homogenous. On the contrary: it means that globally dominant and dominated positions are present within the same national economies, under the jurisdiction of the same states. One of the main problems of semi-peripheral development and governance has been constituted by that heterogeneity—like the coexistence of elements of industrial revolution with forms of second serfdom, or of high-end consumption of Western brands with local production of the same brands under conditions characteristic to peripheral positions. The coexistence of different poles of global uneven development within the same unit of governance historically worked as a source of tensions as well as a base for specific solutions of cooptation and cross-class alliances.

In these contexts, local governance simultaneously needs to organize the integration of local economy into global flows of accumulation dominated by core capital, provide an institutional base for accumulation ambitions of local elites, and manage social tensions following from local and transnational extraction locally (Amin, 1976). Dynamics of local politics therefore are defined by both the tensions and interest alliances arising from fragmented local integration, and by dependent relations within the external interstate system of global accumulation. This dependence of local political forms from internal and external structures of integration has been addressed in critical international studies as the idea of the state as "power connector" (Brunn, 1998: 114; Jessop, 2009: 150, cf. Poulantzas, 1978).

Regarding the structure of internal relations in such positions, the world-systems tradition used the notion of structural heterogeneity to refer to the internal polarization of non-core societies which results from the internalization of requirements of global accumulation. Originally, structural heterogeneity was used in literature dealing with dependent development (primarily in Latin America, Pinto, 1970; Prebisch, 1949; Nurkse, 1952; Sunkel, 1969; Senghaas, 1974, cf: Frank, 1975 on "dualism"). Here, it referred to the specific problem of dependent industrialization where the local polarization of productivity—the simultaneous presence of high technology manufacturing in local subsidiaries of multinational companies and lower tier local suppliers characterized by low profit margins and labor-intensive production—acts as a barrier to local technological development. In a broader sense, dependency literature also used the notion of structural heterogeneity to refer to the coexistence of different levels of productivity within the same economy, as the economic basis of social inequality (Da Costa & Teixeira, 2012). Arrighi (1973) discussed political and ideological polarization arising from the internal fragmentation of integration structures as part of structural heterogeneity. Contemporary reinterpretations of the concept include economic, social, institutional and geographic aspects, and discuss structural heterogeneity in terms of localized characteristics of uneven global development (Hürtgen, 2015). East European traditions reflecting the process of modernization recurrently described effects of structural heterogeneity, but included them within a framework of normative Western modernization, interpreting structural heterogeneity in terms of development pathologies (Boatcă, 2003, 2006).

Along structural heterogeneity, another main characteristic of semi-peripheral politics is the recurrence of projects for global upward mobility in the various ideologies of local political alliances (Chase-Dunn, 1990, 1998; Mouzelis, 1985). In the world-systems tradition, this has been understood as flowing not so much from a drama where projects which endless development potentials consecutively fail, but rather from the relative global stability of semi-peripheral positions. Despite spectacular individual examples of previous semi-peripheral economies raising toward core positions with the occasion of hegemonic shifts across cycles—like the case of the United States, or, arguably, contemporary East Asia—most of the global semi-periphery has been characterized by a relative stability in its global position (Martin, 1990). In this context, individual success stories do not constitute a possibility open to everyone; rather, they represent mobility movements within a hierarchical system of global competition where not everyone can win, and the position of winners presupposes the position of losers.

The main limit of semi-peripheral development efforts is not that specific political conflicts or local inadequacies of developmental efforts too often ruin the chances of global upward mobility, but that mobility ambitions in general meet an "adding-up problem": what is possible for some, is not possible for everyone (Arrighi, 1990). Because of this, world-systems scholars have interpreted semi-peripheral development efforts not in terms of a conflict between real catch-up potential and its local barriers, but as a systemic characteristic of semi-peripheral integration in global competition where local economies are bound to run ever faster in order to stay in one place (Gereffi & Hempel, 1996). From this perspective, the constant crisis of development efforts is a characteristic of semi-peripheral politics as important as the projection of development plans into the future. In the case of East Central European countries, the history of consecutive and competing development efforts has been accompanied by a stable regional hierarchy of development. Comparing the evolution of GDP/capita ratios, Andrew C. Janos (2000) characterized this as the "iron consistency" of developmental difference in the region's modern history. Recent research confirmed the stability of this hierarchy for the postsocialist period, too (Morys, 2020).

Contrary to modernization theory's expectation that all economies will eventually pass through the same stages of growth, and arrive to the stage of highly industrialized, mass consumption societies exemplified by postwar Western countries (Rostow, 1960), in postwar semi-peripheral industrialization catch-up efforts, industrialization worked as a form of dependent integration instead of a tool of catch-up development. The internalization of forms of production characteristic to the core happened in a later phase of innovation cycles, at lower levels of profitability, and among lasting conditions of unequal trade (high technology imports and low-technology/raw material exports). Arrighi (1990) used the notion of developmentalist illusion to describe the mechanisms through which import substitution industrialization, the paradigmatic form of postwar semi-peripheral catch-up projects, actually contributed to the preservation of semi-peripheral positions, while deepening the penetration of capitalist accumulation structures within local societies.

In the following, I will use the notion of developmentalist illusion to refer to ideological projects that organize developmental claims born within uneven systemic interaction into temporary political alliances. While the promises of these ideological projects typically break on the rocks of systemic limitations, developmentalist illusion remains a constant element of semi-peripheral debates, activating new projects within the crises of old ones. Subsequent forms of developmentalist illusion translate conflicts between developmental projects and their systemic limits to the level of ideological conflicts between competing local developmental projects, thus stabilizing long-term integration into developmental competition. In using this notion, I propose to pay equal attention to what Peter J. Taylor (1982) called the "real" and the "ideological" levels of capitalist politics—that is, to system-level integration processes, and their local ideological political representations. In this sense, developmentalist illusion does not simply refer to an illusion as a mistake of understanding or false consciousness. Instead, it refers to a concrete factor of developmental competition, which plays out through political projections of developmental aims that are impossible in systemic terms, but is rooted local actors' in real needs and ambitions conditioned by their positions within the process of capitalist integration, and plays a key role in shaping concrete external-internal articulations of integration.

In terms of the ways versions of developmentalist illusion get projected from local conditions of integration, one important factor is the changes global cyclical shifts engender in the conditions of local integration. In the world-systems tradition, strong states have been defined as states that have the largest capacity to organize, control, and modify flows of global accumulation to the benefit of their allied capital fractions. If we look at the politics of core states from this perspective, political reactions to changing conditions engendered by cyclical shifts can be described as driving, or at least, governing the global conditions of accumulation. The history of Fordism or neoliberalism has indeed been described in such ways, focusing on core states' and core capital's agency (e.g. Harvey,

2007; Van der Pijl, 2014). Semi-peripheral states, on the contrary, are not strong states in the global sense. From this perspective, the fact that semi-peripheral forms of development have been traditionally tied to high levels of state intervention does not reflect the strength of these states in a global sense, but rather a high reliance on the state by different developmentalist alliances across patterns of development projects and their crises. Across developmentalist waves, local developmental alliances that reflect and mobilize local tensions following from dependent integration are strongly contested by the interests they necessarily exclude from their own developmental model, as well as by changes in external conditions of integration that easily break the forms of temporary hegemony they build out. Therefore, instead of stable capitalist coalitions maneuvering cyclical changes to their own benefit, in the case of semiperipheral states we rather see dramatic patterns of the construction and collapse of local developmentalist coalitions (e.g. Martin, 2013), generating shorter waves of developmentalist politics within the long waves of global cycles.

Besides structural heterogeneity and developmentalist illusion, a third significant factor in semi-peripheral politics is political dependence from the dominant states and interstate structures of the world economy. The previous chapter discussed the relativity of state sovereignty according to positions occupied across the global hierarchy of accumulation and its intrastate system. In the case of East Central Europe, besides global centers of power, subordination to regional powers competing over influence over the region has also played a significant role. Local forms of world-economic integration have often been defined through relationships with regional powers and an integration into the distribution of labor within their sphere of influence. Along global hegemony, internal lines of economic and political conflict were also shaped by regional alliances. As Janos (2000: 410–411) put it:

> in Eastern Europe, from the beginning of the modern age, external forces have far outweighed domestic ones as causal factors of institutional change. (...) To use the language of Marxism, the superstructures may well have been in the East, but the base that controlled their movements was in England and in the advanced West. (...) Political change in small powers is not understandable merely as adaptation to socio-economic change within narrow political boundaries, but must be seen as adaptation to the interest and rules of hegemonic powers in the international regime.

Looking at the political history of the region in the modern period, Janos points out that the introduction of parliamentary democracy to the region happened under the influence of the Concert of Europe as a regulator of power relations after the Congress of Vienna, whose function was to maintain intra-European peace in an age of colonial competition, and make the world—including the new states of East Central Europe— safe for the dominant interests of British trade. The creation of legal states capable of enforcing contracts, preferably in a parliamentary form of governance, served that purpose in the region, too. After World War I, universal suffrage and ethnic/minority rights were introduced at the influence of hegemonic powers within the League of Nations. The rise of the radical right in the region happened in connection with German ascent, which gave local fascist politics "their practical weight and meaning" (Janos, 2000: 412). Communist dictatorships typically came to power with the help of Moscow. Postsocialist transitions originated with the Sinatra doctrine in Moscow, and happened under the influence of Western powers. Since then, "many, if not most, of the domestic policies and institutions of East Central European countries have been formulated to conditions set not in Budapest or Bucharest, but in Brussels, Copenhagen, Maastricht and Amsterdam" (Janos, 2000: 412).

The fact that East Central European political systems developed under relations of "hegemony and tutelage" (Janos, 2000: 412) by greater powers does not mean that they completely corresponded to hegemonic models. Such correspondence was limited both by structural restraints— differences in local conditions, like the need to repress local tensions following from external extraction—as well as by diverging interests of local elites and their social alliances. As the other side of the coin of hegemonic domination, corruption and feigned compliance equally characterized the strategies of client elites "laboring under the injuctions of local culture and socio-economic constraints bequeathed by a previous age" (Janos, 2000: 412). In nineteenth-century liberal regimes, political machines combined bureaucratic tools with the force of gendarmeries to guarantee majorities for governments managing subordinated integration. In fascist and communist regimes, local one-party states continued to be prone to deviations from hegemonic models. Writing in 2000, Janos did not expect that the promises of postsocialist democratization would transcend those patterns; rather, he expected that democratization processes dominated by European and US hegemonic tutelage would be riddled by political machineries and increasing bureaucratic and autocratic control.

Janos (1989) referred to the character of local politics that results from the conditions of economic and political dependence as the "politics of backwardness". While in analytical terms this approach is compatible with world-systems interpretations of non-core politics, Janos' use of the term maintains an association of normative value, where the "politics of backwardness" denotes a politics that is not sovereign enough. Janos' "politics of backwardness" is a strong analytical tool for exploring the complexities of East European political life, but it still frames these complexities as distortions following from effects of domination. In this book, I use the "politics of backwardness" in a sense that does not interpret "backwardness" as a subordinated condition that needs remedy through development. Starting from an understanding of global hierarchies as a systemic feature of capitalist development, dominated positions within uneven development are treated in this book as full-value, objective elements of capitalist development, just as important for the constitution of the system as dominant or core positions. Consequently, the notion of "politics of backwardness" (used in quotation marks, due to the slight difference from Janos's usage) is applied not in the sense of distortions of local politics due to external domination, but as a term that summarizes the complex relations within which semi-peripheral politics develop. In this usage, similar to developmentalist illusion, "politics of backwardness" expresses a relation between systemic positions and their ideological projections.

While this application of the notion of "politics of backwardness" addresses complex forms of ideological projections that are often interpreted in terms of illusions, false consciousness or distortions, these forms are understood here as concrete elements of global politics, just as real or significant in terms of the system's global integration as core Western political models. The main conclusion from exploring these contradictions of semi-peripheral politics is not that these are distorted in any way—compared to "normal" Western models—but that the paradigmatic concepts of Western political models need a similar reconsideration, once their embeddedness in systemic relations that normally generate such political forms in non-core situations is realized, and the aspect of ideological projection in Western notions of sovereignty or democracy becomes visible through that realization.

MIDDLE CLASSES AND DEMOCRACY OUTSIDE THE WESTERN CORE

Like democracy, sovereignty, or the idea of civil society discussed in the first chapter, the idea of the middle class has also functioned as a notion that links structural and ideological aspects of normative development marked by Western superiority. Modernization theory defined the co-constitutive relation between free markets, middle class growth, and democracy as an essential condition of development. This idea set Western history as a model of that beneficial relation, and downplayed social contradictions both within and outside Western societies as ones that will be necessarily transcended by the further development of capitalism. In Lipset's (1959) classic model, the main conditions of middle class growth and democratization are industrialization, urbanization, the increase of wealth, the expansion of education, and an open class structure that provides channels for upward social mobility. In his classic study comparing different models of middle class development and democracy across the globe, Barrington Moore (1966) differentiated the contexts of democratic, fascist, and communist regimes of the twentieth century according to the types of transition from agrarian to industrial economies. In what he considers as the successful model of democratization, modernization happened through the development of a broad layer of bourgeoisie and successful bourgeois revolutions.

Moore's summary of this process—"No bourgeoisie, no democracy" (Moore, 1966: 418)—became probably the most quoted line in political science, corresponding to the practice of democracy studies that link democratic theory to Western experience. This statement, however, only covers one aspect of Moore's analysis. He had other two main conclusions from comparing the social conditions of democracy and dictatorship. The first was that each of these roads toward capitalist modernization relied on the violent annihilation of the peasantry as a social class. The second was that the political rights won by bourgeois revolutions were not universal rights, but rules that benefited the bourgeoisie of dominant economies of the modern capitalist world economy (Moore, 1966: 440).

The observation that the chance for a co-development of democracy and a large middle class is distributed unequally across global hierarchies of wealth, has also been a central tenet of democracy studies. As Lipset (1959: 74) put it: "the more well-to-do a nation, the greater the chances that it will sustain democracy". How the opportunity of democratization relates to the hierarchies of the global distribution of labor has been an issue of debate, with standpoints also depending on how authors understood the relation between internal political struggles and external integration. Welfare social democratic approaches have defined higher labor shares from capital's profits as a political aim that can lead to middle class development, and therefore, to a stable democracy, anywhere in the world (e.g. Esping-Andersen, 1996). Critical approaches that have emphasized the interconnection between top and bottom positions of global accumulation, and especially authors who have focused on the conditions of political struggles in the global peripheries, claimed that the hierarchical structure of global capitalist accumulation does not allow for a level of profit redistribution on the peripheries as it does in the center—and therefore, we cannot expect a development of large middle classes and stable democracies in these regions. In non-core positions, to maintain external extraction as a condition of global integration requires the controlled maintenance of local inequalities. These conditions favor authoritarian regimes; democratic institutions, where they are set up, are modified by authoritarian-bureaucratic tendencies, and shaken by intermittent revolts and reorganizations (Frank, 1975). As Amin (1991) put it, in terms of a realistic reference point, the idea of democracy within capitalism is limited to the core; for the peripheries, the stabilization of democracy would only be possible once the external requirements of global capitalist extraction are canceled. Research on semi-peripheries emphasized similar contradictions of semi-peripheral democratization and middle class development (Martin, 1990; for a similar argument on intra-EU uneven development see Becker, 2014).

In terms of structural hierarchies, research that considered the question of middle class in terms of global systemic integration has also emphasized that middle class development in different global positions refer to different systemic functions. The historical development of Western bourgeois middle classes is not a process that could be repeated at any time in any world-economic position, but an aspect of a full systemic transformation, which created the economic and political prerogatives due to which the benefits of system-wide accumulation could be concentrated in Western forms of bourgeois development. In the case of postwar middle class development, too, the spectacular growth of Western middle classes was linked to a system-wide process, where Western labor's growing share in capital's profits was made possible by Western capital's global expansion, and the middle class buying power constituted through that process provided the market for the same capital. Thus, instead of early forms of development that could be replicated elsewhere, Western middle class formation constituted the "embourgeoisement" or "middle class development" of the whole system, with these system-wide functions concentrated in Western core countries.

Research that looked at non-core middle class development from the perspective of systemic integration has emphasized mainly three factors. The first was that in non-core positions, the structure of local economies does not allow for the development of a large economic base for middle class positions. The second is that in face of such economic limitations, local aspirant middle classes claim to acquire a greater share from flows of accumulation within the narrower opportunities due to core actors' domination of accumulation flows. This puts them in a sharp competition against each other and against dominated social groups. The third, related factor is local aspirant middle classes' tendency to emulate consumption patterns of core middle classes. In non-core positions, this ambition is associated with a push to acquire higher shares of local redistribution, and then channel them into core markets through buying Western products. The combination of these factors means not only that non-core middle class development remains limited and prone to competitive struggle and frequent disillusionment, but also that aspirations toward middle class lifestyles in non-core positions act toward non-democratic redistribution of local social wealth, constitute a further channel of core extraction, and act against democratic relations locally (Arrighi, 1990; Cheeseman, 2015; Chirot, 1991; Hinnebusch, 2006; Janos, 2000; López & Weinstein 2012; Mouzelis, 1985; Nurkse, 1952; Portes, 1973; Stokes, 1986). Both of these consequences contradict the expectation that former Western experiences of middle class formation and democratization could be emulated everywhere, leading to the development of middle class democratic societies worldwide.

Since the development of large middle classes has been a feature of top positions in the global hierarchy, the presence of Western middle class characteristics in non-core societies has been associated with the idea of development (global upward mobility) for the whole of society. Beyond just a political or analytical discourse, this connection imbued forms of lived experience through renewing forms of consumption, social interaction, culture, norms, and values, which were perceived as a sign and promise of development for broader social groups too. However, from a systemic perspective, these internalized forms of middle class lifestyle do not signify a generalized process of global upward mobility; rather, they are elements of dependent integration that simultaneously legitimate and deepen uneven development. This structural reality makes the idea of middle class development in non-core positions another example of a notion that unites ideological and structural aspects, linking development hopes and their regular disillusionment to systemic efforts that perpetuate the conditions of these ideological projections.

In the case of Latin America, Alejandro Portes (1973: 272) formulated the contradiction between the perception of local middle classes as the sign of local development, and the actual uneven development effect of local middle class lifestyles in the following way:

> First-time travellers in Latin America are frequently surprised by the sophistication of life in many cities. Especially impressive are the life style, modern opinions and aspirations and general culture of the upper and middle classes. It is almost a cliché to wonder how, with such modern people, the economies of these countries remain quasi-stagnant. When historical reasons for underdevelopment in Latin America are examined, one of the first to emerge is the modernity of its elite groups.

In Eastern Europe, this intimate but contradictory relation between middle class formation and catch-up development has been recurrently addressed in internal debates. In the case of Hungary and Romania, two influential metaphors in such debates have been "dual society" and "forms without foundation". In Romanian debates on modernization, "forms without foundation" was used to denote social forms that emulate Western models without the corresponding internal developmental conditions (Maiorescu [1868] 1978; Boatcă, 2003). In the case of middle classes, "forms without foundation" was applied to middle class formation through a growing number of state functionaries, as opposed to a real economic bourgeoisie (Zeletin [1925] 1997). Similarly, in Hungarian debates, "dual society" was used to refer both to what was seen as an internal structural discrepancy of local social formations (defined according to developmental dualities like feudal and capitalist, Eastern and Western, socialist and democratic, e.g. Erdei, 1976; Kolosi, 1974; Szelényi et al., 1988), and to a contradiction between state-based and economic middle class formation (Karády, 1997). The close association these local forms of social reflection make between the stakes of development and middle class formation is similar to what Adamovsky (2009) described as Argentinian middle class politics' link to the idea of "la grieta", the symbolic construct of a rift that separates "civiliza-tion" from "barbarism", "Europeanism" from "Latin-Americanism", and "white" from "mestizo".

Historians Gyáni and Kövér (2006) showed that the sharpening of an ethnicized symbolic contradiction between Hungarian, Christian, state-based middle classes and Jewish embourgeoisement in Hungary was less based on an actual statistical differentiation, but rather on the internal tensions of a limited middle class development. Their interpretation throws a sharp light on the way competition for state-based channels of limited middle class development produces symbolic differences that become real factors of mobility and social conflict. The numerus clausus introduced in higher education in 1920 to restrict the number of Jewish students in faculties, and the anti-Jewish acts of the 1930s and 1940s illus-trate the merciless application of those differences in using the power of the state to rearrange access to knowledge monopolies, and later, property (Don, 1986; Nagy, 2005).

The fact that non-core middle classes simultaneously serve as a struc-tural motor of uneven development, and an ideological embodiment of development promises, makes local middle class ambitions a prime territory where the dynamics of developmentalist illusion can play out. Politically, this internal contradiction makes local middle classes a strong base for developmentalist coalitions, yet the limitations of development efforts—and the limitations of middle class growth ingrained in them—easily transform middle class ambitions into political revolt. With their high capacity to express their claims on the level of formalized institu-tions, these frequent turns of political loyalties make local middle classes a key element in the ways contradictions and tensions of non-core devel-opment become culturally expressed, politicized and reorganized along new coalitions across cyclical shifts of global integration.

Middle Class Politics in Eastern Europe

Janos (2000) describes middle class politics mobilized by the structural limits of local middle class development as a key element of the "politics of backwardness". He defines the specificity of East European middle class development as one where aspiring middle classes struggle to overcome economic limitations of middle class expansion through mobilizing state support. Due to this characteristic of compensated, state-based middle class development, he conceives of middle classes as relying on political entrepreneurship:

> while the history of the modern Western state may well be described as one of rising middle classes in quest of larger national markets, the history of the peripheral states is one of declining middle classes trying to escape the vagaries of the markets and hoping to find safe haven in political, rather than economic, entrepreneurship. (Janos, 2000: 66)

This definition of the middle class as a "class of political entrepreneurs" (Janos, 2000: 133) implies that aspirant middle classes recurrently make use of state infrastructures and state redistribution to achieve life standards that Western middle classes attain through market positions. This does not imply a constant, unidirectional effort, but an underlying characteristic that manifests in different political-ideological forms according to changes in macroeconomic conditions and political alliances. One main factor in such changes is the difference between phases when aspirant middle classes join political alliances to disrupt and reorganize the existing order, and phases when they integrate into new structures in positions relatively beneficial to their status. In terms of alliances, a similar difference can be made between alliances made with hegemonic elites in times of economic stability, and a reorganization of alliances in times of crisis, where middle classes align themselves with competing or antagonistic groups mobilized by the crisis process.

In times of crisis, middle class politics may ally themselves with social causes, but it may also promote alliances with elites, trying to preserve privileges through selective patron–client relations, authoritarian control, and exclusion. In phases of integration, while both right-wing and progressive versions of middle class politics gain a conservative, prosystemic character, internal tensions can be maintained by alliances to competing projects of development. A typical tension in this respect has been described as one between "internal" and "external" models of dependent development, along alliances favoring national vs. international capital (Wallerstein, 1990). Ideological, cultural, moral, and consumption aspects of middle class political orientation along this duality of "external" vs. "internal" development have been a significant factor in the way intra-middle class struggles politicized developmental contradictions in Eastern Europe, too.

For those strains of middle class politics that build out popular alliances during crisis, one important aspect Janos emphasizes is that in subsequent phases of economic stabilization, these also become part of systemic integration that favors middle class interests vis-a-vis lower strata. In 1848, East European movements followed the social emphasis of Western revolutions, and claimed marketization and liberalization together with the liberation of serfs. However, after the crisis of the 1870s, middle classes who integrated into broadening state structures in the coming decade came to sustain national development based on protectionist industrialization, in alliance with national capital. In the beginning of the twentieth century, universal suffrage and the experience of WWI brought mass participation in politics, together with movements and parties that articulated the interests of lower classes. In the crisis of the 1920s and 1930s, intellectuals struck by unemployment turned toward urban workers and rural peasants, formulating right and left versions of political programs that called for radical social transformation.

After 1945, while former middle classes suffered from socialist redistribution in the early phase of socialism, reintegration into state functions through expertise, together with the broadening of administrative positions, created a situation where upwardly mobile middle classes accepted the legitimacy of the regime. Expert debates of the 1950s revolved around strategic dilemmas within the paradigm of socialist development, with expert alliances supporting Imre Nagy's reformist government even in 1956s Hungary (Bockman, 2000). As the criticism of socialist bureaucracy and intellectuals noted (e.g. Djilas, 1959; Konrád & Szelényi, 1979, cf: Verdery, 1991), despite the official ideology of workers' power, state functionaries occupied a superior position in state redistribution compared to workers. After the 1960s, however, the narrowing and closure of mobility channels led to growing discontent. Socialist intellectuals developed first left-wing critiques of the system, then third-way alternative visions, and finally, liberal critiques tied to the project of abolishing socialism for Western models (Szelényi & King, 2004). During late socialism, liberal criticism of socialism emphasized solidarity with dominated groups together with a critique of state redistribution disfavoring these strata. They promoted political and economic freedom provided by free market and parliamentary democracy as an alternative that would solve the problem of political and economic suppression at the same time (Bockman, 2000; Gagyi, 2015; Szalai, 1995).

In the 1990s, the crisis of former socialist labor and the partial impoverishment of the former socialist middle class was paralleled by the formation of a new, upwardly mobile middle class (Kolosi & Sági, 1996). Correspondingly, in intellectual and political discourse, promises of democratization and middle class development overshadowed concerns about the downward mobility of workers (Ost, 2005; Szalai, 1995; Thoma, 1998). In contrast to former social critiques of socialist redistribution, liberal intellectuals and politicians predominantly supported policies favoring middle class formation (Szalai, 1994). In the wake of the 2008 crisis, a new wave of middle class mobilizations called out governments for unaccomplished promises of the regime change, and requested state help in face of crisis effects (SNSPA, 2016; Szabó & Mikecz, 2015).

For a contemporary analysis of middle class mobilizations, the above considerations suggest three important points for consideration. The first is that in the history of regional middle class politics, revolutionary phases have been followed on a regular basis by phases of integration benefiting middle class positions. These cyclical shifts brought changes in ideological content as well as shifts in political alliances. In Janos's words (2000: 314), if moments of anti-elite mobilization often included solidarity and political alliances with dominated groups, in phases of integration, middle classes' support for the status quo relied on the state acting as

> a grand instrument of income equalization, not, to be sure, among the various economic strata of peripheral societies, but between the elites of the backward and the advanced industrial societies of the Continent.

In moral or ideological terms, such shifts from revolutionary to integration phases are often described as stories of cooptation, treason, or the emptying of political content. Meanwhile, shifts from integration to revolutionary phases are often experienced and represented as a political awakening from earlier illusions of a beneficial order. However, considered as a regular sequence in the patterns of middle class development, these shifts appear as aspects of the same long-term effort to defend and broaden middle class positions under the conditions of limited development. From this perspective, ideological, political, and social visions formulated in different phases of this process need to be considered not only in terms of their momentary aims and alliances, but also in terms of the long-term structural position of middle class politics that produces different versions of these programs in a regular manner.

The second point highlighted by this perspective is the internal contradictions of such ideological projections, which follow from the limitations of their structural conditions, similar to the contradictions of hegemonic compliance and deviation described by Janos (2000). For instance, while East European 1848 movements allied with Western democratic movements in terms of their self-identification and their antagonism with large estates, within local structures of integration, their interest relied in occupying state positions instead of embarking on market enterprises. This contradictory position has been summarized by Janos as being "liberal in their ideology, etatist in their interest" (Janos, 2000: 67). In later integration phases, similar contradictions can be traced in the cases of early twentieth-century socialist or late socialist dissident movements, too.

In terms of the historical fate of progressive middle class ideologies formulated in revolutionary periods, the main consequence of following integration phases is that democratic claims that speak in the interest of dominated groups need to give space to an integration process that benefits middle classes instead of the poor. This condition of middle class status conservation contradicts ideological claims of revolutionary phases. For instance, after 1848, East European middle classes integrated in state positions became actors of hierarchical redistribution. Besides formal wages, this was achieved through informal means such as paid legal advice, various forms of sinecure, trading in political contacts, and gratuities. Along the interest of capitalizing elites, middle classes' interest for beneficial redistribution contributed to political machineries that helped keep up democratic appearances over processes of hierarchical redistribution. Similar contradictions of redistribution have been pointed out by analysts of socialist and postsocialist phases too, from socialist redistribution to postsocialist social policies (Djilas, 1959; Konrád & Szelényi, 1979, Szalai, 1995; Vanhuysse, 2006).

Of course, the fact that middle class revolutionaries' claims for democracy run into ideological contradictions due to structural factors does not necessarily mean that middle class revolutionaries' intention would not be honest. Comparing biographies of main pro-democracy political figures in the modern history of the region, Janos formulated the relation between personal intent and structural limitations as the "victory of structure over design and personality" (Janos, 2000: 143). In moral and ideological interpretations, this kind of defeat is often represented as an unjust and inapprehensible gesture of fate, something that Janos described as the feeling of "gloom and self-pity" (2000: 62) that permeates progressive imagination in the region. From a long-term perspective, however, the fluctuation between progressive intentions and their failure appears as characteristic to a situation where the ideological promise and structural limits of development produce subsequent forms of consciousness in middle classes, who are particularly able and particularly dependent on expressing their interests in the vocabularies of general progress.

A third point by Janos that can inform interpretations of post-2008 movements is that developmental programs and symbolic identities formulated on the ground of middle class ambitions are often seen as abstract, unreal, or theatrical by other local actors. Quoting the example of 1848 revolutionaries in Hungary, Janos (2000: 67) mentions that gestures of identification with the image of the international revolutionary were mocked by contemporary commentators as local revolutionaries behaving like actors in Lamartine's *History of the Girondists*. Gergely Péterfy's, 2014 novel *The stuffed barbarian*, tells the story of a friendship between Hungarian enlightenment figure Ferenc Kazinczy and black Austrian freemason Angelo Soliman, based on historical research. The mirror effect between Kazinczy's efforts to establish Western civilizational standards in the turn of nineteenth-century Hungary, and Soliman's quest to attain fulfillment as an Enlightenment subject while being treated as a barbarian by his Austrian context works as a strong formulation of the simultaneously tragic and comical aspects of developmental theatricality. At one point, Kazinczy and Soliman meet in Vienna, Kazinczy wearing a Hungarian costume that represents the ambition to raise his nation to Western civilizational levels, while Soliman wears an outfit in perfect contemporary Viennese fashion. When they meet, both burst out in hysterical laughter, pointing at each other in recognition of a contradiction that they both suppress in themselves. The mirror effect reaches its dark conclusion when Kazinczy is summoned to Vienna to identify the corpse of Soliman, skinned, stuffed, and exhibited in the Imperial Natural History Collection.

Examples for theatrical forms of middle class developmentalism that have been seen as empty or foreign by contemporaries may range from the expropriation of peasant cultural elements by middle class folklorism to the strained emulation of Western consumption models, or to various versions of progressive claims borrowed from Western social contexts, and therefore seen as unsubstantiated by contemporary compatriots. While critiques often point at these forms as lacking a base in local social realities, in the perspective of this book, they rather represent a real element of structural heterogeneity, following from the process of systemic integration that makes local middle classes define themselves as local embodiments of development projects. This theatrical element is also strengthened by international alliances as well as by enthusiastic reactions against such alliances. Instead of misrepresentations on the symbolic level, Janos also treats these theatrical forms as a real element of the politics of backwardness, pointing out the aspect of power ambitions and internal–external alliances in theatrical symbolic gestures.

Regular shifts between middle class politics' revolutionary and integration phases, and resulting ideological contradictions were discussed by Konrád and Szelényi's classic critique of state socialist middle classes, *The intellectuals on the road to class power* (1979). In building their analysis, Szelényi and Konrád rely on the differentiation between Wirtschaftsbürgertum and Bildungsbürgertum in German embourgeoisment debates (Kocka, 1995). While Wirtschaftsbürgertum refers to segments of economic bourgeoisie, Bildungsbürgertum denotes groups that employ cultural capacities in creating new avenues for modernization. Detaching the notion of Bildungsbürgertum from the German context, Szelényi and Konrád applied it to the situation of an East European "cultural bourgeoisie", which develops on the base of applying knowledge monopolies within state functions, and acts as a driver of new modernization programs:

> In Germany and probably to the East, in Hungary, Poland, or even in Russia, in the lack of a real (national) propertied bourgeoisie, modernization came to be promoted in the eighteenth and nineteenth centuries by the Bildungsbürgertum, the bourgeoisie with intellectual background, a »cultural bourgeoisie«. (Szelényi & King 2004: 41)

Szelényi and King (2004: 105) speak about "cycles" of such modernization programs of the cultural bourgeoisie:

> during the mid-nineteenth century, they constitute themselves as a Bildungsbürgertum, the force to promote capitalist modernization and the making of a propertied class; during most of the twentieth century, they define themselves as the vanguard of the communist modernization process; finally by the end of the century (...) they reconstitute themselves one more time as Bildungsbürgertum. (Szelényi & King, 2004: 116)

Analyzing social alliances of the 1989 regime change, Eyal et al. (1998) claimed that in the coalition between socialist technocrats, bureaucrats and dissident intellectuals toward market-based transition, the historical series of the Eastern European cultural bourgeoisie's modernization projects has come to a full cycle. They saw this point as the era of the second Bildungsbürgertum: after nineteenth-century liberal revolutionaries, and twentieth-century socialists, this time the cultural bourgeoisie once again stepped up to promote a transformation toward capitalism. Following this logic, new left programs gaining voice after 2008 could be described as another round of the same cycle.

However, the cyclical model can obscure several elements that this book seeks to emphasize. From the perspective of systemic integration, projects for socialist or market-based modernization do not fit into a cyclical movement between contradictory social models, but into a continuous history of integration constellations. In this process, socialist and free market programs emphasized by the cyclical model coexisted with other—protectionist, poporanist, national, or third way—projects. How these programs integrated in respective regimes, conflicted with other political projects, and changed throughout different phases, was defined by a broader interaction of internal and external conditions, and not only by ideological choices of their promoters. Therefore, instead of cyclical model of ideological content, what I take to emphasize from Szelényi and his colleagues' work is the link between cultural bourgeois positions and recurrent mobilizations for modernization programs. In terms of actual historical effects, Szelényi and King (2004) also emphasized that modernization projects voiced from cultural bourgeois positions do not necessarily produce situations where they can actually take power. Even if the cultural bourgeoisie occupies vanguard positions in preparatory phases of a transition between integration models, with the consolidation of new forms of integration, these positions are taken over by real systemic elites (with some members of vanguard cultural bourgeoisie having the chance to enter their rows).

From the perspective of historical analysis, differences between the various social positions that can be considered as part of what Szelényi, King and Konrád describe as cultural bourgeoisie is a further question that needs specification. Such aspects have been regularly addressed by empirical research on East European social and intellectual history (e.g. Böröcz & Róna-Tas, 1995; Bockman, 1997; Cucu, 2007; Gyáni & Kövér, 2006; Janos, 2000; Kopeček & Wciślik, 2015; Larionescu et al., 2006;

Popescu, 1995; Szalai, 1997; Trencsényi & Kopeček, 2006; Trencsényi et al., 2016). The book will rely on this background to analyze contextual factors of post-2008 middle class mobilizations; yet instead of a sociological analysis of the complexity of middle class positions, it merely aims to point out the significance of main conceptual link Konrád, Szelényi and Janos identified between limited middle class development, knowledge monopolies, political entrepreneurship and recurrent political projects of development, to the interpretation of post-2008 mobilizations.

THE MIDDLE CLASS AS PROJECT: AN IDEOLOGICAL NOTION OF SYSTEMIC INTEGRATION

East European and Latin American authors quoted above discussed recurrent developmental hopes and failures as a long-term characteristic of dependent middle class development. When researchers of new rising middle classes in China or India speak of tensions following from the limitations of the generalization of middle class lifestyles (Hamel, 2019; Tsang, 2014; Zhou, 2008), the emphasis also falls on the insufficiencies of local middle class development. This implicit focus on local developmental problems easily obscures the fact that the discrepancy between actual middle class formation and the ideological promise of a generalized middle class development has worked as a ground for material and ideological struggles in Western contexts, too. Despite the broadest middle class development compared to other parts of the world, in postwar Western countries, too, tensions around the issue of middle class formation have been broadly politicized—with these debates becoming sharper once the growth of middle class positions stalled, and the crisis of the postwar hegemonic cycle started to place a direct pressure on local middle class livelihoods. This aspect does not only add a new territory to the consideration of current middle class politics, but also problematizes Western middle class development as the origo of the ideological concept of the middle class.

The Notion of the Middle Class in Postwar Developmental Debates

In the context of postwar hegemonic discourses of Western-led modernization, the notion of the middle class was conceived as part of an ideological struggle against socialist critiques of capitalist development. The fact that upward mobility exists, and all workers have the chance to acquire levels of middle class consumption, was conceived as a counter-argument to the Marxist idea of class struggle. The continuous growth of middle classes—or, in individual terms: everybody's chance for upward mobility—was tied to the idea of a harmonious collaboration of classes on the road of economic growth that, on the long term, will benefit everyone (e.g. Nisbet, 1969; Turner, 1984). In terms of class antagonism in the global distribution of labor, the same narrative of Western-led modernization implied that this chance of harmonious growth is available for each country as they follow the consecutive steps of capitalist development. To emphasize the political message of that argument, Rostow (1960) published his theory of modernization as of universal stages of economic growth with the subtitle "A non-communist manifesto".

This notion of the middle class has been debated globally from various critical socialist positions. Western Marxists reacted to the attack on the idea of class antagonism by trying to interpret the growth of postwar middle class not as the transcendence, but as an element of capitalist contradictions. Sweezy and Baran (1966) argued that from capital's side, the New Deal and the Fordist class compromise that allowed Western labor to receive a larger share from Western capital's profits was based in capital's need to create the market for its products within developed economies, and was conditioned by capital's expansion outside of the West. In this interpretation, the growth of Western middle classes was a development based on monopoly capital's temporary strategies to solve the problem of overaccumulation. Instead of solving or transcending class contradictions, it rather manifested them in the form of a new layer of consumers dependent on Western capital's profitability conditions, including that of a fragmented exploitation of the global workforce. Meanwhile, the structural limits of postwar Western middle class formation have been emphasized by empirical research from relatively early on. For example, Richard Parker's 1972 book *The myth of the middle class* argued that since the 1950s, the growth of an upper middle class constituted by white-collar professionals was paralleled by stagnating wages, growing indebtedness, and lack of upward mobility for workers he identifies as the lower middle class. In his book *Labor and monopoly capital: The degradation of work in the twentieth century*, a classic of labor studies, Harry Braverman (1974) pointed out an essential connection between the development of scientific management, and the deskilling, fragmentation, and mechanization of labor. He argued that the monopolization of knowledge in scientific management positions serves the weakening of labor's positions and capital's increased control over the labor process. This analysis underlined that although the growth of white-collar positions engendered by the development of scientific management made upward mobility possible for some members of the working class, the growth of the professional middle class was not due to an equalization of class positions, but rather to their further polarization.

Besides its role in capitalist dynamics, another aspect that critical left commentators discussed was postwar Western middle classes different constitution compared to earlier forms. Nicos Poulantzas (1979) argued that contrary to classic Marxist expectations that the petty bourgeoisie will disintegrate with the intensification of class struggle, a "new" petty bourgeoisie in salaried administrative positions has been growing in the conditions of monopoly capital. While more optimistic interpretations of this growth of professional salaried strata saw it as a promise of a universally educated, value-driven "knowledge society" (e.g. Bell, 1979), left criticism considered it in terms of its structural and political alliances to capital. Early on, C. Wright Mills (1951) discussed the political potential of new professional middle class positions as one driven by a type of self-interest that can only survive through serving other, more powerful groups, and therefore remains in a state of constant volatility.

In a similar vein, Poulantzas assessed the political capacity of the new petty bourgeoisie as being in constant flux between potential social alliances, with its only distinctive characteristic being that it aims to secure and expand the administrative positions on which its livelihood depends. While Poulantzas also characterized the political propensity of the new petty bourgeoisie as structurally underdetermined, he saw petty bourgeois politicization as a significant structural factor. In his analysis of fascism, this was pointed out as petty bourgeois political mobilization providing the fascist state's capacity to transform the crisis of previous accumulation structures into a state-based reorganization of accumulation in favor of big capital (Poulantzas, 1974). Erik Olin Wright et al. (1982) tried to grasp the same position as a contradictory class location, tied to management positions within the process of capital's control of labor. Similar to Mills or Poulantzas, Wright saw the political capacity of this class as undetermined by structure-based alliances, and emphasized the importance of alliances shaped by broader conditions of the class struggle in the politics of the new middle class. Meanwhile, in terms of global aspects, the Western class compromise that allowed the widening of local middle classes based on the global expansion of Western capital was debated along the question whether Western working classes still maintain a capacity for antisystemic struggle (e.g. Brenner, 1977).

In the context of decolonization in the Third World, the role of middle class intellectuals in left politics was discussed in its relation to changing relations of class struggle, imperialism, and neocolonialism. Reflecting local realities of labor distribution where the largest segment of labor was constituted by the peasantry, Third World intellectuals like Amílcar Cabral (1966) saw the emancipative political potential of critical urban petty bourgeois intellectuals in linking up with rural organizations of labor. Cabral saw the political choice faced by these actors as either integrating into the reproduction of global capitalist hierarchies through forming a state-based salaried pseudo-bourgeoisie after national independence—the route that would have symbolically confirmed the hegemonic promise for Western-led development—or committing what he called a "class suicide". In order for petty bourgeois actors to be able to identify with the masses and resist their subordination to global capitalist hierarchies, instead of pursuing middle class self-interests through entering manage-ment positions of integration, Cabral considered, they need to bind their lives to those laboring in the countryside, instead of clinging to urban salaried prospects. This idea has been central to Marxist movements of the Global South which bound political organization to embedded rural work for cultural transformation, from Latin America (Freire, 1972) to India (Dasgupta, 2006). Crystallized in the paradigm of Maoism, this approach was applied by state socialist systems too, and was used as a tool of forming and controlling expert strata in socialist development projects, from Mao's Cultural Revolution and "Down to the Countryside Movement" policy (Lu, 2004) to Castro's Cuba (Heredia, 1993).

In the Socialist bloc, even if less successful than in Western coun-tries, postwar social mobility was a strong structural and ideological element of socialist developmental regimes. Official ideologies empha-sized social mobility as a socialist achievement. Somewhat similar to the developmental narratives of Western modernization ideology, in the Stal-inist doctrine, socialist society was defined as one that has transcended the issue of class conflict. The class structure of socialism was defined as a harmonious collaboration between two classes—workers and peas-ants—and a stratum of intellectuals fulfilling technical and bureaucratic duties (Inkeles, 1950). Critical authors of what came to be defined as the socialist dissident theories of the New Class (e.g. Djilas, 1959; Konrád

& Szelényi, 1979) claimed that contrary to the official ideology of proletarian dictatorship, state socialist systems are actually characterized by the dominance of the party apparatus over workers. Within that system, they claimed, professionals working in bureaucratic positions are becoming a new dominant class, both in terms of management positions at work, and of privileges in state redistribution. This they interpreted as a situation of ideological duplicity and political treason, where a class of professionals whose jobs include the propagation of workers' power in fact use those stances to promote their own benefits, and sustain a system that relies on the subordination of workers. The idea of socialist bureaucracy as a New Class—or, as Konrád and Szelényi (1979) put it: the intellectuals' road to class power—was a diagnosis that grasped the socialist bureaucratic middle class as a simultaneously ideological and structural formation, arriving to a criticism of the state socialist model of emancipation.

In Western debates, socialist dissidents' criticisms of the New Class came to be integrated into ongoing discussions around the politics of the New Left that was developing on the basis of new Western professional strata. Within this debate, optimistic projections expected that the progressive values of new professionals will gain broader influence together with the growth of higher education and jobs tied to professional calling, and identified this process as a desirable route for social development (e.g. Bell, 1979). Meanwhile, conservative criticism pointed at the egalitarian and non-materialist tendencies of new professional classes as an element of power struggle, where a class who deals in non-material knowledge valorized in bureaucratic and management positions tries to increase its own influence by referring to workers' needs. Applying socialist New Class theories to a conservative argument, this critique blamed new professionals' politics as an effort to increase state redistribution and thereby expand their own power, to the detriment of business actors (Bruce-Briggs, 1979).

Within the New Left, the amplification of the middle class debate implied the issue of middle class positions vis-a-vis the capital–labor conflict, including concerns over the class loyalty of middle class left actors vis-a-vis the proletariat. Looking back to a long history in left debates since Bakunin's critique of the project of proletarian dictatorship as a potential dictatorship of the bureaucracy (Hodges, 1960), this debate thematized the differences in position, interest, values, and ambitions that separated the middle class base of the New Left from white workers, black people, and women (Ehrenreich & Ehrenreich, 1977).

Following previous analysis by others (e.g. Bledstein, 1976; Mills, 1951), the Ehrenreichs claimed that on the road of Fordist modernization, the multiplication of white-collar professional jobs in both business and public sectors, together with the expansion of higher education, produced not only a growth in the US middle class, but also a shift in its quality. Compared to the earlier petty bourgeoisie characterized by positions like shopkeepers or small businessmen, this new middle class was developed within the structures of a higher level of capitalist monopolization. Its material positions were based on large technocratic-bureaucratic systems, and the benefits they accessed through managing those systems were based on formal professional education. Unlike optimistic interpretations that saw the multiplication of these positions as the sign of a general move toward a knowledge society, the Ehrenreichs interpreted it as a structural process where the capacities for knowledge and self-organization were increasingly extracted from general social interaction, monopolized in the forms of formal professional education organized according to the needs of capital and state, and then used to manage the flows of capitalist accumulation through the work of a growing number of professional-managerial employees. Similar to other analyses of new middle class habitus (Bourdieu, 1984), the Ehrenreichs pointed out that since their positions were based on non-material knowledge-based assets, which served capitalist interests but were legitimated through references to general progress and social wellbeing, the ideological self-reflection of the professional-managerial class tended to emphasize non-material values like professionalism, meritocracy, or moral good, in front of materialistic claims.

Ehrenreich and Ehrenreich (1977) maintained that the New Left of the 1960s developed on the base of the new professional-managerial class' discontent in face of the bureaucratic and technocratic limitations that capitalist employment imposed over the free application of what they grew to perceive as professional-moral values standing on their own. This analysis did not conceive the professional-managerial class as just a contradictory class location with volatile political options, but saw it as a substantive position in the capitalist distribution of labor, which produces its own interests and efforts for reproduction. Based on this position, the Ehrenreichs formulated the interests of the professional-managerial class as coherent across otherwise contradictory class alliances. While this group's ambitions toward professional and moral freedom drove it to conflict with capital, its interest to maintain and expand the same freedom, based on the actual conditions of the selective extraction and monopolization of social capacities of knowledge and organization, also put it in conflict with blue-collar workers. The Ehrenreichs warned that while its political alliances may alternate between capitalist and labor partners, the political projects coming from this interest position will in each case tend toward expanding professional and managerial control—something that, in the case of left politics, they saw exemplified in the bureaucratic rule of state socialist systems. To avoid such pitfalls of left politics following from the systemic position of professional-managerial middle class actors, the Ehrenreichs emphasized the importance of broad political coalitions with workers, something similar to Cabral's "class suicide"—and criticized the New Left for falling short in face of that prerogative.

Debates on the Middle Class in the Current Crisis

By the 1990s—the time when hopes for middle class based democratic modernization were reactivated in postsocialist countries—the progressive erasure of middle class mobility opportunities that started from the 1970s came to be discussed as a key turn in Western social development. This turn was expected to have significant political effects, too—like in Phillips' argument on the connection between financialization and the decline of the middle class presented in the previous chapter. By 2008, the decline of the middle class came to be seen as a major structural and political problem in Western debates (Mooney, 2008). After the financial crisis, even mainstream supporters of free market globalization like Francis Fukuyama declared an unsolvable conflict between markets and democracy, due to the disintegration of the middle class in the West. In an essay that in its title mirrored his famous earlier statement on the "end of history" (Fukuyama, 1989), Fukuyama asked about *The future of history—Can liberal democracy survive the decline of the middle class?* (Fukuyama, 2012). Here, he argued that the world-historical development of liberal democracy is threatened by the new decline of the middle class, and only a new kind of politics that saves middle classes can save democracy. In an illustrative example to what the Ehrenreichs described in the 1970s as the ideological tendency of the professional-managerial class to maintain and expand its positions, or what Silver and Slater (1999) identified as the typical political stance of junior actors in times of hegemonic crisis, he described this new politics as one that would require enhanced state intervention in order to maintain middle class development, and broaden the areas of technocratic management that serve as a base of middle class livelihoods. This new political line would.

> reassert the supremacy of democratic politics over economics and legiti-
> mate a new government as an expression of the public interest. But the
> agenda it puts forward to protect middle-class life could not simply rely
> on the existing mechanisms of the welfare state. The ideology would need
> to somehow redesign the public sector, freeing it from its dependence on
> existing stakeholders and using new, technology-empowered approaches
> to delivering services. (...) The new ideology would not see markets as an
> end in them selves; instead, it would value global trade and investment to
> the extent that they contributed to a flourishing middle class, not just to
> greater aggregate national wealth. (Fukuyama, 2012: 60)

Since 2008, we have seen this political direction develop in several streams of Western debates, such as a new egalitarian critique of global social polarization (e.g. Piketty, 2013), the mainstreaming of a new Keynesian critique of neoliberalism (e.g. Stiglitz, 2011), or Green New Deal projects that propose to increase state intervention to create new jobs, mitigate climate change effects, and solve the tensions of social polarization by reviving the economy through a knowledge- and technology-driven green development that can provide safe jobs associated with high skills. While these approaches speak of solving global contradictions of the crisis, their focus on broadening the space for expert management reveals a bias toward maintaining levels of professional employment.

Parallel to the new politicization of middle class development in the West, in the context of global transformation following the 1970s, discussions around the rising middle classes of the Global South also addressed the middle class not only as statistical growth in the number of middle-income groups, but as a field of struggle where structural and ideological stakes of systemic integration are negotiated. Ethnographic research on rising global middle classes used the notion of the middle class as project (Fernandes, 2006) to describe the uneasy relationship between the tensions of social polarization, intra-class competition, the structural limits to middle class growth, and new global middle classes' role of representing and promoting themselves as a proof of successful development. Aspects of instability and permanent anxiety that accompany middle class aspirations have been documented even in contexts of spectacular middle class growth. Such effects have been described in various spheres of life, like intensive home education optimized to induce white-collar careers in urban India (Donner, 2012), the sharpening of education competition that inflates competitors' mobility investments in Turkey or India (Rutz & Balkan, 2009; Sancho, 2015), the tensions of home-creation as a social mobility project (Fehérváry, 2013), contradictory ties between black middle class development and financialized debt in South Africa (James, 2015), or new links between mobility anxiety, religious-ethnic ideologies, and nationalist consumption in Indonesia (Jones, 2012), India (Mazzarella, 2003), or Russia (Biziukova, 2020). Donner (2017) describes the accumulation such accounts of new middle class anxiety as a new wave of middle class research that increasingly uncovers the tensions and contradictions of global middle class development, and contrasts them with the idea of a secure and unidirectional process of development. Zhang (2012), an influential author of this wave, writing on new Chinese middle classes, grasped the political edge of this anxiety as an inherent tension between the politics of aspiration and the politics of social exclusion.

Debates around contemporary global movements have emphasized the importance of middle classes in the organization, communication, international networking, and broader political effect of post-2008 movements (e.g. Fowler & Biekart, 2016; Fukuyama, 2013; Mason, 2012). Middle classes' choice of social alliances and political claims has been recognized as a key question in the politicization of the current crisis (Biekart, 2015). One aspect this stream of research emphasized was that the way middle class politics translate structural tensions to ideological claims is linked the different trajectories of middle class development in different global contexts. Looking at patterns of global income distribution, Milanović (2011) showed that besides the top global 1%, those who benefited the most from the transformation of global income distribution between 1988 and 2011 were the middle income groups of China, India, Thailand, Vietnam, and Indonesia. Those who lost most compared to their previous positions were the middle and working classes of former Western core economies (North America, Western Europe and Japan)—while still maintaining a higher share of global income than the rising middle classes of East and South Asia. Milanović's main conclusion was that attitudes toward globalization correlate with this pattern in the reorganization of global income distribution: while middle classes and workers of the former Western core express a disillusionment with the performance of free markets, new rising middle classes are rather optimistic. But how do the politics of either disillusionment or optimism relate to the politics of social alliances?

Considering the relation between mobility patterns and political alliances, Fowler and Biekart (2016) pointed at a significant bifurcation point in the politics of raising middle classes. This is the dilemma of "sharing or self-caring" (Biekart, 2015): the choice whether new middle classes will use their growing political and economic power toward alliances with lower strata and the politics of progressive redistribution (sharing), or use it to monopolize the benefits of world-economic integration, and thereby promote inner polarization and sociopolitical tensions. On a systemic level, the stakes of new middle classes' choice to monopolize growth benefits, and promote polarization further, also involves the question whether their ambitions will promote increasing violent competition over growth resources, and exacerbate the climate crisis.

Looking at downwardly mobile middle and working classes of the former Western core, many commentators have raised concerns over nationalist, racist, and xenophobic reactions, and the rise of authoritarian populist elite politics appealing to those sentiments (e.g. Gest, 2016; Hartleb, 2012). By today, existing streams of political organization along these lines have become manifest in the forefront of electoral politics, too, as exemplified by the storming of the Capitol in January 2021 by Trump's supporters. In turn, Western movements that voiced discontent over downward mobility in terms of democratization claims, have been interpreted within the framework of the crisis of "democratic capitalism" as a new promise for re-democratization and the restoration of past levels of wealth redistribution (e.g. Fominaya, 2017, Mouffe, 2018). Considered on a systemic level, however, these movements carry the same contradictions that follow from contesting downward mobility within a hegemonic crisis. One such contradiction is that while these movements see themselves as part of a global wave of movements struggling for progressive values, their claims are simultaneously tied to recovering previous positions based on Western dominance.

For example, besides claims for democracy, protecting the planet, and ending the war for profit, one program proposed from the rows of Occupy Wall Street (The 99 Percent Declaration, Eissinger, 2012) also included claims tied to the recovery of the dominant world-economic position of the US economy. Such were points like "mandating new educational goals to train the American public to perform jobs in a twenty-first century", "implementing of immediate legislation to encourage China and our other trading partners to end currency manipulation and reduce the trade deficit", or "comprehensive immigration and border security reform including offering visas, lawful permanent resident status and citizenship to the world's brightest People to stay and work in our industries and schools". Corbyn's 2019 program also linked the creation of jobs and better working conditions to technological progress and economic uptake (Labour, 2019). In the case of such examples, Biekart's dilemma of "sharing or self-caring" could be formulated as the question whether movements mobilized by the loss of former privileges will work toward the aim to maintain previous positions, or create new alliances for projects that transcend the logic of systemic competition. While radical proposals like commoning or degrowth also strengthened, the aim to "reclaim their rights to live decent, dignified, middle-class lives" (Hickel, 2008) remained central to post-2008 Western movements, and the structural contradictions between global, antiracist emancipative politics and the project to maintain the status of existing Western middle classes remained underconceptualized even in left political programs.

Attention to differences of global mobility trajectories reveals that similar slogans, repertoires, or mutual support between various mobilizations of the post-2008 wave—like the global spread of the slogan of 99% vs. 1%, the practice of square occupations, claims for real democracy, or the combination of anti-elitist and xenophobic programs in the case of new right movements—do not necessarily reflect the same type of social relations everywhere. Instead, they represent mutual references and partial coordination across actors differently embedded within the same global transformation. When considering how East European new middle class mobilizations enter that discussion, I understand this space of dialogue not as one between similar values and compatible aims of middle class development across the world, but as one where contradictory interests and diverging trajectories of global middle class mobility are expressed in ideological projections that make a negotiated use of shared symbolic forms.

Post-2008 Left Critique of the Middle Class Idea

After 2008, the idea that the present crisis of the middle class can be the carrier of a new wave of left politics, permeated post-2008 left debates, from reformist segments that conceive the "crisis of democratic capitalism" as a potential new driver of pro-welfare politics, to radical voices that saw middle class crisis as a chance for disillusionment with capitalist structures. In the internal critique of new left strategies, the problem of middle class preferences rooted in professional positions resurfaced most sharply in Western debates around Bernie Sanders' 2020 presidential campaign in the US and Jeremy Corbyn's Labour campaign for the UK general elections in 2019. Such critiques noted that new left agendas are biased toward technocratic solutions proposed by professional middle class activists (e.g. Day, 2019; Liu, 2021; Press, 2019), that organizational models favor middle class participation, or that the predominance of disillusioned middle class constituencies has not been balanced by a sufficient reachout to worker constituencies (e.g. Proctor, 2019; Ries, 2020).

In these debates, the issue of the middle class became a ground where the stakes of critical structural analysis and the stakes of new left political identification are explicitly connected. Similar to how the post-2008 mobilization context reorganized the paradigms of social movement research, real-world stakes of middle class politicization penetrated the sphere of left analysis more directly. In analytical texts, this connection is most visible in arguments where the critical analysis of middle class identifications is posed as a key tool that can guide middle class politics away from systemic illusions and alliances, and toward antisystemic coalitions with workers. In this way, the analysis itself is constituted as a highly significant political gesture that acts upon a decisive factor of crisis politicization.

For instance, Hadas Weiss' book *We have never been middle class* (Weiss, 2019) investigated the entanglements of financialization and middle class insecurities as a new stage of capitalist crisis where the critique of the ideological construct of the middle class becomes possible. Just like Hegel's owl of Minerva spreads its wings with the falling of dusk, says Weiss, "the hour of critique chimes at the dusk of the middle-class ideal, when a chorus of voices laments its decline" (Weiss, 2019: 13). In the book's interpretation, this crisis consists in the way financialization intervenes in the structural process of middle class property formation, a systemic function that so far helped maintain the motivation to obey the structures of capitalist employment in the hope of gaining increasing shares from accumulated wealth. Weiss argues that while the volatility of financial markets constitutes a main means of accumulation for financial capital, through the financialization of housing and savings assets, the same volatility makes middle class wealth unstable both on the side of income and property value. The result is a general sense of disillusionment with the promises of middle class ideology globally.

This moment of disillusionment, says Weiss, is generating three main types of critique today. The first looks at worsening conditions of middle class careers from the perspective of individual options, and produces self-help tips for individual gains. The second contests the collective experience of crisis pressure, and promotes projects to mend the system so it can provide again the rewards promised by the ideology of the middle class. The third type of critique, which Weiss adheres to, addresses the social structures that sustain the ideology of the middle class, and unveils the connections through which the promise of "self-made" individual gains helps maintain the stream of labor exploitation. The political reasoning underlying the argument is that through this third type of critique, addressed to what Weiss (2019: 7) calls "an implicated readership", the crisis of the middle class idea can turn into a political project to transform the capitalist order that underpinned earlier middle class ambitions (Weiss, 2019: 158).

Other researchers associated similar political stakes to tracing how biographical experiences, macroeconomic conditions, and political contexts combine into shifts of middle class politics. For example, David Ozarow (2019), in a longitudinal study of middle class mobilization and demobilization in Argentina between the crisis of 2001 and the election of conservative president Mauricio Macri in 2015, traced a cycle of middle class politics that leads from a social movement alliance with workers and the poor to a disillusionment with the idea of collective emancipation, and support of business-oriented, anti-poor policies. Delving into the factors of economic impoverishment, political context, and changes in social sensitivity and consciousness, Ozarow shows how the misery of middle classes struck by the 2001 crisis first drove collectivist modes of mobilization, but then got separated from popular constituencies under the Kirchner governments' corporatist policies. Ozarow (2019: 3) interprets this right-wing shift as a problem of false consciousness. Concluding the lessons from Argentina with regard to possible outcomes of post-2008 new left mobilizations globally, Ozarow points out possible organizational and political tools that can movement can choose to keep middle class politics on the side of worker alliances. Among these, he emphasizes the importance of maintaining movement organizations and solidarity economy practices, which can act as a mixing ground with other social strata, and allow for middle class political consciousness to link with their perspectives.

In East European postsocialist contexts, Don Kalb (2012) discussed from a similar perspective how workers' hopes for middle class mobility acted as an element of the transformation process. To illustrate these dynamics, at one point he quotes his conversations with a former Polish factory worker who became unemployed after the regime change, but bought a second-hand truck, and started to work for the same factory as a private transporter. "Look, I've always been an entrepreneur – of course you know, we were called workers here in Polar, but I've actually been an entrepreneur all my life. Now I'm finally establishing myself formerly as an independent entrepreneur"—he told Kalb in 1998 (Kalb, 2012: 40). However, by 2004, the risks implied in the loan with which he bought the truck and embarked on the optimistic project of middle class entrepreneurship started to show. The French company that bought up Polar in 1998 went bankrupt in 2000; transport contracts got scarcer, and he was starting to have problems paying back the loan. When Kalb met him again in 2007, he had sold his truck, but was still paying for the loan. "Well, you know, in fact we are all workers"—he told Kalb at this point.

Kalb (2012) refers to this dynamic of post-transitional hopes and their failures as "the traumatic symbol of the middle class". Here, middle class is defined as a structurally active ideological concept, which both legitimated and drove postsocialist efforts of catching up with the West. Analytically, this notion is close to what this book conceives of as the structural-ideological aspect of semi-peripheral middle class development as a field of developmentalist illusion. Yet in Kalb's definition, the analytical idea of "the traumatic symbol of the middle class" also implies that the revealing of structural truth can dispel the illusion that constitutes this trauma.

In left discussions about the politics of post-2008 movements, the role of intellectual analysis has often been associated with similar stakes stakes, implying that a correct analysis could point out the right direction amidst systemic diversions. The idea that the rise of the populist right is happening as a result of the left's failure to name and claim the tensions of neoliberalism has been a widespread diagnosis among intellectual commentators of post-2008 politics (e.g. Kalb, 2015; Laclau & Mouffe, 2014; Stavrakakis, 2014; Streeck, 2014). These narratives connected the crisis of "democratic capitalism" to the simultaneous emptying of established left politics and representative democracy in general. In lack of a democratic political infrastructure and left political answer, as Žižek (2008: 275) concluded at one point, populism is filling the void of a left political imagination.

My argument differs from this stream of engaged research in that it does not imply that a critical analysis of the ideological notion of the middle class could induce a "proper" class-based, antisystemic direction in the politicization of middle class disillusionment. First, while I agree with the ultimate perspective of Marxist analyses that see the middle class as an ideological-structural construct that serves to obscure capital–labor conflict, I follow Poulantzas, the Ehrenreichs or Silver and Slater in seeing the middle class as a structural-ideological fact which also produces its own characteristics and its own interest for reproduction. These are not simply dispelled by a critical analysis, and do not stop at the moment of disillusionment: on the contrary, they constitute an active element of middle class politics of crisis.

The second aspect has to do with the the position from which critical analysis is performed—a question with deep implications for the program of antisystemic politics. In classic Marxist approaches, the main carrier of class analysis as systemic analysis was the proletariat in its historical development toward a revolutionary class. Unlike other classes, whose class consciousness formulates necessarily fragmented and ideological views of systemic development, the proletariat was seen as the class whose self-understanding has the capacity to grasp the totality of capitalist relations, and whose conscientization of its interests can go beyond optimizing positions within the existing system. However, even in the case of the proletariat, this leap from optimizing intra-system positions toward a full revolutionary struggle was seen as a challenge. The proletariat was seen as the revolutionary class because it cannot liberate itself in any other way than abolishing capitalism. Yet this final liberation would also involve the self-annihilation of the proletariat as a class within capitalism. Are proletarian struggles ready for this, or do they remain bound within intra-system opportunism? This question has been discussed as a key problem of revolutionary politics (e.g. Lenin, [1920] 1964; Lukács, 1972; Marx, [1865] 1969).

The role of the communist party was conceived as the element of proletarian politics that embodies and encourages the ultimate revolutionary direction within workers' struggles. As the Communist Manifesto put it:

The Communists, therefore, are on the one hand, practically, the most advanced and resolute section of the working-class parties of every country, that section which pushes forward all others; on the other hand, theoretically, they have over the great mass of the proletariat the advantage of clearly understanding the line of march, the conditions, and the ultimate general results of the proletarian movement. (Marx & Engels, [1948] 2000)

But who is the Communist Party? The Manifesto states that communists "have no interests separate and apart from those of the proletariat as a whole" (Marx & Engels [1948] 2000). This presupposes an interest that is perfectly identical with the ultimate revolutionary interest of the proletariat to transcend capitalism, and free from the gravitational pull of existing systemic conditions. In Marxist revolutionary thinking, this position was imagined as progressively constituted by the historical process of workers' organization and thought. However, in historical experience, communist parties' embeddedness in systemic relations of power did generate specific interests, and their references to the ultimate aim of proletarian revolution more often than not implied a distantiation from actual organizations of workers' power. What theories of the New Class voiced as a critique in the context of socialist bureaucratic rule was a sharp formulation of a dormant contradiction between intellectual claims of the ultimate antisystemic program, and workers' struggles on the ground. What New Class theories emphasized was that the silence about the positions from which revolutionary programs are voiced—the idea that the communists who lead the struggle have no interests of their own—can work as a fertile ground for promoting selfish interests in the name of others.

This problem has been addressed recurrently in left political thought, from Bakunin's critique of the project of state power, Lenin's ([1920] 1920) reformulation of the party's role as revolutionary avantgarde, or Western Marxism's reckoning with the history of state socialism to later sociological and philosophical considerations in New Left discussions of the New Class, or renewed debates about middle class based left politics after 2008. One strong stream of this tradition, associated with Karl Korsch ([1923] 2012), Antonio Gramsci (1971), or later, Marxist cultural studies (e.g. Williams, 1983) and New Class theories, explicitly sought to apply materialist analysis to intellectuals' own positions and the left analysis they produce. Regarding the formation of new left diagnoses of neoliberalization in the late 2000s, analyses working in the tradition of the latter stream have emphasized overlaps between academic diagnoses and movement frameworks due to connections between academic precarity, academic mobilizations, and biographical movements between academic and movement circles (e.g., Fominaya & Cox, 2013; Juris & Khasnabish, 2013). In the context of post-2008 movements, similar discussions addressed highly educated participants' influence on movement politics, the issue of academic representation of movements that highlights academic commentators and invisibilizes those who do the ground work, connections between professional middle class ambitions and the political institutionalization of movement politics, as well as geopolitical hierarchies implied in these relations (e.g. Buier, 2014; Karitzis, 2017; Ries, 2020).

In the case of contemporary debates on middle class politics, the same problematic appears in a specific form. Turning middle class mobilizations toward antisystemic aims poses the problem of a leap from intra-system interests toward the ultimate goal of abolishing capitalism, similar to what classic Marxist thought identified on the side of the proletariat. Yet the context of the same problem is different. While Marxist analysis has identified the proletariat as a systemic position where the interest of self-emancipation ultimately implies the abolishment of capitalist relations, the middle class has been described as an intermediary position with contradictory interests and consequently ambiguous class politics. Programs that encourage middle class actors to identify with a revolutionary proletarian position expect a larger antisystemic leap to be carried out through a change of consciousness that would connect momentary disillusionments to antisystemic analysis. In a role similar to that of the communist party in Marxist revolutionary theory, critical analysis is expected to aid this process by dispelling middle class illusions, revealing middle class positions as worker positions, and thereby designating an antisystemic direction to middle class struggles.

What is striking is that in these arguments, the politics of both critical analysis and middle class protest are primarily based in consciousness. This is unlike Marxist programs of proletarian revolution where the formation of revolutionary consciousness was also defined as an organizational process through concrete forms of struggle within the relations of production. This double foregrounding of consciousness as a base for an antisystemic politics that could liberate middle class politics from systemic interests happens in a situation where both the speakers of critical analysis and the audience they address belong to a social position whose material forms are largely based in the monopoly of knowledge-making. Should this make us wary of the promise that an antisystemic turn in middle class crisis politics can be induced by critical analysis? Or shall we, on the contrary, hope that middle class actors' "proclivity to reflect on (…) received wisdoms" can become a carrier of an antisystemic shift, as Weiss (2019: 14) suggests? The impact of knowledge-based positions on middle class ideological capacities is a last aspect of middle class politics that this chapter aims to highlight.

The Political Consciousness of a Knowledge Class

Barbara Ehrenreich (1989) argued that in the postwar US context, the monopolization of organizational and knowledge functions into professional jobs, the foregrounding of the middle class in hegemonic, and the fact that the middle class served as the main consumer market, and therefore, the main addressee of commercial communication, produced forms of consciousness where middle class self-reflection got to be universalized over the whole of society. Besides the idea of knowledge society and other related forms of Western developmental consciousness that treat the middle class as a main protagonist of social and historical narratives, Ehrenreich also included critical voices like Riesman's (1950) *The lonely crowd* as examples where middle class experiences were generalized to the whole of society. Ehrenreich described successive forms of this universalized social consciousness, which she pedagogically termed "the inner life of the middle class", across postwar dynamics of class formation in the United States.

The Ehrenreichs traced how subsequent phases of middle class political consciousness reflected the increasing pressure, internal competition, and finally, post-2008 crisis of US middle classes (Ehrenreich & Ehrenreich, 2013). They showed that in the buildup of these subsequent waves of middle class disillusionment, middle class actors projected political narratives from their own experience over the experience of workers victimized by the same structural process—involving, among others, the cost-cutting measures and financialization that provided alleys for competitive self-preservation for middle class professionals during the 1980s and 1990s. In a similar analysis, Bourdieu (1984) characterized the repertoires, slogans, and claims of 1968 New Left movements as following from the sensitivities of a new postwar middle class that grew to identify itself through immaterial professional and moral values. Faced with systemic limitations of the applications of these skills, he maintained, this new middle class came to express the same values in the form of a revolutionary vision built around the ideal of endless freedom, or, as Bourdieu put it, the lack of the gravitational pull of social and material context. These claims, he argued, were projected from within the conditions of professional new middle class ambitions and their limitations, and were largely incompatible with the situation of workers.

In structural terms, Barbara Ehrenreich (1989) summarized the contradiction between middle class emancipative ideas and the structural position of the professional-managerial class in the question what the middle class can gain from equality. For a group whose position (and consequent moral-political sensitivity) is bound to the extraction and monopolization of organizational and knowledge functions from the social body, more equality can appear as beneficial if it means the further expansion of such positions. In the language of modernization theory, this corresponds to the promise of ever-increasing middle class which also allows upward mobility for workers. This promise is compatible with the tendency of middle class left politics toward claims for redistribution and more mobility. In broader systemic terms, however, the same promise presupposes a further polarization of global labor distribution. If this direction, following organically from middle class perspectives, is not the real way of emancipation, then how can middle classes imagine an antisystemic project of equality that is still beneficial for them?

In the history of left political thought—just like in recent debates—proposals to solve this deadlock of middle class progressivism have been typically linked to transcending middle class structural interests. Next to calls to radicalize middle class consciousness and build alliances with workers, this also involved the idea that middle class leftists should abandon their knowledge monopolies, and concede them to the proletariat. Gramsci (1971) claimed that the task of communist intellectuals is to give their power based in systemic structures over to organic intellectuals of the working class. However, as more than a century of debates over the role of the communist party as that organic intellectual, and the experience of state socialist bureaucratic power indicates, this kind of self-inflicted annihilation of middle class power is not as evident a step to make.

In their critique of socialist intellectuals' betrayal of the working class, Konrád and Szelényi (1979) also raised the problem of middle class consciousness as a key issue of left politics, and offered their own solution to it. Speaking of East European middle classes, but coming close to Western critical sociology of intellectuals (Bourdieu, 1984), this critique identified the root of the problem in the fact that middle class actors can only access forms of power (better livelihood, social respect, right to decision-making) through some kind of knowledge monopoly. On the one hand, this situation implies that the knowledge they produce is tied to the stakes of their own social needs and ambitions. On the other hand, since knowledge monopolies can only be exchanged to actual benefits through powers held by other social groups, the same situation also implies that to pursue their own interests, knowledge professionals need to invisibilize their own interests in the knowledge forms they produce, and instead tie them to the interests of broader social alliances, or of general social progress. Thus, the practical conditions of intellectual knowledge imply that in order to valorize knowledge monopolies, these need to simultaneously contain and mask a complex interplay of partial interests that constitute the practical conditions of their production. Bourdieu (2000: 15) summed up this double aspect of intellectual knowledge production in the statement that "the world in which one thinks is not the world in which one lives". Elsewhere, Smith (2014: 5–6) described the binding force of this situation over intellectual thought as a state where "we know that this [independence of intellectual thought] is untrue (…) but it is a misrecognition that we must retain".

While Konrád and Szelényi emphasized the significance of intellectual capital as something particularly relevant to East European middle class politics, Szelényi's later work (Szelényi, 2011; Szelényi & King 2004) discussed the same question as a problematic of the professional middle class in general, and treated both Eastern and Western theories of the New Class as manifestations of the problems of self-reflection inherent to that position. This placed the idea of East European "cycles" of middle class politics next to claims such as Mills' (1951: 353–354): "They are rearguarders. In the shorter run, they will follow the panicky ways of prestige; in the longer run, they will follow the ways of power, for, in the end, prestige is determined by power".

Szelényi and Konrád noted that the dramatic character of middle class politics in Eastern Europe follows from the contradiction between the universal and particular aspects of intellectual knowledge. Due to this contradiction, the succession of middle class political projects looks like a history of schizophrenic shifts, where moments of universalization of particular interests are followed by moments of disillusionment where these ideas are unmasked as particular (Konrád & Szelényi, 1979, 41). This fluctuation of faith and disillusioned exposure projects ever new visions of the historical landscape around intellectual debates, according to the dynamics of changing conditions and alliances. In order to achieve a more solid grasp on the process whereby the universal image of history is always projected from particularly embedded intellectual perspectives, Konrád and Szelényi propose that instead of the projections themselves, we should look at the historical reorganizations of the contradictions that drive intellectual projections. In other words, they lay out a program of empirical sociology of intellectual ideas which analyzes intellectual visions of history and politics together with the changing conditions and alliances that underpin them.

The method Konrád and Szelényi promote for interpreting intellectual ideologies is based on the classic materialist gesture Marx proposed vis-a-vis idealism (Marx & Engels, [1845] 1970). Their proposal to save intellectual reflection from its self-centered bias is similar to other applications of the same method to the understanding of intellectual thought, from Gramsci's treatment of what he called traditional intellectuals (1971) to Raymond Williams' interpretation of English Romanticism as a perception of the tensions of the industrial revolution abstracted through intellectual positions, or Bourdieu's (1984, 2000) treatment of aesthetics and scholarly production in terms of power fields. Yet, in addition to its analytical value, Konrád and Szelényi (1979) claimed that the sociological critique of intellectual projections can potentially change the political capacities of East European middle classes. They saw this effect of materialist analysis as similar to that of psychotherapy, in that exposing the conditions of desire structures, it reorganizes the perception of reality. The main benefit of this therapy, in their view, was to break the barrier that isolates intellectual forms of consciousness from direct reflection on their own positions and interest. As Szelényi and King (2004: ix) summarized this thought regarding the relationship between the New Class and their politics, this would make it possible for intellectuals.

to dare speak with their own voices rather than feel obliged to present themselves as speaking on someone else's behalf. We believe the history of the New Class will come to an end when we arrive to this brave new world. To put it bluntly: a tour around the history of the idea of the New Class may serve the purpose of some sort of collective psychotherapy for modern intellectuals. It may confront them with their most secret and suppressed desires of the past, and make them more comfortable operating in the real world.

In their political reckoning with the bureaucratic power of the educated middle class in state socialism, Konrád and Szelényi claimed that getting rid of the projection apparatus of those desires, and becoming able to reflect on their own position, was a key condition of resurrecting left politics after the state socialist model. If intellectuals' left politics consists in the program of socialist state power and redistribution, then the evidence of bureaucratic power defines this program as right-wing politics. Is there anything such as an immanent left politics that could salvage intellectual progressivism and drive it beyond self-interest bound to bureaucratic power?—they asked, similar to Ehrenreich's question about the middle class' interest in equality (Konrád & Szelényi, 1979: 311). Their answer was that the recognition of the historical relation between intellectual self-interest and intellectual politics—or, between the interest to monopolize knowledge and claim for power based on portraying that knowledge as serving other people's interest—can provide a base for that. Konrád and Szelényi described this new stage of intellectual left politics, eliberated from the blind universalization of particular interests, as the "transcendental" notion of the intellectual (Konrád & Szelényi, 1979: 317). This solution is similar to Weiss' proposal to use the knowledge-making power of middle class professionals to get rid of their illusionary expectations about valorizing their knowledge. Yet the use of the "transcendental" notion already has ironic undertones in Konrád and Szelényi's book: the idea of "transcending" the historical conditions of knowledge-making easily sounds rather like a reductio ad absurdum of the emancipatory verve characteristic to intellectual politics, than an actual possibility.

On the last pages of their book, Konrád and Szelényi claimed that their critique could only be published when Stalinist bureaucratic rule was abolished, and a new immanent left politics, salvaged by the "transcendental" mode of intellectual activity, brought about a third period of socialism. In contrast to this prediction, *The intellectuals on the road to class power* became a classic of dissident literature already before the collapse of the Soviet bloc. This collapse was not driven by the immanent left politics of intellectuals, and did not bring a third period of socialist history. Instead, it brought a period of dependent capitalist integration. Konrád and Szelényi pursued successful intellectual careers at home and abroad, with Szelényi applying their theory to postsocialist elite formation and to international aspects of the New Class. In this context, their proposal for the intellectual left to pull itself by the bootstraps from the mire of integration interests rather appears as one in the row of delusions described in later formulations of New Left politics.

For the analysis in this book, I follow Szelényi and Konrád's proposal for a historical sociological approach to middle class politics. However, I do not suppose that uncovering the "secret and suppressed desires" inherent in middle class projections could, by themselves, act as a therapy that could eliberate middle class politics from structural effects. Similar to Frank and Fuentes (1990) and Edelman (1999), or the new strain of social movement research that emphasizes research-movement interactions (Cox, 2018), I see research as an act performed within the same interaction space where movements operate. If the analysis of the conditions of middle class projections can help us move toward antisystemic agendas, it is most probably through forms of organization that embody and sustain them within systemic struggles, and not by a "transcendental" force of consciousness that abolishes systemic effects. Instead of such an exceptional moment of reflection, this book's contribution is rather conceived as a side product and potential tool of a larger collective process, where knowledge about systemic contradictions is produced from within their grip.

CONCLUSION

This chapter discussed how the structural and political characteristics of semi-peripheral development impact middle class politics in Eastern Europe, and how this relates to current debates about the significance of middle classes in the politicization of the global crisis. Regarding the characteristics of semi-peripheral politics, it pointed out three main factors. The first was structural heterogeneity as a result of internal polarization in dependent integration. Politically, this involves governments' need to simultaneously maintain conditions of external extraction, and manage local consequences of internal polarization. The second factor was the constant renewal of alliances for development understood as upward mobility within global hierarchies, termed, after Arrighi, as the structural-ideological fact of developmentalist illusion. The third factor was hegemonic tutelage and its corresponding forms of local divergences.

The effects of these factors on local politics were described, after Janos, as the "politics of backwardness".

In these conditions, instead of a co-constitutive development of middle classes and democracy, held up as a general model by modernization theory, we see a contradictory relation between middle class development and democratization. Faced with limited economic possibilities for middle class development, local aspirant middle classes regularly mobilize to reach life standards similar to Western middle classes through state support. The higher share of national wealth distribution this requires contributes to distortions of local redistribution, while in terms of consumption, it channels local savings toward core markets. Therefore, while the—albeit limited—existence of Western middle class lifestyles in East European societies has been usually understood as a sign of development, it actually worked as an element of uneven development.

Looking at middle class politics as a form of "politics of backwardness" in Eastern Europe, the chapter discussed three aspects that could be particularly relevant to understanding contemporary mobilizations. The first was the historical succession of phases of revolutionary upheaval, where middle classes mobilize politically to compensate developmental limitations, and phases of integration, where middle classes integrate in beneficial positions maintained by supportive state policies. The second aspect was the contradictory nature of middle class political ideologies following from this structural position. In the case of progressive ideologies, these contradictions imply that in revolutionary phases, structural differences between middle class interests and the interests of their social alliances are obscured, and the first is expressed in the name of others, or of general progress. In shifts from revolutionary to integration phases, however, democratic and social goals expressed in revolutionary periods come into conflict with middle classes' interest to acquire higher share of state redistribution. A third, related aspect of East European middle class politics was theatricality, understood as a systemic effect of structural heterogeneity.

Going beyond the specificities of East European middle class development, the chapter demonstrated that limitations of middle class development, together with resulting tensions and their expressions in middle class political consciousness, have characterized middle class development everywhere, including postwar Western welfare contexts. Regarding how such tensions are expressed in post-2008 movements, it pointed out that despite mutual references, post-2008 movements express different positions within different systemic dynamics, and cannot simply be understood as a harmonious claim for global middle class futures. In terms of whether those tensions can create a potential for middle class politics to transcend the project of middle class development, the chapter discussed the connection between knowledge-based positions and left politics.

This connection has been emphasized by left traditions as one that poses a specific limitation to the emancipative potential of middle class politics, simultaneously binding it to an interest to expand white-collar positions, and to a need to mask this interest by referring to more general aims. The chapter argued that calls to transcend this limitation by a conscientization of its structural conditions rather repeat the middle class tendency to promote universal programs that point at knowledge as their base, than actually transcend the conditions that recurrently generate this type of gestures. Instead, this book proposed to see the relation between middle class politics and antisystemic analysis as a more complex embedded process, where middle class political projections, moved by the tectonic forces of global transformations, integrate with the broader politics of a crisis. The following chapters look at how this interaction played out in two East European cases since 1973, and how present new left initiatives are struggling to overcome middle class limitations in political practice.

REFERENCES

Adamovsky, E. (2009). *Historia de la clase media argentina*. Planeta.

Amin, S. (1976). *Unequal development: An essay on the social formations of peripheral capitalism*. Monthly Review Press.

Amin, S. (1991). The issue of democracy in the contemporary Third World. *Socialism and Democracy, 7*(1), 83–104.

Arrighi, G. (1973). International corporations, labour aristocracies, and economic development in tropical Africa. In G. Arrighi (Ed.), *Essays on the political economy of Africa* (pp. 105–151). Monthly Review Press.

Arrighi, G. (1990). The developmentalist illusion: A reconceptualization of the semiperiphery. In W. G. Martin (Ed.), *Semiperipheral states in the world-economy* (pp. 11–42). Greenwood Publishing Group.

Baran, P. A. (1966). *Monopoly capital*. NYU Press.

Becker, J. (2014). The periphery in the present international crisis: Uneven development, uneven impact and different responses. *Spectrum: Journal of Global Studies, 5*(1), 21–41.

Bell, D. (1979). The new class: A muddled concept. *Society, 16*(2), 15–23.

Biekart, K. (2015). The choice of the new Latin American middle classes: Sharing or self-caring. *The European Journal of Development Research, 27*(2), 238–245.

Biziukova, V. (2020). Uncertain new middle classes: Changing consumption practices and state policies in Russia. *East European Politics and Societies and Cultures, 34*(2), 464–484.

Bledstein, B. (1976). *The culture of professionalism. The middle class and the development of higher education in America.* W. W. Norton.

Boatcă, M. (2003). *From neoevolutionism to world systems analysis: the Romanian theory of "forms without substance" in light of modern debates on social change.* Leske und Budrich.

Boatcă, M. (2006). Semiperipheries in the world-system: Reflecting Eastern European and Latin American experiences. *Journal of World-Systems Research, 12*(2), 321–346.

Bockman, J. K. (1997). The role of economists in social change: Explaining the end of state socialism in Hungary. *Applied Behavioral Science Review, 5*(2), 141–157.

Bockman, J. K. (2000). *Economists and social change: Science, professional power, and politics in Hungary, 1945–1995.* University of California, San Diego.

Böröcz, J., & Róna-Tas, Á. (1995). Small leap forward: Emergence of new economic elites. *Theory and Society, 24*(5), 751–781.

Bourdieu, P. (1984). *Distinction.* Harvard University Press.

Bourdieu, P. (2000). *Pascalian meditations.* Stanford University Press.

Braverman, H. (1974). *Labor and monopoly capital: The degradation of work in the twentieth century.* New York: Monthly Review Press.

Brenner, R. (1977). The origins of capitalist development: A critique of Neo-Smithian Marxism. *New Left Review, 1*(104), 25–92.

Bruce-Briggs, B. (Ed.). (1979). *The new class?* Transaction Publishers.

Brunn, S. D. (1998). A Treaty of Silicon for the Treaty of Westphalia? New territorial dimensions of modern statehood. *Geopolitics, 3*(1), 106–131.

Buier, N. (2014). The promise of an anarchist anthropology: The three burials of the anarchist project. *Studia Universitatis Babes-Bolyai-Sociologia, 59*(1), 73–90.

Cabral, A. (1966, January). *The weapon of theory. Address delivered to the first Tricontinental Conference of the Peoples of Asia, Africa and Latin America held in Havana in January.* https://www.marxists.org/subject/africa/cabral/1966/weapon-theory.htm. Accessed 26 May 2020.

Chase-Dunn, C. (1990). Resistance to imperialism: Semiperipheral actors. *Review (Fernand Braudel Center), 13*(1), 1–31.

Chase-Dunn, C. K. (1998). *Global formation: Structures of the world-economy.* Rowman & Littlefield.

Cheeseman, N. (2015). "No Bourgeoisie, No Democracy"? The political attitudes of the Kenyan middle class. *Journal of International Development, 27*(5), 647–664.

Chirot, D. (Ed.). (1991). *The origins of backwardness in Eastern Europe: Economics and politics from the Middle Ages until the early twentieth century.* University of California Press.

Cox, L. (2018). *Why social movements matter: An introduction.* Rowman & Littlefield.

Cucu, A. S. (2007). The romanian middle class: A topological analysis. *Studia Universitatis Babes-Bolyai-Sociologia, 52*(2), 17–40.

Da Costa, A., & Teixeira, D. (2012). Structural change for equality: An integrated approach to development. *Conjuntura Internacional, 9*(5), 61–66.

Dasgupta, R. (2006). Towards the 'New Man': Revolutionary youth and rural agency in the naxalite movement. *Economic and Political Weekly, 41*(19), 1920–1927.

Day, M. (2019, August 20). Bernie Sanders and Elisabeth Warren aren't playing the same game. *Jacobin.* https://www.jacobinmag.com/2019/08/bernie-sanders-elizabeth-warren-democratic-party-elite-2020-presidential-race. Accessed 2 April 2020.

Djilas, M. (1959). *Anatomy of a moral: The political essays of Milovan Djilas.* Praeger.

Don, Y. (1986). The economic dimensions of antisemitism: Anti-Jewish legislation in Hungary 1938–1944. *East European Quarterly, 20*(4), 447.

Donner, H. (Ed.). (2012). *Being middle-class in India: A way of life.* Routledge.

Donner, H. (2017, January 18). The anthropology of the middle class across the globe. *Anthropology of This Century.* http://aotcpress.com/articles/anthropology-middle-class-globe/. Accessed 23 February 2020.

Edelman, M. (1999). *Peasants against globalization: Rural social movements in Costa Rica.* Stanford University Press.

Ehrenreich, B. (1989). *Fear of falling: The inner life of the middle class.* Perennial.

Ehrenreich, B., & Ehrenreich, J. (1977). The new left. *Radical America, 11*(3), 7–22.

Ehrenreich, B., & Ehrenreich, J. (2013). *Death of a yuppie dream: The rise and fall of the professional middle class.* Rosa Luxemburg Stiftung.

Eissinger, D. (2012). Occupy Wall Street demands 99% declaration. *International Business Times,* February 14. http://www.ibtimes.com/occupy-wall-street-demands-99-percent-declaration-calls-july-4-general-assembly-philadelphia-410588. Accessed 1 April 2020.

Erdei, F. (1976). A magyar társadalom a két háború között I. *Valóság, 19*(4), 22–53.

Esping-Andersen, G. (Ed.). (1996). *Welfare states in transition: National adaptations in global economies.* Sage.

Eyal, G., Szelényi, I., & Townsley, E. (1998). *Making capitalism without capitalists*. Verso.

Fehérváry, K. (2013). *Politics in color and concrete: Socialist materialities and the middle class in Hungary*. University of Indiana Press.

Fernandes, L. (2006). *India's new middle class: Democratic politics in an era of economic reform*. University of Minnesota Press.

Freire, P. (1972). *Pedagogy of the oppressed*. Penguin.

Flesher Fominaya, C. (2017). European anti-austerity and pro-democracy protests in the wake of the global financial crisis. *Social Movement Studies, 16*(1), 1–20.

Fominaya, C. F., & Cox, L. (Eds.). (2013). *Understanding European movements: New social movements, global justice struggles, anti-austerity protest*. Routledge.

Fowler, A., & Biekart, K. (2016). Navigating polycentric governance from a citizen's perspective: The rising new middle classes respond. *The European Journal of Development Research, 28*(4), 705–721.

Frank, A. G. (1975). *On capitalist underdevelopment*. Oxford University Press.

Frank, A. G., & Fuentes, M. (1990). Social movements. In M. Musheno, D. Altheide, M. Zatz, J. Johnson, & J. Hepburn (Eds.), *New directions in the study of justice, law, and social control* (pp. 127–141). Springer.

Fukuyama, F. (1989). The end of history? *The National Interest, 16*, 3–18.

Fukuyama, F. (2012). The future of history: Can liberal democracy survive the decline of the middle class? *Foreign Affairs, 91*, 53–61.

Fukuyama, F. (2013). The middle class revolution. *The Wall Street Journal*, June 28. https://www.wsj.com/articles/SB10001424127887323873904578571472700348086. Accessed 3 March 2020.

Gagyi, A. (2015). Social movement studies for East Central Europe? . *Intersections East European Journal of Society and Politics, 1*(3), 16–36.

Gereffi, G., & Hempel, L. (1996). Latin America in the global economy: Running faster to stay in place. *NACLA Report on the Americas, 29*(4), 18–27.

Gest, J. (2016). *The new minority: White working class politics in an age of immigration and inequality*. Oxford University Press.

Gramsci, A. (1971). The intellectuals. In Q. Hoare & G. N. Smith (Eds.), *Selections from the prison notebooks* (pp. 3–43). International Publishers.

Gyáni, G., & Kövér, G. (2006). *Magyarország társadalomtörténete a reformkortól a második világháborúig*. Osiris.

Hamel, K. (2019, May 7). Look East instead of West for the future of the global middle class. *OECD Development Matters*. https://oecd-development-matters.org/2019/05/07/look-east-instead-of-west-for-the-future-global-middle-class/. Accessed 9 April 2020.

Hartleb, F. (2012). European project in danger: Understanding precisely the phenomena Euroscepticsm, populism and extremism in times of crisis. *Review of European Studies, 4*(5), 45–63.

Harvey, D. (2007). *A brief history of neoliberalism.* Oxford University Press.

Heredia, F. (1993). Cuban socialism: Prospects and challenges. In C. de Estudios & S. America (Eds.), *The Cuban revolution into the 1990s* (pp. 71–127). Westview Press.

Hickel, J. (2008). How to occupy the world. *Mail and Guardian Thought Leader*, December 16, 2011. https://thoughtleader.co.za/jasonhickel/2011/12/16/how-to-occupy-the-world/. Accessed 12 January 2021.

Hinnebusch, R. (2006). Authoritarian persistence, democratization theory and the Middle East: An overview and critique. *Democratization, 13*(3), 373–395.

Hodges, D. C. (1960). Bakunin's controversy with Marx: An analysis of the tensions within modern socialism. *The American Journal of Economics and Sociology, 19*(3), 259–274.

Hürtgen, S. (2015). *Das Konzept der strukturellen Heterogenität und die Analyse fragmentierter Wachstumsgesellschaften in Europa.* DFG-Kollegforschergruppe Postwachstumsgesellschaften.

Inkeles, A. (1950). Social stratification and mobility in the Soviet Union: 1940–1950. *American Sociological Review, 15*(4), 465–479.

James, D. (2015). *Money from nothing: Indebtedness and aspiration in South Africa.* Stanford University Press.

Janos, A. C. (1989). The politics of backwardness in continental Europe, 1780–1945. *World Politics, 41*(3), 325–358.

Janos, A. C. (2000). *East Central Europe in the modern world: The politics of the borderlands from pre-to postcommunism.* Stanford University Press.

Jessop, B. (2009). The spatiotemporal dynamics of globalizing capital and their impact on state power and democracy. In H. Rosa (Ed.), *High-speed society: Social acceleration, power, and modernity* (pp. 135–158). Pennsylvania State University.

Jones, C. (2012). Women in the middle: Femininity, virtue, and excess in Indonesian discourses of middle classness. In R. Heiman, C. Freeman, M. Liechty, K. Fehérváry, C. Jones, & C. Katz (Eds.), *The global middle classes: Theorizing through ethnography* (pp. 145–168). SAR Press.

Juris, J. S., & Khasnabish, A. (2013). *Insurgent encounters: Transnational activism, ethnography, and the political.* Duke University Press.

Kalb, D. (2012). The traumatic symbol of the middle class. *Visegrad Insight, 1*(2), 38–41.

Kalb, D. (2015). Introduction: Class and the new anthropological holism. In J. G. Carrier, & D. Kalb (Eds.). *Anthropologies of class: Power, practice, and inequality* (pp. 1–27). Cambridge University Press.

Karády, V. (1997). *Zsidóság, modernizáció, polgárosodás.* Cserépfalvi.

Karitzis, A. (2017). Learning from Syriza. In *Shifting Baselines of Europe* (pp. 158–166). Transcript-Verlag.

Kocka, J. (1995). The middle classes in Europe. *The Journal of Modern History, 67*(4), 783–806.

Kolosi, T. (1974). *Társadalmi struktúra és szocializmus*. Kossuth Könyvkiadó.

Kolosi, T., & Sági, M. (1996). Rendszerváltás és társadalomszerkezet. In R. Andorka, T. Kolosi, & G. Vukovich (Eds.), *Társadalmi Riport 1996* (pp. 149–197). TÁRKI, Századvég.

Konrád, G., & Szelényi, I. (1979). *The intellectuals on the road to class power*. Harcourt.

Kopeček, M., & Wciślik, P. (2015). *Thinking through transition: Liberal democracy, authoritarian pasts, and intellectual history in East Central Europe after 1989*. Central European University Press.

Korsch, K. ([1923] 2012). *Kernpunkte der materialistischen Geschichtsauffassung*. Salzwasser Verlag.

Labour. (2019). *Workers' rights manifesto*. https://labour.org.uk/wp-content/uploads/2019/12/13238_19-Work-manifesto.pdf. Accessed 4 April 2020.

Laclau, E., & Mouffe, C. (2014). *Hegemony and socialist strategy: Towards a radical democratic politics*. Verso Trade.

Larionescu, M., Marginean, I., & Neagu, G. (2006). *Constituirea clasei mijlocii în România*. Bucharest: Editura Economică.

Lenin, V. I. ([1920] 1964). "Left-wing" Communism: An infantile disorder. In V. I. Lenin (Ed.), *Collected Works* (Vol. 31, pp. 17–118). Progress Publishers.

Lipset, S. M. (1959). Some social requisites of democracy: Economic development and political legitimacy. *American Political Science Review, 53*(1), 69–105.

Liu, C. (2021). *Virtue hoarders: The case against the professional managerial class*. University of Minnesota Press.

López, A. R., & Weinstein, B. (2012). *The making of the middle class: Toward a transnational history*. Duke University Press.

Lu, X. (2004). *Rhetoric of the Chinese cultural revolution: The impact on Chinese thought, culture, and communication*. University of South Carolina Press.

Lukács, G. (1972). *History and class consciousness: Studies in Marxist dialectics*. MIT Press.

Maiorescu, T. ([1868] 1978). În contra direcţiei de astăzi în cultura română. In *Opere* (Vol. 3). Minerva.

Martin, W. G. (2013). *South Africa and the world economy: Remaking race, state, and region*. University of Rochester Press.

Martin, W. G. (Ed.). (1990). *Semiperipheral states in the world-economy*. Greenwood Publishing.

Marx, K. ([1865] 1969). *Value, price and profit*. International Publishers.

Marx, K., & Engels, F. ([1845] 1970). *The German ideology*. International Publishers.

Marx, K., & Engels, F. ([1948] 2000). *Manifesto of the Communist Party*. Marx/Engels Internet Archive (marxists.org). https://www.marxists.org/arc hive/marx/works/1848/communist-manifesto/ch02.htm. Accessed 20 May 2021.

Mason, P. (2012). *Why it's still kicking off everywhere: The new global revolutions*. Verso.

Mazzarella, W. (2003). *Shovelling smoke: Advertising and globalization in contemporary India*. Duke University Press.

Milanović, B. (2011). *Worlds apart: Measuring international and global inequality*. Princeton University Press.

Mills, C. W. (1951). *White collar: The American middle classes*. Oxford University Press.

Mooney, N. (2008). *(Not)keeping up with our parents: The decline of the professional middle class*. Beacon Press.

Moore, B. (1966). *Social origins of democracy and dictatorship*. Beacon.

Mouffe, C. (2018). *For a left populism*. Verso.

Morys, M. (Ed.). (2020). *The economic history of Central, East and South-East Europe: 1800 to the present*. Routledge.

Mouzelis, N. P. (1985). *Politics in the semi-periphery: Early parliamentarism and late industrialization in the Balkans and Latin America*. Macmillan International Higher Education.

Nagy, P. T. (2005). The numerus clausus in interwar Hungary. *East European Jewish Affairs, 35*(1), 13–22.

Nisbet, R. A. (1969). *Social change and history: Aspects of the western theory of development*. Oxford University Press.

Nurkse, R. (1952). Some international aspects of the problem of economic development. *The American Economic Review, 42*(2), 571–583.

Ost, D. (2005). *The defeat of solidarity: Anger and politics in postcommunist Europe*. Cornell University Press.

Ozarow, D. (2019). *The mobilization and demobilization of middle-class revolt. Comparative insights from Argentina*. Routledge.

Parker, R. (1974). *The myth of the middle class*. HarperCollins.

Péterfy, G. (2014). *A kitömött barbár*. Kalligram.

Phillips, K. (1993). *Boiling point: Republicans, democrats, and the decline of the middle-class prosperity*. Random House.

Piketty, T. (2013). *Capital in the 21st century*. Harvard University Press.

Pinto, A. (1970). Naturaleza e implicaciones de la" heterogeneidad estructural" de la América Latina. *El trimestre económico, 37*(145(1)), 83–100.

Pop, C. (2015). Stratificarea claselor sociale în România. Aspecte metodologice. *Studii şi cercetări din domeniul ştiinţelor socio-umane, 28*, 432–452.

Popescu, L. (1995). Clasa mijlocie si proiectul modernizării României (1900–1940). *Revista De Cercetari Sociale, 1995*(2), 18–30.

Portes, A. (1973). Modernity and development: A critique. *Studies in Comparative International Development, 8*(3), 247–279.

Poulantzas, N. (1974). *Fascism and dictatorship: The Third International and the problem of fascism.* New Left Books.

Poulantzas, N. (1978). *State, power, socialism.* Verso.

Poulantzas, N. (1979). *Fascism and dictatorship: The third international and the problem of fascism.* Verso.

Prebisch, R. (1949). *The economic development of Latin America and its principal problems.* UN-CEPAL.

Press, A. (2019, October 22). On the origins of the professional-managerial class: An interview with Barbara Ehrenreich. *Dissent.* https://www.dissentmagazine.org/online_articles/on-the-origins-of-the-professional-managerial-class-an-interview-with-barbara-ehrenreich. Accessed 2 April 2020.

Proctor, K. (2019, December 25). Five reasons why Labour lost the election. *The Guardian.* https://www.theguardian.com/politics/2019/dec/13/five-reasons-why-labour-lost-the-election. Accessed 2 April 2020.

Ries, C. (2020, September 8). Our path forward after Bernie must include rank-and-file unionism and class-struggle elections. *Jacobin.* https://jacobinmag.com/2020/08/bernie-sanders-campaign-unions-class-struggle. Accessed 8 February 2021.

Riesman, D. (1950). *The lonely crowd. A study of the changing american character.* Yale University Press.

Rostow, W. W. (1960). *The stages of growth: A non-communist manifesto.* Cambridge University Press.

Rutz, H. J., & Balkan, E. M. B. (2009). *Reproducing class: Education, neoliberalism, and the rise of the new middle class in Istanbul.* Berghahn.

Sancho, D. (2015). *Youth, class and education in urban India: The year that can make or break you.* Routledge.

Senghaas, D. (1974). *Peripherer Kapitalismus: Analysen über Abnhängigkeit und Unterentwicklung.* Suhrkamp.

Silver, B. J., & Slater, E. (1999). The social origins of world hegemonies. In G. Arrighi & B. Silver (Eds.), *Chaos and governance in the modern world system* (pp. 151–216). University of Minnesota Press.

Smith, G. (2014). *Intellectuals and (counter-)politics: Essays in historical realism.* Berghahn.

SNSPA. (2016). *Studiu SNSPA: "Piata Unirii – noiembrie 2016".* http://www.snspa.ro/snspa/info-snspa/stiri/item/670-studiu-snspa-piata-universitatii-noiembrie-2015. Accessed 7 April 2020.

Stavrakakis, Y. (2014). The return of "the people": Populism and anti-populism in the shadow of the European crisis. *Constellations, 21*(4), 505–517.

Stiglitz, J. (2011, July 6) The ideological crisis of Western Capitalism. *Project Syndicate.* https://www.project-syndicate.org/commentary/the-ide ological-crisis-of-western-capitalism?barrier=accesspaylog. Accessed 12 January 2021.

Stokes, G. (1986). The social origins of East European politics. *East European Politics and Societies, 1*(1), 30–74.

Streeck, W. (2014). *Buying time: The delayed crisis of democratic capitalism.* Verso Books.

Sunkel, O. (1969). National development policy and external dependence in Latin America. *The Journal of Development Studies, 6*(1), 23–48.

Szabó, A., & Mikecz, D. (2015). After the Orbán-Revolution: The awakening of civil society in Hungary. In G. Pleyers & I. Sava (Eds.), *Social movements in central and eastern Europe: A renewal of protests and democracy* (pp. 34–43). University of Bucharest Press.

Szalai, E. (1994). Political and social conflicts arising from the transformation of property relations in Hungary. *The Journal of Communist Studies and Transition Politics, 10*(3), 56–77.

Szalai, E. (1995). The metamorphosis of the elites. The Metamorphosis of the Elites. In B. Király & A. Bozóki (Eds.), *Lawful revolution in Hungary, 1989–94* (pp. 159–174). Social Science Monographs.

Szalai, E. (1997). *Az elitek átváltozása.* Cserépfalvi.

Szelényi, I., Manchin, R., Juhász, P., Magyar, B., & Martin, B. (1988). *Socialist entrepreneurs: Embourgeoisement in rural Hungary.* University of Wisconsin Press.

Szelényi, I. (2011). The rise and fall of the second Bildungsbürgertum. In P. H. Reil & A. Balázs (Eds.), *Cores, peripheries, and globalization.* Central European University Press.

Szelényi, I., & King, L. P. (2004). *Theories of the new class: Intellectuals and power.* University of Minnesota Press.

Taylor, P. J. (1982). A materialist framework for political geography. *Transactions of the Institute of British Geographers, 7*, 15–34.

The 99 Percent Declaration. (2012). http://www.freerepublic.com/focus/f-news/2794951/posts. Accessed April January 2020.

Thoma, L. (1998). Védtelen társadalom. A rendszerváltásés a szakszervezetek (1988–1992). In T. Krausz (Ed.), *Rendszerváltás és társadalomkritika. Tanulmányok a kelet-európai átalakulás történetéből* (pp. 244–269). Napvilág.

Trencsényi, B., & Kopeček, M. (Eds.). (2006). *National romanticism: The formation of national movements: Discourses of collective identity in Central and Southeast Europe 1770? 1945* (Vol. 2). Central European University Press.

Trencsényi, B., Janowski, M., Baár, M., Falina, M., & Kopeček, M. (2016). *A history of modern political thought in East Central Europe: Volume I:*

Negotiating modernity in the 'long nineteenth century'. Oxford University Press.

Tsang, E. (2014). *The new middle class in China: Consumption, politics and the market economy*. Springer.

Turner, J. H. (1984). *Societal stratification: A theoretical analysis*. Columbia University Press.

Van der Pijl, K. (2014). *The making of an Atlantic ruling class*. Verso.

Vanhuysse, P. (2006). *Divide and pacify: Strategic social policies and political protests in post-communist democracies*. Central European University Press.

Verdery, K. (1991). *National ideology under Socialism: Identity and cultural politics in Ceausescu's Romania*. University of California Press.

Wallerstein, I. (1990). Culture as the ideological battleground of the modern world-system. *Theory, Culture & Society, 7*(2–3), 31–55.

Weiss, H. (2019). *We have never been middle class*. Verso.

Williams, R. (1983). *Culture and society, 1780–1950*. Columbia University Press.

Wright, E. O., Costello, C., Hachen, D., & Sprague, J. (1982). The American class structure. *American Sociological Review, 47*, 709–726.

Zeletin, S. ([1925] 1997). *Burghezia română: originea şi rolul ei istoric*. Nemira.

Zhang, L. (2012). *In search of paradise: Middle-class living in a Chinese metropolis*. Cornell University Press.

Žižek, S. (2008). *In defense of lost causes*. Verso.

Zhou, X. (2008). Chinese middle class: Reality or illusion. In C. Jaffrelot & P. van der Veer (Eds.), *Patterns of middle class consumption in India and China* (pp. 110–126). Sage.

CHAPTER 3

Crisis, Regime Change, Movement: Comparing Mobilization Cycles in Hungarian and Romanian Constellations of Global Integration After 1973 and 2008

This chapter applies the insights of previous chapters to a comparative analysis that considers local East European mobilizations in the historical context of world-economic and geopolitical integration. The cases it highlights are the Hungarian environmental movement and Romanian workers' mobilizations in late socialism, and post-2008 mobilizations in the two countries. In regional terms, the comparison of Hungarian and Romanian examples is especially illustrative in that successive forms of the two countries' integration regimes have been radically different (even seemingly contradictory) despite occupying quite similar positions in the postwar hegemonic cycle. After Stalin's death, Romania performed an early opening toward Western economic collaborations, while maintaining a neo-Stalinist political and social regime. Hungary's regime after 1956, on the other hand, acted as a pioneer of post-Stalinist liberalization. In the 1980s, the surge of foreign debt that characterized the whole region was treated in Romania with extreme austerity measures, coupled with state repression and nationalist populism. Hungary tackled the same debt problem by promoting market liberalization. After the regime change, Hungary was praised as a regional success story of liberalization (e.g. Jeffries, 1993), while Romania followed a policy of protectionism with undertones of political nationalism, causing concern with international

A. Gagyi, *The Political Economy of Middle Class Politics and the Global Crisis in Eastern Europe*, International Political Economy Series, https://doi.org/10.1007/978-3-030-76943-7_3

lenders. Since 2010, Hungary's nationalist government builds its political campaigns on the delegitimation of the liberal economic model of the previous decades and follows a policy of state-aided development of national capital. Meanwhile, Romania's state structure is increasingly dominated by liberal-technocratic blocs of power promoting a regime of "extreme neoliberalism" (Ban, 2014), with the country receiving a new wave of Western capital inflow after 2010. The book traces links between local forms of mobilizations, national meso-levels of different integration constellations, and broader dynamics of the global cycle.

In a broader regional comparison, such illustrative differences between Hungarian and Romanian cases fit in a broader pattern of regional developmental differences. Various authors have categorized the two countries into different typologies of regional development, based on criteria like local versions of contradictions between agrarian and industrial development, historical relations between regional powers and national independence, the scale of ethnic homogeneity, geopolitical alliances (e.g. Berend, 2009; Bohle & Greskovits, 2012; Bottoni, 2017; Shields, 2014; Stokes, 1986). The differences in Hungarian and Romanian integration constellations identified in the present analysis serve to illustrate the significance of links between movements, meso-structures of integration, and global processes. They do not provide theoretical models for a regional typology integration; for that, a broader cross-regional comparison would be necessary. While the apparent spectacularity of these differences allows me to emphasize the connection between integration constellations and movement dynamics, this does not imply that the cases of Hungary and Romania would constitute two opposite extremes of potential regional constellations. In a broader regional scope, various aspects of Hungarian or Romanian development can be placed closer to each other in a broader scale of comparison. For instance, in a recent study that compares states' capacity to roll back the effects of financial vulnerability after 2008 in the cases of Latvia, Romania, and Hungary, Cornel Ban and Dorothy Bohle (2020) treat Romania as an in-between case, where an FDI-based growth model allows more maneuver space than in the case of finance-dependent Latvia, but political and institutional conditions foreclose a strong national financial agenda like in the case of Hungary.

This chapter starts the analysis of Hungarian and Romanian constellations from the global crisis of the 1970s, and follows the transformations of both constellations across the long downturn of the postwar global cycle. Obviously, local reactions to the global crisis are built on the heritage of earlier forms of integration—like Hungary and Romania occupying different levels in the long-term developmental hierarchy of the region, or like the different local histories of class differentiation based on different economic and geopolitical integration histories (Chirot, 1991; Stokes, 1986). While a deeper comparative perspective would need to consider the full spectrum of modern capitalist integration, this chapter will only highlight links between integration shifts caused by the 1970s crisis, related forms of postsocialist economic and political development, and local versions of post-2008 movements.

SOCIALISM, POSTSOCIALISM, EUROPEAN INTEGRATION: SITUATED NOTIONS OF SYSTEMIC INTEGRATION

Before turning to details of local movements and integration constellations, two notions that played a central role in contemporary formulations and later analysis of post-1970s development need to be addressed: that of socialism/postsocialism, and that of European integration. Like democratization or middle class development, these concepts have functioned as notions tied to developmental projects (and shifts within) systemic integration. In local contexts of pre-1989 or post-2008 movements, one important difference from Western contexts was that local regimes and their political contestations expressed their politics in terms of these notions, tied to ambitions of catch-up development.

Debates on socialism and postsocialist development tied references to state socialist systems to the broader horizon of long-term developmental stakes. Along these stakes, the use of the term socialism also activates left and right traditions of modern politics across local and international contexts of debates. This multi-referential character of the idea of socialism in late socialist, postsocialist, and current debates is an important factor in the way local movements formulate and express their politics, and it poses a specific challenge for the comparative understanding of East European and other global movements. At the same time, catch-up ambitions and political programs related to postsocialist transition coincided with another major process that defined macrostructural, institutional, and political conditions of contemporary developmental projects: European integration. This notion also expressed long-term developmentalist ambitions in specific ways tied to struggles and alliances along with contemporary constellations of dependent integration.

Contrary to Cold War or postsocialist developmentalist usages of the term, the world-systems tradition does not conceive of socialism as a system of social organization that would have been separate from capitalism (Frank, 1977). Instead, state socialism is analyzed along the dynamics of the import substitution industrialization efforts that characterized noncore postwar developmentalist projects across the world. Despite political differences, and what József Böröcz (1992) characterized as the geopolitical condition of "dual dependency" from Western capital and Soviet power, the project of socialist industrialization in Eastern Europe happened according to the conditions and limitations of the capitalist world economy, was dependent from the external dynamics of these conditions, and internalized them as its own priorities. This did not only mean that besides military competition with Western powers, socialist states engaged in external relations of commerce or finance with global markets, but also that the socialist development effort followed the priorities of global capitalist competition. Upgrading technological capacity in order to ameliorate terms of trade, and thereby achieve upward mobility in the hierarchies of the world economy, was a necessity that stood at the base of industrialization efforts in socialist countries as well as non-socialist semi-peripheries and peripheries. This development effort, with its priorities and conditions fixed in the external environment of global capitalism, came to be internalized in the form of forced industrialization and urbanization, the exploitation of agricultural resources in order to support technological imports and development, and stood at the basis of the debt spiral that led to the final crisis of socialist economies in the 1980s.

In comparison with non-socialist semi-peripheries or with the social destruction of the postsocialist era, state socialist systems were more egalitarian and accommodated a larger volume of reproductive needs. However, even in the most successful years of socialist development, these measures were characterized by a clear hierarchy between socioeconomic functions that figured among the priorities of catch-up development (urbanization, industrialization, development of expertise and technology), and socioeconomic functions that served as a reproductive base. The latter (agriculture, rural labor and demography, self-supporting agriculture, self-built housing, kin and community level reproductive cooperations, etc.) were used as a "cheap" resource for development

(Patel & Moore, 2017). The same socialist project that created socioeconomic infrastructures of high modernity simultaneously deepened these internal hierarchies.

The main aspect of internal contradictions that followed from external conditions of world-economic integration was the double pressure for high technology imports and corresponding exports that could compensate their costs. Catch-up industrialization aimed to reach higher levels of technology, in order to ameliorate the terms of external trade. This presupposed a simultaneous effort to import higher levels of technology and maintain lower technology exports in order to be able to pay for those imports. While Stalinism bridged this contradiction through the forced centralization of resources and proletarianization of the agrarian workforce, on the longer term state socialist systems could not fulfill these simultaneous needs, and resulted in international loans to cover trade bills (Gerőcs & Pinkasz, 2018).

The world-economic crisis of the 1970s had several major consequences on state socialist development efforts. First, the explosion of oil prices in 1973 and 1979 had an impact on the costs of industrial production, as the Soviet Union started to withhold the export of cheap oil to satellite countries. The same step cut the possibility to cover Western trade bills by reexporting Soviet oil. Second, global money markets swollen by petrodollars provided a temporary source of cheap credits to finance growing deficits. Third, the crisis of the 1970s signaled the crisis of the postwar hegemonic cycle, with the US, West European, and Japanese capacities of Fordist production reaching the limits of an overproduction crisis. This process fueled the financialization of the whole world economy (Brenner, 2003; Harvey, 1989). In the incipient phase of financialization, within global struggles for capital access, the fate of semi-peripheral import substitution economies going into debt in this period was defined by major moves of international financial governance, which influenced global financial markets to alleviate crisis symptoms in the United States. One such major move was the Volcker shock of 1980, when FED Chairman Paul Volcker raised the federal funds rate to a peak of 20%. This changed the direction of global financial flows toward US investments, causing an exponential growth in the debt service of noncore debtors. Resulting debt spirals of East European socialist countries were part of a global sweep of debt crises that struck noncore industrialization efforts (Walton & Seddon, 1994). Meanwhile, starting from the late 1960s, the incipient overproduction crisis of core economies also brought a willingness by core actors to expand into the Socialist bloc, leading to a series of joint ventures under various socialist regimes.

While the subordination and continued dependence of socialist industrialization efforts from core economies—from technological imports under unequal terms of trade to relations of debt—is one of the manifest results of their global integration, state socialism's relationship with the Global South also needs to be emphasized. While socialist countries politically supported Third World initiatives against the unequal development of the global economy, in terms of crude economic relations, their priority remained to optimize their position within global economic hierarchies. This priority did not simply mean that they joined efforts with Third World countries for global reform with the expectation that it will also contribute to their own development. It also meant that in terms of world-economic flows, they occupied positions very similar to non-socialist semi-peripheries, where unequal relations with core economies were expected to be compensated through unequal trade with peripheral countries (Frank, 1977). This tendency was intensified by the growth crisis and increasing debt problems after the 1970s, when socialist regimes increased Third World cooperation as a means of compensating their losses.

In the United States, capital reacted to the crisis of Fordist production by the outsourcing and destruction of local production capacities, and a redirection toward financial investments, facilitated by a deregulation of global financial markets. This process, the results of which came to be characterized as the formation of the 1% vs. the 99% by the Occupy movement after 2008, was celebrated by elites in the 1990s as a new boom period of the US economy. Reforms of the Clinton administration facilitated a new wave of international investments fueled by financial markets. This was the late flowering of a declining hegemony that Arrighi (1994) called the phase of "belle époque". Besides the global markets opened up by structural adjustment programs forced by international lender organizations on peripheral countries, part of these investments flew to East European markets and fueled the privatization of former socialist economies. While on a systemic level, these investments were part of core capital's crisis management measures, political programs of postsocialist transformation treated them as an opportunity to overcome what was perceived as a backwardness caused by socialism, and catch up with capitalist core economies.

The process of privatization reflected the conditions and hierarchies of global crisis. Local capital institutionalized in the socialist state came to be privatized at subdued prices, through hierarchical bargains that reflected power relations between international and local capital. In many cases, foreign direct investment in privatization was used to close local capacities, in order to create export markets for home production. Capacities that were kept active were typically integrated into production chains in low positions, reflecting the priorities of outsourcing and flexibilization that served to compensate decreasing profitability in core enterprises (Gerőcs & Pinkasz, 2017). Local private capital played a subordinate role to these processes, often in the role of second- or third-tier supplier to foreign-owned companies. Varieties of capitalism authors referred to postsocialist East European economies' dependence on such subordinated integration into global production chains as the emergence of dependent market economies (Bohle & Greskovits, 2006; Nölke & Vliegenthart, 2009).

With the exhaustion of privatization, the inflow of foreign direct investment into the region halted, while profits and dividends kept leaving the countries. As a result, by the 2000s, regional economies engaged in a new cycle of debt, this time public as well as private. This wave of lending was part of the pre-2008 financial boom, in a subordinated position where regional structures of lending increasingly served to compensate the saturation of core markets by more expensive and more risky loans (Raviv, 2008). During the 2000s, another main source of financing came from European transfers, as part of formal processes of European integration. These transfers contributed to keeping budget balances in order, but were tied to requirements that fixed regional economies in subordinate roles (e.g. they excluded financing productive sectors, and did not allow for acquiring competitive technologies). In global comparison, the function of these transfers has been likened to development aid given to peripheral economies that help avoid economic collapse and sustain "normal" flows of extraction (Amin, 1977; Gerőcs & Pinkasz, 2017).

In the second half of the 2000s, and especially after 2008, a new wave of outsourcing of productive capacities reached the region, as a result of core capital's renewed efforts for profit compensation (Chivu et al., 2017; Lux, 2015). In political programs of local allied elites, this wave was represented as an opportunity to create jobs and reach higher levels of development in the midst of economic crisis (e.g. Dragnea, 2017; Orbán, 2017). As this wave of reindustrialization was strongly based on cheap local labor utilized in subordinated positions of the production chain, experts have recurrently emphasized that surpassing the low-cost production model that made reindustrialization possible would require the upgrade of local production to higher positions in global value chains (e.g. Adăscăliței & Guga, 2016; Szent-Iványi, 2017). However, as reindustrialization is subordinate to the aim of compensating a deepening profitability crisis, such hopes remain limited (Gerőcs & Pinkasz, 2017).

To address the relation between economic subordination and the political-ideological level of hopes tied to Europeanization, the systemic context of European integration needs to be emphasized. In mainstream narratives, the history of the creation of common institutional systems in Europe is told in terms of a series of agreements and regulations, led by the values of international cooperation and democracy, in a collective effort to avoid the horrors of WWII in the future (e.g. Dedman, 2009). However, in the hierarchies of global accumulation reorganizing under US hegemony, European reconstruction was tied to the expansion of Fordist production dominated by US transnational companies, as well as the formation of its markets and consequent structures and norms of mass consumption (Apeldoorn, 2003). In this phase, European integration was supported partly by US private capital and geopolitical interests, and partly by the interest of West European capital to build competitiveness in key economic sectors through European collaboration and common markets (Van der Pijl, 1998). The gradual expansion of these collaborations was accompanied by new institutional forms of international cooperation. Contrary to mainstream narratives that represent this integration as a mainly intra-European process, the main scale of operation of integration policies was that of global competition. If the norms of sovereignty and international diplomacy established by the Westphalian system were based on colonial wars outside of Europe, from the same perspective, post-WWII European integration served to compensate the loss in global economic weight imposed by the loss of colonies, by selectively protecting European markets while deepening European capital's global expansion (Böröcz, 2009). From this perspective, the birth of the EU signifies not so much the avantgarde of global political progression, but rather an effort to maintain a global position gained by colonial rule earlier.

While initially the institutionalization of the common market served to protect internal markets and promote European industry within global competition, starting with the crisis of the 1970s, the politics of European integration increasingly served European capital's crisis management (Overbeek, 1993). Monetary integration or the integration of Southern and later Eastern European economies providing cheaper labor and new markets served those purposes. By the 1990s, the deepening of the overproduction crisis led to the abolishment of previous social democratic-ordoliberal policies within European politics. The Treaty of Lisbon and the introduction of the common currency signaled a turn in European policy that abolished models of mass consumption and welfare institutions that stabilized internal markets in times of expansion, and started to charge the costs of profitability crisis directly on member states' societies, too (Drahokoupil & Horn, 2008; Nousios et al., 2012). The uneven distribution of the weight of these policies has been reflected in intrastate social polarization as well as cross-European regional polarization, leading to Southern European and East European crises after 2008.

The first phase of European neoliberalization has been described by the term "embedded neoliberalism", referring to pro-capital measures with a selective retention of social institutions and guarantees (Apeldoorn, 2009). By the time of Eastern enlargement, however, this model has been abandoned for a full-fledged program of European neoliberalism (Ban, 2016). At the moment, however, integration was widely understood in Eastern Europe as a beneficial opportunity of development. In maintaining this symbolic hegemony, the raw effect of power relations was complemented by the discursive activation of long-term traditions of East–West modernizational hierarchies, coupled with developmentalist understandings of Cold War differences between socialism and democracy/capitalism, and postsocialist developmentalist hopes promoted by internal–external alliances of the transition. If East European societies were not enjoying the effects of European integration, that was interpreted by dominant coalitions managing integration as the effect of these societies' backwardness.

On the side of EU institutions and discourses, this ideological aspect was strengthened by a specific characteristic in the constitution of the EU, which allowed for the maintenance of an image of moral and political goodness decoupled from economic and social effects of extraction. Böröcz and Sarkar (2005) described this effect in terms of a decoupling of policymaking power and coercive power. While the formation of the European Union continuously expanded the institutions of economic collaboration and political coordination, the function of military power was left in the hands of US-dominated NATO, and coercive functions of economic and political governance were left to be done by national governments. This outsourcing of coercive functions allowed the EU to become an international institution that, comprising about 6% of the global population, could claim more than one fourth of global GDP, without having to bear the responsibility for direct measures that established the conditions of these hierarchical relations. Keeping institutional rules of representation unclear allowed the EU to step up either as one actor, or in the form of multiple countries' representatives, providing a base for uneven representation in international institutions. This institutional structure helped maintain an ideological image of the EU as a representative of political-moral values and developmental promises, while charging the blame for the social effects of transition to local governments. As Böröcz and Sarkar put it:

> By contracting out the burden of strategic defence to NATO, the EU can maintain an elegant and convenient distance from matters of coercion without endangering its own defence. In the process of 'eastern enlargement', much of the transformative 'dirty' work in the economies on the EU's eastern and southeastern flanks is done by the state apparatuses and the political elites of those societies themselves. EU-based multinational companies do much of the coercive work in the economic, environmental, social and legal realms worldwide, without the EU itself ever having to utilize conventional tools of state-based coercion. Surviving colonial ties, re-emerging relationships with the historically dependent parts of the German and Austrian-dominated, land-based European empires, and constantly renewed neocolonial linkages to virtually the entire 'former second' and 'third worlds' provide the EU with terms of exchange, raw materials, energy, labour, capital and services that continue to subsidize the EU's accumulation process without the EU ever having to get involved in the messy business of the social and environmental violence associated with the extraction of surplus. To a large extent precisely because of its distance from institutional locales where direct coercion happens, the EU is widely portrayed as the epitome of goodness in world politics today, reinforcing a centuries-old, Eurocentric ideology of superiority. (Böröcz & Sarkar, 2005: 166–167)

The entanglements of long-term developmental hierarchies with short-term postsocialist politics have been analyzed widely. Researchers have looked at forms of cultural internalization of dependent relations within

European integration (Böröcz, 2006; Buchowski, 2006; Dzenovska, 2018; Kideckel, 2002; Klumbyte, 2009; Kuus, 2004; Thornton et al., 2012; Zarycki, 2009 or Arfire, 2011), demonstrated correlations between perceptions of national development levels and world-economic hierarchies (Thornton et al., 2012), analyzed economic, political, and cultural relations of domination within European integration in terms of empire and imperialism (Bakić-Hayden, 1995; Behr & Stivachtis, 2015; Böröcz, 2006; Böröcz & Sarkar, 2005; Böröcz et al., 2001; Petrović, 2008; Todorova, 2009; Wolff, 1994; Zielonka, 2007), identified constructs of symbolic hierarchies as results of intra-regional competition within the hierarchical space of integration (Bakić-Hayden, 1995; Petrović, 2008), and examined the ideological role of European values in the process of integration—something Böröcz (2006) described in terms of the "moral geopolitics" of integration, and Arfire (2011) defined as "the moral regulation of the second Europe". Analysis that looked at more small-scale differentiations of ideological attitudes toward integration in terms of actors' positions within the hierarchical space of integration (Gagyi, 2016; Scheiring, 2020; Szalai, 2005; Zarycki, 2000; Zarycki & Nowak, 2000).

In Western and Southern Europe, pro-capital measures of crisis management after 2008 exploded the tensions built out during the decades of European neoliberalization. Within EU politics, the crisis of Southern economies, and the authoritarian nature of European responses—with the outstanding example of the Greek crisis (Lapavitsas, 2018)—exposed and deepened the delegitimation of European institutions. The European Union has become the target of criticism by left and right movements and political parties. Right-wing political forces, combining strategies of protectionist politics with new tactics of populist political communication, increased their power in several member states. In the eyes of many, the Brexit referendum of 2016 sealed the end of the idea of a unilinear process of European integration. While some fractions of European left movements argued for the abolishment of the EU, a broader trend targeted the reform of European integration toward a more social Europe.

After the failure of the left program of Syriza, the party's minister of finance Yanis Varoufakis initiated a political movement to democratize European institutions (DiEM25). Several left parties and party fractions after 2008 conceived of their own politics as a way to reform European politics from within (e.g. Razem, 2016), or building out new channels of political representation through which these institutions can be held in check—like in the case of municipalism. Meanwhile, following the alter-globalist direct action model of summit hopping, the Blockupy movement organized demonstrations at core locations of European capitalist power like the headquarters of the European Central Bank. Left-wing arguments for a social reform of the European Union have intensively relied on the rhetoric of European goodness and claimed a return to the original values of European integration. For instance, DiEM25 defined itself in the language of the EU's ideological founding narrative, evoking a democratic collaboration against the threat of xenophobia and nationalism exemplified by the 1930s, and refers to the dismantling of the EU as a fatal threat:

> DiEM25 is a pan-European, cross-border movement of democrats. We believe that the European Union is disintegrating. Europeans are losing their faith in the possibility of European solutions to European problems. At the same time as faith in the EU is waning, we see a rise of misanthropy, xenophobia and toxic nationalism. If this development is not stopped, we fear a return to the 1930s. That is why we have come together despite our diverse political traditions - Green, radical left, liberal - in order to repair the EU. The EU needs to become a realm of shared prosperity, peace and solidarity for all Europeans. We must act quickly, before the EU disintegrates. (DiEM25, 2016)

Similarly, Another Europe is possible, a group of the British Left that campaigned for the remain position in 2016, refers to the reform of neoliberal European institutions as "rebuilding hope":

> Brexit is a national disaster for Britain, but it is not a "British problem". All over Europe faith in the project of unity has eroded. Free-market thinking has dominated EU institutions for too long. Many people no longer have faith in the capacity of European democracies to deliver social justice by working together for the common good. To rebuild this hope, the EU requires radical and far-reaching reform, breaking with austerity economics and pioneering a radically new development strategy. That's why we are actively working together with international partners, such as European Alternatives, to campaign for political change across the continent. (Another Europe Is Possible, 2016)

Such gestures of rekindling the ideological promises of European integration have been opposed by other fractions of the post-2008 left, from Eurocritical positions like that of Spanish Podemos (Gago, 2017) to expressions of a new Euroscepticism. The latter position includes proposals to exit from the European Union as a way to increase left movements' and governments' maneuver space. As Thomas Fazi and William Mitchell (2018) put it in the case of Brexit: a left-wing pro-Brexit argument could provide "a once-in-a-lifetime window of opportunity to show that a radical break with neoliberalism, and with the institutions that support it, is possible". Conflicts over Euroscepticism became a strong factor of internal tensions and external alliance strategies in post-2008 left politics, especially in a situation where debates between a declining liberal hegemony and the new right feeding on postcrisis dissatisfaction make an intense ideological use of the question—with UK Labour losing 2019 general elections in the context of high-intensity Brexit debates standing out as an exemplary case.

Attac Austria (2018), gathering contributions by long-time activists and analysts of European neoliberalism in a collection entitled *The European Illusion: Why we need new strategies toward the EU and beyond,* declared the European institutional system to be beyond any possibility for reform. It called the European left to think beyond the unproductive dilemma of exit or remain, toward internationalist strategies to change the balance of forces at various levels simultaneously in order to achieve change. Relying on decades of previous analysis, the collection describes European integration as a capitalist project, and argues that European ideology hinders meaningful debate on the political significance of the EU. Still, the realization that the European institutional system is designed to block control from below is pictured in the book as a new occurrence—illustrated by the subchapter title *Hopes shattered.* A 2019 manifesto authored by the activist alliance ReCommonsEurope similarly argued that European institutions serve to block popular influence on pro-capital policies, yet it also defined the debate within the limits of "activists and citizens of Europe" addressing the crisis of Europe (ReCommons, 2019: 2).

From the point of view of a systemic analysis of European integration, most new critical arguments still rely on the ideological narrative of the European project and core European states' welfare experience. Left reform stances, like that represented by DiEM25, propose to bring back the promise of universal welfare and democracy through the mere force of more democratic representation of welfare claims, neglecting the conditions of postwar welfare capitalism in global expansion and the actual context of global crisis and hegemonic shift. Left exit stances hope to realize the same promise through deliberating national policy from the control of European institutions. These latter arguments tend to neglect the force of world-economic dependencies and respective internal interests ingrained in national economies that bind non-member nation-states into the same structures of capitalist coercion. In Attac Austria or ReCommonsEurope's critical assessments, the idea of awakening to a recent crisis risks to obscure the problems inherent in the non-crisis phase. The fact that the promise of European welfare as such is an ideological expression of postwar capitalist expansion, that the Western experience of capitalist welfare states relied on global hierarchical accumulation, and that its crisis organically followed from the former process of expansion, and not from a mere ideological turn in policy, tends to remain hidden in all three types of analysis.

In this book, I conceive of these stances as variations of what the first chapter called the narrative of the crisis of "democratic capitalism". What is important in such stances in terms of the politicization of the crisis is that after announcing the "crisis" of a previous ideological model of welfare development, together with actors' own disillusionment with its promises, the same models are brought back in the form of new projects. This survival of postwar Western political models is an important aspect in analyzing relations between movements in different global positions. In the case of East European movements, this characteristic of Western post-2008 progressive stances connects with dynamics of East European disillusionments with the promises of postsocialist transition, and new claims to mend that process. While this creates the impression of consensus and mutual support on the surface, this connection obstructs movements' capacity to understand the structural process they are part of and identify the possibilities and limitations of cross-regional and cross-class collaborations.

LATE SOCIALIST REGIMES OF GLOBAL INTEGRATION—HUNGARY AND ROMANIA AFTER 1973

Although typical tensions and contradictions of socialist industrialization efforts were characteristic to both Hungary and Romania, the two countries saw different regimes of world-economic and geopolitical integration and followed relatively different tracks during the socialist period. In Hungary, After Stalin's death, between 1953 and 1956, the pressure of external debt that resurfaced after the first years of Stalinist centralization, the contradictions of technology development and export pressure, and internal tensions of resource centralization, crystallized in a political conflict between party leader Mátyás Rákosi and his challenger Imre Nagy. Rákosi promoted the Stalinist program of resource centralization and industrialization, supported by the industrial lobby, while Nagy proposed the relaxation of centralized industrialization, and a greater reliance on lower technology, export-capable sectors—a model more favorable to agriculture and to population segments most struck by forced resource centralization (Rainer, 1996: 525–537). From 1954 on, reform economists allied with Nagy began to develop the idea of the "economic mechanism" as an objective, autonomous economic model that substituted direct administration with a system of economic incentives.

While Nagy was executed after the Soviet invasion of Hungary that suppressed the 1956 revolution, the reform direction he prepared was integrated into the politics of the post-1956 regime. János Kádár, put in office by Soviet leadership, engaged in a politics of compromise, reducing political pressure on citizens, and substituting the aggressive centralization of resources with a politics favoring living standards. From 1962 on, previous "hardliner" and "softliner" economists worked together under the leadership of finance minister and central committee member Rezső Nyers to prepare the economic reform. The reform's economic politics were marked by the revolution as well as a new compromise between agricultural and industrial lobbies through marketization, made possible broader geopolitical processes: the scheduling of Soviet economic reform 1961, and the incipient overproduction problems of Western economies, which prompted Western companies to look for markets in Eastern Europe (Feitl, 2016; Gerőcs & Pinkasz, 2018). Meeting the technology need of socialist economies, this turn brought a wave of joint ventures and increased East–West commerce (Kozma, 1996). The tendency toward market reform was also aided by East–West knowledge exchange. Starting in 1956, the US National Security Council supported educational exchange with socialist countries, with the aim of strengthening internal critique based on Western professional knowledge. In Hungary, the Ford Foundation worked closely together with the State Department, focusing on reform economists who would have the most impact on the new mechanism (Bockman, 2000: 259–264). By the 1960s, Hungary occupied a bridge position between Comecon and Western markets: it imported Western technology which it integrated into technological products exported to Comecon markets, and compensated the costs of technology imports by exporting cheap Soviet oil and raw materials to the West (Gerőcs & Pinkasz, 2017; Vigvári, 1990).

A major reorganization of the institutional settings of economic governance in line with this direction was prepared implemented in 1968 under the name New Economic Mechanism (NEM). The NEM emphasized supply and demand over planning, and substituted direct administrative tools with a system of incentives favoring profitability. This system aimed to favor Western export capacities (generators of convertible currency), and disfavor lower technology industry which could only export to Comecon countries. The NEM also institutionalized a transformation of the field of power. It reduced the significance of the classic loci and actors of direct planning like the ministries for particular economic branches or the National Planning Office and transferred power to units associated with reform functions like the Economic Policy Division or the Ministry of Finance (Bockman, 2000: 301). In terms of professional personnel, controllers, engineers, and technicians working on the concrete details of fulfilling the plan lost position and decision power to economists and accountants dealing with decisions based on financial concerns. More economists were trained and employed in the apparatus, new research institutions were created, while the general numbers of state personnel were reduced (Bockman, 2000: 296–298).

Research on state socialist systems traditionally emphasizes the role of intellectuals as actors who acquire especially significant roles due to the ideological nature of the regime—both as supporters and as critiques of the system (Konrád & Szelényi, 1979; Verdery, 1991). Due to this ideological exposure, forms of expert and intellectual knowledge, and their support or criticism of the regime, are treated as important elements of socialist politics. Besides this ideological factor, two other aspects need to be mentioned in terms of intellectuals' roles. The first is that in the context of the Cold War, any expressions of opposition or critique toward the regime were treated as particularly significant by the political communication of Western powers. In this process, educated, explicit, and detailed forms of criticism were prioritized versus implicit, hidden, or politically less explicit forms of opposition or critique, more characteristic to dominated groups. The second aspect is the institutional and political weight of positions occupied within the state apparatus.

The Hungarian model of post-Stalinist socialist development effort was characterized by a decrease of the ideological control over experts and intellectuals, and their broad and favorable integration into state positions (Szalai, 1995; Szelényi et al., 1998)—a process read by Konrád and Szelényi (1979) as the intellectuals' road to class power. This process, of course, did not imply that programs proposed by experts and intellectuals in such positions were automatically carried through, or that experts and intellectuals did not formulate strong forms of criticism against the system. On the contrary: the highly developed nature of Hungarian criticisms of the regime was equally conditioned by frustrations due to a halt of the economic expansion that conditioned middle class growth, a relatively large space to express criticism due to decreased ideological control, the fact that many experts themselves were employed in positions where they were supposed to work on various aspects of the market reform, and the fact that the growing influence of international lenders lent a stronger voice to internal critiques (Gagyi, 2015a).

In the early 1970s, reforms were halted by an orthodox political turn, induced by an anti-reform turn in Moscow (Tőkés, 1996: 103), as well as the crisis of expansive growth that reached all socialist economies once the cheap demographic resource of agrarian labor was exhausted, and by the oil crisis of the 1973 which had a detrimental effect on Hungary's external integration model. From 1973 on, the boom in oil and raw material prices required new efforts to restore the balance of payments (Berend, 1990: 234). Based on the supply of cheap credits from petrodollars, the leadership resorted to Western loans, with the aim of using them for technological development in industry, which could generate Western exports and therefore, hard currency for debt repayment. The orthodox turn brought a reinforcement of big industry and central planning, a weakening of reform institutions, and a wave of repression against dissident critique. This repression turned intellectuals against the regime. Throughout the 1970s, the type of critique that aimed to reform socialism based on socialist values gradually gave space to critiques aligned with the liberal criticism of socialism. In lack of broader social connections, dissidents relied on samizdat publications circulating among intellectual readerships, the amplification effect of the Hungarian program of BBC and Radio Free Europe, and connections with other Eastern dissident movements.

The conditions of the orthodox turn were soon exhausted: the new industrialization effort did not produce competitive products that could meet Western demand, and the Volcker shock caused Hungary's debt to increase exponentially (Vigvári, 1990). Unable to service its debt,

Hungary resulted in an IMF loan, and after Romania, became the second country in the socialist bloc to become its member in 1982. These conditions re-prioritized export-led specialization as the main point of economic policy, and after initial efforts to maintain it, dissolved import substitution efforts (Comisso & Marer, 1986). This reinforced the positions of actors and institutions allied with the reform process, who used the situation to struggle for a new wave of reform (Gagyi, 2015a, Fabry 2018). One major ally of reform economists became the IMF (Bockman, 2000: 329), whose influence increased with further debt shocks. Locally, two further expert groups allied with economists in the reform struggle: sociologists and dissident intellectuals. Within this system of alliances, a consensual form of the criticism of socialism developed into an intellectual common sense in the years leading up to the regime change. In this consensus, the analysis of world-economic requirements, social inequalities, and democratic deficits all seemed to point in the same direction: the necessity of marketization and the rolling back of party state power (Fabry, 2019; Gagyi, 2015a; Sebők, 2019).

The politics of liberalization contributed to a growth of consumer prices, while increasing costs of debt service resulted in cuts in welfare policies. By 1982, the growth of life standards halted. Labor was made increasingly flexible, and under the surface of the official ideology of full employment, unemployment started to spread (Pittaway, 2012). To compensate for the political effects of this turn, in 1982 the regime legalized the second economy, a sphere of semi-illegal activities through which households strove to complement their formal incomes by working non-paid second shifts in small businesses, self-supporting agriculture, or self-built housing (Galasi & Kertesi, 1985). For many households, combining incomes from double jobs in state and second economy activities, and complementing them with free reproductive labor and mutual self-help, meant a significant potential for accumulation. For instance, for the first time in the history of socialist modernization, the hierarchy of urban and rural home construction was overturned: after state home building programs were halted due to debt repayment, in the 1980s, the largest growth in home building was provided by rural constructions based on self-build financed from state loans (Szelényi, 1988). Contemporary dissident commentators tended to describe the second economy as an incipient version of bottom-up marketization that simultaneously serves social welfare, economic equality, and a form of emancipation that could be the base of a new, democratic, market-based society—a potential route to embourgeoisement (Galasi & Sik, 1988; Róna-Tas, 1990; Szelényi, 1988). However, in systemic terms, the second economy rather played the role of an economic and political puffer for the socialist austerity of the 1980s, channeling workers' discontent into new investments into systemic integration (Vigvári & Gerőcs, 2017). Contrary to dissident commentators' expectations, the second economy did not wither away or turn into market successes after 1990, but continued to form a puffer made up by extra reproductive work, that absorbed much of the contradictions of capitalist polarization (Gagyi & Vigvári, 2018).

When the Plaza Accord in 1985 depreciated the dollar in relation to the Japanese yen, Hungary's debt—in a large part denominated in yen—peaked again, giving a final blow to anti-reform stances. From 1986 on, market reforms were issued with an unprecedented pace. Experts and managers who gained state positions during the marketization reforms became core actors of first "spontaneous", then formal privatization (Gagyi, 2015a; Stark, 1990). Former intellectual dissident groups, gathered around two-party initiatives of liberal and conservative fractions, mobilized to carry out the process of political transition and gain positions within it.

Discussing the effects of the 1970s global crisis on the politics of socialist and non-socialist semi-peripheries, Wallerstein (1976) attributed a specific importance to the role of technocratic strata developed on the base of favorable redistribution within catch-up development efforts. He expected that the halt of economic expansion might instigate technocracies of both socialist and non-socialist semi-peripheral systems to step up as a political force that demands an ideological alignment with the politics of the capitalist core and promotes economic and political opening to the influence of core actors. In this situation, Wallerstein saw the political dilemma in whether socialist governments would build alliances with workers to maintain their power, or lean toward reform alliances and fully engage with the process of and liberalization. Hungary and Romania's politics of the 1970s crisis seem to follow the two different paths of this dilemma. Yet instead of a dilemma between systemic and anti-systemic politics, what they demonstrate are two ways toward similarly subordinated modes of postsocialist integration.

Unlike in Hungary, the Romanian elite of the Stalinist period managed to hold power after de-Stalinization. The government of Gheorghe Gheorghiu-Dej made the already marginalized Muscovite fraction of the party carry the blame for the crimes of Stalinism, and continued the program of centralized import substitution industrialization (Crowther, 1988). With references to connections with the Hungarian "counter-revolution", the regime carried out retaliations that equaled the level of those in Hungary. These served to subdue the resistance of peasants and the urban petty middle class and prepared a nationalist political turn against ethnic minorities (Bottoni, 2017). This model of de-Stalinization combined the maintenance of the Stalinist model of industrial development with a strong discourse on the national interest.

The emphasis on nationalism was supported by several factors. First, it served to discredit Muscovites, as many fraction leaders belonged to ethnic minorities. Second, it maintained a continuity with interwar right-wing programs for import substitution industrialization, which grew out from opposing Romania's subordinated role in world trade tied to agricultural exports. Third, this tradition was reactualized in Dej's opposition to Moscow's economic politics of intra-Comecon labor distribution, which relegated Romania to the role of agricultural producer. The industrial development project of the Dej government followed the tradition of interwar protectionist industrialism when it contradicted Khrushchev's plan for Comecon economic coordination, and in turn opted to break from Soviet dependence (Ban, 2014). When Soviet troops were withdrawn from Romania in 1958 as part of a larger international move, Dej represented this development as a success of his own politics of independence. In 1964, the Romanian Workers' Party demanded equal rights for every communist party, going into explicit ideological conflict with Moscow. During the Cuban missile crisis, Romania openly confronted the Soviet stance. After the Sino-Soviet split, Romania did not halt its Chinese relations, and China in exchange supported Romania's claims for national independence. Romania was also the first socialist country that officially acknowledged West Germany. During the Six-Day War, it was the only socialist country that did not break its diplomatic ties to Israel. Due to these gestures of independence, Romania became a significant partner for Western powers as a potential ally within the Soviet bloc. After Romania condemned the occupation of Chechoslovakia in 1968, Nixon traveled to Bucharest, making Romania the first socialist country where a US president made an official visit.

Due to these conditions, the industrialization wave of the late 1950s was not based on Soviet energy and raw materials, but instead on economic cooperations with Western and, increasingly, Third World countries. After 1958, the share of Soviet trade in the Romanian economy decreased, while Western technology imports, and corresponding raw material and agrarian exports to Western markets started to grow (Lavigne, 1991). In the 1960s and 1970s, Romania strongly participated in the incipient wave of joint ventures with Western companies, accompanied by agreements of technological and economic cooperation. It became a member of IMF in 1972, and a member of GATT (General Agreement on Tariffs and Trade) in 1971. In 1975, Romania was listed by the United States among the countries benefiting from the largest trade benefits. The effects of this industrialization model were spectacular: 1955 and 1965, industrial capacities grew threefold (Crowther, 1988: 68).

In order to exceed the economic and political limitations of extensive industrialization that started to become explicit by the 1960s, after the 1965 Soviet economic reform, all socialist regimes of the region started to experiment with reforms. Hungary and Romania followed different routes in the process: while Hungary's New Economic Mechanism had the strongest market character in the region, Romania reinforced the model of centrally planned forced industrialization. Aspects of geopolitical and internal power relations played an important role in the Romanian regime's preference for centralized industrialization. Crowther (1988) emphasizes that the withdrawal of Soviet troops left the Romanian party in a situation where it needed to build out a strong control over the state apparatus and the military. The withdrawal of Soviet troops meant that unlike other satellite regimes, local leadership could not rely on Soviet military help in the face of popular discontent and competing for elite fractions. At the same time, the withdrawal of troops also turned the Soviet Union into the number one military threat against the regime. After 1964, Soviet control over the Romanian security service was disbanded. The military became a main reference of the ideology of national independence—and a main tool of control over the population (Bottoni, 2017)—in support of the centralized industrialization model.

Nicolae Ceaușescu, who succeeded Dej in power in 1965, continued the program of centrally planned forced industrialization. Turning the heritage of power centralization to his own use, Ceaușescu reorganized the system of regional governance and built out a strongly hierarchical and center-dependent structure of cadres. This politics of centralization involved another specific element of the post-Stalinist Romanian model: unlike most other socialist regimes, the Ceaușescu regime did not forge an alliance with the educated middle class, but instead strove to build

out power structures that made it capable to govern directly, circum-
venting intellectuals and experts of the apparatus. Directly after coming
to power, in order to dominate Dej's former entourage and to attain
legitimacy, Ceaușescu made concessions to the second line of bureaucracy and intellectuals, opening temporary professional and administrative
career routes (Tismăneanu, 2005). The acceleration of industrialization
also contributed to the multiplication of expert jobs (Petrovici, 2006).
But intellectuals and technocrats were not allowed to grow into a strata
that participate in power. Ceaușescu's 1967 reform program entailed a
shift from extensive to intensive industrialization, supported by managers
and technocrats, which would have provided a stronger influence of
experts on economic processes. But by 1969, the implementation of the
reform returned to a neostalinist program of centrally planned forced
industrialization. Politically, it became a tool of attack against economic
and administrative elites and middle managers. Contrary to the case of
Hungary, where the New Economic Mechanism promoted the power
of the technocracy, by reinforcing the model of centrally planned industrialization, the Romanian regime reduced the function of experts to
executives, and regularly used them in this role as scapegoats for the
political treatment of internal tensions (Pasti, 1995).

   Crowther (1988) interprets the marginalization of technocrats as an
internal condition of Romania's centralized industrialization effort after
Soviet independence. Here, too, expertise produced by socialist development became a significant social and political factor by the 1960s:
like elsewhere, technocrats became a privileged group that was able
to promote its own demands within the state administration. Yet the
program of shifting from extensive to intensive industrial development,
supported by managers, posed a danger to central power which strove
to remain in control without Soviet support. Next to that, limitations of
the growth projection of the five-year plan for the second half of the
1960s prioritized industrial acceleration in the politics of the regime.
While the plan initially foresaw equal growth in industry, agriculture,
and consumption, its implementation saw a decline in agricultural output
and consumption, while industrial growth surpassed planned numbers. In
other words, when industrial growth met the limits of extensive growth,
the regime chose to maintain its power by accelerating centralized industrialization and abolishing reform plans together with technocratic power
ambitions. This model, expanded and deepened throughout the next

decades under worsening conditions of external trade—and later: indebtedness—, implied an ever-increasing centralization of power, shrinking life standards for the larger part of the population, an extreme exploitation of rural resources which by the end of the 1970s led to a general lack of male workforce in rural regions (Crowther, 1988: 66–78), and increasing repression of experts' power. Compared to Hungarian reform struggles, the Romanian case shows a victory of centralist alliances in the competition for managing late socialist contradictions of external integration.

While the Romanian regime refused to cater to the needs of all the larger new social strata it created (collectivized peasants, industrial workers, and educated middle classes), the marginalization and alienation of expert and intellectual cadres played a special role in its techniques to control social discontent. Attacks against the members of the middle-level apparatus in 1969 were followed by the "small cultural revolution" of the early 1970s, (Chirot, 1978: 485), a campaign which represented cultural and technocratic cadres as the obstacles of socialist development, or even a direct threat to it. Thousands have been moved from administrative positions to production lines, cultural institutions were brought under extremely strict ideological control, and intellectuals and their supporters were demoted within the party (Crowther, 1988: 98). The marginalization of intellectuals and high levels of ideological control did not allow for the development of complex political critiques of the regime as in Hungary or Poland (Verdery, 1991). The experience of relative deprivation in educated strata under these conditions is well illustrated by the fact that by the turn of the 1980s, the levels of satisfaction with income, career progress, everyday work environment, life standard, future possibilities, and social integration were lower among their rows than among manual workers in the lowest positions (Chelcea, 1979: 97; Zamfir, 1984: 158–79).

Parallel to its condemnation of experts and intellectuals in mediating positions, the regime set up symbolic institutions of direct popular inclusion to emphasize its legitimacy through a direct connection with the people. These included the Workers' Councils, a system modeled after the example of Yugoslavian self-management but without any real decision-making capacity, the Great National Assembly as the formal legislature of Romania, collaboration with the Orthodox Church, and a series of official mass events and symbolic moments of the people's direct contact with Ceaușescu and his family. In the late period of the regime, under the conditions of increasing pressure by economic decline, external debt, and internal tensions, these political tools were complemented by the rhetorics of siege, the discourse of national martyrdom, and attacks against the Hungarian minority (Gabanyi, 1987; Novák, 2015).

Although Romania's socialist development effort started from a lower level of industrialization, and therefore could build on a larger reservoir of agricultural hinterland, by the second half of the 1970s the exhaustion of rural resources of agrarian labor and the subsequent labor shortage reached the levels that more industrialized neighbors experienced in the 1960s. The countermeasures that aimed to keep up the growth of industrial production through new legislation and reorganizations met an increasing dissatisfaction of workers. Shortages in capital goods combined with labor shortage and workers' dissatisfaction contributed to a decrease of industrial productivity. While domestic oil production played a large role in shielding the direct effects of the 1973 oil crisis, internal production capacities peaked in 1977. The effect was felt both by internal industrial production and in the decline of external terms of trade. One main tool for compensation that the Romanian regime employed was increasing the trade with Third World countries. Replicating hierarchies of uneven exchange by exporting industrial products and importing agrarian products and raw materials, Romania could capture some trade surplus in hard currency, and use it to compensate for the deficits of trade with Western partners. This broadening of trade relations with Third World countries was accompanied by a shift in foreign policy. In 1972, Ceauşescu declared Romania a socialist developing country, and started to step up in various international organizations as a representative of this position (Barnett, 1992).

These compensation strategies managed to delay economic crisis until the early 1980s. Yet by 1981, the external deficit was exacerbated by continued investment into energy-intensive industry under the conditions of raising prices of oil import and the halting of oil barters with Iran and Iraq due to the war, as well as by the growth of debt service rates from earlier loans. The regime resulted in an IMF loan. The conditions of the loan included decreasing the pace of industrialization and increasing investment in agriculture. In a few months, the IMF stopped the lending process, as Romania did not succumb to these conditions. In order to avoid pressure for economic reforms like in Poland under similar conditions, Ceauşescu proposed an extreme austerity package to service the loan, which was accepted by the IMF. This package prescribed the increase of exports (to gain hard currency for debt service) and radical cuts in internal consumption. Industrialization efforts were maintained, despite the fact that severe shortages and lack of technology led to low quality and uncompetitive products (Ban, 2012). At the end of 1982, Ceauşescu announced a program to pay back all existing loans using the same method, with the aim to eliminate lenders' influence on economic and political governance. This answer to the debt crisis of the 1980s followed a path contradictory to the Hungarian one: while in Hungary external debt contributed to increasing liberalization, the 1980s in Romania were characterized by extreme forms of austerity, deepening centralization, the maintenance of forced industrialization, and efforts to eliminated dependence from international lenders. By 1987, Ceauşescu halted the communication of economic data (which was among the conditions of the IMF loan), with the argument that Romania does not need Western financing anymore.

Interpretations of the Ceauşescu regime tend to attribute a decisive role to the dictators' personal character and ambitions. This kind of explanation seems to be supported by the politics of personality cult. Besides personal aspects, Ban (2014) attributes the seemingly illogical maintenance of forced industrialization under the conditions of extreme austerity as an effect of the regime's specific neostalinist ideology. However, Crowther (1988) argues that the politics of the Romanian regime in the 1980s correspond to the objective possibilities to maintaining power within the external circumstances of the country's world-economic integration at the time, and in this sense, do not merely follow from personal psychology or ideology.

In the 1980s, the politics of extreme austerity went hand-in-hand with the deepening of authoritarian suppression. While workers' discontent was also suppressed, the control of experts and intellectuals constituted a special focus for security forces (Poenaru, 2013). In the perception of these strata, regular persecution, together with institutional and political marginalization, came to be connected with the increasing national populist rhetoric the regime used to legitimate its centralization of power. Even though manual workers lived and worked under more severe conditions, participated in rebellions that were violently suppressed, and were part of the 1989 December revolution, the perception of an anti-intellectual alliance between communist dictatorship and popular strata remained a significant element of postsocialist middle class politics.

The Hungarian Environmental Movement and Romanian Workers' Mobilizations in Late Socialism

In Hungary, the largest movement that later came to be acknowledged as a mover of the regime change was the environmental movement (Fleischer, 1993). The two main issues that the movement targeted were both connected to the specificities of world-economic integration, and the internal pressures they produced. The first was the plan of the Gabčíkovo–Nagymaros barrage and hydroelectric power plant, which was initially forged by industrial planning in the 1950s to service the future growth in energy consumption, and became actualized by the repercussions of the 1973 oil crisis. As cheap Soviet oil became inaccessible, energy procured central priority in economic policy. Energy import to sustain the industry required hard currency, a cumbersome weight on an economy caught between the needs of technology imports and the incapacity to sustain those imports by exports to hard currency markets. In the narrative of the anti-waterworks movement, the Gabčíkovo–Nagymaros plan was criticized as an expression of an outdated, aggressive, and megalomaniac project, which serves no other aim than reinforcing the logic of central planning, and ruins the intricate living tissue of natural and human habitats (Bossányi, 1989; Pajkossy, 2006; Szabó, 1994; Vargha, 1981). Environmentalist arguments about intricately balanced ecological systems threatened by the barrage were formulated as a metaphor of the contrast between the artificial, rigid, and coercive nature of planning, and more spontaneous and democratic forms of social organization. In line with dissident narratives, planning was thought of as irrational, its irrationality following from the logic of a system built on the maximization of bureaucratic power.

The second main issue of environmental activism in late socialist Hungary was toxic chemical waste, produced in increasing quantities by chemical plants and stored in unprotected sites that held dangers for nearby settlements. In the narrative of the environmental movement and its international communication, this unsafe treatment of toxic waste followed from the repressive and irresponsible character of the socialist system toward its citizens and nature. From the perspective of world-economic integration, the increased production of chemical waste was linked to two main factors: the general lack of investment capacity to improve waste management due to the conditions of debt repayment to improve waste managemen, and the pressure toward exports that are able to generate hard currency. Hard currency pressure pushed industrial policy toward solutions that have a relatively low level of investment, but can still generate export capacity. Toxic chemical technologies were particularly suitable for that purpose. An illustrative example is a case conveyed by Zsuzsa Gille's (2007) research on waste regimes in socialist Hungary. The chemical company Budapest Chemical Works, one of the biggest firms in the sector, produced TCB for export to Austria. TCB was a component so toxic that it was also used for the herbicide Agent Orange, a substance applied by the US military in the Vietnam War. It was precisely the toxicity of TCB why Hungary could capture much-needed export capacities from its production, due to the stronger environmental regulations in Austria that made its local production impossible. This kind of cheaper and more risky production of chemicals for external trade was a tool that was also used by other noncore economies maneuvering under similar conditions. As a Hungarian article put it in 1977, explaining why the costs of environmental protection cannot be included in chemical production:

> It is impossible to realize these costs in our export prices. Industrial capacities founded on the oil and gas fields of Arabic countries present a strong competition in industrial markets, as they do not undertake ecological costs, and can work with consequently low prices. This is also one of the factors why we are not able to realize costs of ecological measures in our exports (Breitner, 1977: 3)

The environmental movement played an important role in the internal criticism of the regime, and became an important actor of the demonstrations of the regime change (Romsics, 2003; Szirmai, 1999). In this process, the issue of environmental protection came to be linked with demands to employ more developed and environment-friendly Western technologies, and a corresponding critique of the backwardness of socialist technology that causes environmental harm. Like in other fields, the abolishment of socialism was conceived in the environmental debate as implying a promise that would make it possible for Hungary to catch up with Western environmental norms. On the structural level, however, the relation of economic subordination that governed both the plan of the Gabčíkovo–Nagymaros barrage and the problem of toxic chemical waste, continued to define environmental policies after 1989.

In the process of the regime change, the issue of environmental measures came to be entangled with questions of new technology imports, and the parallel elimination of local, lower technology products from local markets. Examples include cases like the NEFCO venture capital trust funded by Scandinavian countries to foster ecological-technological investments in Eastern Europe administered by the Nordic Investment Bank, or the Kemira–Trabant–Wartburg catalizador joint company, whose sales were subsidized by the state and boosted by a ban on two-stroke engines (Gagyi, 2015b). In the period of privatization-led foreign direct investment, the issue of toxic chemical waste dumps transformed into the issue of new waste incinerators built by Western companies in Hungarian locations, which also burnt waste exported to Hungary from Western countries. In debates around the location and building of these incinerators, investors pointed at the toxicity of existing waste dumps, and argued that their investments would provide higher level, Western technology to eliminate their risks. However, incinerators also produced toxic effects, which started new conflicts locally (Gille, 2007). This process came to be criticized by environmental activists in terms of "wild capitalism" and "ecocolonialism" (Harper, 2005).

In 1989, an investigative article tracing a case of soil pollution presents a snapshot of the changing social landscape in the Hungarian countryside, providing a short summary of internal–external relations of environmental harm from late socialism to postsocialist transition. Starting from the socialist chemical company dumping toxic waste due to lack of investment capacity, the story continues with the incineration of toxic waste by new Western companies and zooms in on the appearance of local middlemen who buy the barrels emptied from toxic waste for making brandy. This results in a series of toxic poisoning in the rows of day laborers to whom the brandy is sold. The story is particularly telling in terms of the new postsocialist social hierarchy where locals produce half-illegal income from the waste of the new, environmentally friendly incineration, and the toxic effect this produces on the lowest local social strata remains outside of the jurisdiction of institutional concern:

> the surface of toxic soil has been collected and dumped in concrete containers. Yet the plastic barrels which have been emptied from toxic waste before the incineration were sold at a cheap price to locals, who used them for making brandy. (…) An alcohologist physician from Szekszárd was surprised to see how fast alcoholics in Kiskőrös degraded. It is

not easy to monitor toxic brandy, since it is consumed by the new stratum of day laborers employed by wine farmers. (Tanács, 1989)

In Romania, the most significant mobilizations against the regime in the late period of socialism were those of heavy industry workers and miners. The largest strike was that of the Jiu Valley miners in 1977, resulting in severe repercussions (Deletant, 1995; Rus, 2007). Three years later, the Free Trade Union of the Working People of Romania was formed with twenty founding members. After their founding document was read in Radio Free Europe, their numbers grew to 2400. The union aimed to represent demands against worsening working and life conditions and the repression of workers' rights. The regime reacted with fast and violent measures—hundreds of people were arrested, followed by persecution, physical violence, psychiatric confinement, deportation, or prison sentence (Karatnycky et al., 1980: 80). In 1986–1987, another series of smaller conflicts broke out in factories around the country. The series peaked in the strike of industrial workers in Braşov, followed by similar retaliations.

In the case of the 1977 Jiu Valley strike, the immediate cause that sparked coal miners' protest was the extension of workdays to aid the reconstructions following the 1977 earthquake and a transformation of the pension system that forbid those on disability pension to continue to work and raised the general retirement age. These acute grievances only constituted the peak of discontent that has been building up due to low wages and poor living conditions, and the fact that workers were expected to exceed planned production targets despite these conditions, and were punished by paycheck cuts if they remained below them (Rus, 2007). This extreme pressure on coal miners reflected the regime's efforts to maintain the pace of forced industrialization despite the pressure of growing energy prices and internal labor shortage. Coal mining as a source of internal energy production became important in alleviating the pressure for oil imports and thereby slowing the pace of indebtedness. This pressure was handled rather by the means of coercion than that of rewards, while life standards were nationally reduced in order to maximize industrial investment.

On August 1, 1977, 35.000 miners put down work in the Jiu Valley mines. They claimed that they would only accept to speak to Ceauşescu in person about their demands. The next day, two high-level members of the Politburo visited the scene, one of whom came from a miner background himself. Strikers held both of them captive, and demanded a direct meeting with Ceaușescu. On 3 August, Ceaușescu traveled to the valley's central city of Lupeni from his Black Sea vacation. He was greeted by the slogan "Ceaușescu and the people", a line produced within the regime's official direct populist ideological communication, and "Lupeni 29!", referring to the 1929 Jiu Valley strike which was also used as an element of the party's official historical narrative. These references to the regime's own legitimation ideology served to optimalize miners' bargaining position; but the bargain also included elements of threat. Worrying for his physical safety amidst the angry crowd, Ceaușescu made promises to radically ameliorate miners' situation, and avoid retaliations (Deletant, 1995: 243–245; Gosu, 2004). He blamed middle management for the mistakes causing miners' plight. This move, also fitting into the regime's general legitimation strategy, resonated with workers' discontent with strong workplace hierarchy that stood in sharp contrast with the slogans of workers' power. This grievance was expressed in the antibureaucratic slogan "down with the communist bourgeoisie!" (Cesereanu, 2004).

The appearance of an alliance between Ceaușescu and the miners, that could solve miners' problems by eliminating middle management's mistakes along the lines of the regime's ideological narrative of direct populism, did not last long. As soon as Ceaușescu left the valley, thousands of soldiers marched in. The presence of the secret service was scaled up, and retaliations started with violent interrogations. Main organizers of the strike were declared missing in a few weeks. Many participants were taken to the hospital or psychiatry. Others were sent to prison and to work camps. On the whole, up to 4000 miners lost their jobs, and hundreds of families were deported to other regions of the country (Cesereanu, 2004; Rus, 2007; Varga, 2011, 2013). Once the threat of workers' self-organization was successfully subdued, concessions regarding working conditions and food supply were canceled.

The industrial strike series of 1986–1987 also reacted to growing workplace pressure linked to maintaining forced industrialization, coupled with the drastic austerity measures introduced as a condition of external debt repayment. As part of the debt repayment program started in 1982, most of the agricultural production was reoriented to export, leading to a severe food shortage. In 1987, strikers in Cluj and Turda justified work stoppage by claiming that they needed time to stand in line for bread (Gabanyi, 1987). These strikes were also handled by a combination of temporary concessions and violent retaliations. After the Brașov strike, food supply was temporarily increased in large industrial centers; meanwhile, a hundred were arrested, tortured, and deported. Some went missing without a trace (Oprea & Olar, 2003).

Based on the above, the conditions of the Hungarian environmental and Romanian workers' mobilizations in late socialism were connected not only to the generic traits of the socialist regime (such as central planning or lack of political freedom), or to local variations of it, but also to the specific constellations of how the two national economies integrated into world-economic processes following 1973. Looking at specific constellations of world-economic integration may explain why the plan of a megaproject for a hydroelectric plant, toxic chemical waste, the unbearable workload in coal mining and industry, or the lack of basic foodstuffs emerged as conditions for local protests rooted in transnational processes. Of course, like any condition of movement formation, these do not explain the exact buildup of the movements, but they do cast some light on the particular kind of agencies activated in these mobilizations.

In Romania, what made coal miners and industrial workers likely subjects of protest was not only the fact that the industrial effort put a strong burden on their shoulders, but also because these were the sectors crucial to sustaining that effort. This was expressed by work requirements as well as by symbolic statements about the importance of their work, embedded in a discourse of work heroism that granted some selective privileges in wage and living allowances (which came to be eroded after 1973). Ceaușescu's political strategy to marginalize the technocratic power of intellectuals and emphasize a political alliance with the working masses on the symbolic level was institutionalized in various forms of workers' "autonomy" and "consultation", which, even if not able to influence real decision-making, could provide the illusion of a symbolic resource in bargaining. Istvan Hosszu, one of the Jiu Valley strike organizers, remembered his own reliance on this rhetoric during his interrogations in the following way:

> He looked at me as if I were an idiot for confessing such outrageous charges.
>
> – Comrade Hosszu, what kind of explanation can you give, how can you account for your deeds?

– Very simply – I said. - I only need to quote the words of the general
secretary on the IX. Congress. (…) the general secretary encouraged
everyone to be outspoken, and explore all problems in an honest
way. This is what he said; but I think that in order for his message to
become reality, and not merely a turn of speech, we need to prove
his point by our action. (Csalog, 1989)

That workers' mobilizations utilized the regime's ideology as a resource
for bargaining was not only based on the Ceauşescu regime's specific anti-
technocracy and direct populist strategy, but also on a longer tradition of
direct bargaining with high-rank communist leaders. Since the 1950s, in
cases of workers' discontent in main industrial units that bore a strong
structural significance, but also had a stronger tradition of workers' organization, the party sent high-rank communist leaders with backgrounds
in the local plant to bargain with workers. These functionaries stepped up
as personal mediators between workers and the party, often promising
special proceedings and privileges. This technique of pacification was
typically complemented by combinations of concessions and repressive
measures. Strikers' strategies also relied on the technique of personal
bargaining with a high-rank leader who had local roots, and even initiated
such moments of mediation. In the Jiu Valley, besides the 1977 strike, this
pattern of bargaining was applied also in 1972, 1980, and 1981. Previously, Dej also personally acted as such a mediator in 1952 or 1957 in face
of striking railway workers, using his legitimacy as a party member who
started his political career from organizing the 1933 strike at the Grivița
plant of the Romanian Railways (Gagyi, 2015b). In 1957, when Grivița
workers protested cuts in the base wage that were announced in punish-
ment for not fulfilling the production plan, the informant of Radio Free
Europe reported the following conversation. Dej claimed that problems
were due to management, and exempted workers.

ordering that they must be excused of things that are really the fault of bad
organization (…) Source asked the official accompanying him why something is not done to avoid this discontentment, that is why the collective
work contract is not changed. Smiling, the Rumanian official replied: 'Then
Gheorghiu-Dej could not be the 'father of the railroads' any longer, and
would lose forever the popularity he enjoys now in the shops'. (HU OSA
300-60-1, 424)

The quote is illustrative of the way tactics of personal contact were tied to both leaders' and workers' positions and their maneuver space within the same structure of power. This pattern of conflict management has been described by studies of workers' mobilizations after the regime change, too (Rus, 2007; Varga, 2011, 2013).

In the case of the 1977 Jiu Valley strike, the contrast between the use of the slogan "Ceauşescu and the people!" and the harshness of retaliations also illustrate the difference from forms of protest where intellectuals formulate highly developed, coherent, and abstract expressions of political criticism. The latter forms of critique, embodied in text documents, could be easily represented, disseminated, and amplified in Western media. Romanian workers' mobilizations produced few such documents, and the process of their struggle was less suitable to be represented in the form of abstract political criticism of the socialist system. As a parallel case, Bottoni (2017) mentions that spontaneous protest by ethnic minorities was easier to suppress and cover up, as they rarely reached the threshold of international media attention. Formulated within the power logic of direct personal bargaining, and addressed against structural conditions of overtime work and food shortage, the expressions of Romanian workers' struggles were not suited to become abstract models of political critique. From among the thousands of workers who became the victims of retaliations, very few rose to positions similar to dissident intellectuals whose name became symbols of political struggle after 1989.

In Hungary, the anti-socialist critique of the environmental movement was formulated by the movement's intellectual members in a highly detailed, abstract form, compatible with Western criticism (Bossányi, 1989; Dobos et al., 1988). Actors directly affected by environmental problems, like inhabitants of villages threatened by dam construction, or people living close to toxic chemical waste dumps, participated in mobilizations only intermittently. More significant protests took place in the capital, and addressed not only environmental issues, but expressed a more general critique of the system. Due to the fact that environmentalism was a cause supported by the system (Gille, 2007), and to the broader space allowed for intellectual politics, environmentalism could become a preliminary ground for oppositional politics (Pickvance, 1998). Oppositional arguments formulated in the terms of environmentalism would later become part of transition narratives, as many of the prominent members of the movement became important actors and voices of the regime change (Gagyi & Ivancheva, 2017). Growing control by Western lenders also meant that appeals to Western audiences by local opposition forces could function as a political resource and protection. The capacities of intellectual critique were also increased by overlaps with and support from reformer segments within the party apparatus (Bockman, 2000; Gagyi, 2015a). Finally, East–West movement dialogues enhanced the intelligibility of local movement narratives in Western circles. In contrast, in Romania, workers' mobilizations themselves did not speak the language of abstract political critique, and the marginalization and suppression of intellectual critique and the lack of significant contacts between intellectual dissidents and workers' mobilizations reduced the possibility for intellectual critique to mediate and translate between workers' demands and Western audiences. Meanwhile, the regime's central effort to reduce Western influence through debt repayment limited the effect of Western communication.

From Postsocialist Development to Middle Class Mobilizations After 2008

Late socialist constellations of integration set different conditions for postsocialist politics in the two countries. In Romania, the maintenance of the program of forced industrialization, the strong centralization of power, and the marginalization of experts and intellectuals foreclosed the formation of reform fractions supporting liberal reforms within the party. Unlike in most late socialist regimes, in Romania there was no internal debate between "orthodox" and "liberal" fractions within the party. Internal opposition strove to gain power through coups rather than reform. Indeed, the December revolution of 1989, the only bloody revolution in the series of regime changes in the region, was used in the manner of palace coups to put the second line of party leaders in power. Based on this continuity with the previous party line, early postsocialist policies aimed to maintain a model of national development tied to industrialization supported by protectionism. The Postolache commission that laid down the program of marketization prescribed a gradual transformation toward a mixed economy with a strong state sector, similar to the French indicative planning of the postwar years (Ban, 2016). This new version of national development policies carried strong continuities with the principles of industrial development promoted by interwar right-wing regimes as well as with socialist neostalinist industrialization. In terms of class aspects, in the context of privatization this new version can be described as a project to create and promote state-supported domestic capital (Ban, 2014). Liberalization that actually opened domestic economy for foreign investment, like the process that started in Hungary after 1986 did, only started in Romania with the reforms carried out by the Romanian Democratic Convention government between 1996 and 2000, and reached its full verve with the process of NATO and EU integration during the 2000s.

In contrast to Hungary, Czechoslovakia or Poland (Eyal, 2003; Szelényi et al., 1996), in Romania dissident intellectuals did not become dominant actors of the regime change. The National Salvation Front, the political organization formed from bureaucrats, technocrats, and dissident intellectuals which stepped up as the organizational representative of the revolution, soon became the terrain of competing bureaucratic and technocratic fractions. Humanistic intellectuals soon withdrew from the coalition, and joined other political initiatives—mostly the reestablishment of historical parties, or liberal NGOs (Petrovici, 2006). This fraction of intellectuals, which has also been the most marginalized during late socialism, felt that it was losing the power struggle of the transition, and started to interpret the coalition of bureaucrats and technocrats as the survival of communism, and joining reestablished historical parties (the National Liberal Party and the National Peasants' Party) in an effort to reinforce its political opposition.

After January 1990, these parties, both supporting liberal reforms, started to organize demonstrations in Bucharest demanding that previous members of the communist party be forbidden to participate in democratic elections. Despite the demonstrations, the National Salvation Front, led by Ion Iliescu, a high-level former party cadre, won a secure victory in the first free elections, thanks to the broad mobilization machine inherited from the communist party. When the liberal opposition continued to demonstrate after the election results came out, claiming the nullification of the results, Iliescu declared the situation as a threat to the stability of post-revolutionary democracy. Relying on the former party apparatus' penetration of miners' organizations, Iliescu called Jiu Valley miners to Bucharest to defend the results of the December revolution. In June 1990, miners directed by the Securitate were transported to Bucharest, and attacked demonstrators and other citizens, targeting individuals with intellectual appearance (e.g. people wearing glasses, Rus, 2007). In the eyes of educated strata across the country, the horrible pictures of the 1990 "mineriad" sealed the symbolic opposition between "communism" as the alliance of ex-communists and popular strata, and "democracy" as the program of Western integration represented by educated people. University Square, the location of the liberal opposition's demonstration, became a geographical symbol of this symbolic conflict, which came to be recurrently reactualized in later mobilizations. In postsocialist public discussions dominated by intellectuals, the image of miners with sticks attacking urban intellectuals under the direction of Securitate officials in 1990 permanently overwrote memories of former worker mobilizations and workers' participation in the revolution, and invisibilized the anti-government politics of later mineriads. Anthropologist David Kideckel (2008) noted that in the 1990s, the image of physical workers suffering under the economic repercussions of the transition crisis was associated with the memory of communism and the sentiments of anti-communism contributed to their exclusion from political debates.

In 1992, the National Salvation Front broke into two platforms—a group of bureaucrats and financial experts led by Prime Minister Petre Roman, which proposed further liberalization, and a group dominated by technocrats and industrial managers led by Ion Iliescu, which strove to maintain the previous direction of industrial policy, and a politics of slow privatization (Pasti, 1995; Petrovici, 2006). After the break, Iliescu's fraction was formalized under the name Democratic National Salvation Front (the later Socialist Party). After winning the 1992 elections, this party promoted the politics of protectionism and limited privatization, in line with industrial managers' interests to maintain domestic industrial structures. Politically, these policies were legitimated by references to the priority to maintain jobs and protect domestic industrial sectors that are of key importance to national security (Ban, 2014; Pasti, 1995, 2006).

In terms of protecting workplaces, the slowdown of privatization did not only follow from the economic and political priorities of former technocratic party elites. After the revolution, industrial workers reorganizing into independent unions outside the former socialist union alliance constituted a significant pressure on the government, which was already struggling in terms of governance capacity due to the erosion of former bureaucracy. Varga (2011, 2013) demonstrates that in regional comparison, Romanian unions manifested the strongest protest capacity after 1989. Strikes, factory occupations, and street blockades, often leading to violent clashes with the police, made unions a strong actor of struggles around economic policy in the 1990s. These struggles peaked by the end of the decade. The heat and scope of conflict are well illustrated by a strike in Braşov, *1999*, *where* workers held the minister of finance captive, applying the same model of personal bargaining that Jiu Valley miners used in 1977. This protest capacity of postsocialist unions was only dismantled in the 2000s. Within the EU accession process, the rewriting of the labor code was supported by the escalation of police repression (reaching the level of protracted battles with police and gendarmerie), a communication smear campaign that stigmatized unions as the hotbed of corruption, as well as informal actions by foreign parties interested in privatization. In the case of TEPRO Iaşi, the latter included the murder of a union leader (Varga, 2013). In Varga's assessment, this violent top-down action against unions in the early 2000s resulted in Romanian unions achieving relatively little lasting concessions despite their regionally outstanding protest capacity.

From the perspective of Iliescu's party, the alliance with workers—represented ideologically in terms of job protection, industrial development, and national security—was a tactic induced by workers' pressure as well as by industrial technocracy's interest to hold internal and external promoters of liberalization in check. In carrying out a subdued privatization that favored domestic capital formation, symbolic alliances with workers helped show political strength, and references to workers' resistance could help sustain their standpoints in face of the IMF, World Bank, EU accession conditions, and local actors like the Bank of Development, opposition parties, and liberal NGOs. Meanwhile, under the facade of the same symbolic alliance, unions could pressurize Iliescu's party to support the slowing of industrial closures and concessions of social policies. The symbolic communication of this alliance reinforced the idea of a political connection between workers and the socialist party, reverberated equally in the political communication of socialist and oppositional politics. Contradictions between workers' struggles and socialist politics were obscured by this representation.

After the 1996 elections, the Democratic Party established by the liberal faction of the National Salvation Front formed a common government with the Front's liberal opposition. Their program for a shock therapy was prepared under the instructions of Leszek Balcerowicz, assessed by the *Economist* as the most radical reform package of the region (Ban, 2014: 160). This coming to power of a liberal coalition also shifted the position of human intellectuals. From marginal oppositional positions in liberal NGOs, many entered positions of expertise and consultancy within the process of economic reform and the preparation of

EU accession. The regime's shift toward liberalization—also perceived by liberal oppositional politics and their Western allies as welcome opening toward proper democratization—implied a shift in funding channels for these experts' work, too, moving from NGO communication to applied expertise within governance structures (Ban, 2016: 169–179).

The social effects of shock therapy soon destroyed the political legitimacy of the liberal coalition and brought a new electoral victory of the socialists in 2000. However, by now, the stage of structural adjustment and privatization, together with the unbroken popularity of the idea of European accession (which required approval by the IMF) only made possible a moderation of neoliberalization, despite this elite group's interests colliding with the process. In 2004, Traian Băsescu, representing the liberal fraction of the Front, became president, and held on to that position until 2014. Consecutive governments during the Băsescu presidency promoted a neoliberal model of integration, focused on attracting foreign direct investment through lowering wages, cutting labor rights, and state subsidies directed at investors, in line with the requirements of EU accession.

Despite growing social polarization, the symbolic and economic effects of NATO and EU accession helped maintain the legitimacy of this direction for a relatively long period. Besides high hopes associated with entering these Western clubs, these included the possibility of labor migration to the EU, which soon grew to millions in numbers, a partial reindustrialization based on foreign investments, and increasing debt-based consumption. In major cities, the inflow of foreign investments resulted in the formation of a new, postsocialist middle class, and the proliferation in Western forms of consumption and services in which they could engage (Petrovici, 2007; Petrovici & Poenaru, 2017). The political power base of the socialist party and its broader network of state-dependent domestic capital and bureaucracy was significantly eroded (Poenaru, 2017a: 69–78). As this political bloc could hardly provide any benefits to its constituency beyond narrowing patron–client relations, its political discourse increasingly shifted toward nationalist slogans and conspiracy theories (Poenaru, 2017a: 79–89). Meanwhile, the National Anticorruption Directorate, an organization funded by an emergency decree in 2002 with the support of international partners like the US State Department, acquired ever expanding capacities. Interlacing with secret services, throughout the years it became a parallel pole of power next to the system of governance based on electoral representation (Bottoni, 2017).

In Băsescu's politics, the support for neoliberal integration and the struggle against socialists' power was complemented on the symbolic level with a sort of top-down populism or "neo-populist elitism" (Shafir, 2008). This promoted a symbolic opposition between corrupt political elites and forward-looking citizens who support the project of Western integration. The political narrative built on this opposition questioned the legitimacy of elected governments and parliamentary parties by claiming that the process of elections is distorted by corrupted alliances between socialists (ex-communists) and uneducated lower classes. Against this coalition, progress needs to be sustained by the efforts of the presidential office, anti-corruption organizations, and their Western and international allies. During the process of EU accession, Băsescu solidified this narrative by a symbolic alliance with anti-communist humanist intellectuals. In 2006, he created a presidential committee to analyze the communist dictatorship, with the participation of historians and anti-communist intellectuals. The committee's task was to prepare a report (Tismăneanu et al., 2006), based on which Băsescu could officially condemn the crimes of communism. This gesture rose anti-communist human intellectuals' image of communism to the mainstream of liberal politics, reinforcing the symbolic opposition between educated, Westernized middle classes, and the alliance between ex-communist political elites and their uneducated clientele, which hinders the progression of catch-up development (Buier, 2007; Poenaru, 2013).

In Romania, too, the 2008 crisis brought a debt crisis. The budget deficit was also deepened by the political decision to delay crisis measures for the campaign period of 2008 parliamentary and 2009 presidential elections, and instead raise wages and pensions. Crisis measures started from 2009, in a context where the financial sector was dominated by foreign banks and relevant policies were dependent on lenders' control, and the real economy depended on an export sector dominated by multinational investors, who also stepped up as main actors defining crisis management (Ban, 2016: 218–219). Ban argues that even within this extremely narrow maneuver space, Romanian austerity measures surpassed expectations by the Troika (Ban, 2016: 230). He explains this by a lack of up to date, deeper knowledge of international expert debates on the side of Romanian neoliberals, and by the fact that in internal political struggles, even measures acknowledged in the international mainstream like progressive taxation were stigmatized as communist heritage that holds progress back. In political discourses on crisis management, Băsescu attributed the negative effects of the crisis to lower strata still carrying the communist heritage of low work ethics and state dependence, and therefore supporting the postcommunist politics of free gifts. It is this vicious circle, he claimed, why the wealth produced by the middle classes cannot be used to promote progress (Băsescu, 2011). Within this logic, anti-corruption campaigns against politicians and austerity measures were expected to cut the ties between political corruption and low-income strata expecting state gifts, and thereby create the possibility of progression:

> Reality created a chance for Romania by unveiling our weak points. What we need now is dedication and determination to get rid of them. (...) If examined well, we see that in Romania the main problem is not poverty, but laziness and abuse of the welfare system. (Băsescu, 2011)

Austerity measures were soon followed by demonstrations. Protests by unions culminated in a general strike in October 2009 (Trif, 2014). In response, in 2011, modifications of the labor code practically abolished the right to national collective bargaining (Stoiciu, 2016). In the winter of 2011, a wave of street demonstrations was sparked by the plan to partially privatize the emergency rescue service, an exceptionally efficient and popular system. When deputy health minister Raed Arafat, the founder and coordinator of the service since its inception in the 1990s, criticized the move, he was forced by Băsescu to resign, a move that caused widespread resentment. As a result of 2011 winter protests, the liberal government failed, and from 2012, socialist Victor Ponta took the position of prime minister. The next years were characterized by a growing conflict between socialists relying on their still significant political networks, and liberal-technocratic groups using external economic and geopolitical dependence to erode socialist power. In the context of economic crisis, austerity measures and series of political scandals, waves of street demonstrations followed each other.

After the case of the emergency rescue service, immediate causes of new demonstration waves included environmentally harmful investments supported by corruption in the case of the Roşia Montană goldmine plan and Chevron's investment into shale gas fracking at Pungeşti; limitations of voting opportunities for the liberally inclined diaspora at the 2014 presidential elections; a fire at the Bucharest night club Colectiv that killed over 60, and continued in a scandal of a Romanian pharmaceutical company supplying over 350 hospitals with heavily diluted disinfectants that contributed to the death of further Colectiv victims due to bacterial infections; and a socialist plan for an emergency ordinance in 2017 that would have made possible for leading politicians—including socialist party leader Liviu Dragnea under criminal investigation at that point—to be dismissed from corruption charges. In 2018, the mobilization series was continued by the "Diaspora at Home" protests, where Romanians working abroad protested against the modification of the penal code, the dismissal of the head of the National Anticorruption Directorate, the gaffes of the socialist Prime Minister Viorica Dancila seen as a symbol of incompetent socialist leadership, and the fact that Dragnea still headed the Chamber of Deputies despite having been sentenced to prison. Since the violent repression of union protests in the late 1990s and early 2000s, and the force applied against local resistance in Pungeşti to open the way for Chevron's investment, the 2018 diaspora protests were the first instance of violent clashes with the police (and the first where such measures were applied against middle class protesters, Reuters, 2018a). Meanwhile, counterprotests organized by socialists also reached the volume of hundred thousand by 2018 (Reuters, 2018b).

Throughout the years, political conflict between competing elites became an integral part of protest dynamics. While in the early years, anti-austerity claims did not exclude social demands, and small groups of new left activists made efforts to thematize protests in lines similar to Western anti-austerity social demands, protest frameworks later came to be closely aligned with the political narratives of the liberal fraction of political struggles. On the one hand, instances of protests were often followed by resignations and changes of government, and electoral victories by political competitors—in 2012, the failure of Emil Boc's liberal government; in 2014, the election of President Klaus Iohannis despite the higher mobilization capacity of his socialist opponent; in 2016, the establishment of a technocratic government in place of Victor Ponta's socialist government that resigned at the pressure of the Colective protests; in 2017, the withdrawal of the original bill for the modification of the penal code, etc. On the other hand, while protesters often expressed discontent in face of the whole political class, throughout the years the political effects and frames of the protests were successfully channeled on the side of liberal-technocratic elites, and utilized to support their struggle to destroy the power of socialist political networks, and increase the parallel power of technocratic anti-corruption institutions independent from electoral politics, symbolically expressed in the narrative of anti-communist anticorruption (Bottoni, 2017; Poenaru, 2017b; Tamás, 2016).

For instance, the liberal presidential election campaign of 2014 opposed the image of Klaus Iohannis as a person of Saxon origin, representing Western protestant progression and efficiency, to socialist Victor Ponta who had been charged by corruption and plagiarism at the time, and whose steps to compensate political marginalization by populist methods were characterized by the international press as akin to Putin's or Orban's (e.g. Traynor, 2013). In this context, demonstrations were sparked by the charge that Ponta's government does not provide sufficient conditions for the liberally inclined diaspora to cast their votes. Protests reinforced the opposition between modern, educated, Westernized strata vs. corrupt socialist elites, and incompetent lower strata (Gherasim-Proca, 2016). This opposition, shared across protesters and liberal political campaigns, was illustrated by social media memes like one contrasting a picture of Ponta standing among a group of old peasant women to an Iohannis campaign photo where the presidential candidate is pictured in a group of middle class youth on bikes, on a bike lane in the first district of Bucharest.

In 2015, slogans of the first demonstrations reacting to the Colectiv accident addressed the responsibility of postsocialist political elites as a whole for the failure of the transition project (Crețan & O'Brien, 2019). However, the communication of Iohannis' presidential office soon helped to impose the slogan "corruption kills" as the dominant interpretation of the events. The resignation of the Ponta government and the setup of a technocratic government was represented as moves to set the country on the road of progress as demanded by demonstrators. Despite this success in channeling protest energies into political support, the 2016 parliamentary elections brought a socialist victory. While the 2017–2018 protest wave was immediately directed at the corruption aspects of the socialists' emergency ordinance plan, on a more general level it also expressed protesters' frustration with what they perceived as a political victory going against the will of the people. At this point, demonstrators' claims to hold ex-communist political elites accountable for the failure of the regime change already fit the symbolic frameworks of socialists' liberal competitors. "Red plague" became a widespread slogan of the protests, comprising the full scope of the anti-communist liberal narrative on socialism, transition, and the limits of postsocialist development. By 2019, Iohannis' successful reelection campaign, framed along the same lines, was widely represented as the political expression of the discontent that has been building up throughout the protests (Rogozanu, 2019).

At the same time, new center-right and neonationalist party initiatives that built on the political energy of the demonstrations (Save Romania Union, USR, and the Alliance for the Union of Romanians, AUR) also became successful and grew into the third and fourth strongest parties by 2020. USR, founded in 2016 after a successful local electoral campaign in Bucharest, promoted an anti-corruption and pro-business agenda, defining its political line as closest to Emmanuel Macron's La République En Marche! (Gotev, 2018). With a growing support that allowed it to enter a coalition government after the 2020 parliamentary elections, the electoral geography of Save Romania Union reflects the positions of young and educated urban middle class voters concentrated in major cities.

AUR, getting into parliament in 2020 with almost 10% of the votes despite only being founded in 2019, promoted nationalist slogans such as anti-Hungarian sentiments and the unification with Moldova, next to claims similar to other new right parties, like anti-LGBTQ and anti-abortion campaigns and opposition to Covid-19-related restrictions or vaccines (Clark, 2020). Like USR, AUR also built on a younger voter base, but had similar levels of rural and urban support, with a slight majority of men with mid-level education (Protv.ro). The large diaspora of Romanian migrant workers, who played a central part in the anti-corruption protests of 2017–2019, and have previously voted with pro-European center-right parties like the Liberals (PNL) and USR, also played a significant role in AUR's success. Raul Castorcea, an expert on Romanian interwar fascism, to which AUR's politics bears strong and explicit resemblances, emphasized that the neonationalist turn in diaspora votes was linked to diaspora workers' dire experiences during the Covid-19 crisis, where the usual hierarchies of intra-European labor migration turned into an outright treatment of East European migrants as expendables (Boatcă, 2020; Castorcea, 2021).

While AUR's direct references to the interwar legionary movement (including external symbols like representatives wearing folk costumes in Parliament) stand in sharp contrast with USR's self-portrayal as the representative of European civilization, the differences in their political background are not watertight. From as early as the environmentalist protests, both center-right and neonationalist currents have been present in demonstrations (Abăseacă, 2018). When in 2017, the Coalition for the Family, an organization tied to AUR, initiated a referendum against gay marriage, not all USR members committed to the party's majority liberal stance, and the party's leader Dan Barna declared the issue not to be a priority (Gotev, 2018). AUR took votes from USR both in the diaspora and at home, and in the 2020 electoral campaign of AUR, several USR representatives, including one of its founding members, joined AUR (adevarul.ro). Initially, left and left-leaning activists joined USR too, in the hope to channel the left potential of protests toward political institutionalization. These standpoints did not succeed in informing the party's political line—illustratively, in 2019, USR promoted a proposal for any use of communist symbols to be punished by jail. An alternative left party initiative, Demos, founded by highly educated activists, attempted to merge anti-austerity protest with redistributive agendas, but did not succeed in gathering enough signatures either in 2019 or 2020. While commentators often portrayed post-2019 mobilizations as a political incubator where the disillusionment with the postsocialist political system breeds new forms of democratic politics, the new forms of political institutionalization supported by the protests were characterized by the strengthening of incumbent neoliberal forces as well as the rise of neoliberal center-right and neonationalist extreme right parties.

Since 2011, street protests were dominated by middle class actors—not only in terms of symbolic frameworks and media representation, but also in terms of organization (through NGOs and social media), and in terms of sheer numbers. Research showed that participants were dominantly urban middle class, male, with university diplomas, politically conservative, and took part in subsequent waves of protest (CeSIP, 2017; SNSPA, 2016). While demonstrators and commentators of the protests often represented new mobilizations as an awakening from political passivity after the 1989 revolution, Varga (2015) notes that the specificity of the demonstration series starting in 2011 was rather that it was the first mobilization wave of large volume that had not been organized by unions. Although unions continued to protest against the continuous rolling out of austerity measures, with railway workers, healthcare practitioners, and teachers protesting cuts in various state sectors, social topics represented by unions did not become a lasting part of street protests' agenda. This was partly due to different modes of organization and different frames of protest, as unions largely contested reforms of the pension system and taxation, while middle class demonstrations focused on political corruption (Margarit & Rammelt, 2020). As the symbolic contradiction between educated middle classes and liberal-technocratic elites vs. corrupt ex-communist politicians and uneducated lower classes looking for state assistance became the major framework of protest narratives, contemporary forms of unions' protests and demands were increasingly erased from protest narratives, in conformity with the anti-communist narrative of the regime change. As one analysis of post-2008 mobilizations in line with this narrative put it, union mobilizations (including the 2009 general strike) "were splintered, represented narrow interests and did not lead to unified political pressure" (Olteanu & Beyerle, 2018: 805). Instead, street protests were considered as bringing about a true "civic awakening" after the long pause of political participation after 1989, with citizens "reclaiming the state and democracy" (Olteanu & Beyerle, 2018: 819).

The fact that middle class mobilizations could be channeled into elite political struggles to the benefit of liberal-technocratic groups was also backed by overlaps between crisis effects felt by new urban middle classes and constellations of political crises. Petrovici and Poenaru (2017) analyzed the social context of the post-2008 demonstrations in terms of how the wave of foreign direct investment starting by the mid-2000s conditioned transformations of local class relations together with the opportunities of political actors. This wave of foreign investments, occurring relatively late in regional comparison, was due to the dismantling of the protectionist national-capitalist program of ex-socialist elites upheld throughout the 1990s, and to a precrisis wave of Western capitalist outsourcing. In consequence, while the 1990s were characterized by a protracted process of deindustrialization, unemployment, repeasantization, and a surge in labor migration to the West, the 2000s wave of foreign investment brought a reorganization in the constitution of both urban and rural workforce. Multinational companies moving to Romania started to employ educated middle class experts in big urban centers. While on the side of companies, this process was motivated by lower wages, compared with earlier local conditions, it was experienced by local middle classes as an opportunity to enter Western-style workplaces, make proper professional careers, and enjoy Western-style service sectors developing around new urban middle class consumption capacity. This type of urban development acted toward the further marginalization of urban workers and the poor. Struck by previous waves of unemployment, these strata were increasingly driven out from urban public spaces turned into middle class consumption grounds.

In 2008, the inflow of foreign investment temporarily halted, and the first wave of austerity measures, involving basic state services like healthcare and education, were also felt by urban middle classes. As Petrovici and Poenaru (2017) point out, the first waves of middle class protest stepped up against the austerity aspects of the same tendency of liberalization that created the ground for the formation of new urban middle class lifestyles. While new left groups at the time hoped that this factor would make it possible for politicized middle classes to ally with social groups suffering from the transformations of the 2000s, this window of opportunity was soon closed. By 2011, foreign investments started to flow in again. The growth of IT and services sectors, as well as of new management functions tied to a new wave of reindustrialization through outsourcing to former socialist industrial areas provided a new sense of optimism for new urban middle class careers.

As a relocation wave following from Western parent companies' crisis management, these investments were also built on low costs of local labor, and rarely created career paths or forms of workplace security characteristic to former Fordist Western regimes. Instead, new urban expert employees were encouraged to invest in the competitiveness of their individual portfolios. Paired with personal experiences of upward mobility in a period of expanding opportunities, this situation solidified a moral norm of individual competition and meritocracy. Contrasted to the models of individual success based in this structural context of educated middle class employment and its related moral norms, the "lack of success" manifested in the situation of blue-collar workers working under unfavorable conditions in manufacturing positions created by the same investment wave, or in new rural unemployment created by land concentration following agrarian investments, were depicted in new middle class discourses as a consequence of communist, state-dependent, incompetitive mentality (Simionca, 2012; Simionca & Gog, 2016). In these discourses, Western neoliberal criticism of the rigid and bureaucratic character of Fordist organization was identified with a local criticism of socialist production. In contrast, the work conditions of new middle class experts were held up as a model of competitive meritocracy that provides the conditions of historical progress.

Petrovici and Poenaru (2017) argue that this competitive individualist image of middle class development gained a political expression after 2013, when street protests became part of anti-socialist political campaigns, and demonstrators started to identify the cause of economic crisis and transition failure in a corrupt political alliance between socialists and the poor. The electoral success of the socialists after 2014 overlapped with the restabilization of new urban middle class positions shaken after 2008. Petrovici and Poenaru interpret the political edge of the 2016 and 2017 protests as the reaction of the new urban middle class to the political power of socialists representing alliances with social strata different from their own position and elite alliances: domestic capital fractions, smaller entrepreneurs and rural bureaucrats, and the rural and urban poor, whose interests have partially been considered in the redistribution politics of socialists. Competition for state support, as well as issues of worldview and taste set new urban middle classes in sharp contrast with petty middle classes of smaller municipalities. Besides images of the uneducated poor, the image of party-dependent backward petty middle classes has been a frequent element of protest discourse.

Protest participation and its media representations also became an element of new urban middle class identification and lifestyle. Gubernat and Rammelt (2020a, 2020b) described the lifestyle element as a specific form of protest organization, where forms of alternative cultural consumption and noncommittal/nonideological participation at protests generate a type of liminal cohesion, which spurs protest politics, but also hinders the development of more direct debates on political agendas. In terms of the connection between middle class ambitions and developmental claims, what stands out is that syltistic aspect simultaneously expresses a sense of tragedy due to the collapse of transition expectations despite middle class efforts and merits, and a rebirth of hope and entitlement in the collective action of protest. Protests were depicted as the reenaction and historical fulfillment of the martyrdom of the 1989 revolution and earlier historical efforts, expressed in slogans like "Our grandparents in the war, our parents in the revolution, now it is our turn!". In this vision of historical change, imagined as an effort to correct the historical failure of transition due to backtracking by the corruption of ex-communist politics, representations of middle classness as a proof of merit and capacity for progress gained a central function. This capacity of middle class becoming was linked to a narrative of successive generations, where parents' unsuccessful martyrdom, represented by symbolic

locations like University square, or by singing chants from 1990 oppositional demonstrations, is fulfilled by a new generation who finally becomes
the actor of progress its parents could not be. The generational aspect
of achieving middle class standards was emphasized by the adjectives
"young and free beautiful people" in descriptions and self-descriptions
of protesters (Crăciun & Lipan, 2017). Protesters simultaneously claimed
to be "the true representatives" of Romania (as opposed to corrupt politicians), and of a "well-mannered European society"—in other words: the
embodiment of Romania's long-awaited attainment of Western progress
(Gubernat & Rammelt, 2020a: 258, 260).

Similar to Pepsi's 2011 advertisement inspired by Occupy protests,
a 2017 advertisement of Ciuc Beer made use of this narrative, representing drinking Ciuc Beer and going to protests as the fulfillment of
middle class lifestyle. More than just a class position and consumption
environment, the advertisement represents the new generation of politicized middle class as the fulfillment of the country's hopes for becoming
a properly developed actor of its own future. The story of the advertisement runs from this generation's socialist childhood, represented by
a pioneers' song about a golden future to be reached by 2000, to the
postsocialist realization of that future in scenes where stylish youngsters
reuse former socialist factory spaces for leisure, skate and dance through
the city, raise a drone above a socialist mega-sculpture, protest and kiss
among the protest. In a well-placed advertising gesture, the arrival of
Ciuc Beer to the party—a brand owned by Heineken but belonging
to the group of postsocialist brands that were maintained to reap sentiments of nostalgia and longing for continuity across historical rupture—is
immediately preceded by an 1989 reference, with a young man's and
woman's faces transforming into their parents' sad and tired faces among
the protesting crowd.

In the Ciuc advertisement, the words of the pioneer song about the
golden future are applied to the expression of middle class fulfillment,
creating a victorious narrative bridge between parents' hardships and
youngsters' consumption of the "Beer from the new world", as the final
slogan puts it. However, in the actual protests, attempts at the same narrative of fulfillment carried shades of grave and tragic sentiments, as the
victory of developmental achievement was always understood to be under
vital threat. This contradiction in the stakes of middle class mobility was
often expressed in terms of historical derailment and personal death, especially after the Colectiv incident. In this context, bringing about change

through protest appeared as a life-and-death stake of both personal and historical rebirth, a question of the possibility of the future in general. The lines of the Romanian metalcore band Goodbye to Gravity, played in the Colectiv club before the fire broke out, became a slogan of the Colectiv protests in this sense: "We're not numbers / we are so alive, / 'cause the day we give in / is the day we die". In the protests' usage, these lines simultaneously referred to the tragedy of those who died in the fire and in hospitals by inadequate treatment due to instances of corruption, and to the fate of what protests referred to as a generation, whose chances are hindered due to corrupt politics that backtrack the country's development into the past. In social media memes, images depicting Colectiv victims were transformed into symbolic images of protesters as victims/ghosts who come back to take their revenge on the system. The slogan "corruption kills" was associated with a generational martyrdom, like in memes representing a youngster whose eyes and mouth are covered by tape, with the inscription "Corruption kills your future!".

Ozarow (2019: 207) notes that after delinking from social claims and alliances, middle class politicization in Argentina increasingly turned toward abstract and moral concepts like death or the moral opposition between corruption and uprightness. Crăciun and Lipan (2020) conclude from anthropological studies of postsocialist East European middle class identifications that the interchangeability of the notions of middle class and good life as a consensual field of aspirations contributed to perceiving these aspirations as inherently ethical and apolitical. In a critique of protest discourses, formulated from a left perspective, Cirjan (2016) emphasized the sharp contradictions of structural politics hidden under the image of an ethical and universally collective revolution of a generation of beautiful youngsters:

> This vision of politics as an altruist solution-search has begotten a well-rooted ideal of a pure protest of anonymous dissatisfaction which somehow surpasses class interests and political affiliations here is a stubborn reluctance to accept what for a lot of women, Roma and workers are actually very strong daily realities: that class interests don't match, that they lead to powerful conflicts and that, somehow, those who lose keep on being the same over the years. There is no democratic chorus of citizens, no "Facebook generation", no beautiful youngsters who would magically find the perfect solution under the conductor's baton of technocracy or civic unity. Such political imageries are the result of violent political exclusions, they rely on the enforced silence of millions for Romanians who are excluded

from the political process, whose voices are hardly heard and whose poverty seldom becomes a matter of concern.

While Crăciun and Lipan do not speak of protesters per se, I agree with their point that the formulation of the idea of middle class development as an unproblematic and apolitical notion of good, proper, and normal life should be read as an ideological element that sustains the continued idealization of middle classness in face of recurrent frustrations and disillusionments. In the vocabulary of this book, this kind of moral politicization may be described as a political condition of reproducing middle class identifications as a form of developmentalist illusion in the context of the crisis. In this reading, the fact that middle class ideologies express political discontent in universalizing moral terms does not exclude their political edge. Indeed, in later moments of the protest wave, conflicts with other strata whom new urban middle classes perceived as competitors dragging back the state policies they would favor expressed the structural politics of the protests in sharper terms, while still maintaining the ideological level of moral and taste-based reflection. Depictions of the uneducated and uncivilized poor, or class-based discrediting of socialist politicians as uneducated or looking below middle class standards, like caricaturing Socialist Prime Minister Dragnea for having bad teeth, belong to this category.

The local constellations of postsocialist development that set the conditions of post-2008 demonstrations in Hungary differed from those of Romania to a significant extent. Here, it was the internal–external alliances supporting liberalization that won the struggle over managing late socialist crisis. Already in the second half of the 1980s, alliances between reform fractions of the party, managerial-technocratic elites involved in incipient privatization, international lenders, and Western capital managed to carry out significant reforms for economic opening. Dissident intellectuals, although temporarily marginalized in the early 1970s, grew into internationally recognized voices of political transition. Organizing in two competing camps—liberal and national-conservative—, they mobilized to achieve political power. In the process of the Round Table Talks, new parties and the socialist party (reorganized as a democratic party) set the foundation of a constitutional democracy. As Szalai (1994b) or Bruszt (1995) pointed out, these talks were a negotiation among Hungary's future political elite. Their main stakes revolved around political institutional power. Stakes of economic power were implicitly involved through political groups' different economic alliances in the already ongoing privatization process.

In the process of the regime change, new parties joined forces in the collective condemnation of socialist centralization and in the struggle for political democratization, as a means to broaden their own space of maneuver. At the same time, in the competition between future political elites, a lasting conflict between liberal and protectionist visions of post-socialist development crystallized. Liberal fractions, including the Alliance of Free Democrats and Fidesz (Federation of Young Democrats) favored a model of world-economic integration through liberalization and foreign direct investments. The conservative-nationalist Hungarian Democratic Forum promoted more protectionist policies favoring domestic embour-geoisement. While new parties wrought severe battles over questions of political influence (like media control and cultural politics), or symbolic issues representing national or Western-led development (like the choice of the coat of arms), their differences implied a strong consensus over the need to overcome popular resistance to marketization, as both liberal and national-capitalist models of postsocialist integration involved processes of privatization, unemployment, and further welfare cuts that harmed workers' interests.

The Hungarian Democratic Forum was formed by the fraction of dissi-dent intellectuals who had been criticizing socialist modernization by reviving poporanist traditions. In the interwar era, poporanist writers and the peasant party criticized capitalist modernization for destroying peasant livelihoods. After 1945, the movement was forced to integrate with the communist party, with one of its main representatives, Ferenc Erdei, becoming a prominent actor of collectivization. Starting from the 1970s, dissidents revived poporanist discourses. This revival carried further a tradition of sociography infused by nationalist sentiments, but omitted the perspective of economic conditions. Instead, the representation of the people was imagined as a work of representing national cultural identity (Papp, 2012). As a party, the Hungarian Democratic Forum relied on this tradition, welding it to expressions of grievances by former middle classes harmed by socialist redistribution. The party's actual constituency was broader than the descendants of interwar bourgeoisie, involving socialist middle classes and lower middle classes, mainly in rural and municipal environments, who saw their interests harmed by the privatization process dominated by alliances between socialist managers and liberal politics (Körösényi, 2000). While struggling to create space for the formation of national capital within conditions dominated by its Western competitors (Szalai, 1994a: 478), the Hungarian Democratic Forum reactualized poporanist slogans in gestures that portrayed its efforts as saving national wealth for the nation as a whole. Beyond symbolic expressions, such gestures included measures like creating farmers' markets where small producers could sell their products, or an ambivalent support provided to workers' struggles for workers' share of property in the privatization process.

While workers' politics during the privatization process was largely characterized by technical coalitions with industrial interests that temporarily opposed or strove to delay privatization, there have been incipient attempts to promote workers' share of property as an element of privatization, and form Workers' Councils that could promote this cause. These instances came to be supported by an anti-bureaucratic Marxist group, Left Alternative, as a possible way of decreasing the social damage and improving workers' position within the privatization process. Left Alternative represented this claim at the Round Table Talks, but the inclusion of workers' share of property as a legitimate element of privatization was consensually rejected by liberal, ex-socialist, and conservative sides. A pact between the two major new political parties, Hungarian Democratic Forum and the Alliance of Free democrats, signed after the first democratic elections, included the point that the principle of workers' self-management and workers' property will be excluded from the new constitution (Szalai, 1994a; Thoma, 1998). On the level of the movement, left alliances were soon superseded by alliance offers from the side of the Hungarian Democratic Forum, from whom workers hoped to gain direct help after their electoral victory. The Forum was motivated to support the movement as a tactic to gain positions against industrial management allied to socialists and liberals; however, it was not interested in promoting results that benefited workers. After a long delay, the Forum government legalized the possibility of workers' property share as an intermediary stage of privatization, at a point where the main struggles of privatization were already over (Szalai, 1994a). The Alliance of Hungarian Workers' Councils gave up its demands for workers' property share in 1992, and continued to exist as a Christian union, in a dependent relationship to right-wing politics.

The other main party of the regime change, the Alliance of Free Democrats followed the tendency of the liberal wing of the dissident tradition, and linked the causes of democracy and human rights to the promotion of market liberalization. If before 1989, this link has been promoted by dissident intellectuals as a means to alleviate problems of poverty and workers' repression, in the politics of the regime change liberals ceased to refer to workers' interests, and the issue of poverty came to be restricted to the area of philanthropy and social policies targeted at most disenfranchised groups. Like all new political initiatives, the liberal fraction of the democratic opposition also created a new union in 1988, when the opportunity to fund new unions was opened before the possibility to create new parties. This union (LIGA) was to fulfill the role of aiding political work and to decrease the infrastructural power of the former national union tied to socialist party structures. In line with this mission, LIGA suspended the representation of workers' interests for the time of the Round Table Talks, defining its aim as supporting the process of political democratization (Thoma, 1998).

The Forum government's efforts to increase its maneuver space within conditions dominated by external-internal alliances promoting liberalization were severely attacked by the liberal opposition as attempts to recentralize political power. In the symbolic frameworks of political struggle, this conflict was represented as a duality of Western-led democratic development versus national embourgeoisement. In these debates, the conflict between liberals and ex-socialists, after constituting a main legitimation framework of liberal politics in 1989, gradually shifted to second place. The main rift of postsocialist politics became that between nationalist development and liberalization, the latter coming to be represented by an increasingly explicit alliance between liberals and socialists. This rapprochement was accelerated by a political scandal where a Forum MP, István Csurka (1992) argued in an article that the failure of the Forum government's economic program is caused by the power of ex-Kádárist networks allied with external lenders. This power, he argued, is so strong that it can govern the economic process outside of the frameworks of parliamentary politics. He interpreted the seemingly contradictory alliance between ex-socialist managers, Western capital, and liberal dissidents as a result of Jewish conspiracy. As a response to this argument, evoking dark memories of interwar right-wing discourses, the Alliance of Free Democrats and the socialists created a common front, stepping up in the name of democracy against nationalism and anti-semitism. After the 1994 elections, these two parties formed a coalition government. As Erzsébet Szalai (1995) pointed out, this solidification of the political field muted social critiques of liberalization: in the liberals' discourse, any argument against liberalization was marked as allied with nationalism and potentially anti-semitism, while on the conservative side, social critiques were merged with, and expressed in the vocabulary of, national capital's interests.

On the level of capitalist alliances, liberal and conservative parties' politics represented the two main political-economic elite blocks that crystallized in the first years after the regime change and continued to define the politics of the next decades (Böröcz & Róna-Tas, 1995; Kolosi & Sági, 1996; Stark & Vedres, 2012; Szalai, 1995; Szelényi et al., 1996). The alliance of liberal and reform socialist politics had strong connections to the managers of earlier state companies and to various international organizations. Due to the significance of earlier company managers in privatization, and the essential role of lack of capital and pressing debt, this block had the upper hand country's FDI and credit-led development. The second block, promoting the interests of an aspiring national bourgeoisie, continued to rely ideologically on the symbolic nationalism of anti-communist interwar bourgeoisie, but struggled to forge a powerful alliance from its constituency scattered across conservative elites, rural middle classes, and entrepreneurs or farmers struggling under the dominance of liberal alliances. In terms of political parties, in the first period of the transition this block was largely represented by the Hungarian Democratic Forum; from 1998 on, Fidesz took over this role, changing its program from liberal anti-communism to that of national embourgeoisement. While political efforts to promote domestic capital were long suppressed by the dominance of liberal internal-external alliances, from 1998, Fidesz engaged in developing allied domestic capital as an economic hinterland (Szelényi, 2016).

In their strategies of political communication, the political representation of each block developed symbolic bridging techniques to paper over the contradiction between the foreign or domestic capitalist interests they promoted and the interests of local workers. Conservatives referred to the need to defend national wealth from Western capital and its allied interests which work for the survival of socialist power. This definition of national wealth obscured interest conflicts between domestic capital and labor by merging them into the idea of an organic national community. In turn, liberals and socialists defined themselves as a democratic front against anti-semitic nationalism. They promoted liberalization as the sole guarantee of catching up with Western standards of democracy and condemned any expression of economic discontent as allied with nationalism. This formal, normative, ascetic notion of democracy represented by the socialist-liberal coalition was solidified by the austerity package they implemented after their election victory in 1994. In portraying expressions of economic grievances as threats against democracy, they could always refer to conservatives' symbolic gestures that blurred the difference between "national wealth" and labor's interests. This mutually reinforcing framework of political bridging techniques I described earlier as an interplay between liberal's "democratic antipopulism" and conservatives' "antidemocratic populism" (Gagyi, 2016: 357).

In the above dynamics, the notions of political left and right came to signify different positions in the case of Hungary than in Romania. While in Romania, the political left was identified with socialists' efforts to continue the main lines of socialist industrializing policies, keep strategic industries, and channel them into domestic hands, in Hungary the political left came to be constituted by reform fractions of the state party that had been already carrying out liberalizing reforms in the 1980s, and their liberal allies. This version of the "left" promoted the type of foreign investment-led neoliberal politics that in the same years in Romania was represented by the liberal opposition (dominated, at the time, by socialists). In Hungary, the protectionist line that favored domestic capital formation, such as the one represented by Romanian socialists, was promoted by the conservative opposition of dominant "left" coalitions.

While competing for elite blocks' mutually reinforcing bridging techniques successfully obscured expressions of class tensions in political debates, these tensions have been nevertheless accumulating in the years following the regime change. Hungary's reintegration into global markets happened under the unfavorable conditions of high levels of public debt, the loss of Comecon export markets, and a severe need for capital (Éber et al., 2014). Throughout a privatization process carried out from that unfavorable bargaining position, international capital entered the country to create export enclaves producing tradable goods, and to capture strategic positions in banking, utilities, retail, telecom, and energy (Böröcz, 1992, 2000; Drahokoupil, 2009; Nölke & Vliegenthart, 2009). The downsizing of local production transformed large segments of the previously full-employed population into a reserve army, a condition for the cheap labor offered to investors. After the issue of labor was sidelined in favor of political bargaining between parties in the process of the regime change (Bruszt, 1995; Szalai, 1995; Thoma, 1998), it was successfully kept from transforming into a political force on its own. Besides gestures of symbolic bridging and the narrowing unions' maneuver space, pacification through social benefits also played a part in the subduing of labor's voice. Unemployment, together with a new system of state subsidies divided between multiple types of pensions and unemployment benefits, set affected groups in competition against each other, resulting in a strategy Pieter Vanhuysse described as "divide and pacify" (2006). Literature on the lack of politicization of postsocialist unemployment in Hungary has also emphasized the individualization of systemic risks (Bartha, 2011b), patience induced by catching-up expectations (Beissinger et al., 2014), and the capacity of newly installed infrastructures of political democracy to channel dissent into protest votes (Bohle & Greskovits, 2012).

While foreign direct investment sustained Hungary's solvency during the 1990s, its benefits were hardly felt by workers, who struggled to find new employment under conditions of steep depreciation and new investments that created low positions in manufacturing chains. As privatization exhausted by the end of the decade, investments slowed, but profits and dividends continued to leave the country. Under these conditions, regional competition for foreign investments sharpened, further weakening and depreciating local labor. While the shock therapy of the 1995 austerity package stood out as a symbolic moment of anti-labor policies, successive left and right governments continued to weaken workers' rights, suppress unions, and further flexibilize labor, to keep in line with regional competition. Despite these measures, by the early 2000s, the slowdown of foreign investment led to a new increase in deficit and external debt. After the full convertibility of the Forint was introduced in 2001, and the country joined the EU in 2004, foreign banks owning 70% of the local market started to push foreign exchange loans. In a few years, private companies, households, the state and local governments all became indebted in foreign currencies (Éber et al., 2019). If the swift process of Hungarian privatization was a model case of property shift in the service of core capital's crisis management, the debt wave of the 2000s incadrated in a move where the exhaustion of Western and Southern European loan markets was compensated by more risky and more profitable constructs directed at East European markets (Raviv, 2008). This second, debt-led phase of the neoliberal regime of accumulation and world-economic integration already showed signs of crisis by the mid-2000s. Problems in the public budget attracted inspection by international lenders, while the cumulative effects of liberalization and austerity policies led to public discontent. Another source of delegitimation was that under conditions of trade deficit and growing public and private debt, state policies became fully dependent on European transfers, which fixed state action within the frameworks of European policies characterized by several researchers as a phase of authoritarian neoliberalism (Bohle & Greskovits, 2012; Bruff, 2014; Medve-Bálint & Šćepanović, 2019). Despite the efforts of the socialist-liberal government to alleviate the political effects of this situation by private Keynesian policies promoting debt-led consumption, by the mid-2000s not only unions, but also national-capitalist fractions based in former alliances between socialist managers and liberal politics were alienated from the coalition—the latter regrouping around contender nationalist politics of Fidesz.

Meanwhile, right-wing contender politics developed under the domination of the neoliberal integration model successfully created a broader political subculture of right-wing anti-neoliberalism, and channeled popular discontent into the organizational structures of right-wing politics through various means. As several studies showed, the extreme right movement Jobbik, which turned into a party in 2003, and Fidesz' strategy to create a nation-wide network of citizens' circles as an alternative institutional system of political mobilization after losing the 2002 elections, successfully established the idea of national resistance as the answer to grievances suffered by former industrial and agricultural workers during the decades of neoliberal integration (Bartha, 2011a; Halmai, 2011; Greskovits, 2017; Szombati, 2018); Varga, 2014). The stiff resistance of socialist-liberal politics and related expert and cultural publicity to give any space to expressions of economic grievances supported this process. As an activist of the alterglobalization movement put it, in terms of any left critique, the liberal-dominated public sphere of the 2000s worked as a "vacuum press": "you had to be extremely cautious with every word, because the smallest expression of social critique could mark you forever as an antisemite" (Gagyi, 2011: 184).

In 2006, following a leaked speech by socialist Prime Minister Ferenc Gyurcsány in which he admitted to have lied about the public budget, a series of violent protests broke out in Budapest. While right-wing groups dominated the front lines, the protests were largely spontaneous, and demonstrators came from various backgrounds. However, the government's reaction which reached the level of police abuse helped to channel discontent toward vocabularies already prepared by previous constellations of the political sphere. While Fidesz initially delimited itself from the politics of the streets, it soon came to position itself on the side of suppressed protesters (for instance by a media event where Fidesz leaders destroyed the cordon that had been set up to keep demonstrators away from the Parliament). Next year, Fidesz initiated a national referendum against a new system of personal payments that the Gyurcsány government planned to introduce in public healthcare and education as a first step toward marketization. The success of this referendum fortified Fidesz as the representative of anti-neoliberal struggle. When in response to the referendum, Gyurcsány dismissed the healthcare minister delegated by the Alliance of Free Democrats, the latter withdrew its delegates from the government and broke the coalition. The 2009 European and 2010 parliamentary elections institutionalized the change in political power: Jobbik became a parliamentary party, the classic parties of the regime change (Hungarian Democratic Forum and the Alliance of Free Democrats) were disbanded, and Fidesz, winning a landslide victory that allowed itself to govern with a supermajority, embarked on transforming external-internal structures of Hungary's integration to the benefit of its own alliances. Politics Can Be Different, a party established on the base of the alterglobalist version of 2000s anti-neoliberalism also got into parliament.

The new Fidesz government declared the program of "central power space" in internal politics, and the program of "economic freedom fight" in external politics (Wiedermann, 2014). What these slogans expressed on the symbolic level was an endeavor to reconfigure internal–external relations of systemic integration in a way that could re-boost growth, allow the regime to stabilize its power (including support by external capitalist alliances), and carve out a broader maneuver space to benefit state-supported domestic capital (Éber et al., 2019). This program relied on the conditions of strong centralization of administrative power. The government repeatedly rewrote the constitution, changed the electoral law, increased media control, narrowed the autonomy of the judiciary, centralized the decision-making power of local governments, reorganized institutions of science, culture, and education, and disbanded remaining forms of public consultation (Kovács & Trencsényi, 2019; Magyar & Vásárhelyi, 2017).

Relying on the centralization of administrative power, the regime started to realign internal–external class relations along with a complex portfolio where dependent modes of external integration were combined with alleys of internal accumulation. Research by the Working Group for Public Sociology "Helyzet" (Barna et al., 2019; Jelinek & Pinkasz, 2014) linked the regimes' policy types to different aspects of that portfolio. The first aspect is macrostability: policies aiming to reduce deficit and external debt served to simultaneously increase investment appetite into the Hungarian economy, and reduce direct dependence on lenders in order to gain policy autonomy for measures that serve domestic capital. In external financing, a related aspect was the shift from exclusive dependence on Western lenders to other—dominantly: Russian and Chinese—capital, in the hope to create more autonomy vis-a-vis Western lenders.

The second aspect of the regime's integration portfolio is the encouragement of foreign direct investment into export manufacturing. As Hungarian companies do not have the capacities to compete on external markets, keeping up export in order to maintain the balance of trade, create trade surplus, and produce foreign currency reserves was a key condition of macroeconomic stability and policy autonomy (Becker et al., 2015; Éber et al., 2014). Benefiting from a new wave of industrial outsourcing that started after 2008, the regime invested heavily into attracting export industrial capacities. Besides providing the most generous subsidies for industrial relocations within regional competition (Gerőcs & Pinkasz, 2019), it amended labor regulation to fit investors' needs, reorganized education to channel labor into cheap semi-skilled positions, and introduced a corporate tax level that is the lowest among EU states. Some of these industrial policies were co-drafted with German lobby organizations, such as the German—Hungarian Chamber of Industry and Commerce (Dull, 2018). Further amended at later points to follow investors' needs, these policies created a cheap and flexible labor source for investors, reduced trade union activity, and for a while, provided a source of symbolic legitimation based on the idea of technological development creating new jobs. At the same time, the same policies created a strong exposure to the global crisis of manufacturing—and within it, dominantly: the long crisis of the German automotive industry—, specializing in a position where the production of elements declining in their product life-cycle was outsourced in order to maintain their profitability temporarily through increasing standardization and cheap labor (Gerőcs & Pinkasz, 2019).

In the sphere of domestic service industries, where the state has a larger capacity to shape market conditions, economic policy served to broaden domestic capital accumulation. In branches like retail, media, telecommunication, transport, energy, or construction, policies favored domestic actors and discriminated against foreign capital. In banking, a less conflictual but similar shift took place. The government bought insolvent assets of foreign banks hit by the financial crisis in a relatively high price. This move allowed the regime to reestablish domestic financial capital and start building protected circuits of domestic capital across financial and domestic service industries sectors (Gagyi et al., 2019; Mihályi, 2015; Pósfai et al., 2017). Together with tax policies and redistribution favoring the capitalization of a new upper middle class, whose savings are channeled into domestic consumption, new circuits of state-supported housing mortgages directed into new construction, as well as Forint state bonds, these measures constitute a third aspect of policies, which aims the broadening and protection of domestic capital.

Finally, the regulation and control of labor and the unemployed is a fourth aspect of the regime that has been increasingly imposed throughout the years. Besides the reconfiguration of labor regulation and education, an important element of these policies has been the introduction of the workfare model (first proposed by the Socialists after 2008). This scheme substituted universal unemployment benefits and tied participation in the program to "invitations" laid out by local governments. The high discretionary power of local governments made the workfare program a successful tool of political control over the most disadvantaged groups—illustrated by regions with the highest unemployment reaching the highest shares of pro-government votes in subsequent elections (Jandó, 2018). This shift expanded and radicalized the trend that continuously decreased the universality of social policies and distorted redistribution to the benefit of middle classes since the 1970s (Ferge, 2017; Szalai, 2007). However, due to the immense pressure put on labor by the double extraction stream the regime's model rested upon, by the mid-2010s a strong wave of work migration started, and both foreign and domestic capital faced an increasing problem of labor shortage. In these conditions, rural unemployment started to serve as a source of internal work migration, and the strategic significance of the workfare program shrunk (Czirfusz et al., 2019). Measures of control of the poor also included more direct and coercive steps, like anti-homeless legislation (Udvarhelyi, 2014). Related ideological campaigns linked the idea of job creation through reindustrialization and the introduction of workfare to the idea of transcending the "welfare state" toward a "work-based state". As Viktor Orbán put it:

every state needs to carry out the correction of the welfare state. This is harder to do in the West, because there you have broad structures of welfare state, in Eastern Europe it's easier, because we don't have them. We are stumbling across the ruins and half-built new constructs of post-socialist economic systems, but have no welfare state. Our program is that instead of the uncompetitive model of Western welfare states, we create a work-based society. (Napi.hu, 2012)

Ideological gestures of inclusion and exclusion were strongly employed by the government to complement and compensate for effects of new policies. The middle class, a key topic of Fidesz' politics since its first cycle between 1998 and 2002, remained central government communication. While actual policies increased the polarization of the middle class, enriching a narrower circle of new middle class and letting others—teachers, doctors, or the largest part of professionals squeezed into increasingly precarious market jobs—suffer the effects of downward mobility, government communication continued to address the middle class as the universal subject of the nation. Reorganizations of social policy or housing support that increased social polarization were expressed in the general language of "families" (Scharle & Szikra, 2015), translated on billboards and loan advertisements into images of middle class family life. The ideological use of the idea of the family was completed by a communication campaign that promoted traditional female roles as a symbolic cover for increasing the burden of care work on women while denying the fact that it is work (Csányi, 2019; Kováts, 2018). Blue-collar workers, while being channeled into structures of reindustrialization that were made possible by freezing their potential for advocacy, were included into ideological discourses by emphasizing decent work versus the state dependence of the undeserving poor. The workfare model also functioned as a public dramatization of this ideology, representing the idea that the regime puts the unemployed—defined with ethnic undertones alluding to the Roma—to work. Next to punitive measures such as anti-homeless legislation, the main tool of symbolic delimitations that served to include groups otherwise disfavored by the regime's policies into the circle of deserving citizens was the against migration that started in 2015. Reacting to a problem of declining popularity after the elections of 2014, this campaign forged a successful ideological tool that was able to portray the regime as beneficial to all Hungarians, despite its strongly exploitative character.

In its first cycle after 2010, the Fidesz government included some selective measures of economic inclusion into its policies, in line with the social lines of its anti-neoliberal discourse practiced in the election campaign. These included measures like distributing nationalized tobacco shop licenses to politically loyal families or providing state subsidies to energy bills (practically subsidizing providers with growing domestic shares). In the following cycles, however, tensions generated by aggressive wealth concentration were rather tackled by stepping up ideological campaigns, around a narrative that charged Western powers' ("Brussels") and internal opposition with a conspiracy that aimed to replace Hungarians by migration (kormany.hu, 2017). After years of political campaigns, by 2017 Hungarians who never came in touch with migrants mentioned migration as the number one threat to their security (Pew, 2017). NGOs were targeted as an element of that alliance, with references to George Soros's support for main liberal NGOs (Gagyi, 2017). Conflicts with European politics over issues of de-democratization (Staudenmaier, 2018), were made use in government communication as a proof of international attacks against Hungary, strengthening the position of the government as the nation's defender.

Meanwhile, local opposition's alliance with Western critiques of de-democratization was largely associated with the delegitimation of previous socialist-liberal politics (Böcskei, 2016; Scheiring, 2016; Sebők, 2016). The significance of local "left" politics was arguably upheld rather by government communication's image of a mighty enemy, than its actual influence. The stronger political contender was Jobbik, which grew into the largest oppositional party. Jobbik applied the same national rhetoric as the government without carrying the responsibility for economic extraction and started to criticize the regime from a right populist stance. By 2018, Jobbik was also defeated: taking over its ideological statements, and pushing it to reframe its politics as a more mainstream one, the Fidesz managed to divide and then break the party. Fidesz won a third supermajority in the 2018 parliamentary elections, with the strong application of all tools of political control and electoral machinery built out in previous years. However, the 2019 local elections brought a series of victories by oppositional coalitions. This was due to oppositional negotiations reaching an agreement on a joint electoral strategy, as well as to local electoral coalitions that expressed the discontent of local elites and middle classes affected by the regime's extreme accumulation measures. While oppositional governments are struggling with a narrow maneuver space due to Fidesz' centralization of power, their organizational and political base might play an important role in the 2022 elections, the first parliamentary elections that Fidesz meets under the conditions of a new economic crisis instead of post-2008 recovery.

In the above context, in Hungary, the mobilizations that could be considered as part of the post-2008 global wave appeared along with specific splits. The burst of discontent and disillusionment with the neoliberal project of development that happened in 2006 was dominantly thematized in the frameworks of right-wing anti-neoliberalism, developed by dominated conservative postsocialist elites and new right movements of the 2000s. The fact that Fidesz successfully channeled this discontent into electoral struggle against the socialist-liberal coalition, and then used it to legitimate its own accumulation regime, defined the political space in which discontent with postcrisis policies came to be expressed after 2010.

During the time of liberal hegemony, right-wing oppositional politics formed networks that connected party structures to grassroots mobilizations (Halmai, 2011; Szombati, 2018), with constituencies ranging from conservative elites to lower middle class and workers' participation in new right political subcultures. For these networks, the Fidesz government brought an increasing fragmentation. Jobbik was pushed to reformulate its political lines and finally broke along tensions between hardliners and those seeking more populist directions. The broader hinterland of right-wing movements came to be simultaneously nurtured by Fidesz communication and fragmented by its practical politics of centralized control. One important example of the political and class aspects of pre-2010 anti-austerity movements is that of the forex debtors' movement. This kind of mobilization rose in the wake of a sweeping debt crisis affecting families who took mortgages in foreign currencies (Dancsik et al., 2015). Initially, Fidesz' communication incorporated debtors' problems, promising to punish banks and save debtors in line with its "economic freedom fight". But its actual measures to tackle the debt crisis served the restabilization of the banking sector and property shifts benefiting domestic financial (Gagyi et al., 2019). While debtors in better positions were helped to reintegrate in domestic circuits of lending, families who took mortgages out of necessity rather than as an investment remained without help.

Disillusioned by earlier promises, by 2013 the debtors' movement turned against the Fidesz government, but struggled to make its voice heard. The government's sweeping communication campaign which stated that the problem of forex debt had been solved, as well as its steps to make debtors' contestations legally impossible (Kiss, 2018) effectively silenced the debtors' movement. The "left" opposition's distancing from the debtors' movement contributed to this effect. In contrast with European and North American cases where housing debt became a leading issue of anti-austerity pro-democracy politics after 2008, in Hungary the issue of forex debt was not included into oppositional agendas—both because former professional elites of the neoliberal regime did not acknowledge their claims as legitimate, and because left fractions of oppositional politics felt alienated by their use of right-wing anti-neoliberal frameworks of the pre-2010 oppositional culture.

Like elsewhere, major demonstration waves after 2010 were defined by middle class constituencies. While the Fidesz government's economic policies actually favored (upper) middle classes, and were most detrimental to the poor (Kolosi & Fábián, 2016), its dismantling of political and cultural institutional systems of the former liberal hegemony (from media centralization or the reorganization of research and higher education to a full transformation of cultural financing and the attacks against NGOs) put a strong pressure on experts and intellectuals previously integrated into those structures. The dismantling of these structures and Fidesz' attacks on cosmopolitan liberal values were also rejected by younger generations aspiring to future professional careers. After 2010, demonstration waves regularly erupted in response to specific measures or at the occasion of historical anniversaries of 1848 or 1956 revolutions. Most demonstrations thematized problems that these groups found most important: the rewriting of the constitution, the centralization of the media, the reorganization of higher education, a plan to tax internet traffic as part of an austerity package in 2014, the closure of the Central European University, and the abolishment of the independent status of the Hungarian Academy. Demonstrations were organized ad hoc, based on networks and skills brought from previous civil society or professional connections, or gathered throughout protest events (Krasztev & Til, 2015; Szabó & Mikecz, 2015). The preparation of demonstrations happened along with informal networks, most often by invitation. Unlike Romanian or other post-2008 movements that rejected central organization and public speeches, and only used speakers and human mic, in Hungary demonstrations were organized in a more traditional manner, with stages, sound systems, selected speakers, and pre-written speeches. This was largely due to the existence of previous liberal civic networks which got activated as one of the main organizational channels of the protests (Rammelt, 2018).

Unions responding to anti-union legislation (like in the case of police or firefighters' unions in 2011), or to reorganizations of respective branches—most emphatically: teachers and healthcare workers—also took part in these demonstrations, and organized their own protests as well. Next to other issues like students' protests, advocacy groups' protests against anti-homeless legislation, anti-Roma discrimination, women's rights, anti-migration campaigns, or mobilizations responding to specific local decisions like that of the reconstruction of the Városliget park, unions' issues were often included in big demonstrations' agendas in the form of invited speakers, including their claims among demonstrators' demands, and providing organizational or communication support to their own initiatives. However, they remained in a status of illustrations to main political narratives that attributed all grievances to the anti-liberal and anti-Western stance of the Orbán regime and demanded a return to the path of Western-type modernization and democracy. Geopolitical metaphors expressing this division permeated demonstrations from speeches or slogans to European flags and red flags featuring Putin and Orban's portraits. Attempts to put the European flag on the parliament or other public institution, sometimes with the aid of oppositional politicians, became a recurrent element of demonstrations.

Due to the strong delegitimation of socialist-liberal coalitions that represented this idea, and their close association with the idea of corruption, demands to return to the path of European democracy risked to run into a contradiction when translated into the language of party politics. Protesters made recurrent efforts to keep themselves at a distance from illegitimate political actors of the "left"—who, on their own side, did everything to portray protests as expressions of popular support for their politics. Coming close to the 2014 parliamentary elections, informal leadership formed within the networks that organized demonstrations, together with architects of political maneuvering from oppositional parties tried to channel demonstrations' energy to support a new party (Together), established around the figure of entrepreneur and economist Gordon Bajnai, former neoliberal minister of economy and then prime minister of the Gyurcsány government.

While democracy was the main slogan of demonstrations, and protest organizers made gestures to reinforce this message by symbolic gestures of inclusion—e.g. by distributing symbolic press cards at demonstrations, symbolizing the message that when media becomes dominated by the government, everyone becomes a journalist—the fact that organizations representing demonstrations' energy are joining Bajnai's party was decided in closed informal circles, and brought a surprise not only to protest participants, but even to many organizers. This relation between democratic claims and informal power practices was reminiscent of dissidents' democratic claims and practice in 1989. Lacking a deeper embeddedness and carrying the stigma of socialist-liberal delegitimation, Together failed at the elections. Meanwhile, Politics Can Be Different went through a party split over the issue of alliance with Together. In a conflict resembling postsocialist political debates, one fraction of the initially anti-neoliberal party rejected the alliance with former neoliberal socialists, yet another claimed that this alliance is the only way to block the spread of the extreme right, and interpreted internal opposition to the alliance as coming from internal right-wing tendencies. Politics can be Different made it through the parliamentary threshold, but some of its members continued to represent not the party but the formation that split from it (Dialogue for Hungary). This, in turn, gave space for government critiques portraying Dialogue for Hungary as the opposition that nobody voted for.

After the elections, protests renewed, once again delinking from the political infrastructures of the earlier "left". Based on representative surveys with protesters demonstrating against the issue of internet tax in autumn 2014, Szabó and Mikecz (2015) defined protesters as voters without a party, meaning that while their political preferences match the ideological profile of the former "left", this preference does not result in a party choice in present conditions. Szabó and Mikecz conclude that due to this identification with the ideological position of the former political "left", post-2010 demonstrations cannot be regarded as a spontaneous outbreak of general civic activity, or the embodiment of a more general critique represented by Occupy-type movements, but rather a protest movement of former "left" voters who were left without a legitimate political choice. Once again, liberal civil society networks became an important base for protest politics both in terms of organization and of conceptual frameworks. As one organizer of the new group "We won't be silenced!", formed from 2014 internet tax demonstrations, put it:

We are indignant and angry with the political elite that had 25 years at its disposal to put the country in order but didn't do it. We are not here to protest for a specific issue, like the internet tax, we want a new regime change. Not only the resignation of the Orbán government: our aim is that new communities are formed, that there be a paradigm change in politics. We need a bottom-up, civic initiative that can form the base on which we can build in the future. (Dalbóczy, 2014)

Such general programs of re-democratization based on civic participation were similar to those of Occupy-type movements. However, in their claims to recreate and reactualize the regime change as a chance of catch-up development, as well as in their contradictory relation to democratic participation, they were more similar to dissidents' civil society programs. Just like in the case of pre-2014 pro-democracy mobilizations, post-2014 protests continued to be organized by informal networks and did not build broader organizations of democratic representation and control.

The organization that followed Occupy's idea of horizontal participatory democracy the closest was the Students' Network. Founded by a left student group in 2011, the organization consciously avoided to define its political line and hoped to coalesce it through participative deliberation. The Network organized protests and occupations against the reorganization of higher education and joined general anti-regime protests. Despite its broad practices of participative deliberation, the Network also shifted toward the Together coalition in 2014, by a combined effect of informal meetings and government communication which lumped it together with the "Bajnai guard" (MTI, 2013). On the side of protest participants, the lack of broader organizational structures was reflected in spontaneous moves at protests, like rallies that attempted to take symbolic buildings like the national television headquarters or the Parliament, which broke off from previously organized and coordinated protest agendas, with organizers struggling to take responsibility for their consequences (Dalbóczy, 2014).

Throughout post-2014 demonstrations, networks of mobilization groups skilled in protest organization and communication were reinforced. New left and independent media initiatives (like Mérce, Új Egyenlőség, or Slejm—later: Partizán) started to play an increasing role in the representation and interpretation of protests, in parallel with the government's narrowing of former liberal media space. Still, the main symbolic opposition between national and Western-led development, established by postsocialist political divisions, continued to dominate the discourse and public interpretation of protest events. These interpretations were strongly supported by Western political and media commentary, and its domestic use by protesters, political opposition, and the government. Western political and media commentary dominantly interpreted the Orbán regime's illiberal turn by reactualizations of Cold War East–West geopolitical differentiations supported by references to new geopolitical tensions with Russia, China, or Turkey. In these frameworks, anti-government protests that demanded a return to Europeanization and democracy were portrayed in ways very similar to Cold War portrayals of local dissidents.

If Romanian protests were represented as a political "awakening" (LA Times, 2017), reactualizing the framework of postsocialist development as a long-dragging but finally fulfilling process, where civic organization finally becomes able to "nurture a fragile democracy" (MacGoy, 2019), Hungarian protests were portrayed as elements of a historical drama centered around the dismantling of earlier achievements of democratization. Here, it was the destruction of Western-oriented development and the turn toward Eastern models of despotism that constituted the main narrative, understood as a dark warning sign regarding populist threats against Western democracies themselves (e.g. Krugman, 2012; Traynor, 2014). If media pictures of Romanian protesters casting light from their smartphones could be associated with the idea of a final victory of democratization, reinforcing transitional narratives, similar pictures of Hungarian protests were interpreted in a more melodramatic tone, portraying protesters—especially after Trump's electoral victory—as the last representatives of the true direction of historical development amidst a world-historical decay exemplified by the Orbán regime (Gagyi, 2014). As one protest banner described the historical implosion of the democratization project as an incomprehensible failure in the logic of history: Hungary was downloading democracy, but ran into a "fatal error".

This perception was not limited to the streets, but shared widely across various levels of protest slogans and commentaries. Historians János Mátyás Kovács and Balázs Trencsényi, as editors of the scholarly volume *Brave new Hungary*, described the Orbán regime as an anti-modern power that is "rolling back time" (Kovács & Trencsényi, 2019: 381). If Romanian protests were recurrently represented as the first and largest mobilization event after decades of passivity, the final culmination of the transition story, and obscured previous mobilizations, the idea of a historical failure in Hungary's case was so strong that, even in the eighth year of anti-government protests developing along relatively similar scenarios, protests could be described as a "rare display of dissent" in Orban's Hungary (Kingsley, 2018).

A major metaphor around which this alignment of internal and external voices coalesced in Hungary was the government's attack on NGOs and the Central European University, as an element of its campaign for the 2018 parliamentary elections (Gagyi, 2017). The government's narrative linked both liberal NGO activity and the CEU to the person of George Soros, Hungarian-American billionaire and philanthropist. While this campaign followed lines set by international political advisors who applied similar strategies around the vilification of Soros's figure worldwide (Grassegger, 2019), in Hungary similar references to Soros were present on the political right since the early 1990s (Bátorfy & Tremmel, 2019), and in the eyes of many, were supported by Soros's strong role in funding the institutions that prepared liberal hegemony from arts to business education, as well as his speculative action against the Forint in 2009. CEU, funded by Soros, was attacked by the government as a representative of Soros's unwelcome interference with Hungarian politics. On the side of Hungarian anti-government protesters, it was seen as a last bastion of links to superior Western standards. In a context where Hungarian institutions of higher education and the academy were already going through reorganizations, solidarity actions, and protests against attacks on CEU expressed last hopes in the strength of Western links—as the saying went among protesters: "If they can do it to CEU, they can do it to everyone". Meanwhile, Western commentaries treated attacks against CEU as a symbol of attacks against the historical project of liberal democracy.

Such links between local and Western reactualizations of transitional narratives effectively obscured the contradictions of postsocialist uneven development, including the connections between limited democratization, the social effects of neoliberal politics, and East–West hierarchies of economic and political "Europeanization", which ultimately prepared the ground for the shift in the balance of forces toward a right-wing local hegemony. Mutual support among Western and local oppositional commentaries reinforced a reactualization of normative transitional frameworks, colored by a grief over the historical defeat of superior values. If in Romania, demonstrations' emotional charge was defined by middle class self-pity over the loss of mobility possibilities (despite superior merits), in

Hungary a very similar emotional charge was expressed in terms of feelings of melancholy over the victory of political evil over political good, and the uplifting effect of collective experience in demonstrations was often formulated as the experience that people with the right ideals and political character still exist.

In post-2010 Hungarian politics, social and liberal streams of critique were pushed in the same corner of oppositional politics. Demonstrations did not reject social issues, but rather embraced them as further arguments toward their own cause, similar to pre-1989 dissidents. After the failure of Together at the 2014 elections, politicians and experts of the former socialist-liberal bloc turned from blaming people's lack of political culture toward standpoints of left populism, emphasizing the importance to react to people's needs and reach out to them with political messages that they find relevant. The socialists started their 2018 election campaign with the slogan "Let the rich pay!", in close competition with Jobbik's "You work. They steal". While the main political framework of anti-government politics continued to be defined by the reactualization of transition ideals and claims return to the European path of development, and a new, explicitly centrist liberal party, Momentum, grew out from protest waves, the general oppositional direction came to be colored by a social sensitivity and an association of European models with that of broadening the welfare state. This posed another contrast to the Romanian case, where middle class demonstrators' reclaiming of the transitional program implied explicit anti-poor stances.

Conclusion

The chapter followed transformations of systemic integration in the case of Hungary and Romania after the crisis of the 1970s, and pointed out linkages between global cyclical shifts, local regimes, and their contestations after 1973 and 2008. The aim of the analysis was to show how movements reacting to the same global crisis develop within different local constellations of global integration, and express effects of long-term processes through alliances and vocabularies shaped by the conditions of those constellations. The ideas of socialism/postsocialism and Europeanization were interpreted within these contexts as symbols of developmentalist illusion activated in particular contexts of internal–external alliances. The chapter maintained that socialist state economies have always been integrated into the capitalist world economy, their import substitution industrialization efforts internalized its priorities, and the crisis of late socialist economies was organically tied to global dynamics of the 1970s crisis. Late socialist crisis measures, and increasingly, postsocialist transition and Europeanization, constituted an integration of these economies into the process of core capital's crisis management in a subordinated position. Despite this structural background, ideas of postsocialist transition and Europeanization were strongly associated with promises of catch-up development. In post-2008 movements, expressions of disillusionment over failed promises reactualized these symbols along with contemporary sociopolitical alliances. The chapter argued that similarities between European left narratives of the crisis of "democratic capitalism" and East European claims to resurrect and fulfill the promises of transition provided a ground for symbolic connections, yet these connections in fact obscure a closer understanding of mutual positions within the same crisis process.

The reaction of Hungarian and Romanian regimes to the challenges posed by the 1970s global crisis differed significantly, based on conditions set by different paths of de-Stalinization. In Hungary, consolidation after the 1956 revolution gave space to socialist market reforms, which strengthened reform fractions within the party, weakened the power of centralist alliances favoring forced industrialization, and built out a strong expert strata within reform institutions. In the context of surging external debt after 1973, these alliances, supported by the influence of international lender institutions, ultimately won the struggle over managing the crisis. The alliance between lender institutions favoring marketization, reform socialists and socialist managers benefiting from privatization, and dissident intellectuals mobilizing for political positions came to dominate Hungary's integration model from the years of privatization throughout the debt-led development of the 2000s. The exhaustion of capitalist growth based on Western capital inflow, together with the political delegitimation of the liberal coalition that represented it, opened space for a shift of power relations that allowed previously dominated contender elites to take control of the state, and engage in the reorganization of integration in favor of state-supported domestic capital.

In Romania, former party elites managed to retain their power during de-Stalinization and continued the program of forced industrialization. This included a larger autonomy from the Soviet Union and the Comecon international labor distribution, stepping up power centralization and military control in lack of Soviet support, and the reorientation of external trade toward Western and Third World collaborations. In this context, Ceauşescu's initial opening toward experts' reform ideas by the end of the 1960s gave space to the reinforcement of forced industrialization under central control, the marginalization and scapegoating of experts and intellectuals, and a form of populism that symbolically emphasized direct contacts between the leader and the people. This regime reacted to the crisis of the 1970s by increased efforts to maintain control and continue industrialization. To avoid the influence of external lenders on policy, in the 1980s the Ceauşescu regime engaged in a program of extreme austerity to pay back debt. While social tensions accumulated within the regime led to the only bloody revolution in the region in 1989, in the lack of a strong reform fraction within the party and broader alliances with intellectuals and movements favoring liberalization, the political elite that came to power after 1989 was dominated by ex-socialist cadres who continued the program of protectionism and industrialization, in a version that favored the protected development of domestic capital. This political line remained dominant throughout the 1990s, despite contestation by anti-communist dissidents and international institutions. It was only broken in the 2000s, as contender internal–external alliances gained ground with NATO and EU accession. The 2000s brought a relatively late wave of foreign direct investment and loans, which reinforced liberal positions. After the crisis of 2008, the struggle between still powerful ex-socialist networks and liberal-technocratic elite blocs intensified, working toward a power shift to the benefit of the latter.

In terms of party politics, Hungary's political spectrum came to be polarized between two competing elite blocs, which supported competing models of capitalist integration favoring Western vs. domestic capital. Supporters of the former model, represented politically by the coalition between liberals and socialists, portrayed their politics of transition as that of democratization and marketization following Western models in order to catch up with Western standards. Contender elites built out a nationalist-conservative critique of liberalization, which contrasted the program to save national wealth to what they portrayed as the exploitation of the nation by Western capital and its internal allies. With left critiques successfully subdued, popular discontent with the liberal model by the mid-2000s came to be expressed in the frameworks of nationalist anti-neoliberalism formulated by conservative contender elites and contributed to the landslide victory of Fidesz in 2010. Making use of a parliamentary supermajority, Viktor Orbán's government engaged in a process of power centralization, and used the state to reorganize internal–external capital alliances in a way that combined providing favorable conditions to industrial foreign direct investment, carving out new space of maneuver for building domestic capital, and a geopolitical diversification of financial dependence.

The chapter looked at post-1973 and post-2008 protests in the two countries in terms of their embeddedness in local integration constellations. In the case of late socialist mobilizations, it showed that while both Hungarian environmental and Romanian workers' movements reacted to similar pressures of world-economic integration, the agency, alliances, and symbolic memory of the movements differed significantly in the two contexts of integration constellations. In Hungary the environmental movement was organized and represented by dissident intellectuals who used intellectual arguments to produce an abstract political criticism of the system. Due to stronger Western connections, to the influence of Western publicity due to lenders' influence, and to organizers' participation in the politics of the regime change, narratives of the regime change included the environmental movement as an organic part of the process that led from socialism to democratization. In Romania, on the contrary, workers' mobilizations focused on material claims and operated within a personal bargaining framework set by the regime. They were less in the position to produce abstract expressions of political critique that could resonate well in Western publicity, and lacked alliances with dissident intellectuals who could mediate such critiques. They had weaker Western connections, and the regime's enmity toward Western influence did not allow for using Western publicity as a resource. The regime's double strategy that repressed intellectuals and symbolically emphasized direct connections to workers came to be internalized by intellectuals' resentment against the regime as an idea of an actual coalition between communism and uneducated workers. This framework was reinforced by the ex-socialist party's use of miners to suppress anti-government demonstrations in 1990. Due to these conditions, workers' struggle under late socialism did not become an organic part of intellectual narratives of the regime change, and the idea of an unholy alliance between ex-communist politics and the uneducated masses remained a lasting element of intellectual politics.

After 2008, both countries saw a protracted series of large demonstrations, dominated by middle class constituencies of major cities. The politics of these demonstrations were strongly marked by the different contexts of postsocialist integration. In Hungary, Fidesz channeled the energy of anti-neoliberal demonstrations in 2006 toward its own electoral success in 2010. After 2010, it was elements of educated middle classes who lost positions or career hopes within former institutions of liberal hegemony that politically dominated the protests, organizing around issues like changes of the constitution, media centralization, or higher education reform. This particularly politicized segment of the Hungarian middle class defined the direction of demonstrations in the terms of the formerly dominant liberal bloc's transitional program. In these frameworks, reverberated across Western commentaries, Orbán's politics was interpreted as a fatal error in the normal process of Western-oriented development. In Romania, the first instances of middle class protests after 2008 included reactions to austerity politics that were potentially open to alliances with workers and the poor. By 2013, however, the recovery of crisis-driven foreign direct investment and respective possibilities of competitive mobility for new urban middle classes resulted in a new combination with the intensification of intra-elite struggles, which channeled protest energies into the political support of liberal-technocratic blocs against the socialists. Within the framework set by this alliance, protests expressed the disillusionment with the promises of the regime change as the problem of corruption, sustained by the alliance of ex-communist politics and the uneducated poor. Tensions of middle class mobility were expressed in political narratives that represented protests as a new chance to embark on the road of Western-led catch-up development. In spite of their anti-poor stances, protests were widely represented in Western publicity as a "political awakening" of Romanians that finally can bring the hopes of democratic transition to fulfillment.

In both countries, the effects of the 2008 crisis intensified the contradictions of postsocialist integration and facilitated power shifts along with external-internal coalitions that mobilized to optimize integration functions within narrowing possibilities of world-economic crisis. Post-2008 protest waves selectively politicized the effects of these changes, linking middle class ambitions to reactualizations of transitional developmentalist programs. While they did this from positions that drove toward opposite poles of the local political palette, both reactualizations of transitional narratives obscured the social tensions implied in the transition process—including workers' mobilizations within the post-2008 wave. Research on these movements, including Henry Rammelt's (2018) comparative study of Hungarian and Romanian mobilizations after 2008, have described them as a new wave of civic democratization that might make up for the inadequacies of postsocialist transition. In contrast to such approaches, this chapter argued that when new Hungarian and Romanian movements emphasize the ideas of democracy and development as universally beneficial claims, these notions play the role of an ideological element in a selective struggle, where middle class fractions mobilize along with specific internal–external alliances for developmental projects within a narrowing space of global capitalist competition.

REFERENCES

Abăsează, R. (2018). Collective memory and social movements in times of crisis: The case of Romania. *Nationalities Papers, 46*(4), 671–684.

Adăscăliței, D., & Guga, S. (2016). *Tensions in the periphery: Dependence and the trajectory of a low-cost productive model in the Central and Eastern European Automotive Industry.* Center for Policy Studies, Central European University.

Adevarul.ro. (2020, July 22). Un partid recent înființat intră în bătălia pentru alegerile locale. Val de plecări din USR către noua formațiune politică. *Adevarul.ro.* https://adevarul.ro/news/politica/un-partid-recent-infiintat-intra-batalia-alegerile-locale-val-plecari-usr-noua-formatiune-politica-1_5f17 676d5163ec42713c8f6b/index.html. Accessed 1 February 2021.

Amin, S. (1977). *Imperialism and unequal exchange.* Monthly Review.

Another Europe Is Possible. (2016). https://www.anothereurope.org/about/. Accessed 3 February 2021.

Apeldoorn, B. (2009). The contradictions of 'embedded neoliberalism'and Europe's multi-level legitimacy crisis: The European project and its limits. In J. Drahokoupil & L. Horn (Eds.), *Contradictions and limits of neoliberal European governance: From Lisbon to Lisbon* (2008, pp. 21–43). New York: Springer.

Arfire, R. (2011). The moral regulation of the second Europe: Transition Europeanization and the Romanians. *Critical Sociology, 37*(6), 853–870.

Arrighi, G. (1994). *The long twentieth century: Money, power, and the origins of our times.* Verso.

Austria, A. (2018). *The European illusion: Why we need new strategies towards the EU and beyond.* Rosa Luxemburg Stiftung.

Bakić-Hayden, M. (1995). Nesting orientalisms: The case of former Yugoslavia. *Slavic Review, 54*(4), 917–931.

Ban, C. (2012). Sovereign debt, austerity, and regime change: The case of Nicolae Ceaușescu's Romania. *East European Politics and Societies, 26*(4), 743–776.

Ban, C. (2014). *Dependență și dezvoltare: economia politică a capitalismului românesc*. Tact.

Ban, C. (2016). *Ruling ideas: How global neoliberalism goes local*. Oxford University Press.

Ban, C., & Bohle, D. (2020). Definancialization, financial repression and policy continuity in East-Central Europe. *Review of International Political Economy*, 1–24.

Barna, E., Csányi, G., & Éber, M. Á. (Eds). (2019). 2008–2018: Válság és hegemónia Magyarországon. Special issue of *Fordulat*, 26.

Barnett, T. P. (1992). *Romanian and East German policies in the third world: Comparing the strategies of Ceaușescu and Honecker*. Praeger Publishers.

Bartha, E. (2011a). It can't make me happy that Audi is prospering: Working-class nationalism in Hungary after 1989. In D. Kalb & G. Halmai (Eds.), *Headlines of nation, subtexts of class: Working class populism and the return of the repressed in neoliberal Europe* (pp. 92–112). Berghahn Books.

Bartha, E. (2011b). *Magányos harcosok: munkások a rendszerváltás utáni Kelet-Németországban és Magyarországon*. L'Harmattan.

Băsescu, T. (2011, January 18). Speech at joint ISP-KAS workshop. ANEIR Jubilee, December 19, 2011.

Bátorfy, A., & Tremmel, M. (2019, February 10). Data visualization: The definitive timeline of anti-Soros conspiracy theories. Átlátszó. https://eng lish.atlatszo.hu/2019/02/10/data-visualization-the-definitive-timeline-of-anti-soros-conspiracy-theories/. Accessed 9 February 2021.

Becker, J., Jäger, J., & Weissenbacher, R. (2015). Uneven and dependent development in Europe: The crisis and its implications. In J. Jäger & E. Springler (Eds.), *Asymmetric crisis in Europe and possible futures: Critical political economy and post-Keynesian perspectives* (pp. 101–117). Routledge.

Behr, H., & Stivachtis, Y. A. (Eds.). (2015). *Revisiting the European Union as empire*. Routledge.

Beissinger, M. R., Sasse, G., Bartels, L., & Bermeo, N. (2014). An end to "patience". *Mass politics in tough times: Opinions, votes and protest in the Great Recession*, 334, 238–245.

Berend, I. T. (1990). *The Hungarian economic reforms 1953–1988*. Cambridge University Press.

Berend, I. T. (2009). *From the Soviet bloc to the European Union: The economic and social transformation of Central and Eastern Europe since 1973*. Cambridge University Press.

Boatcă, M. (2020, May 11). [Thou shalt] Honour the asparagus!: Romanian agricultural labour in Germany during the Covid-19 season. LeftEast. https://www.criticatac.ro/lefteast/thou-shalt-honour-the-asparagus%EF%BB%BF-romanian-agricultural-labour-in-germany-during-the-covid-19-season/. Accessed 1 February 2021.

Bockman, J. K. (2000). *Economists and social change: Science, professional power, and politics in Hungary, 1945–1995.* Doctoral dissertation, University of California.

Böcskei, B. (2016). Új autoriter rezsimek, a magyar illiberalizmus és a "létező liberalizmus" válsága. In A. Antal & G. Földes (Eds.), *Holtpont. Társadalomkritikai tanulmányok Magyarország elmúlt 25 évéről* (pp. 79–95). Napvilág.

Bohle, D., & Greskovits, B. (2006). Capitalism without compromise: Strong business and weak labor in Eastern Europe's new transnational industries. *Studies in Comparative International Development, 41*(1), 3–25.

Bohle, D., & Greskovits, B. (2012). *Capitalist diversity on Europe's periphery.* Cornell University Press.

Böröcz, J. (1992). Dual dependency and property vacuum: Social change on the state socialist semiperiphery. *Theory and Society, 21*(1), 77–104.

Böröcz, J. (2000). Informality rules. *East European Politics and Societies, 14*(2), 348–380.

Böröcz, J. (2006). Goodness is elsewhere: The rule of European difference. *Comparative Studies in Society and History, 48*(1), 110–138.

Böröcz, J. (2009). *The European Union and global social change: A critical geopolitical-economic analysis* (Vol. 58). Routledge.

Böröcz, J., & Róna-Tas, Á. (1995). Small leap forward: Emergence of new economic elites. *Theory and Society, 24*(5), 751–781.

Böröcz, J., & Sarkar, M. (2005). What Is the EU? *International Sociology, 20*(2), 153–173.

Böröcz, J., Kovács, M., Mauro, E. D., Sher, A., Dancsi, K., & Kabachnik, P. (2001). *Empire's new clothes: Unveiling EU-enlargement.* Central Europe Review e-books.

Bossányi, K. (1989). Szólampróba: beszélgetések az alternatív mozgalmakról. Láng.

Bottoni, S. (2017). *Long awaited West: Eastern Europe since 1944.* Indiana University Press.

Breitner, M. (1977). Gazdaság és környezetvédelem. Figyelő, 1977 May 25, 1–3., HU OSA 300-40-1 631, Környezetvédelem 1977, Radio Free Europe / Radio Liberty Research Institute (RFE/RL), Open Society Archives at Central European University, Budapest.

Brenner, R. (2003). *The boom and the bubble: The US in the world economy.* Verso.

Bruff, I. (2014). The rise of authoritarian neoliberalism. *Rethinking Marxism, 26*(1), 113–129.

Bruszt, L. (1995). Reforming alliances: Labour, management and state bureaucracy in Hungary's economic transformation. *Strategic choice and path-dependency in post-socialism: Institutional dynamics in the transformation process* (pp. 261–286). Edward Elgar.

Buchowski, M. (2006). The specter of orientalism in Europe: From exotic brother to stigmatized other. *Anthropological Quarterly, 79*(3), 463–482.

Buier, N. (2007). Officializing the past. An analysis of the presidential commission for the analysis of the communist dictatorship in Romania. MA dissertation, Central European University.

Castorcea, R. (2021, January 11). First as tragedy, then as farce? AUR and the long shadow of fascism in Romania. LeftEast. https://www.criticatac.ro/lefteast/first-as-tragedy-then-as-farce-aur-and-the-long-shadow-of-fascism-in-romania/. Accessed 1 February 2021.

Cesereanu, R. (2004, August 3). Greva minerilor din Valea Jiului, 1977. Revista 22.

CeSIP. (2017). Corupție si contestare. http://cesip.ro/cercetare-proteste-05-02-2017/. Accessed 20 December 2020.

Chelcea, S. (1979). *Chestionarul în investigarea fenomenelor sociale.* Editura Științifică și Enciclopedică.

Chirot, D. (1978). Corporatism, socialism and development in Romania. *Amsterdams Sociologisch Tijdschrift, 5*(3), 389–409.

Chirot, D. (Ed.). (1991). *The origins of backwardness in Eastern Europe: Economics and politics from the Middle Ages until the early twentieth century.* University of California Press.

Chivu, L., Ciutacu, C., & Georgescu, G. (2017). *Deindustrialization and reindustrialization in Romania.* Palgrave.

Cirjan, D. (2016, January 4). *Did it ever happen? Social movements and the politics of spontaneous consensus in post-socialist Romania.* LeftEast. https://www.criticatac.ro/lefteast/social-movements-and-politics-of-spontaneous-con sensus-in-romania/ Accessed 2 February 2021.

Clark, R. (2020, December 22). Is fascism returning to Romania? Open Democracy. https://www.opendemocracy.net/en/countering-radical-right/fascism-returning-romania/. Accessed 1 February 2021.

Comisso, E., & Marer, P. (1986). The economics and politics of reform in Hungary. *International Organization, 40*(2), 421–454.

Crăciun, M., & Lipan, S. (2017, February 12). Manicheism, middle class and the Victoria Square protests. Crețan, R. & O'Brien, T. (2019). Corruption and conflagration: (In)justice and protest in Bucharest after the Colectiv fire. Urban Geography 41(3): 368–388. In *Bucharest. The material culture of Romanian middle class blog.* https://clasamijloc.wordpress.com/2017/02/12/manichaeism-the-middle-class-and-the-victoria-square-protests-in-buchar est/. Accessed 2 May 2020.

Crăciun, M., & Lipan, Ş. (2020). Introduction: The middle class in post-socialist Europe: Ethnographies of its "Good Life." *East European Politics and Societies, 34*(2), 423–440.

Crețan, R., & O'Brien, T. (2019). Corruption and conflagration: (In)justice and protest in Bucharest after the Colectiv fire. *Urban Geography, 41*(3), 368–388.

Crowther, W. E. (1988). *The political economy of Romanian socialism.* Praeger.

Csalog, Z. (1989). *Börtön volt a hazám:-Hosszú István beszél.* Európa Könyvkiadó.

Csányi, G. (2019). Genderrezsim és nőpolitika Magyarországon 2008–2018 Történeti Politikai Gazdaságtani Elemzés. *Fordulat, 26,* 116–141.

Csurka, I. (1992). Néhány gondolat és nyolc társgondolat. *Magyar Fórum, 1992,* 36–64.

Czirfusz, M., Ivanics, Z., Kovai, C., & Meszmann, T. (2019). A magyarországi munkásság a hosszú lejtmenetben. *Fordulat, 26,* 143–170.

Dalbóczi, M. (2014, November 20). Ne csak Orbán takarodjon. *Origo.* http://www.origo.hu/itthon/20141120-nem-csak-az-orban-kormany-lemondasat-akarjuk.html, 30 May 2020.

Dancsik, B., Fábián, G., Fellner, Z., Horváth, G., Lang, P., Nagy, G., & Winkler, S. (2015). *Comprehensive analysis of the nonperforming household mortgage portfolio using micro-level data* (No. Special Issue 2015). Budapest: MNB Occasional Papers.

Dedman, M. (Ed.). (2009). *The Origins & development of the European Union 1945–2008: A History of European Integration.* Routledge.

Deletant, D. (1995). *Ceauşescu and the securitate: Coercion and dissent in Romania, 1965–1989.* ME Sharpe.

DiEM25. (2016) What is DiEM25? https://diem25.org/what-is-diem25/. Accessed 2 February 2021.

Dobos, L., Rácz, J., & Vit, L. (Eds.). (1988). *Utánunk az özönvíz.* Duna Kör és ELTE-ÁJK Politikatudományi Tanszékcsoport.

Dragnea, L. (2017, February 14). Fondul Suveran de Dezvoltare şi Investiţii a generat interes uriaţ în mediile financiare internaţionale. *Mediafax.* http://www.mediafax.ro/politic/liviu-dragnea-fondul-suveran-de-dezvoltare-si-invest itii-a-generat-interes-urias-in-mediile-financiare-internationale-din-sua-pana-in-norvegia-16161884. Accessed 9 June 2020.

Drahokoupil, J. (2009). *Globalization and the state in Central and Eastern Europe: The politics of foreign direct investment* (Vol. 48). Routledge.

Drahokoupil, J., & Horn, L. (Eds.). (2008). *Contradictions and limits of neoliberal European governance: From Lisbon to Lisbon.* Springer.

Dull, S. (2018, November 26). A Fideszben egyszer már megfúrták a 400 órás túlórát. *Index.* https://index.hu/belfold/2018/11/26/a_fideszben_egyszer_mar_megfurtak_azt_amit_most_kosa_lajos_ujra_eroltet_tulora_mun kaido_munka_torvenykonyve/. Accessed 30 September 2020.

Dzenovska, D. (2018). *School of Europeanness: Tolerance and other lessons in political liberalism in Latvia.* Cornell University Press.

Éber, M. Á., Gagyi, A., Gerőcs, T., & Jelinek, Cs. (2019). 2008–2018: Válság és hegemónia Magyarországon. *Fordulat, 26,* 29–75.

Éber, M. A., Gagyi, A., Gerőcs, T., Jelinek, Cs., & Pinkasz, A. (2014). 1989: Szempontok a rendszerváltás globális politikai gazdaságtanához. *Fordulat, 21*(1), 10–63.

Eyal, G. (2003). *The origins of postcommunist elites: From Prague Spring to the breakup of Czechoslovakia.* University of Minnesota Press.

Fabry, A. (2018). The origins of neoliberalism in late 'socialist' Hungary: The case of the Financial Research Institute and 'Turnabout and Reform'. *Capital & Class, 42*(1), 77–107.

Fabry, A. (2019). *The political economy of Hungary.* Springer.

Fazi, T., & Mitchell, W. (2018, April 29). Why the Left should embrace Brexit. Jacobin. https://www.jacobinmag.com/2018/04/brexit-labour-party-social ist-left-corbyn. Accessed 19 April 2020.

Feitl, I. (2016). *Talányos Játszmák: Magyarország a KGST erőterében 1949–1974.* Napvilág.

Ferge, Z. (2017). *Magyar társadalom-és szociálpolitika, 1990–2015.* Osiris.

Fleischer, T. (1993). Jaws on the Danube: Water management, regime change and the movement against the Middle Danube hydro-electric dam. *International Journal of Urban and Regional Research, 17*(1993), 429–443.

Frank, A. G. (1977). Long live transideological enterprise! the socialist economies in the capitalist international division of labor. *Review (Fernand Braudel Center), 1,* 91–140.

Gabanyi, A. U. (1987). Gorbachev presents "Restructuring" to the Romanian Public'. *RFE Research, Romania SR, 4,* 29.

Gago, L. (2017, June 10). *Is Podemos an Eurosceptic party?* Eurovisions. Available at http://www.euvisions.eu/is-podemos-a-eurosceptic-party/. Accessed 4 April 2020.

Gagyi, A. (2011). *A civil globalizáció 'univerzális' eszméje a 'periférián'. Magyarországi és romániai globalizációkritikus csoportok.* Doctoral dissertation, University of Pécs.

Gagyi, A. (2014). Smartphones and the European flag: The new Hungarian demonstrations for democracy. *Studia Universitatis Babes-Bolyai-Sociologia, 59*(2), 75–86.

Gagyi, A. (2015a). A moment of political critique by reform economists in late socialist Hungary. Intersections. *East European Journal of Society and Politics, 1*(2), 59–79.

Gagyi, A. (2015b, May 1–July 31). Social movements as transnational constructs: Hungarian environmental and Romanian workers' mobilizations in the

Records of RFE/RL Research Institute 1973–1990. Visegrad Scholarships at the Open Society Archives Final Report. http://www.osaarchivum. org/files/fellowships/visegrad/reports/2015/GAGYI-201504.pdf. Accessed 2 February 2020.

Gagyi, A. (2016). "Coloniality of power" in East Central Europe: External penetration as internal force in post-socialist Hungarian politics. *Journal of World-Systems Research, 22*(2), 349–372.

Gagyi, A. (2017, September 12). Hungary's 'Lex CEU'and the state of the open society: Looking beyond the story of democratic revolutions. *Cultures of History Forum.* https://www.cultures-of-history.uni-jena.de/focus/lex-ceu/hungarys-lex-ceu-and-the-state-of-the-open-society-looking-beyond-the-story-of-democratic-revolutions/. Accessed 30 April 2020.

Gagyi, A., & Ivancheva, M. (2017). The rise and fall of civil society in East-Central Europe. In M. Moskalewicz, & W. Przybylski (Eds.), *Understanding Central Europe.* Routledge.

Gagyi, A., & Vigvári, A. (2018). Informal practices in housing financialisation: The transformation of an allotment garden in Hungary. *Critical Housing Analysis, 5*(2), 46.

Gagyi, A., Jelinek, C., Pósfai, Zs., & Vigvári, A. (2019). Lakhatási helyzet a válság után. Financializációs folyamatok, kettészakadó lakáspolitikák és a háztartások túlélési stratégiái. *Fordulat, 26,* 200–224.

Galasi, P., & Kertesi, G. (1985). Second economy, competition, inflation. *Acta Oeconomica, 35*(3/4), 269–293.

Galasi, P., & Sik, E. (1988). Invisible incomes in Hungary. *Social Justice, 15*(3/4), 160–178.

Gerőcs, T., & Pinkasz, A. (2017). Debt-ridden development on Europe's eastern periphery. In M. Boatcă, A. Komlosy, & H. H. Nolte (Eds.), *Global inequalities in world-systems perspective* (pp. 131–153). Routledge.

Gerőcs, T., & Pinkasz, A. (2018). Conflicting interests in the Comecon integration: State socialist debates on East-West-South relations. *East Central Europe, 45*(2–3), 336–365.

Gerőcs, T., & Pinkasz, A. (2019). Relocation, standardization and vertical specialization: Core–periphery relations in the European automotive value chain. *Society and Economy, 41*(2), 171–192.

Gherasim-Proca, O. (2016). Presidential elections in Romania (2–16 November 2014). Hypermobilization and administrative failure. In Bogdan Gheorghiță (Ed.), *Alegeri, alegători și aleși în România 2009–2014* (pp. 117–169). Lucian Blaga University Press.

Gille, Z. (2007). *From the cult of waste to the trash heap of history: The politics of waste in socialist and post-socialist Hungary.* Indiana University Press.

Gosu, A. (2004, August 24). *Ceaușescu și minerii.* Revista 22. http://revista22 online.ro/3966/.html. Accessed 2 February 2021.

Gotev, G. (2018). *Dan Barna: Save Romania Union similar to Macron's En Marche.* https://www.euractiv.com/section/elections/interview/dan-barnas ave-romania-union-similar-to-macrons-en-marche/. Accessed 25 May 2021.

Grassegger, H. (2019, January 1). *The unbelievable story of the plot against George Soros.* BuzzFeed.News. https://www.buzzfeednews.com/article/hns grassegger/george-soros-conspiracy-finkelstein-birnbaum-orban-netanyahu. Accessed 2 February 2021.

Greskovits, B. (2017). Rebuilding the Hungarian right through civil organization and contention: The civic circles movement. *Robert Schuman Centre for Advanced Studies Research Paper No. RSCAS, 37.*

Gubernat, R., & Rammelt, H. P. (2020a). Liminality and activism: Conceptualising unconventional political participation in Romania. In I. R. Lamond & J. Moss (Eds.), *Liminality and critical event studies: Borders, boundaries, and contestation* (pp. 247–262). Palgrave.

Gubernat, R., & Rammelt, H. P. (2020b). "Vrem o țară ca afară!": How contention in Romania redefines state-building through a Pro-European discourse. *East European Politics and Societies.* https://doi.org/10.1177/088 8325419897987.

Halmai, G. (2011). Possessed by the spectre of socialism: Nationalist mobilization in "transitional" Hungary. In D. Kalb & G. Halmai (Eds.), *Headlines of nation, subtexts of class: Working class populism and the return of the repressed in neoliberal Europe* (pp. 113–141). Berghahn.

Harper, K. (2005). "Wild capitalism" and "ecocolonialism": A tale of two rivers. *American Anthropologist, 107*(2), 221–233.

Harvey, D. (1989). *Postmodernity.* Basil Blackwell Publishing.

HU OSA 300-60-1. Open Society Archives Item no. 1025/57, Cases of rebellion at Grivita Rosie on payday, Labor: Strikes, 1951–1979, 424.

Jandó, Z. (2018, April 21). Az állásteremtés és a közmunka piszok jól bejött a Fidesznek. *G7.* https://g7.hu/kozelet/20180421/az-allasteremtes-es-a-koz munka-piszok-jol-bejott-a-fidesznek/. Accessed 30 April 2020.

Jeffries, I. (1993). *Socialist economies and the transition to the market: A guide.* Routledge.

Jelinek, C., & Pinkasz, A. (Eds.). (2014). Rendszerváltás. Special issue of *Fordulat, 21.*

Karatnycky, A., Motyl, A. J., & Sturmthal, A. F. (1980). *Workers' rights, East and West: A comparative study of trade union and workers' rights in Western democracies and Eastern Europe.* Transaction Publishers.

Kideckel, D. (2002). The unmaking of an East-Central European working class. In D. Kideckel & M. Hann Chris (Eds.), *Post-socialism: ideals, ideologies and practices in Eurasia* (pp. 114–132). Routledge.

Kideckel, D. (2008). *Getting by in post-socialist Romania: Labor, the body and working-class culture.* Indiana University Press.

Kingsley, P. (2018, December 16) Opposition in Hungary demonstrates against Orban, in rare display of dissent. *The New York Times*. https://www.nyt imes.com/2018/12/16/world/europe/hungary-protests-viktor-orban.html. Accessed 30 April 2020.

Kiss, Z. L. (Ed.). (2018). *Devizahitel?* Rejtjel.

Klumbyte, N. (2009). The geopolitics of taste: The 'Euro' and 'Soviet' sausage industries in Lithuania. In E. C. Dunn & M. Nestle (Eds.), *Food & everyday life in the post-socialist world* (pp. 130–153). Indiana University Press.

Kolosi, T., & Fábián, Z. (2016). Vagyoneloszlás Magyarországon. In T. Kolosi & I. G. Tóth (Eds.), *Társadalmi Riport 2016* (pp. 98–112). Tárki.

Kolosi, T., & Sági, M. (1996). Rendszerváltás és társadalomszerkezet. *Társadalmi riport 1996* (pp. 149–197). Tárki.

Konrád, G., & Szelényi, I. (1979). *The intellectuals on the road to class power*. Harcourt.

Kormany.hu. (2017, July 21). Orbán Viktor a Kossuth Rádió 180 perc című műsorában. http://www.kormany.hu/hu/a-miniszterelnok/beszedek-publik aciok-interjuk/orban-viktor-a-kossuth-radio-180-perc-cimu-musoraban-201 70721. Accessed 30 April 2020.

Körösényi, I. (2000). *Értelmiség, politikai gondolkodás és kormányzat*. Osiris.

Kovács, J. M., & Trencsényi, B. (2019). Hungary—Brave and new? Dissecting a realistic dystopia. In J. M. Kovács & B. Trencsényi (Eds.), *Brave new Hungary: Mapping the system of national cooperation* (pp. 379–432). Lexington Books.

Kováts, E. (2018). Questioning consensuses: Right-wing populism, anti-populism, and the threat of 'gender ideology.' *Sociological Research Online, 23*(2), 528–538.

Kozma, F. (1996). *Külgazdasági stratégia*. Aula.

Krasztev, P., & Van Til, J. (Eds.). (2015). *The Hungarian patient: Social opposition to an illiberal democracy*. Central European University Press.

Krugman, P. (2012). Why Hungary matters? *The New York Times*, March 3, 2015. https://krugman.blogs.nytimes.com/2012/03/15/why-hungary-mat ters/?mcubz=3. Accessed 2 February 2021.

Kuus, M. (2004). Europe's eastern expansion and the reinscription of otherness in East-Central Europe. *Progress in Human Geography, 28*(4), 472–489.

LA Times. (2017). Romania is engulfed in protest in a political awakening of the young. *Los Angeles Times*. https://www.latimes.com/world/europe/la-fg-romania-protests-2017-story.html. Accessed 2 February 2021.

Lapavitsas, C. (2018). *The left case against the EU*. Wiley.

Lavigne, M. (1991). *International political economy and socialism*. Cambridge University Press.

Lux, G. (2015). The institutional conditions of reindustrialization in post-crisis Central Europe. *Journal of Economics & Management, 19*, 16–33.

Margarit, D., & Rammelt, H. (2020). The revitalization of social and civic participation in Eastern Europe? Industrial conflict and popular protests in Romania. Intersections. *East European Journal of Society and Politics, 6*(4).

MacGoy, D. (2019, December 12). Romanian civil society has proved its strength. Now it can help nurture a fragile democracy. *EuroNews*. https://www.euronews.com/2019/12/11/romanian-civil-society-proved-its-str ength-now-can-help-nurture-a-fragile-democracy-view. Accessed 1 December 2020.

Magyar, B., & Vásárhelyi, J. (Eds.). (2017). *Twenty-five sides of a Post-Communist mafia state*. Central European University Press.

Medve-Bálint, G., & Šćepanović, V. (2019). EU funds, state capacity and the development of transnational industrial policies in Europe's Eastern periphery. *Review of International Political Economy*. https://doi.org/10.1080/096 92290.2019.1646669.

Mihályi, P. (2015). *A privatizált vagyon visszaállamosítása Magyarországon 2010–2014* (No. MT-DP-2015/7). Budapest: IEHAS Discussion Papers.

MTI. (2013, May 31). Fidesz: *"Bajnai csapatában focizik"* a Hahások nagy része. HVG. https://hvg.hu/itthon/20130531_Fidesz_Bajnai_csapataban_focizik_ a_HaHaso. Accessed 2 February 2021.

Napi.hu. (2012, October 13). Orbán: nem jóléti állam épül. *Napi Gazdaság*. https://www.napi.hu/magyar_gazdasag/orban_nem_joleti_allam_ epul.534599.html. Accessed 3 February 2021.

Nölke, A., & Vliegenthart, A. (2009). Enlarging the varieties of capitalism: The emergence of dependent market economies in East Central Europe. *World Politics, 61*(4), 670–702.

Nousios, P., Overbeek, H., & Tsolakis, A. (Eds.). (2012). *Globalisation and European entegration: Critical approaches to regional order and international relations*. Routledge.

Novák, C. Z. (2015). *Holtvágányon: A Ceauşescu-rendszer magyarságpolitikája II. (1975–1989)*. Pro Print.

Olteanu, T., & Beyerle, S. (2018). The Romanian people versus corruption. The paradoxical nexus of protest and adaptation. *Partecipazione e Conflitto, 10*(3), 797–825.

Oprea, M., & Olar, S. (2003). *Ziua care nu se uită. 15 noiembrie 1987*. Braşov, Polirom.

Orbán, V. (2017). *2017-ben Magyarországon magasabb fokozatba kapcsol az iparosítás*. Speech at the occasion of the opening of the Samsung SDI accumulator factory in Göd. http://www.kormany.hu/hu/a-miniszterelnok/ videok/2017-ben-magyarorszagon-magasabb-fokozatba-kapcsol-az-iparositas. Accessed 3 February 2021.

Overbeek, H. W. (Ed.). (1993). *Restructuring hegemony in the global political economy: The rise of transnational neo-liberalism in the 1980s*. Routledge.

Ozarow, D. (2019). *The mobilization and demobilization of middle-class revolt: Comparative insights from Argentina*. Routledge.

Pajkossy, G. (2006). *Viktor Vida: Interview with Gabor Pajkossy*. 1956 Institute Oral History Archives. www.vedegylet.hu/Duna_Kor/legepelt_interjuk_ Duna_Kor/Pajkossy.doc. Accessed 3 February 2021.

Papp, I. (2012). *A magyar népi mozgalom története, 1920–1990*. Jaffa.

Pasti, V. (1995). *România în tranziţie: căderea în viitor*. Editura Nemira.

Paşti, V. (2006). *Noul capitalism românesc*. Polirom.

Patel, R., & Moore, J. W. (2017). *A history of the world in seven cheap things: A guide to capitalism, nature, and the future of the planet*. University of California Press.

Petrović, T. (2008). Nesting colonialisms: Austria, Slovenia, and discourses on the Western Balkans in the context of the EU enlargement. In L. Kreft & J. Benderly (Eds.), *Do good fences make friendly neighbors? Inclusion and exclusion in and on the borders of Europe* (pp. 917–931). The Peace Institute.

Petrovici, N. (2006). Relaţii de putere în cadrul elitei politice româneşti la sfârşitul anilor '80 şi începutul anilor'90. *Sociologie Românească, 4*, 119–145.

Petrovici, N. (2007). Excluderea muncitorilor din centrul Clujului. Gentrificare într-un oraş central-european. *Sociologie Românească, 5*(03), 42–70.

Petrovici, N., & Poenaru, F. (2017, December 9). *Class and urban integuments in Romanian protests (2012–2017)*. Paper delivered at ISA-RC21, Leeds.

Pew. (2017, January 8). Globally people point to ISIS and climate change as leading security threats. http://www.pewglobal.org/2017/08/01/globally-people-point-to-isis-and-climate-change-as-leading-security-threats/; 30 April 2020.

Pickvance, K. (1998). Democracy and grassroots opposition in Eastern Europe: Hungary and Russia compared. *The Sociological Review, 46*(2), 187–207.

Pittaway, M. (2012). *The workers state: Industrial labor and the making of socialist Hungary, 1944–1958*. University of Pittsburgh Press.

Poenaru, F. (2013). *Contesting illusions: History and intellectual class struggle in post-communist Romania*. Doctoral dissertation, Central European University.

Poenaru, F. (2017a). *Locuri Comune: clasă, anticomunism, stânga*. Tact.

Poenaru, F. (2017b, January 2). Ceai sau cafea? CriticAtac. http://www.critic atac.ro/29387/ceai-sau-cafea/. Accessed 3 February 2021.

Pósfai, Z., Gál, Z., & Nagy, E. (2017). Financialization and inequalities: The uneven development of the housing market on the eastern periphery of Europe. In S. Fadda & P. Tridico (Eds.), *Inequality and uneven development in the post-crisis World* (pp. 167–190). Taylor & Francis.

Protv.ro. (2020, December 8). Cine sunt românii care au votat cu AUR. Profilul alegătorilor partidului-surpriză de la parlamentare. *Ştirile ProTv*. https://sti rileprotv.ro/stiri/alegeri-parlamentare-2020/cine-sunt-romanii-care-au-votat-

cu-aur-profilul-alegatorilor-partidului-care-a-luat-prin-surprindere-lumea-pol
itica.html. Accessed 2 January 2021.

Rainer, J. (1996). *Nagy Imre: Politikai életrajz. Első kötet: 1896–1953.* 1956-os
Intézet.

Rammelt, H. (2018). *Activistes protestataires en Hongrie et en Roumanie.*
Editions L'Harmattan.

Raviv, O. (2008). Chasing the dragon east: Exploring the frontiers of Western
European finance. *Contemporary Politics, 14*(3), 297–314.

Razem. (2016). Razem za Unią solidarną. Przeciw Brexitowi. Partia Razem -
Inna polityka jest możliwa! http://partiarazem.pl/stanowiska/razem-unia-sol
idarna-przeciw-brexitowi/. Accessed 2 February 2021.

ReCommons. (2019). *Manifesto for a new popular internationalism in Europe.*
https://www.cadtm.org/IMG/pdf/recommons-2019_eng.pdf. Accessed 3
February 2021.

Reuters. (2018a, October 8). Anti-government protest in Romania turns
violent. Reuters. https://www.reuters.com/article/us-romania-protests/anti-
government-protest-in-romania-turns-violent-idUSKBN1KV1YO. Accessed 3
February 2020.

Reuters. (2018b, June 9). *Romania's ruling coalition stages rally against alleged
abuses by anti-graft legislators.* Reuters. https://www.reuters.com/article/us-
romania-politics-rally/romanias-ruling-coalition-stages-rally-against-alleged-
abuses-by-anti-graft-prosecutors-idUSKCN1J50XK. Accessed 4 February
2021.

Rogozanu, C. (2019, May 28). Alegeri 2019. Concluzii. CriticAtac. http://
www.criticatac.ro/alegeri-2019-concluzii-si-o-notita-despre-inchiderea-lui-dra
gnea/. Accessed 4 February 2021.

Romsics, I. (2003). *Volt egyszer egy rendszerváltás.* Rubicon-Ház.

Róna-Tas, A. (1990). *The second economy in Hungary: The social origins of the
end of state socialism.* Doctoral dissertation, University of Michigan.

Rus, A. (2007). *Mineriadele: între manipulare politică şi solidaritate munci-
torească.* Curtea Veche.

Scharle, Á., & Szikra, D. (2015). Recent changes moving Hungary away from
the European Social Model. In D. Vaughan-Whitehead (Eds.), *The European
social model in crisis: Is Europe losing its soul?* Edward Elgar Publishing.

Scheiring, G. (2016). A nemzeti burzsoázia diszkrét bája - A demokrácia hany-
atlásának politikai gazdaságtana. In A. Antal & G. Földes (Eds.), *Holtpont.
Társadalomkritikai tanulmányok Magyarország elmúlt 25 évéről* (pp. 11–45).
Napvilág.

Scheiring, G. (2020). *The retreat of liberal democracy: Authoritarian capitalism
and the accumulative state in Hungary.* Springer.

Sebők. (2016). A modernizációs konszenzus, mint a rendszerváltás ideológiája és közpolitikája. In A. Antal & G. Földes (Eds.), *Holtpont. Társadalomkritikai tanulmányok Magyarország elmúlt 25 évéről* (pp. 46–76). Napvilág.

Sebők, M. (2019). *Paradigmák fogságában. Elitek és ideológiák a magyar pénzügyi kapitalizmusban.* Napvilág.

Shafir, M. (2008). From historical to "dialectical" populism: The case of post-communist Romania. *Canadian Slavonic Papers, 50*(3–4), 425–470.

Shields, S. (2014). *The international political economy of transition.* Routledge.

Simionca, A. (2012). Neoliberal managerialism, anti-communist dogma and the critical employee in contemporary Romania. *Studia Universitatis Babes-Bolyai-Sociologia, 57*(1), 123–149.

Simionca, A., & Gog, S. (2016). Sociological and anthropological perspectives on religion and economy: Emerging spiritualities and the future of work: Guest editors' foreword. *Studia Universitatis Babes-Bolyai Sociologia, 61*(2), 5–9.

SNSPA. (2016). *Studiu SNSPA: "Piata Unirii – noiembrie 2016".* http://www.snspa.ro/snspa/info-snspa/stiri/item/670-studiu-snspa-piata-universitatii-noiembrie-2015. Accessed 3 February 2021.

Stark, D. (1990). Privatization in Hungary: From plan to market or from plan to clan? *East European Politics and Societies, 4*(3), 351–392.

Stark, D., & Vedres, B. (2012). Political holes in the economy: The business network of partisan firms in Hungary. *American Sociological Review, 77*(5), 700–722.

Staudenmaier, R. (2018). *EU Parliament votes to trigger Article 7 sanctions procedure against Hungary.* Deutsche Welle 9 December 2018. https://www.dw.com/en/eu-parliament-votes-to-trigger-article-7-sanctions-procedure-against-hungary/a-45459720. Accessed 4 February 2021.

Stoiciu, V. (2016). *Romania's trade unions at the crossroads.* Friedrich-Ebert Stiftung.

Stokes, G. (1986). The social origins of East European politics. *East European Politics and Societies, 1*(1), 30–74.

Szabó, A., & Mikecz, D. (2015). After the Orbán-revolution: The awakening of civil society in Hungary. In G. Pleyers & I. Sava (Eds.), *Social movements in Central and Eastern Europe: A renewal of protests and democracy* (pp. 34–43). University of Bucharest.

Szabó, M. (1994). Greens, cabbies, and anti-communists: Collective action during regime transition in Hungary. In E. Larana (Ed.), *New social movements: From ideology to identity* (pp. 155–185). Temple University Press.

Szalai, E. (1994a). *A civil társadalomtól a politikai társadalom felé: munkástanácsok, 1989–1993.* T-Twins.

Szalai, E. (1994b). Political and social conflicts arising from the transformation of property relations in Hungary. *The Journal of Communist Studies and Transition Politics, 10*(3), 56–77.

Szalai, E. (2005). *Socialism: An analysis of its past and future*. Central European University Press.

Szalai, E. (1995). The metamorphosis of the elites. The Metamorphosis of the Elites. In B. Király & A. Bozóki, (Eds.), *Lawful revolution in Hungary, 1989–94* (pp. 159–174). Social Science Monographs.

Szalai, J. (2007). *Nincs két ország...?: társadalmi küzdelmek az állami (túl) elosztásért a rendszerváltás utáni Magyarországon*. Osiris.

Szelényi, I. (1988). *Socialist entrepreneurs: Embourgeoisement in rural Hungary*. University of Wisconsin Press.

Szelényi, I. (2016). Weber's theory of domination and post-communist capitalisms. *Theory and Society, 45*(1), 1–24.

Szelényi, I., Eyal, G., & Townsley, E. (1998). *Making capitalism without capitalists*. Verso.

Szelényi, S., Szelényi, I., & Poster, W. R. (1996). Interests and symbols in post-communist political culture: the case of Hungary. *American Sociological Review, 61*, 466–477.

Szent-Iványi, B. (2017). Introduction: The changing patterns of FDI. *Foreign Direct Investment in Central and Eastern Europe* (pp. 1–22). Palgrave.

Szirmai, V. (1999). *A környezeti érdekek Magyarországon*. Pallas Stúdió.

Szombati, K. (2018). *The revolt of the provinces: Anti-gypsyism and right-wing politics in Hungary*. Berghahn.

Tamás, Gáspár Miklós. (2016, March 3). *Mi van Romániával?* Transindex. http://tgm.transindex.ro/?cikk=1217. Accessed 4 February 2021.

Tanács, I. (1989, March 24). *Zöldhullám*. Népszabadság.

Thoma, L. (1998). *A rendszerváltás és a szakszervezetek 1988–1992*. Villányi úti könyvek.

Thornton, A., Binstock, G., Abbasi-Shavazi, M. J., Ghimire, D., Gjonca, A., Melegh, A., & Young-DeMarco, L. (2012). Knowledge and beliefs about national development and developmental hierarchies: The viewpoints of ordinary people in thirteen countries. *Social Science Research, 41*(5), 1053–1068.

Tismăneanu, V. (2005). *Stalinism pentru eternitate: O istorie politică a comunismului românesc*. Polirom.

Tismăneanu, V., Dobrincu, D., and Vasile, C. (2006). *Comisia prezidențială pentru analiza dictaturii comuniste din România*. Raport final. https://archive.org/stream/ComisiaPrezidentialaPentruAnalizaDictaturiiComunistedinRomania-Raport/ComisiaPrezidentialaPentruAnalizaDictaturiiComunistedinRomania-RaportFinal-coord.VladimirTismaneanu_djvu.txt. Accessed 4 February 2021.

Todorova, M. (2009). *Imagining the Balkans*. Oxford University Press.

Tőkés, R. (1996). *Hungary's negotiated revolution: Economic reform, social change and political succession 1957–1990*. Cambridge University Press.

Traynor, I. (2014, October 29). Budapest autumn: Hollowing out democracy on the edge of Europe. *The Guardian*. http://www.theguardian.com/world/2014/oct/29/budapest-viktor-orbandemocracy-edge-hungary. Accessed 4 February 2021.

Traynor, I. (2013, August 13). Eastern European autocrats pose new test for democracy. *The Guardian*. https://www.theguardian.com/world/2013/aug/13/eastern-europe-autocrats-return-test-democracy. Accessed 4 February 2021.

Trif, A. (2014). Austerity and collective bargaining in Romania national report–Romania. http://doras.dcu.ie/22268/1/Romania_Final.pdf. Accessed 21 May 2021.

Udvarhelyi, É. T. (2014). "If we don't push homeless people out, we will end up being pushed out by them": The criminalization of homelessness as state strategy in Hungary. *Antipode, 46*(3), 816–834.

Van Apeldoorn, B. (2003). *Transnational capitalism and the struggle over European integration*. Routledge.

Van der Pijl, K. (1998). *Transnational classes and international relations*. Psychology Press.

Vanhuysse, P. (2006). *Divide and pacify: Strategic social policies and political protests in post-communist democracies*. Central European University Press.

Varga, M. (2011). *Striking with tied hands: Strategies of labor interest representation in post-communist Romania and Ukraine*. Doctoral dissertation, University of Amsterdam.

Varga, M. (2013). Refocusing studies of post-communist trade unions. *European Journal of Industrial Relations, 19*(2), 109–125.

Varga, M. (2014). Hungary's "anti-capitalist" far-right: Jobbik and the Hungarian Guard. *Nationalities Papers, 42*(5), 791–807.

Varga, M. (2015). Trade unions and austerity in Central and Eastern Europe: Did they do something about it? *Transfer: European Review of Labour and Research, 21*(3), 313–326.

Vargha, J. (1981). Egyre távolabb a jótól. *Valóság, 1981*, 1–23.

Verdery, K. (1991). *National ideology under socialism: Identity and cultural politics in Ceauşescu's Romania*. University of California Press.

Vigvári, A. (1990). Adósság: Tanulmányok adósságunk multjáról és jövőjéről. *Szakszervezetek Gazdaság-és Társadalomkutató Intézete*.

Vigvári, A., & Gerőcs, T. (2017). The concept of 'peasant embourgeoisement'in the perspective of different historical conjunctures. *Studia Universitatis Babes-Bolyai Sociologia, 62*(1), 85–104.

Wallerstein, I. (1976). Semi-peripheral countries and the contemporary world crisis. *Theory and Society, 3*(4), 461–483.

Walton, J. K., & Seddon, D. (1994). *Free markets and food riots: The politics of global adjustment*. Wiley.

Wiedermann, H. (2014). *Sakk és póker: krónika a magyar gazdasági szabadságharc győztes csatáiról*. Kairosz Kiadó.

Wolff, L. (1994). *Inventing Eastern Europe: The map of civilization on the mind of the Enlightenment*. Stanford University Press.

Zamfir, C. (Ed.). (1984). Indicatori și surse de variație a calitații vieții. *Ed. Acad. RSR*.

Zarycki, T. (2000). Politics in the periphery: Political cleavages in Poland interpreted in their historical and international context. *Europe-Asia Studies, 52*(5), 851–873.

Zarycki, T. (2009). The power of the intelligentsia: The Rywin Affair and the challenge of applying the concept of cultural capital to analyze Poland's elites. *Theory and Society, 38*(6), 613–648.

Zarycki, T., & Nowak, A. (2000). Hidden dimensions: The stability and structure of regional political cleavages in Poland. *Communist and Post-Communist Studies, 33*(3), 331–354.

Zielonka, J. (2007). *Europe as empire: The nature of the enlarged European Union*. Oxford University Press.

CHAPTER 4

Long-Term Middle Class Politics and Contemporary New Left Initiatives in Hungary and Romania

Similar to other countries in the region (Gagyi, 2019a; Unkovski-Korica, 2016), by the end of the 2000s, a new generation of left activism appeared in both Hungary and Romania. After decades of delegitimation and marginalization of left political and analytical frameworks in postsocialist contexts, by the mid-2000s new instances of left intellectual critique and activism started to appear, connected to local waves of the alterglobalist movement (Gagyi, 2013). After 2008, left formulations of the critique of transition started to gain ground and constitute a distinguishable segment of postcrisis middle class mobilizations. In both countries, the first half of the 2010s brought a multiplication of left projects and incipient infrastructures that connected them. Although workers' organizations as well as ethnic or womens' groups also stepped up for aims that could be considered as part of potential left agendas, the new left that defined itself in terms of politically explicit left positions was dominantly developed on an educated middle class background, and initiated social alliances from that background. As a middle class political phenomenon, it was as part of a new wave of middle class politicization that started from the 2000s and went against former dissidents' status quo.

© The Author(s), under exclusive license to Springer Nature Switzerland AG 2021
A. Gagyi, *The Political Economy of Middle Class Politics and the Global Crisis in Eastern Europe*, International Political Economy Series, https://doi.org/10.1007/978-3-030-76943-7_4

A New Moment of Intellectual–Political Thought

Like in other East European countries, new left actors faced specific challenges in formulating left political stances in postsocialist contexts. In the same period, for Western new left circles, the common ground of political critique became anti-neoliberalism. This framework focused on the era after the 1970s crisis, and put the emphasis on struggles on the level of regulatory frameworks that allowed the neoliberal strategy of capital's crisis management to be rolled out. In Western contexts, post-2008 movements' critique (unlike the globally more open alterglobalism before) lumped this partial historical and institutional focus together with the indignation over the decline of the Western welfare standards, and linked anti-neoliberal critique to what I earlier called the narrative of the crisis of "democratic capitalism". In turn, in global contexts where neoliberal reforms were directly linked to Western actors—like in Latin America—, anti-neoliberal critique was associated with a critique of Western global hegemony.

In Eastern Europe, new left critique could not rely on such clear alignments between local constellations and the framework of anti-neoliberalism that was growing into a transnational currency of new left discussions. While new left actors would criticize the transition process for destroying the welfare systems provided by socialism, the formulation of such critiques had to be weighed against the challenge of reckoning with the history of state socialism from a left perspective (Horvat & Štiks, 2015; Kalb, 2009; Poenaru, 2013). Doing this implied a task of reorganizing the meaning of local social experience, and finding new ways to make left alternatives politically no capitals relevant to people living with that experience. This constituted a major challenge to which Western models of reckoning with state socialism were only selectively relevant. It posed a specific problem in the way local left initiatives could connect to dominant Western ones and apply their frameworks and strategies locally—especially in a context where the delegitimation of state socialism and overall hierarchies of postsocialist transition contributed to Western hegemony in movement networks, too. As a Hungarian alterglobalist activist told me in an interview[1] in 2008:

---

[1] All research interviews quoted in this chapter are anonymized.

There were too many red flags. We believed that with time the Western European wing of the alterglobalist movement would understand and internalize the East European historical experience. That is, red flags yes, Stalin no, red star yes, but carefully. Because a few decades ago, millions died under those signs. Today we know our hopes were futile. (R. G., 2008)

In the case of alterglobalist networks, not only Western movements' use of red flags and socialist slogans, but also their strategies seemed impossible to replicate in East European contexts, due to a more narrow context of supporting movement infrastructures. Eastern activists felt that their voice is not heard by Western partners when they try to discuss the conceptual levels of left politics after socialism. When they tried to apply Western movement repertoires at home, they felt left alone with the challenge to integrate an analytical understanding of local contexts with the frameworks of transnational left frameworks, and produce political tactics relevant to both. Caught between dominant hierarchical models of postsocialist development and alterglobalist frameworks of horizontality mediated by Western partners, they started to identify themselves as actors of a horizontal global collaboration who are nevertheless limited by the postsocialist backwardness of their own social conditions (Gagyi, 2013).

As new left orientations grew stronger after 2008, discussions increasingly turned toward the task to reinterpret the history of state socialism and postsocialist transition as part of global history, and thereby reintegrate East European struggles into global narratives. This was a strong challenge both in terms of movement and academic dialogue. Academic structures recurrently imposed the dominance of Western frameworks over questions arising from East European discussions, due to the power of academic funding infrastructures. Movement interactions, too, were more often than not characterized by a hierarchical relation, composed of a self-assumed superiority on the side of Western activists—based on a better knowledge and longer experience in frameworks understood as universal—, and an acceptance mixed with puzzlement or frustration on the side of Eastern activists who could not express local differences in ways that could be recognized as relevant by their dialogue partners. "They always make us take an exam in their own frameworks before they let us speak about our issues"—one activist told me about his experience in East–West discussions among cooperative initiatives (G. L., 2018).

One illustrative example involves People's Global Action (PGA), an alterglobalist network that was initiated as a more horizontal version of the Social Forums. On a tour that served the inclusion of local groups into PGA's Balkans unit (conceived as ranging from Hungary to Turkey) PGA activists asked local activists on local issues by reading and ticking a list of problems compiled by Western activists in a notebook. More common examples include instances where East European situations are comprised within frameworks that can make these cases relevant to Western audiences by recognizing them as the same problems as their own (or extreme versions thereof). After 2008, listing local issues as products of neoliberalism in general has been a prominent case of the latter—a strategy that risked to downplay elements of local social constellations that did not fit into paradigms of anti-neoliberal critique developed in Western contexts. In Hungary, for instance, fitting the Orbán regime into the definition of neoliberalism has been a constant challenge faced by activists in international left discussions. If simply criticizing the regime's authoritarianism and xenophobic nationalism put them on the same platform with liberal critiques, proving that in fact, economically, the regime is neoliberal, could emphasize a common platform with Western new left stances. However, just as the critique of authoritarianism de-emphasized class-based tensions, the critique of neoliberalism obscured many of the regime's key characteristics.

The challenge to reformulate new left positions vis-a-vis socialism and postsocialist transition invoked the question of East–West hierarchy on multiple levels. Beyond unequal relations within academic and movement networks, East–West hierarchy as the dominant framework of postsocialist transition constituted a major element of the political, cognitive, and emotional order against which new left activists rebelled against, with varying degrees of implicit and explicit elements. In explicit expressions, rejecting the West's superiority as the leading note of the postsocialist integration project was as important for the new left as it was for right-wing answers to the same process, and it was often also expressed as part of a necessary political alternative to the new right: "We need a new mythology, collective narratives that restore a certain type of identity, and not let the right seize this problem" (Popovici & Schwartz, 2015). On more implicit levels, the same hierarchy was present in a mix of diligent study and internal frustration in face of dominant Western frameworks: "It is an anger I know from these circles. It is the expression of a cognitive frustration – when you want to express a different truth, but are not able say it yet" (C. Z., 2015). In meetings between East European activists, besides the inspiration that regional comparison provided, sharing the cognitive and emotional burden of Western domination was an important binding force. Developing these stances in theory and practice, however, implied further challenges.

First, the critique of Western dominance was hard to translate infrastructurally into East–East and global transnational collaborations. New left projects relied primarily on movement self-help and Western-dominated networks of academic or NGO funding (Unkovski-Korica, 2016). The complex task of comparing and translating between East European contexts in order to contextualize one's own diagnosis was subdued in face of a more prominent model where Eastern analysis was developed vis-a-vis various Western frameworks, as respective sub-cases—from PhDs written in Western doctoral programs to East–West collaborations set in terms of Western movement frameworks, or projects composed according to Western donors' funding schemes. While more global academic and movement frameworks and globally embedded activist biographies inherited from alterglobalism existed in both Hungary and Romania, infrastructural connections to broader global partnerships proved hard to maintain. This relative lack of global connections allowed for the critique of Eurocentrism to also be dominantly mediated by Western actors and institutions. In terms of frameworks, it allowed for the development of a critical direction where questions regarding Eastern Europe's relations to the Global South were, with some exceptions (e.g., Dialoguing Posts, 2019; Ginelli, 2018; Ginelli & Mark, 2021; Țichindeleanu, 2018), subdued compared to a focus on its subordination to Western capital and geopolitical interests. The latter, narrower focus responded more directly to both local liberal and nationalist stances on East–West hierarchies, but also opened space for left versions of developmentalist frameworks, conceived as more state-led, more welfare-oriented versions of catch-up development.

Beyond direct East–West movement dialogue and its infrastructural conditions, local new left actors' efforts to reinterpret socialism/postsocialism also posed the question of East–West relations in terms of the frameworks and vocabularies that could be used to reinvigorate local left critique. Even in criticizing East–West relations, the relevant political and academic standpoints from where critique could be developed were typically produced or mediated through Western positions. To orient local new left political thought in terms of local historical and contemporary contexts, to (re)discover their connections with global transnational threads of left thought and social struggles, to understand and contextualize dominant frameworks of present international debates, and to contribute local insights to them not only as sub-cases, but as perspectives that speak to key conceptual questions, required an effort beyond the relatively easy gains of identifying local issues as sub-cases of Western frameworks. This effort required a cumulative, collective work, which slowly developed with the growth of new left scenes. In both countries, various streams of new left research reinterpreted local Marxist traditions (Cistelecan & State, 2015; Guga, 2015), placed local modernization debates in global context (Boatcă, 2006), integrated local labor and urbanization histories into global capital-labor processes (Cucu, 2019; Petrovici, 2018), analyzed contemporary regimes in terms of long-term dynamics of world-economic integration (Éber et al., 2014; Scheiring, 2020), or provided empirical sudies on the politicization of local labor and reproductive conditions (Adăscăliţei & Guga, 2017; Bartha, 2011; Halmai, 2011; Kováts, 2018; Szombati, 2018; Vincze et al., 2018; Simionca, 2012). Together with similar trends in other countries, despite its barriers, by today this process resulted in a relatively broad and mutually shared space of regional new left thought in postsocialist contexts, that can be considered a new phase in the region's history of political thought.

Finding an alignment between the reinterpretation of local histories of global integration, respective international left viewpoints, actors' local embeddedness and empirical knowledge of local contexts, and repertoires of political action that could translate between these aspects, was a task that was key not only to forming the political program of the new left, but also to its self-understanding and identification. The formation of new left diagnoses and political programs was not only a question of analysis and political conviction, but also a process through which new political identities and respective life projects took shape, and integrated into newly reorganized landscapes of historical imagination. This chapter looks at the sensitive connection between new left political identities and new left programs that refer to external social processes.

Writing about the birth of the intellectual group that founded the left forum *CriticAtac* in the early 2010s in Romania, Poenaru (2013) developed an argument on their political becoming that links the recognition of biographical conditions to the formation of left identities. In line with broader left traditions that discuss this problem in terms of a meeting point between class position and political consciousness, Poenaru claimed that *CriticAtac* members' shift toward left positions was motivated by a basic inconsistency between their biographies as intellectuals coming of age after 1989, and the dominant narratives of postsocialist transition. Poenaru argued that this tension alienated them from the intellectual roles prescribed within those narratives and respective institutions. Instead of engaging in intellectual positions as mediators of Western-oriented progress, these people started to view their own life course in the context of the material realities of the transition process. Instead of representing intellectual superiority in the name of Western-led development, they started to see themselves on the side of workers downplayed by the process of transition (Poenaru, 2013: 324).

In this interpretation, Poenaru linked the formation of new left identities to a straight alignment between the failure of the transitional promise, the analysis of postsocialist integration as capitalist integration, and the revaluation of the intellectuals' role based on group members' own biographical experience, which led to the substitution of aspirations toward Western middle class standards with a solidarity with local workers. This process is described as a political awakening to a class consciousness that recognizes the realities of the region's capitalist integration behind the transitional projections of development, together with intellectuals' actual material subordination within it. Poenaru's analysis linked *CriticAtac* members' biographical trajectories to regional and world-historical shifts that overlap in their lifetimes: the transition from agrarian to industrial society during the socialist developmental effort; the global shift from Fordism to neoliberalism after the 1970s, and the postsocialist transition from socialist industrialization to a subordinated integration into the structures of neoliberal capitalism. In his interpretation, the disillusionment with the bourgeois role of the intellectual, and the awakening to a wage worker position happens as a result of the close overlaps of these shifts within the same biographies. Later, assessing the development of the new left in Romania in 2017, Poenaru argued that the petty bourgeois class background and respective cultural sensitivities of new left actors eventually hindered this process of identification with workers, despite close similarities in their material positions (Poenaru, 2017).

Poenaru's argument points at a key issue in the formation of new left analysis: namely, that the social actor whose class consciousness is illuminated by class analysis coincides with the agent of that analysis—in the position of the disillusioned educated middle classes. This point recalls the stream of engaged new left research discussed in Chapter 2, which posed critical analysis as an important actor that can connect particular grievances to antisystemic politics. In Chapter 2, I argued that this treatment of antisystemic political consciousness risks to omit the element of embedded structural process implied in Marxist conceptions of revolutionary consciousness, and to place all the guarantees of an antisystemic direction on the level of consciousness. I claimed that this foregrounding of the knowledge aspect falls close to what has been described as a characteristic of New Class or professional middle class politics—the tendency to experience and express one's own interests in terms of knowledge constructs framed as universal. As Poenaru's account of the birth of new left perspectives from disillusioned middle class actors' turn of consciousness suggests, the issue of consciousness as a base for a new left politics has been amplified in Eastern Europe by the lack of continuous left traditions, organizational links or movement alliances that could embed the birth of middle class new left consciousness into real-world interactions. On the one hand, the sense of an unprecedented and radical change in the understanding of the world increased the importance of intellectual conceptualization in the eyes of new left actors, making it appear as capable to inflict an ontological break that dissolves the earlier world and opens a new one. On the other hand, the lack of social contacts that could provide weight and structure to this turn of consciousness became a long-standing source of self-doubt and mutual accusations.

The present analysis does not start from the question whether forms of new left political consciousness correspond to a universal antisystemic program, and does not expect its own analysis to have a direct impact on that connection. Instead, it conceives both intellectual analysis and middle class political ambitions as real elements of the politicization of systemic tensions. In this perspective, the systemic relevance of new middle class diagnoses and programs is assessed in terms of the ways they are embedded within specific positions of systemic processes. Looking at the ways this embeddedness works within new left middle class perspectives allows us to think empirically about the relation between left political imagination and the positions from where it is born from.

Due to East European middle class new left's relative lack of significant social embeddedness (outside of its own trajectories that motivate its own mobilization), the cases discussed here offer a particular angle on the specific relationship between new left positions and new left imaginaries. This chapter delves into that question, but the analytical perspective proposed here does not aim to create a universal theory of that relation. Rather, it serves to contribute to understanding the specific conditions of further political work and alliance-making, as implied in the dynamics of East European middle class politics. A full-fledged monographic approach to the sociology of the new left would need to consider macro- and meso-level contexts together with biographical trajectories and a detailed mapping of activist and intellectual fields, including the presentation of the diverse fields of thought new left authors have produced during the last decades. The present analysis only aims to pinpoint linkages between new left positions, meso-level integration constellations, and long-term tendencies of regional middle class politics, in order to demonstrate how a perspective focused on political perspectives' contextual embeddedness can help the understanding of their stances.

New Left Positions in Post-2008 Mobilization Waves

Different meso-level constellations of postsocialist integration provided different grounds for the development in new left stances in the two countries. In Romania, the entry of new left voices into public debates happened through a direct and conflictual break with the intellectual anti-communism represented by dissident intellectuals, and with the politics of liberal-technocratic coalitions that dissident anti-communism became part of by the mid-2000s (Poenaru, 2013). Reacting to the report on communism published by Băsescu's intellectual committee, in 2008 a group of intellectuals published a collective volume (Ernu et al., 2008) that reflected critically on the political embeddedness of the report, and the limits of the moral stance it represented. A strong backlash from dominant intellectual circles condemned this kind of criticism not only as dangerous, but as practically allied to the crimes of communism. This reaction attributed the volume a significance beyond the actual influence of its authors, or the actual coherence of their stances. Exaggerated debates around the book contributed to fixing its new left perspectives' moment of debut in broader political publicity.

While this debate was the most visible publicly, the formation of new left perspectives was not limited to it: various subcultural, philosophical, artistic, sociological, and activist streams of new left criticism of postsocialist catch-up efforts were on the way to create an increasingly complex field of new left thought (Abăseacă, 2018; Ban, 2015; Gagyi, 2011). After

2010, parallel with the waves of street demonstrations, new institutional-ized forms of new left thought and activism started to multiply. In the first years of the protests, the main public forum of left debates was the portal *CriticAtac*. Founded in 2010, the mission of this portal was defined by its editors as going against the politics of the liberal-anticommunist alliance. Meanwhile, new left organizations actively participated in protests, and in some cases also started them, like in the case of Roşia Montană protests sparked by activists in Cluj. New left groups also started to build more dense relations among each other, and made first attempts at formu-lating common agendas. Throughout the following years, however, these attempts did not succeed to create a united left movement, and parallel with the right-wing shift of protests, left voices also became increas-ingly marginal within protest politics. Poenaru (2017) argued that the potential of new left groups to influence protests was terminated with the 2014 elections, when the broader middle class environment of new left actors, which used to be willing to express its discontent through left slogans before, voted for the political right against socialist candidate Victor Ponta. This alliance of demonstrators with the political right, in many of my activist conversation partners' views, led to the fragmentation and public marginalization of the new left.

Some protesters who initially identified with new left positions joined the Save Romania Union party (USR). However, their hope to promote a left political line from within the party was not fulfilled. In 2018, another, center-left platform was registered, under the name Demos (Democracy and Solidarity Party). Next to transparency, this platform emphasized the issue of social solidarity in an anti-neoliberal key, and promoted welfare reforms similar to Western anti-austerity pro-democracy parties, under the slogan of Social Europe (Demos, 2018). Yet so far, Demos was not able to produce an electoral outreach beyond highly educated urban intel-lectuals, and it could not collect sufficient signatures to join the 2019 European elections or the 2020 Bucharest local government elections. Besides USR, the second new party that came out as a winner of the protest waves was extreme right AUR. Below the electoral level, the right-wing shift of protests has been described by researchers and activists Ioana Florea and Veda Popovici (2020) as a process which started before the 2014 elections, and has been intensifying ever since. Already before the 2014 elections, left activists had been attacked several times by right-wing elements within the protests and their broader countercultural environ-ment like the FânFest festival in Rosia Montana (diycraiova, 2014), and had a hard time pushing organizers to react to those incidents. Other conflicts included instances like USR's initiative to punish the use of communist symbols by jail in 2019, an idea that was received by new left circles as a direct attack, or the attack of queer activists at a march promoting the Coalition for the Family's anti-gay marriage referendum, organized by the Romanian Orthodox Church (GAP, 2017).

Parallel to the right-wing shift of protests, and the political institution-alization of reform left stances next to more successful center-right (and later, extreme right) positions, those new left groups who criticized local crisis management not only in terms of corruption and bad economic governance, but also in the terms of an anti-capitalist critique of the post-socialist project, were marginalized in public debates. Paradoxically, this happened in parallel to a process where new left positions became increasingly popular within educated circles of the politicized new middle class. Compared to the unanimous dominance of anticommunist discourse in intellectual circles before 2008, this created a situation where new left voices were met by a growing middle class cultural demand—despite having lost their influence on the broader political process fueled by the energy of protest waves. As a *CriticAtac* member described this connec-tion: "This strata of aspirational middle-class youth, many of whom now act as volunteers at NGOs and new parties, this is where we recruit our public from" (C. G., 2016).

Poenaru (2017) argued that under these conditions, the new left's potential for an identification with workers' positions largely evaporated, and instead people turned toward pursuing middle class careers—either through political initiatives, or through the cultural embourgeoisement of anti-capitalist new left initiatives. By the latter process, Poenaru meant the professionalization of new left political expressions, which was made possible by the opening of a cultural space for expressing left standpoints in public, and by some opportunities for funding that can sustain such activities. Poenaru claimed that this apparent opening of possibilities had the effect of focusing anti-capitalist activism in the field of culture and professional activism, and promoted its integration into the customary frameworks of intellectual activity. This, in his view, acted as a barrier against perceiving the insecurity of activists' own conditions as similar to that of workers. (Poenaru, 2017: 242–244).

However, in Hungary, where the new left was not marginalized, but rather increasingly integrated into post-2010 protests, the professional-ization of new left activism shows a similar trend. While in the majority of cases, this trend indeed focuses on intellectual and representative activities characteristic to middle class politics, it does not forbid building out new alliances with workers or subaltern groups. Examples of middle class voluntary downshifting and solidarity economy also suggest that practices beyond cultural embourgeoisement exist in both countries. What stands out in terms of comparison is not so much the level of cultural embourgeoisement of the Romanian new left, but rather some characteristics of professional new left positions that follow from the specific position of new left critique within postsocialist Romanian politics.

One such characteristic consists in the fact that within the field of public intellectual debates, new left positions were constituted in a sharp contrast to the dominant alliance of political liberalism and intellectual anti-communism. From these positions, anti-neoliberal stances in the local new left could be more easily fitted to Western post-2008 anti-neoliberalism. The identification of mainstream welfare policies (like progressive taxation) with the heritage of communism by local liberal discourses made possible a swifter identification of new left positions with Western claims for bringing back welfare measures. The fact that liberal anticommunism stigmatized social critique as communist also facilitated the crystallization of a more conflictual break with liberalism and its critique of the previous regime. Against this background, despite the extremely repressive character of the Ceaușescu regime (and its clear acknowledgment by new left actors), several new left intellectuals self-identified as communist, a term other regional new left scenes typically tend to avoid, or do not communicate as a public self-definition.

Within the field of intellectual debates, the explicit break with dominant liberal models of postsocialist intellectual positions also meant that left arguments were rarely accepted in, and rarely addressed in the conventional venues of intellectual publicity. It also implied that new left intellectual styles and identities developed as outsiders, largely without the pressures and support of existing intellectual infrastructures. On the one hand, this provided a certain freedom and sense of power compared to Hungarian cases, an experience of carving out new realities in a space that did not exist before. On the other hand, the almost watertight marginalization of new left voices from mainstream debates—both in politics or academic circles—maintained the frustrating elements of this position as a lasting characteristic of new left stances.

For example, in 2015, a collective volume on Romanian Marxists— a significant milestone of the crystallization of the new left field both in terms of publishing infrastructure, collaborative work, the reevaluation of local left traditions, and in terms of related debates on relations among local new left voices—was published under the title *Exotic plants* (Cistelecan & State, 2015). This metaphor was taken from nineteenth-century Romanian debates, which discussed modern political ideologies, including Marxism, in the framework of developmental backwardness expressed in the idea of "forms without substance". As a title, *Exotic plants* reactualized this framework by defining the volume—otherwise intended as a proof of an existing tradition and a gesture of showcasing contemporary left thought—as alien and extremely vulnerable in its relation to the broader intellectual–political field. Despite the differences in various left circles' intellectual and political orientation, this element of marginality, together with a heads-on, conflictual response to it, remained a recurrent characteristic of Romanian new left stances. In sociology or philosophy, the marker "Marxist", which functioned as a stigma in mainstream discourses, was used explicitly by new left actors. In programs that expressed emancipatory claims in decolonial frameworks, the idea of speaking from the margins was simultaneously applied to the question of global subordination, speakers' own marginal position, and the gesture of opposing dominant Western frameworks mediated through local liberal bourgeois hegemony (e.g. Popovici & Pop, 2016).

Gestures of distantiation from mainstream intellectual positions and frameworks did not only involve political stances and a class identification that defied the norm of intellectuals' role as mediators of Western-led development. They also involved shifts in intellectual style and habitus. Several new left authors describe the latter as turning away from models of intellectual expression that connect the systemic function of developmental mediator to symbols of intellectual-aesthetic superiority consecrated by Western references. For instance, Rogozanu (2006) pointed out a continuity between interwar, dissident, and postsocialist literary styles, which consists in gestures of expressing superiority through the aesthetic form. He analyzed these gestures as an aesthetic abstraction or mystification of a power claim characteristic to the role of intellectuals as developmental mediators. Rogozanu opposed this to an intellectual attitude that denies solidarity with the value claims implied in the traditional role of developmental mediator.

Besides denying developmental claims per se, this attitude also implies that intellectual practice places itself outside of the range of aesthetic mystification, and defines its reference in terms of the social struggle. In

Poenaru's (2013) interpretation of the formation of the group behind *CriticAtac*, this rejection of aesthetic and habitual solidarity with intellectual positions coincided with the identity shift and political choice through which new left actors break the surface of intellectual mystifications that project the idea of development over postsocialist integration, and come to define themselves in terms of their material conditions, as wage workers. While the actual stances through which this aesthetic and habitual break is carried out differ across groups, the effect of distantiation from mainstream intellectual positions is a specificity that stands out in comparison to Hungarian cases.

In Hungary, in contrast, the former liberal hegemony that silenced left voices in the 1990s and 2000s imploded after 2010. In response to the Orbán regime's explicitly anti-poor and anti-labor stances, oppositional politics opened toward social issues. This created a space within oppositional publicity where left messages not only could be voiced more freely, but were also eagerly integrated into oppositional arguments. However, the same situation also implied that left elements of arguments became integrated into dominant oppositional frameworks defined by the reactualized transitional narrative of Western-led development, and remained limited to the status of minor complementary arguments within those frameworks. The integration of left ideas into oppositional arguments happened along lines similar to dissidents' social politics before 1989, which presupposed an overlap between democratization, market liberalization, and the end of poverty. While this fit well with less radical formulations of European new left narratives that reactualized the ideal of European democratic capitalism through the diagnosis of the crisis of "democratic capitalism", it also put limitations on the scope of leftist critique within oppositional coalitions.

In this context, unlike in the Romanian case, the Hungarian new left became increasingly acknowledged and visible in the oppositional publicity. Despite the implosion of liberal hegemony, this sphere was still dominated by highly acclaimed and erudite liberal intellectual circles whose career and legitimacy reached back to dissident years. While gestures of marginalization were not completely absent, compared to earlier decades, these circles' resistance to left stances significantly softened after 2010. Besides the regime's antisocial character and the solidarity of oppositional struggle, what also contributed to this opening was a sense of professional collectivity. In a context where research, higher education, culture, and media were swiftly reorganized under the domination of centralized power, higher levels of intellectual erudition often came to be seen as valuable even if expressed in left stances. This effect was reinforced by an increasing leftward trend in the younger intellectual generation, which limited the pool of young intellectual disciples and allies to ones with left perspectives. On the side of new left actors, this rapprochement was also supported by a sense of solidarity following from the context of oppositional struggle. Despite their criticism against the neoliberal model of the regime change and its political and intellectual proponents, in a context where former power holders of liberal hegemony were pushed into marginalization and unemployment, and institutional systems transformed in ways that threatened with the annihilation of former professional standards in various branches of intellectual activity, new left actors stood in solidarity with actors of the previous liberal hegemony who became victims of the Orbán regime. In demonstrations against the closure of CEU, the reorganization of higher education or the academy, as well as in the various smaller actions against reforms that substituted old institutions with new ones in hands loyal to the government, redrew whole cultural fields through new funding schemes, or moved museums to new locations risking the destruction of their material, new left actors joined opposition movements' struggle, and only expressed their alternative views as side notes.

The relative closeness of new left and former liberal spheres supported the development of several characteristics of new left stances that differed from the Romanian case. One of these was a more dialogical attitude toward local liberalism, which did not allow for the sense of iconoclasm and foundational freedom characteristic to Romanian new left positions. Instead, it bound new left orientations in a considerable manner to the professional and cultural knowledge developed within former liberal infrastructures. On the one hand, this often resulted in binding the development of new left frameworks to legitimating them in the face of liberal frameworks still experienced as dominant. Liberal intellectuals' erudition in Marxist frameworks and in the dissident traditions of refuting those frameworks with liberal arguments, together with liberal intellectual elites' high-level empirical knowledge of postsocialist contexts made them strong debate partners. On the other hand, relative mutual openness to dialogue allowed Hungarian new left stances to benefit from, and build upon the erudition of liberal intellectual circles. In terms of political identification, the same closeness resulted in a relative toning down of differences between left and liberal positions. While critique was part of new left expressions, Hungarian new left actors typically developed their claims in a language that balanced between expanding the social aspects of politics still acceptable to liberal audiences and claims similar to those of Western anti-austerity pro-democracy movements. Correspondingly, Hungarian new left circles seldom used controversial identity markers such as communism or Marxism.

If in terms of institutional positions, new left activists met previously powerful actors of former liberal hegemony on a relatively common ground of institutional marginalization, in the broader political publicity government communication pushed them even more explicitly in the same corner of oppositional politics. Building on the tradition of postsocialist right-wing politics, government communication regularly referred to liberalism and Marxism as interconnected aspects of Western ideological penetration. The very notion of the "left", canonized in Hungary as a label for socialist-liberal coalitions, also contributed to the blurring of differences between new left and oppositional liberal stances. In this context, the defining point of new left political stances became a moral identification with the values of democracy, solidarity, and antiauthoritarianism. This allowed to reject the politics of former socialist-liberal coalition while engaging in a collective struggle with broader oppositional protests. In public expressions of their difference from liberal stances, new left actors typically recurred to arguments of moral responsibility or claims of social justice tied to developmental promises and avoided more conflictual forms like emphasizing contradictory class interests.

This kind of balancing limited the scope of critique in several areas. The idea of Europe, for instance, remained a positive reference point: despite criticisms of European neoliberalism and transitional subordination, references to European standards of democracy and welfare remained a recurring element of new left arguments—underlined, of course, by a context of deepening of authoritarianism and antisocial measures. The case of new left stances on Europe is also illustrative to the way the effect of a dual ideological space, dominated by internal and external liberal critiques of the regime, and the government's use of these to support its image as the defender of the nation, could contain the development of alternative forms of critique that did not fit the logic of that division. In other areas, however, the same type of balancing opened space for a certain mainstreaming of left ideas. Welfare claims, the idea of workers' rights, and the relegitimation of unions as actors of progress are examples of this kind of development.

Another important difference from the Romanian context was that in Hungary, there was a narrow but existing continuity of left criticism, active since the regime change. The intellectual group around Left Alternative has been criticizing postsocialist reorganization in terms of materialist analysis in their journal *Eszmélet* (Consciousness) since 1989. The College for Advanced Studies in Social Theory, founded in 1981, functioned as a school of left theory that inspired many of the activists of the alterglobalist and post-2008 waves. Despite their marginalization from dominant intellectual publicity, the work of left intellectuals linked to the *Eszmélet* circle like Tamás Krausz, Erzsébet Szalai, Attila Melegh, József Böröcz, or that of Gáspár Miklós Tamás served as existing orientation points for the new wave of left activism.

This background was built upon by a publicly less visible stream of new left intellectual and activist work, which engaged less with the current events of oppositional politics, and focused more on developing types of collaborations and knowledge that could orient left political action. Next to a more dialogical relation with established intellectual frameworks, the existence of local left traditions in Hungary contributed to a sense of context that differed from Romanian new left actors' experience of marginality and new beginnings. Even where contacts with representatives of earlier left traditions did not provide a full continuity with their ideas and politics, new left actors acknowledged and respected these traditions as a source of learning and as an example. This context contributed to a more silent tendency toward learning and empirical research. In internal organizing, below the level of public demonstrations and more visible political movements, the tradition of the College for Advanced Studies in blending left theory with self-organizing spilled over in several new initiatives that with time, became significant institutions and models of new left organizing.

Earlier initiatives for left politics also existed in Hungary—although none of them managed to transcend the dominant divisions of the political field, and assert left politics as an alternative on its own right. Politics Can Be Different, which initially seemed to successfully channel the energy of the alterglobalist movement into parliamentary politics, broke along the lines of the traditional left–right division of postsocialist Hungarian politics. Fourth Republic (4 K!), a left movement that was founded in response to the right-wing tendency of the 2006 demonstrations, and turned into a party after 2010, was initially a prominent participant of oppositional demonstrations. After it declined the invitation into the Together alliance due to its neoliberal continuities, 4K! was excluded from oppositional publicity, and could not gather the higher number of signatures required by Fidesz' new electoral law in 2014. Meanwhile, transforming organizations of the orthodox postsocialist left, starting with the Workers' Party in 1990, remained on the fringe of the political system, and did not manage to appeal to the new wave of left activism.

The local elections of 2019, and the preparations for the 2022 parliamentary elections brought a new wave of interest for party politics within the new left. In 2019, several new left initiatives engaged with the opposition's coordinated campaign for local elections. A community campaign behind independent candidate András Pikó won the leadership of Budapest's 8th district, based on a model of grassroots organization that merged left community organizing and liberal civil society expertise. A new initiative for left political organizing, Szikra (Spark) mobilized activists to aid the campaign of selected candidates in Budapest, including that of Gergely Karácsony, who became the mayor of Budapest. After a series of oppositional victories, several leading new left activists enrolled in oppositional local government positions. While oppositional local governments struggled against a narrow maneuver space, governmental attacks, and the task to build oppositional capacity for the 2022 elections, Szikra and other left groups tried to use their connections to promote left agendas. For instance, when the government allowed local governments to modify legislation regarding Airbnb (in a move to channel tourism toward the pandemic-stricken hotel industry owned by party-related oligarchs), left activist groups responding to the call of The City is for All organized an anti-Airbnb campaign, and oppositional mayor Karácsony organized hearings where these groups were also present. For the 2022 parliamentary elections, Szikra supports the preselection campaign of an independent candidate.

It can be argued that despite a slowly growing new left scene, so far all initiatives of the Hungarian new left either integrated into oppositional politics, broke along the lines of dominant political divisions, or remained confined to marginal circles with little social outreach. Yet the simultaneous growth of social tensions and of new left infrastructures might also prepare the ground for new types of dynamics. Throughout the 2010s, groups representing social claims were as welcome in oppositional politics as new left elements, with their participation similarly relegated to a complementary function within the main lines of pro-European, pro-democracy arguments. However, the case of the demonstration wave reacting to a new amendment of the labor code in 2018, nicknamed by protesters as the "slave law" (Gagyi & Gerőcs, 2019) illustrates a potential shift in the relation between these two groups.

The independent news site *Mérce*, which became a major media site of the new left wave, had been founded with an explicit mission to represent social issues in a media space dominated by right-wing and liberal arguments. Normally *Mérce*'s content was dominated by intellectuals' opinion pieces similar to other opposition media, but in 2018, through its choice to follow up on unions' claims and focus on unions' presence in its regular on-site reports on protests it came to play a strong role in the thematization of demonstrations. Like in other cases, opposition parties and extra-parliamentary opposition initiatives thematized the issue of the labor code amendment as part of their general oppositional agenda. Across established communication networks, these efforts soon made it to international publicity, framed according to narratives of Europeanization vs. democratic backsliding. For instance, a campaign by female opposition politicians who stepped up in the parliament and at demonstrations wearing white caps to distinguish the group, was presented by *The Guardian* as representing protesters' cause in general: "a new wave of female politicians and protesters are offering an alternative to the Hungary PM's macho politics" (Walker, 2018).

In contrast to this usual stream of protest representation, *Mérce*'s protest reports and opinion pieces continued to keep a focus on unions' standpoints and role within the protests, and did not cease to emphasize that the "slave law" is primarily an issue of labor, not one of Europeanization or democracy in general, or a sub-case of oppositional politics. This opening in a media space that is generally closed to unions' communication was taken on by unions, and *Mérce*'s articles became a two way link between unions' public communication and public articles that unions could use internally. A small example in itself, this case represents a significant change compared to a decades-long trend, where any expression of social grievances was either closed out from publicity, or translated into the language of liberal vs. nationalist political discourse. Gille (2010) called this effect the epistemological "decapitation of society" in transnational communication, where the role of translation between local social issues and international publicity was fully dominated by mainstream neoliberal frameworks, and resistance to these was channeled into nationalist politics. The fact that *Mérce*'s reports managed to keep the issue of labor on the agenda in the case of the "slave law" protests, differentiate new left stances from that of the oppositional "left", and create practical links with unions, was a development that pointed toward a potential shift compared to the previously established order of politicization.

LEFT POLITICS AS THE EXPERIENCE OF THE SELF

In 2015–2016, I had the occasion to complete (and reevaluate) my understanding of Hungarian and Romanian new left scenes that I had a participant, through a research conducted according to the methods of anthropological fieldwork. To gain a broader understanding of new left scenes beyond my own embedded perspective, I took part in events, personal and group discussions beyond the regular paths defined by my own activist work, analyzed materials and media communication by various groups and projects, and made 22 biographical interviews with Hungarian and Romanian new left activists and intellectuals. The main lesson I learned was the actual multiplicity of political programs and sensitivities, something which tends to be toned down or translated to dismissals of others' standpoints in participants' embedded perspectives.

If Poenaru (2013) argued that the birth of new left political perspectives is a result of biographical experience across overlapping global and regional shifts of capitalist development, what I found in my interviews was that activists' narratives connect biographical experience to the story of political formation in significantly different ways, arriving to strong variations in the ways personal experience and sensitivity becomes aligned with political vocabularies and forms of action. In sense of a linear and necessary connection, this variability contradicts the argument that new left stances would follow from biographical experience. Instead of such a direct connection, what my interviews suggest is that pressures experienced in middle class positions are given a political meaning through a complex and socially embedded process of intellectual and emotional labor, where personal memory, attitudes, and ambitions are continuously negotiated vis-a-vis changing relations of local and international activist scenes, creating different alignments between biographical narratives, political conviction, and activist work.

The way my conversation partners formulated the connection between biographical experience and political orientation often pinpointed the significance of contradictions between personal experience and transitional ideologies that represented local realities as a process of catching up with Western standards. However, the actual reference points of these contradictions, and the political conclusions associated with them, varied largely. For instance, situations where parents' employment and careers were broken by deindustrialization were marked as a strong motivation for seeking new interpretations and political answers in the case of several of my interlocutors. However, these connected in different ways to actual political orientations, and the personal feelings and convictions associated with them varied. A feminist left activist spoke about her father's depression, an issue she struggled with during her teenage years, as an issue that combined the aspect of male roles as necessarily dominant within the family with the humiliation effect of deindustrialization, and its unresolved conflict with the symbolic promises of the regime change. Elsewhere, my interlocutor's understanding of his parents' experience of unemployment due to deindustrialization was first associated with the nationalist current of anti-neoliberalism, and his story of political formation pinpointed the steps of revaluating that perspective through learning left theories and participating in left activism in Western contexts, and then integrating those inspirations with a deeper knowledge of rural deindustrialization locally through ethnographic work. In another case, parents' hardships were pointed out as an experience that sparked the need to explain local processes as elements of neoliberal globalization, and reinvent local left politics in terms of a twenty-first-century ecopolitics that goes beyond former historical models, and opens the way to a potential future:

> I started to be irresistibly interested in what is going on with us, what is globalization, why people's lives are being destroyed, what happened to my family in fact (...) I realized that the only way I can tell my own story is the language of left politics (...) green politics is an attempt to reinterpret progress. For me, this is the entering of left politics into the 21th century. (D. G., 2016)

Like the idea of green politics here, in most cases, the perception of the link between personal experience and the political paradigm of present activism was expressed in the form of a necessity. In other cases, however, the same necessity pointed in different directions. In another interview, the main aspect of political necessity was to use intellectual work for the restoration of an emancipative form of collective dignity:

> To speak from the margins, the position of those who are suppressed and marginalized, but in another way! With pride, with aggression, without fear (...) those years were dominated by a public discourse that was either based on contempt or self-pity, you know, a combination of these two, as if we never did anything worthy of mentioning, this is what we are, we have always been taken advantage of, we are so miserable (...) This combination of contempt and self-pity instead of a consciousness of being oppressed, it's a very perverse situation. To learn to speak about oppression with force, I realized that this is what we need to do. (B. P., 2015)

Class analysis was one of the various ways in which biographical experience was linked to new left political frameworks. In the case of *CriticAtac*, Poenaru described this link as one that induced a shift from intellectual positions and corresponding frameworks of mystification to a materialist analysis and identification with workers' positions. As a member of the Working Group for Public Sociology "Helyzet" in Budapest, I also promoted class analysis as a necessary element in the development of new left politics (e.g. Éber & Gagyi, 2015). In Helyzet's practice, this ambition was tied to a more austere and professional version of analysis, which aimed rather to eliminate the influence of researchers' own class perspective on the result of analysis, rather than express it through it. While Helyzet also sought to depart from existing intellectual frameworks and institutions, and to build alternative infrastructures of knowledge creation, this dissociation was not accompanied by an identification with workers' position. Instead, Helyzet members saw their own position as rooted in the crisis of earlier intellectual infrastructures, and remained suspicious of their own positions' effect on political practice. Helyzet kept a distance from both left-liberal alliances of oppositional movements and public stances that claimed labor-based left politics from intellectual positions. Instead, they organized public sociology activities to build a research-inspired shared orientation in newly forming left constituencies and continued to struggle with the limitations of outreach that bound this work to already mobilized middle class segments.

Although central in some accounts, the class analysis did not appear in my interviews as a general condition of new left orientation. For instance, one feminist activist told me that structural analysis in itself does not have the capacity to orient political action, in the sense that it does not necessarily lead to inaction, and does not build actual relations of solidarity and identification that are indispensable elements of left politics. Instead, she perceived the universalizing tendency of structural analysis as a potential— and often practical—barrier in building left alliances, as it keeps sustain the appearance of a general relevance of intellectual claims that are not bound to actual political work and social coalitions. Instead, she emphasized the capacity of empathy that arises from one's own experience and political understanding of suffering as the main base of left politics. She saw this capacity as one that is able to make different experiences of suffering visible for each other, and link them together in forms of solidarity that do not overwrite each others' perspectives with their own programs, but rather open the way toward new collaborations.

> If you went through such struggles yourself, you will develop a capacity to understand those people who are living among oppressive conditions – that is, to understand them from their own perspectives, and not from the perspective of your own expectations. I think that this kind of sensitivity is more important than theory and Marxism. The sensitivity that makes you capable to perceive the complexity of the world. (C. P., 2016)

In terms of conclusions regarding the possibilities and significance of personal action, different narratives reflected similarly varied conclusions. One frequent type of conclusions was the idea of an urgent, necessary, and undoubtedly relevant action, formulated according to the scope of actions available to politicized intellectuals:

> I feel that I have a responsibility in this situation as an intellectual (...) In politics sometimes you cannot go for compromise (...) there are moments that allow no doubt, where you need to stand your ground and fight the battle. (F. A., 2016)

Other standpoints, however, reflected less unanimous relations between intellectual responsibility and practical engagement. In the case of social theater experiments which worked with real biographical stories of marginalized communities, actor-activist Katia Pascariu (2016) spoke about the gap between political representation and palpable solutions as an implicit contradiction of this kind of work:

Social theater is a complex issue; you open Pandora's box, but then it remains open, and you don't have the solutions to the problems that it reveals. You act as a funnel that makes problems audible. But it is frustrating as we do not solve these problems. We cannot solve them.

In other cases, the shift toward left perspectives was associated with a sense of limitation and irrelevance of intellectual capacities. One Budapest activist described her political trajectory throughout the 2010s as starting from a mutually reinforcing experience of participation in the political actions that opposed the government's reorganization of the art field, and a parallel shift toward left perspectives on art and politics. However, her internalization of left viewpoints soon started to question the relevance she earlier attributed to political art and to its professional frameworks:

Later, when I started to actually think in terms of practice, I could not live [art] any more. The real world broke into my field of vision. And art seemed less and less important. My conscience started to block me (...) We wanted to criticize the whole system, to deal with reality and make art into a tool for this. But when you try to do that, it becomes unavoidable to start to learn about that reality. It was an awfully rough moment when I realized how much actually I should know in order to do anything relevant. Then I saw that this duty of learning kills practice. (T. A., 2016)

The variety of narratives and political conclusions suggests that there is no direct, necessary link between global integration dynamics, transitional careers, biographical experience, and new left politics. At the same time, the multiplication of new left voices after 2008 suggests that there is a connection between structural crisis and new left politics. In line with the analytical perspective proposed in this book, I interpret this connection not as one established by a transparent reflection on structural conditions, which would necessarily engender a certain type of political stance, but as a differentiated process through which crisis effects become politicized through various ideological and social alliances embedded into local constellations of global transformation.

The previous section argued that different constellations of postsocialist integration provided different positions for new left actors in Hungarian and Romanian contexts, and this influenced the political and intellectual stances they took. In the following, I highlight characteristics that I saw as largely similar in the two countries in 2015–2016. I understand these as situated expressions of the long-term tendency of middle class politics to formulate middle class experience in terms of general political programs. The situated aspect of these long-term characteristics that I emphasize here has to do with an initial stage of development of new left fields, after the sweeping marginalization of left stances in post-transition decades. This, of course, is only one aspect of the contextual factors among which new left politics develop in these contexts. The characteristics and examples highlighted here do not provide a complex analysis of either group's practice or ideology and do not provide a monographic analysis of the two fields. Instead, they serve to demonstrate the relevance of long-term patterns of middle class politics to the understanding of present dynamics and bring them the attention of present debates over new left politics.

One of the characteristics that I saw as common across various groups in both Hungary and Romania in 2015–2016 was the high intensity of symbolic debates over authenticity. In discussions and interviews, activists often referred to new left fields' fragmentation and the intensity of symbolic struggles as a major source of tensions and barrier to collective action. These characteristics were often explained by specificities of certain groups or intergroup dynamics, yet I found that symbolic struggles over the authenticity of left political positions were generally present in both new left fields. While instances of conflicts over specific resources or power positions did exist, patterns of symbolic divisions did not seem to reflect a geography of resource conflicts. Instead, I understood the intensive, but constantly shifting fields of symbolic debates as following from a situation where various actors initiate new models of left politics, but do not dispose of the "proof" of those models in terms of actual social embeddedness. The gap between the universal ambition of such projects and their minimal forms of realization came to be reflected in symbolic struggles where mutual differences were exaggerated and projected into the future, and their significance was assessed not in terms of initiatives' present state, but in terms of their prolongation in a potential future where their universal programs would be realized. Thus, in debates of authenticity, new left actors could accuse each other of various types of negative tendencies even if none of them possessed any significant power or was responsible for significant outcomes.

The question of relevant social alliances that could sustain the authenticity of political claims was a key element of symbolic debates. The sensitivity of the issue was enhanced by the fact that most new left projects were initiated by politically mobilized middle class groups. This aspect of social alliances exposed virtually any project to the possibility of mutual critique. In my experience, the actual measures different projects applied to ensure equal participation of other social groups, or to control and reduce the effects of middle class privilege in such relations, did not count as significant factors in deterring such criticism. Projects upheld as examples of political authenticity in one moment could be unmasked by critiques in a new wave of debates as hypocrites, without any change occurring in their internal organization that served as the reference point of debates.

The intensity of symbolic struggles within new left fields might seem esoteric from an external perspective. This was commonly reflected in my interviews, with people telling me that the conflict lines they are speaking about are probably indistinguishable even for the relatively few people who are aware of the new left groups involved. From the inside, however, these struggles constituted an unavoidable reality that requires a constant investment of energy. Quoting Durkheim, Randall Collins (2001) used the concept "collective effervescence" to name similar situations of move-ment building. Thinking about moments of mobilization in terms of affective investments, Collins wrote about collective effervescence as a social state where actors experience the transformation of existing social bonds and norms, including that of their own attachments. In these situ-ations, Collins claimed, group relations are characterized by a heightened sensitivity to trends of reorganizing social connections and meanings, and an intensified state of collective attention to each other. This also implies a competition for collective attention and the potential benefits of newly forming tendencies of norms and group boundaries—a type of resource that is not (only) based in the external conditions of movement formation, but in its internal dynamics. Collins also describes this state as a factor of radicalization, in case stances disregarded or stigmatized by external norms come to be acknowledged and valued within group dynamics, and internal competition reinforces a shift toward more radical ones.

This environment of intense collective attention, extremely sensitive to tendencies of internal norms and differentiations, which are experi-enced by actors as something like a collective resource, was a characteristic that I frequently recognized in both Hungarian and Romanian new left scenes. I also found Collins' concept of collective effervescence indicative in thinking about the simultaneous but contradictory presence of group solidarity and mutual control. In the environment of symbolic struggles, the authenticity of one's political position works as a type of symbolic capital that requires constant maintenance. On the one hand, this acts as a motivating force and a source of intergroup solidarity, but on the other hand, it also provides an interface of vulnerability for interventions that question or harm this kind of symbolic capital. In such tense situations, actors' authenticity was questioned and required to be proved in a rhetorical framework that implied a sense of urgency combined with that of a final and irrevocable decision. However, in terms of later dynamics of debates and collaborations, in fact such instances did not necessarily have irrevocable effects. Similarly, the stakes of such debates in most cases did not connect to actual effects of actors' practice, but rather to the significance of potential further implications of their direction of thought and action. Comparing instances of such debates, my impression was that the sense of urgency and high stakes of the debates were rather characteristic of how field dynamics came to be expressed in moments of debates, and followed less from concrete characteristics of debate situations.

While the environment of mutual critique and intense symbolic debates was often condemned as an unnecessary hindrance in new left discussions, the volume of time and attention dedicated to them suggested that they cannot be dealt away with as a minor side effect. In Western new left debates, long-term critiques of left sectarianism have been actualized by Mark Fisher (2013) with respect to the shift of middle class left practice toward identity politics. Fisher's metaphor "vampire castle" epitomized a description of the dynamics of British new left scenes as one that consists of exercises of moral critique formulated in terms of victimhood defined in the paradigm of identity politics. In the lack of actual movement organizations and respective coordinated forms of political action, Fisher argued, these exercises reproduce the appearance of political action and corresponding forms of political capital by identifying moments of speech or action as symbolically implying catastrophic consequences of oppression, and initiating actions of exorcism that produce the political situation of struggle, and fortify the position of good through victory over evil.

While forms of Western new left identity politics were integrated into some segments of both Hungarian and Romanian cases, neither of the fields was wholly characterized by symbolic struggles fought within the frameworks of identity politics. Instead of an effect of petty bourgeois reflexes and peasant backgrounds, a direct effect of resource and power struggles, or the consequence of identity politics, I grew to understand symbolic struggles over authenticity as following from a stage of development of new left fields. This stage I saw as a moment where actors politicized as part of a larger mobilization wave already started to reorient their symbolic investments into new left political projects, but these projects did not yet reach a stage of materialization that would bind these investments into concrete forms of social alliances, organizational structures, and political practice. In this situation, the value of symbolic investments into various political programs relies on the capacity of maintaining their promise in lack of external proof for it, and is exposed to the constant risk of inflation—especially in a context where projects framed in universal terms mutually question each other's relevance.

Authors writing about the politics of symbolic competition in environments of contemporary Western middle class crisis have also emphasized the issue of symbolic inflation—like in the case of the value of taste displayed in consumer choices in hipsters (N+1, 2014), or the value of virtue signaling in situations where virtue becomes a currency speculatively invested into mobility hopes in the lack of corresponding social or material capital. Nagle (2017) pointed out that since virtue signaling is threatened by inflation, the need to create scarcity to maintain virtue's value fuels mutual symbolic attacks. While these descriptions fall close to the way I understood the field dynamics I saw in 2015–2016 in Hungarian and Romanian new left environments, following developments in later years reinforced my idea that these dynamics did not constitute a general characteristic, but rather that of a stage in development. By the end of the decade, the deepening of various projects that bound them to specific forms of organization and social alliances, as well as the strengthening of cross-group collaborations created a new environment in which the significance of authenticity debates was reduced or solidified along with stable divisions between different projects.

In terms of rhetorical expression, a characteristic related to the symbolic nature of new left expressions was a type of theatricality that manifests in a highly ambitious, but overly brittle claim to represent one's political expression as carrying a broad social significance. The brittleness of this construct follows from a situation where that significance is only maintained by the act of speech, and is not sustained by real structures of organization and political power that could translate them to broader social effects. While already in 2015–2016, some groups did work with marginalized groups or—like in the case of party initiatives—did build larger structures of representation, the main dynamic of new left fields was dominated by symbolic expressions of left analysis and political stances. Since the authenticity of these stances was defined in terms of social relevance, the situation where new left activity was more often than not limited to middle class actors' expressions of their own political reorientation created an uncomfortable contradiction. One way this contradiction was bridged was what I came to call the extension of symbolic chains of reference to the authenticity of real fieldwork examples.

In international activist debates, the relationship between daily fieldwork and grand political expressions has been a long-debated issue, raising questions of gender- and class-based hierarchies in the distribution of labor between fieldwork and political representation. While these issues were also at play in the circles I interacted with, together with conscious efforts to counterbalance them, what I would like to pinpoint here is the relation between new left politics based in middle class mobilization and the extension of symbolic chains of reference. Here, the extension of the chain refers to instances where relatively small initiatives that do practical work and do connect to other social groups are referred to by other new left actors as a reference point that authenticates acts of uttering symbolic political programs that exceed the actual scope and effects of the project in question. While traveling through these reference chains, the symbolic significance of such concrete projects as potential models or prefigurative realizations of broader political programs is amplified, while the pragmatic context, everyday work, or concrete challenges and contradictions of the same projects tend to be obscured. In one interview, the term my conversation partners used for this effect was "symbolic gentrification". This referred to their perception of a discontinuous and hierarchical relation between their own everyday work, and their project's symbolic representations which framed it as a successful and politically broadly significant initiative, but also obscured and misrepresented their actual experience:

> [Our project] has built up this superb image (...) half of which is not true in practice. (...) Our communication was so successful, even if it was not our main focus at all, that many [cultural] professions now are pushing it as an example, in circles where you can gain some position by claiming left stances. And by now this became a mutually reinforcing circuit. (T. A., 2016)

Another characteristic that I saw as common to various segments of Hungarian or Romanian new left fields was a rhetorical structure of political expressions which implied a major historical crisis and turning point, with regard to which the speakers' own thought, speech, and action were attributed central significance and responsibility. This centrality of speakers' own perspective to what was defined as an external crisis reflected a close overlap between speakers' own experience of a crisis and their definition of a broader historical turn.

A series of examples for this close connection can be seen in Hungarian political essays written in response to the open question "WTF left?", posed by *Kettős Mérce* in 2015 as part of an effort to establish the site as a forum for new left debates. Most answers to *Kettős Mérce*'s question formulated the diagnosis of historical crisis and the corresponding need for action in terms of new left actors' own stakes; yet both diagnoses and proposals for solution differed according to actors' different positions. Most often, these stakes were defined by the position of new left actors as intellectuals voicing new left standpoints, or as activists working in oppositional initiatives and projects of representative politics. For instance, in several cases, the conditions for the formation of the new left were associated with the relation between formerly dominant liberal intellectuals and new left intellectuals, where the key to the solidification of new left political stances was seen in liberal intellectuals providing space for new left voices (e.g. Gyenge, 2015). In other cases, the key to the formation of new left politics was seen in new left actors being able to make themselves seen and acknowledged by voters: "The audience/community has to see that we are strong, capable, that we move well in the ring, and they have to feel that we are fighting for them and not for ourselves. When all this is achieved, we can say "Hello, the left has arrived!" (Krasztev, 2015).

Another type of examples for the connection between new left perspectives and actors' own positions is provided by answers which defined left politics as a fulfillment of the habitus and values speakers identified with: "In the present political environment, the left is condemned to insignificance. It is the ideology if idealists. I am an idealist, and I don't want this to be burnt out within me, ever" (Eperjesi, 2015). "I want to amplify human values. To emphasize my professionalism. As an independent, free civilian" (Ritók, 2015). "My leftism is the base of my mental hygiene" (Cserháti, 2015) "As mere words, these ideas mean nothing, but it is wonderful to live according to them" (Selyem, 2015) "In my family, leftism is not more than an instinctive rejection of all forms of premodern traditionalism, mythologizing, exclusion, social injustice. On a more conscious level, it is a stubborn fidelity to 'common sense rationality', the values of the Enlightenment, and the achievements of the history of civilization, future-centric thinking, and collective responsibility" (Krasztev, 2015).

In other examples, besides their habitus and values, it is the intellectual erudition of middle class new left actors that is identified as the key condition of new left politics:

> Today's new left might strike one as too theoretical and refined. It is full of delicate details, it's not a type of leftism where you are shouting slogans. And this new left is constituted by very nice, highly cultured individuals with a strong sense of self-reflection, who regularly lose the battle against evil intentions, violence, shameless lies and open manipulations – so how can we trust them? For me, it is exactly these gentle figures that represent the guarantee for the potential of left politics to become the antidote to abandonment, vulnerability, exploitation. (Nemes, 2015)

> But something is happening today. I feel that these days, it becomes cool to be a leftist. A new left generation appeared. They are amazingly well prepared and educated, consequential, and make no compromises. They represent everything that being on the left means for me, with an enthralling resolution. They are at ease in using even Marxist terminology, accurately and correctly. (Kósa, 2015)

> It is only an educated and materially independent middle class that is able to operate, sustain and defend the institutions of democracy. Societies that mostly consist of uneducated people are unable to participate in today's increasingly complex public debates in a relevant way. They think in simple schemes, and easily fall prey to populism. (Pogátsa, 2015)

The third type of examples consists of cases where speakers define the actions that are necessary for the birth of new left politics in terms of questions and programs formulated according to authors' own professional profiles. Intellectuals who deal with political ideology or political theory emphasized the necessity to formulate new ideological and theoretical diagnoses and programs that could orient new left politics:

> We need to become able to recognize what kind of *semiotic regime* it is that manifests itself in all these diverse forms (...) we need to aim for the

critique of the semiotic regime, not only the substitution of delegitimated figures with others (...) without a systematic critical theory, political fantasy remains empty. (Sipos, 2016)

Speakers involved in humanitarian studies, or working as pedagogues or in helping professions emphasized the importance of dignity, creativity, and education, as the necessary tools to create a new political imagination that can serve as a basis of social transformation:

> Now we need to take a radical step, and create, on the one hand, a much more egalitarian pedagogy, and on the other hand, much braver forms of art, philosophy and science. Pedagogy needs to become local, participatory, democratic. Art and philosophy need to be universal, non-applied and without compromise, but first of all: constructive. It needs to produce new imagination. (...) To create new imagination is a slow process, but if we don't start producing it, we will forever remain captive of the fantasy of others. (Bagi, 2015)

Political scientists, historians, or sociologists spoke about the significance of empirical and historical research in providing a ground for evidence-based orientation, finding relevant inspiration for new left political imagination. "We need to accomplish a critical reevaluation of those Hungarian political traditions that can be associated with left politics, or values related to left politics"—a writer and historian of literature wrote (Schein, 2015). While I did not contribute to the essay series, in other fora I made similar statements in the same period. In my case, I pointed at the analysis of contemporary social transformation and its links to dynamics of global capitalism as an essential condition of left political orientation. I do not think back to this stance as irrelevant, and still believe that this kind of analysis has a contribution potential to new left thought. But viewed in the context of other intellectual stances, my standpoint also integrates into the row of rhetorical expressions that place speakers' own professional capacity at the center of the historical drama of new left formation. As I grew to understand, being able to understand this connection can be as important to political orientation as the analysis of external social processes.

Analyzing the "WTF left?" series, Erzsébet Szalai (2017) noted that only two of the authors, *Eszmélet* editor Mihály Koltai and long-term civil activist Éva Cserháti addressed other left actors as fellow thinkers or colleagues. Instead, most texts are characterized by a rhetorical gesture where speakers announce universal programs for left politics addressing a seemingly empty space. Reading the articles next to each other, this adds up to an impression of a collection of parallel monologues. Szalai adds that it is only Éva Tessza Udvarhelyi (2015), a scholar-activist with a practical experience reaching back to the early 2000s, who directly addressed the topic of practical steps.

The series itself is not representative of the whole spectrum of the new left in 2015–2016. *Kettős Mérce* opened the debate with the motivation to start a larger debate in the lack of existing common fora, and contributions were voluntary. Many important actors remained silent, while others who might not be considered as part of the new left by others participated. Also, the selection of participants reflected a situation where more explicit left standpoints which later became more influential in the new left were often formulated within relatively closed circles, while in public debates, the leftward shift of new segments of anti-government mobilizations happened through less explicit, more fluid stances, expressed by references to moral values or concrete harms done by government reforms. In this environment, participants of the "WTF left?" debate were not only actors who later became key players of new left politics, but also intellectuals who used to be part of dissident circles or integrated into NGO or intellectual infrastructures during the years of liberal hegemony, and were opening toward left stances in the context of anti-government protests. Their contributions made the characteristics of dissident politics—like the emphasis on intellectual-moral considerations as the basis of politics, or the lack of a requirement of larger social alliances and organizational structures for what they conceive of as democratic politics—more emphatic in the series.

However, as Szalai points out, in the series these characteristics are almost unanimously present. Authors typically speak about issues related to their own intellectual-professional work as key questions of new left politics and do not address relational and organizational aspects of political work. From this perspective, the series illustrates how new left political perspectives are projected from specific intellectual-professional positions, and how this characteristic connects back to the tradition of dissident politics. If in the years of the regime change, dissident politics shifted from more socially oriented statements to exclusively liberal programs, and actors who maintained socially oriented political work were marginalized, the newly forming consensus illustrated by the series shows a shift in the opposite direction, where socially sensitive actors of former liberal spheres join new left voices in announcing the need for a left political turn.

Another aspect of the close connection between actors' intellectual-professional perspectives and their definitions of new left imaginaries can be seen in the reformulations of their relation to their own professional and institutional backgrounds. In such gestures, the reorientation of actors' investments into their social environment in terms of professional careers and mobility, and the formulation of this reorientation in terms of a political shift, is expressed as an experience of breaking through the illusion sustained by former paradigms and institutions, and their substitution by a new type of intellectual-political work that allows more immediate social intervention. This kind of reinvention of intellectual and activist work is imagined to simultaneously provide a direct access to reality, and a reconstitution of the cognitive and political relevance of intellectual-professional work. In Poenaru's (2013) description of the *CriticAtac* group, this shift was portrayed as a turn from dominant aestheticizing models of intellectual habitus toward new left actors understanding themselves and their social context in terms of Marxist categories of class analysis. Elsewhere, the same turn is formulated in terms of similar conversions of the frameworks of other types of cultural and artistic work.

In contemporary art, the disillusionment with previous paradigms has been expressed as the emptying of art from meaning due to its social irrelevance: "if it is not connected to reality, art remains but a pile of self-referential metaphors" (h.arta, 2013). Elsewhere, the formation of a new left segment of artists' anti-government protests in Hungary was described in similar terms:

> This disillusionment, this distantiation from our whole profession also comes from a break that happened parallel to [the demonstrations against the Orbán government's transformation of the system of cultural institutions]. (...) Before, I used to have dreams like it would be a good thing to work in [the contemporary museum of arts]. Then this system suffered a significant twist. Suddenly I started to see problems that were always present, and I realized: it's over. (...) For several members of my generation, the twist that the cultural infrastructure suffered showed that the way the whole sphere used to be constituted made this twist possible. That this was not a stable reality, but only a bubble that was easy to burst. (T. A., 2016).

This type of shift induces a fundamental change in the way artists experience the quality and relevance of their own work: "There was a video that we exhibited several times. At that time, we really believed that it is a political work, but now I see it as completely irrelevant. And it's embarrassing"—a Hungarian artist explained his disillusionment with institutionalized art forms (Z. A., 2016).

While the disillusionment with the established paradigms of intellectual-professional work is linked to the experience of a larger sociopolitical crisis, the positive answers formulated in face of that disillusionment often propose new models of professional work, defined as ways to reactualize the relevance of intellectual professions through more immediate links to the broader social transformation. For instance, dramaturgist Michaela Michailov (2014), writing about the new Romanian documentarist political theater, argued that in documentarist projects which recount life stories in front of the same communities where they happened, actors "rediscover the real task of the actor" in the intimate relationship with the audience. Through this connection, she wrote, "theater descends into the sphere of the existential".

The blurb of a Hungarian edited volume on Lukács's work, published in 2017, described the significance of the volume in the following way:

> Without a fantasy in politics and social theory, action is impossible. When authors of *The infinity of the revolution* start from the reconstruction of the philosophy and political theory in Lukács's oeuvre, and turn towards the concreteness of contemporary political action, they engage in a journey through which politics, life itself, is reborn. (Böcskei, 2017)

The communique of a key piece of the new Romanian documentary political theater wave, *What we would be if we would know* (Ce-am fi dacă am şti?) described its aim as portraying "the resistance of the vulnerable, who make up for their repression through making their stories visible" (GAP, 2015). In the latter examples, descending into the "sphere of the existential", making up for the suffering of the oppressed, or the rebirth of politics refers to a process where intellectuals' own activity starts an essential social transformation. However, viewed from outside of these program's own perspective, the same process can rather be described as one where intellectual actors, motivated by their own worldview shift, turn toward their broader social environment, and experience a merge between their own stakes with what they think of as the key problems of their external environment. In other words, it is a situation where intellectuals experience and address a general social crisis as a projection of the reorientation of their own professional perspectives. Arguably, in these political expressions, the significance of theater "descending into the sphere of the existential", taking retribution for the suffering of the oppressed through telling their story, or the rebirth of politics through an edited volume is measured less in terms of these actions' actual social implications, but rather in terms of how significant this kind of foundational reorientation appears for intellectuals' own perspectives.

By pointing out that speakers tend to express historical change in terms of their own experience of political and professional reorientation I don't imply that there can be no relevant connections between intellectuals' perspectives and the broader crisis, or that new left actors' action programs formulated in terms of their own professional reorientation would necessarily be irrelevant to the creation of broader political alliances. What I imply is that there is an element of new left politics that links political imaginaries to middle class actors' intellectual-professional perspectives, and represents subjective experience and political programs characteristic to these perspectives as key turning points of the general historical process. The bias that follows from this connection does not only constitute a cognitive limitation in the analysis of broader social relations, but it can also be transposed as a real factor of political work, which contributes to the imposition of the dynamics of middle class politics over other social perspectives in the politicization of the crisis. Previous chapters described this effect as a regular element of long-term patterns of middle class politics in the region and pointed out its effects in maintaining middle class positions across changes between revolutionary and integration-based strategies. The examples above do not imply that all new left initiatives are equally and necessarily limited to this connection between left political imaginary and intellectual-professional perspectives; they were selected to illustrate the effect of this connection, and demonstrate its permanence despite variations across various political models and vocabularies.

I understand the traits outlined here as characteristic to a situation where middle class actors experience the crisis and formulate their political responses to it primarily through a reorganization of their own professional perspectives. In this stage, new political projects are defined by these reorganizing perspectives rather than external alliances and organizational structures to which they could connect to. Relations between various projects are constituted rather by communication and mutual references than collective modes of organization. Within these relations, political programs are voiced mostly on the symbolic level, in a parallel and often competitive manner. This stage where middle class political activity does not connect yet into concrete organizational structures and respective political frameworks of broader social alliances, provides a highly illustrative case to the significance of the experience of the self in middle class new left politics, but it does not in itself explain the further dynamics through which middle class politicization is embedded in the crisis process. The next section discusses the cumulative effect of activist work which, in later stages of development, links middle class left projects into various forms of broader collaborations.

BUILDING SUBSTANCE

In its initial phase of development, new left politics in both cases was defined by an intensive search for local political traditions and repertoires, transnational alliances, as well as local contextual knowledge and social outreach. External commentators often criticized this search as indicative of the irrelevance of new left stances: their lack of local social embeddedness and adequate knowledge of local contexts. However, the motivation for this search was rooted in a change of perspective that followed from contextually embedded shifts in new left actors' own positions and experiences. What I call the question of building the substance of new left politics refers to how, based on this political motivation, new left groups working within local sociopolitical constellations came to construct alignments between reactualizations of left traditions, new interpretations of local and international contexts, political repertoires crystallized in new movement institutions, connections to local social groups, and respective political alliances among local political infrastructures and international left circles. The building of substance, in this perspective, does not simply imply the question of correct or wrong politics (as in class consciousness vs. false consciousness), but rather refers empirically to a diverse and open-ended process where new left segments of new middle class mobilizations integrate into and become an actor within the process of the politicization of crisis.

The alterglobalist phase of incipient new left organization in the 2000s provides a picture of the immense challenge that building substance constitutes in contexts where left traditions and institutions were dismissed, and new left activists struggle to align local orientation and action with external alliances and frameworks. While alterglobalist initiatives produced some precedents that inspired post-2008 movements, and also exerted influence through the continuity of activist biographies, neither in Hungary or Romania did they manage to construe lasting alignments between local contexts, transnational frameworks, and political repertoires that could mediate between the two. In Hungary, the birth of the alterglobalist movement was marked by a split between a stream of postsocialist Marxist tradition represented by actors around Left Alternative, and new initiatives who emphasized the aspects of horizontality and civil networks in alterglobalist politics. After the split, the major branch of alterglobalist activism was built on a collaboration between green NGOs built on the tradition of the dissident green movement, and grassroots new left initiatives that followed the model of horizontal alterglobalism (Gagyi, 2011).

By the mid-2000s, these networks were mobilized by leading figures of the movement to form a party. Politics Can Be Different became relatively successful in electoral politics, yet the question of political alignment was not solved in its foundation. In terms of Hungarian political traditions and sensitivities, rural fractions favored conservative stances, while the party's initiators from the capital rather defined themselves as being on the left, combining an alignment with left anti-capitalist stances of the international alterglobalist movement with anti-nationalist, pro-democracy stances of Budapest intellectual circles. The party's initiators hoped that the idea of a twenty-first-century ecopolitics, which goes beyond twentieth-century traditions of left and right politics, will bridge between the two stances (D. G., 2016). However, in real political struggles, the duality of the political space enforced decisions along left and right cleavages, and in the end broke the party.

While Romanian altergobalism did not take the path of party politics, the same dominance of existing frameworks and political-infrastructural conditions over alterglobalist groups' own politics was present in this case, too. In Romania, too, the early phase of alterglobalist activism was characterized by conflicts between representatives of a more continuous tradition of left politics and a new generation of activists identifying with horizontalist alterglobalist frameworks. Here, the association of the former with socialist heritage was perceived as even more problematic by the latter, due to connections to the heritage of socialist dictatorship. For instance, the Romanian branch of Attac was funded by an association that bore Ceauşescu's epithet on ornans, "the genius of the Carpathians" in its name. The fact that Western actors managing the process of Eastern expansion of the European Social Forum paid little attention to such local details escalated internal conflicts. This was even more significant in a context where participation in Western networks provided a key resource and a stake of internal competition for local activists.

The other stream of Romanian alterglobalist activism was composed of cultural initiatives, a few transnational NGOs, and anarchist and subcultural groups who built local movement infrastructures in major cities. This network could not rely on existing broader local networks like that of green NGOs in Hungary; broader contacts with existing movements, unions, or supporting parties, characteristic to Western or Latin American branches of the movement, were similarly lacking. In 2008, Romanian groups attempted to organize a countersummit to the 20th NATO summit in Bucharest, according to the model of alterglobalist summit hopping. Working in close collaboration with Western partners, Romanian organizers worked according to Western models of organization, and the context of a very limited local base, and stronger repression potential of the state was obscured in the process. The violent repression of the protest action worked as a strong blow of discouragement for the movement, and many considered it as the end of alterglobalism locally (Gagyi, 2011).

If the alterglobalist movement's failure to build stronger alignments between movement frameworks, political institutions, and internal–external alliances could be seen as an end of the movement wave, in a longer term alterglobalist initiatives seem to constitute first attempts in a longer process of trial and error experiments that cumulated with time. After 2008, in both countries new initiatives to institutionalize left political stances started to multiply. In public communication, such institutions that came to play a significant part in the formation of new left scenes were *CriticAtac* and *Gazeta de Artă Politică* (GAP) in Romania, and *Kettős Mérce* (later: *Mérce*) and *Új Egyenlőség* in Hungary. Intellectual debates and new left research were grouped around institutions like the Tranzit House, a new left group at the Sociology Department in Cluj or the new left publishing house Tact in Romania, and the Working Group for Public Sociology "Helyzet", the journal *Fordulat* published by the College for Advanced Studies in Social Theory, and a new social theory working group of the Institute for Political History in Hungary.

New left activist groups working on specific subjects produced expertise, social contacts, and institutions that later served as inspiration and basic infrastructure for further initiatives. The housing activist groups The City is for All in Hungary (Misetics, 2017), and Common Front for Housing Rights (Popovici, 2020), both of which built their advocacy on creating horizontal alliances with people affected with extreme forms of housing poverty, are major examples to this trend. New left cultural initiatives multiplied in both countries, with Romania's new political theater movement becoming probably the most clearly canonized example (Michailov & Schwartz, 2017; Schwartz, 2019). Finally, initiatives that aimed to create physical spaces for new left debates and organizing, such as Claca and later Macaz in Bucharest, Acasa in Cluj, Gólya or Auróra in Budapest, also grew to have an effect in gathering and blending new left experiments.

In the first half of the 2010s, in both Hungary and Romania, several initiatives attempted to gather new left groups in a unitary political platform, with little success. These failures were often interpreted by new left actors as following from an internal problem of new left organizing. If Poenaru (2017) explained fragmentation by a specific Romanian historical class heritage of petty bourgeois reflexes mixed with a familism, in Hungary the same effect was often interpreted as a national characteristic of internal divisions. Comparing Hungarian and Romanian cases, my understanding is that instead of group-level or national characteristics, these similarities reflected a momentary state of the development of new left fields. I see this state a moment where initiatives powered by middle class political motivations have already started to build out various diagnoses, programs, and activist practices, yet these efforts were still framed as parallel, initial answers to the big question of left politics. What is the main issue in today's capitalist reality? How does the social and political situation in our country relate to global capitalism? What are the social relations where political action can most relevantly address the vectors of power? What kind of internal organization suits best the challenge of left politics in Eastern Europe today? Different initiatives comprised different paradigms of answering those questions through small-scale experiments, which were imagined and assessed according to their greater significance to the general question of left politics. This resulted in a situation where debates among various initiatives addressed the stakes of present initiatives on the level of more general strategies and consequences, projecting the significance of small-scale initiatives to larger scopes of historical political organization.

By the second half of the 2010s, several tendencies signified a surpassing of this moment in the development of new left scenes. Besides the further development of institutionalization and mutual contacts, these included the deepening of expertise, growing connections with other social groups based on sustained activist work, and practices of voluntary downshifting that substitute white collar livelihoods with livelihood based on material self-organization. By the deepening of expertise, I refer to a cumulation of contextual and strategic knowledge through years of activist work on certain topics. Instead of a state of generalized forward thinking over major questions of left politics, the deepening of expertise tied new left actors' thought to specificities of given contexts, including alliances that they built out within the conditions of those contexts. In the case of housing activism, for instance, this implied gaining a detailed knowledge on the economic, social, and political conditions of housing and housing injustice in the contexts respective groups worked in, creating and continuously adjusting strategies according to that knowledge, and binding activist groups' politics into alliances that could control and influence their direction. In intellectual research, the deepening of expertise implied the formation of paradigms, horizons of reference, local and international collaborations, bodies of empirical knowledge, as well as institutional and funding frameworks, which gave a concrete shape to the ways critical analysis connected empirical data to political questioning. Connections with other social groups—most prominently: unions, Roma, people affected by housing poverty, and international alliances—, were slowly expanding along the lines of activist work in various groups and paradigms. These connections also started to become a factor that bound groups' thinking and action into "really existing" forms of substantive politics that arose from the combination of activist work cumulating along with various paradigms and strategies, and the influence of external actors and conditions to which new left initiatives grew to bind themselves to. By downshifting and material self-organization, I refer to initiatives that respond to the crisis of middle class livelihoods and career expectations by performing a shift from white collar jobs to self-help economic initiatives that are conceived as examples of broader left political alternatives. The cooperatives Macaz in Bucharest and Gólya in Hungary, or the initiatives for housing cooperatives in both countries are examples of this trend.

Political Substance in Party Politics

In terms of political institutionalization, so far neither Hungarian nor Romanian new left scenes succeeded in organizing political parties that could sustain left agendas in the political sphere. Until today, the history of new left party politics provides a picture where new initiatives recurrently adapt to or break on the rocks of the political establishment. Politics Can Be Different split along the division line of Hungarian politics, Save Romania Union shifted to the right, and Fourth Republic and Demos did not pass the threshold of electoral participation. Smaller party initiatives, like the Workers' Party, Green Left and Left Party in Hungary, which associated themselves more closely with the state socialist heritage, or Mâna de lucru, a member of the Trotskyist Committee for Workers' International in Romania, maintained programs explicitly tied to orthodox left political traditions, but remained marginal in new left circles, and did not succeed in reaching out to broader constituencies.

If we define building political substance as creating linkages between political program, external conditions, organizational form, and social alliances, new left party initiatives can be described as characterized by the dominance of the external political sphere over relatively weak linkages that these parties establish between left political programs, real constituencies, and shared political imaginaries. The fact that these parties were organized from the base of the politically mobilized middle class made them capable of using resources like free voluntary work, middle class actors' interest and relative understanding of formal politics, and their capacity and willingness to express grievances in vocabularies of formal politics. However, the apparent shortcut that organizing on a politically mobilized middle class base provided also implied limitations. Ideologically, it bound new left party programs to middle class mobility claims. In terms of social outreach, the relatively fast political institutionalization that middle class capacities made possible also allowed the program and institutional structure of these parties to be closed down on the perspective of middle class bases, and be defined by their tendency to bind universal claims to ambitions for expert and decision-making positions to be gained through electoral campaigns. These conditions contributed to new left programs' integration into developmentalist paradigms that combined claims to fulfill transitional promises of catching up with European standards with a rearguard struggle defending existing welfare institutions similar to Western left programs.

In terms of the structural base of political imagination, the developmentalist tendency of new left party programs reflected a situation where programs were based on a combination of political frameworks reactualized from past or contemporary foreign traditions, and generic expert empirical knowledge on the local context. A conclusion at hand would be that in these cases, the combination of middle class political resources, abstract political frameworks and expertise, and a reliance on established political infrastructures did not lead to electoral success. From the perspective of buliding political substance for left politics, these stories also raise a further question: how the political energy generated in middle class trajectories within the present crisis can become part of political alliances that are able to produce paradigms that break with the priorities of systemic integration and address the imminent challenge of the climate crisis based on symbolic and organizational paradigms developed within alliances with other social groups.

New Expertise

By the end of the 2010s, in both Hungary and Romania, sustained work by several new left initiatives has produced forms of expertise and organizational practice that built out new, strengthening paradigms of political orientation, as well as movement structures and alliances that linked political programs into actual forms of organization. Media projects like *Mérce*, *GAP*, *Új Egyenlőség*, *A Szem*, the journal *Fordulat* or the publishing house Tact created professionalized forms of content production and diffusion, with organizational models developed according to different political programs of left publicity as well as the available conditions of resources and supporting alliances. In exchange, the actual structure of such publicity projects itself became a factor of the specific ways new left publicity developed.

Expertise accumulated by new left actors working in applied activist projects as well as academic research dedicated to left political questions became a significant source of orientation, and an unavoidable landmark within the broader field of left political thought. For instance, the political alliances, activist expertise, and organizing experience built up by housing activist groups like The City is for All or the Common Font for Housing Rights made housing a key issue of left politics, but instead of deducing it from a general political paradigm, it posed the question according to the specific knowledge and organizational paradigms produced by these groups. Academic research projects initiated by activist-academics, like the Working Group for Public Sociology "Helyzet", the social theory working group of the Institute for Political History, the urbanism thinktank Periphery Center, or collaborations around the Cluj Sociology Department or the Institute for Social Solidarity developed forms of knowledge-making and cumulated empirical knowledge along with various paradigms of engaged research. These forms of knowledge created in detailed paradigms of empirical diagnosis along with questions posed according to specific conceptions of left research, highlighting aspects that enabled certain types of political action. While their outreach is necessarily smaller than that of publication projects aimed at a larger audience, to the extent of their actual integration into new left cultures, frames of knowledge produced by research projects also work as tracklaying mechanisms, whose direction becomes a factor in the further development of new left perspectives.

By claiming that cumulating effects of organization-building and knowledge production build a substance around new left programs, binding them to specific, contextually embedded forms of organization, alliances, and knowledge paradigms, I do not mean that this kind of substantial rootedness would correspond to a necessary progression in the proper direction of left politics. The type of political substance various projects create, and thereby make into a factor in the formation of the broader new left field, are different, and produce varying surfaces for collaboration and conflict. For instance, The City is for All operates with a paradigm close to the US tradition of community organizing, and relies strongly on the idea of political rights based on citizenship. The group has been promoting this paradigm across its alliances and provided it as a model for the various new initiatives that it inspired. In contrast, the Common Front for Housing relies on a paradigm of intersectional solidarity, and criticizes forms of activism relying on citizenship as ones that bind protest practice to "the civilizational narratives of Western becoming" and "the aspirational paradigm of becoming a white middle-class West" (Popovici, 2020). Yet, unlike in the case of political programs voiced as universal theoretical projections, this difference between paradigms does not hinder the two initiatives from collaborations on practical issues in the same field.

Material Self-Organization

Another sphere where new left initiatives built new structures of left politics was that of various practices in voluntary downshifting and material self-organization. Probably the most influential cases of such initiatives were the movement community spaces Gólya in Budapest and Macaz in Bucharest. These were run as cooperatives, with activist founders coming from intellectual backgrounds sustaining themselves and the space through working physical jobs. In both cases, the fact that cooperative members created the space for political debate with the work of their own hands, and that their livelihoods were organized within a cooperative structure of economic democracy, served as a prefigurative political model for the new left publicity organizing around the two places. On the one hand, it can be argued that in this way, two relatively small cooperative businesses were elevated to a political significance that far exceeded their actual scope. On the other hand, the material base and the actual models of economic democracy they developed weren't only symbolic. In the case of Gólya, this potential was taken further by moving into a larger space in 2019 which gives home to 8 more organizations, and by starting new blocks of activities in face of pandemic lockdowns in 2020. Gólya's experience and activities serve as a base for Solidarity Economy Center, an initiative which organizes solidarity economy networks in fields like food, care work, cooperative housing, or green energy.

Another example of material self-organization is that of cooperative housing, initiatives for which developed in Hungary and Romania alike. The effects of community living as a political-cultural innovation of economically weak middle class actors have been described elsewhere as producing cheap resources for urban rejuvenation and the cultural and tourism industries (e.g. Arnoldus, 2004). The capacity of such initiatives to fulfill their social and ecological aims was found to be often limited by structural constraints (e.g. Hagbert et al., 2019). In other cases, however, like in that of Uruguay's FUCVAM, housing cooperatives played a strong role not only in providing accessible housing to workers, but also in building a base for political movements. Working together with unions and groups in housing poverty, Hungarian and Romanian initiatives make conscious efforts to build this capacity in their operation, and to apply professional skills in creating models that can scale accessible cooperative housing solutions beyond middle class circles.

In terms of constituency, the new left self-help models I know are dominantly based in circles with a middle class background. While this is not exclusionary, and initiatives do aim to broaden their inclusion of members from other social backgrounds, their founders' middle class background seems to me to be an essential condition of these initiatives, which defines the ways their practical characteristics bind with political potential. One of the effects of middle class backgrounds is the high capacity to embed initiatives for downshifting into symbolic levels of middle class professional and political networks. This kind of embedding can mobilize forms of symbolic, professional, but also material help that would not be possible without middle class backgrounds. It also delivers a symbolic validation of physical work that elevates it above regular blue-collar jobs, creating forms of recognition that compensate the element of downshifting. Here, it is the background of middle class crisis and mobilization that provides the political motivation and symbolic frameworks that attribute material downshifting a value beyond its concrete form.

This phenomenon is close to what research on precarious cultural workers has described as new wave of self-employed forms of micro-enterprises. From craft beer to vegan lifestyle or body therapy, these enterprises convert cultural capital into commercial forms whose product mostly consists of some added cultural, aesthetic, or moral value. Michael Scott (2017) described this form of "hipster economy" as a contemporary version of Bourdieu's new petite bourgeoisie, adapted to the context of economic austerity. Bourdieu (1984) claimed that with the halt of the postwar boom of middle class development, many who initially mobilized to reach higher positions through education found that their credentials have been inflated by mass access. Bourdieu described a resulting stratum of new petite bourgeoisie whose day jobs do not completely correspond to their high levels of education, yet who compensate for this experience of halted mobility by fashioning themselves as models of new aestheticized and culturally charged lifestyles. These models are associated with a general direction of social development—serving to simultaneously obscure the class position of their promoters, and sell their businesses like lifestyle coaching or interior design.

Scott adapts this description to the situation of new hipster micro-entrepreneurs, where a more emphatic danger of downward mobility meets a context of austerity, and the pressure toward self-employment is stronger. Here, too, as in Bourdieu's new petty bourgeoisie, "the cultural intermediary shifts from employee to self-employed" (Scott,

2017: 61), and applies her tendency to obscure her position and preach broader social programs to managing a micro-enterprise instead of broader institutionalized projects. However, due to its more dire economic conditions, Scott claims that the new hipster enterprise relies more heavily on nonmarket elements—the various networks of mutual help and professional-cultural exchange, which constitute the "'back-stage' modes of integration" that then make the "'frontstage' conversion of style into livelihoods" possible (Scott, 2017: 72). While this reliance on informal/reproductive resources in lack of stable formal incomes is a general tendency, and a constant characteristic of lower social positions, their combination with cultural entrepreneurship in the case of middle classes reached by new levels of the crisis has generated a new sensitivity toward community and cooperative initiatives, particularly in culture-related sectors (e.g. Patti & Polyák, 2017).

New left initiatives for downshifting associated with the values of economic democracy and worker ownership can be interpreted as specific versions of this trend, where the cultural/aesthetic value associated with new micro-enterprises also extends to a political narrative. However, besides symbolic references, the political nature of these initiatives also involves a transformation of the material forms of market integration. Instead of merely valorizing cultural messages on the market, new left solidarity economy initiatives involve a conscious construction of countermeasures that help resist the pressure of market logic and strengthen economic relations of solidarity. Like in other instances of cooperative or solidarity economy forms, this characteristic itself does not provide a full break with systemic relations, but it does create a situation of mixed economic logic which might provide more space for antisystemic organizing.

It is a question whether applying middle class political energies activated by the crisis to creating solidarity economy forms can provide a lasting break with the structural pull of middle class developmental preferences. In the context of the present crisis, and reinforced by the Covid-19 pandemic, solidarity economy solutions have been increasingly promoted as part of new left political agendas (e.g. Sacks, 2019). Arguably, just like the broader trend of new left politics, this tendency implies a channel for self-promotion of middle class expertise. Meanwhile, self-help projects can be limited to middle class segments and produce exclusionary models. Solidarity economy aspects of new left politics may end up as survival projects tied to administrative positions fulfilled in reforms stabilizing and adjusting capitalist extraction. Ozarow (2019) argued that the solidarity initiatives middle class actors engaged in during the 2001–2002 Argentinian protests remained relatively separated from those of workers and the poor, and ultimately did not hinder middle class actors from turning toward conservative political stances. Previous examples to such applications of middle class skills include instances where these efforts constituted temporary symptoms of a crisis of left politics, like in the case of New Left members' alternative professional projects in the 1970s (Ehrenreich & Ehrenreich, 1977). However, we also see examples where similar efforts linked into broad and successful social alliances, like the Landless People's Movement in Brazil, where the production and application of expertise are controlled by a larger movement based on solidarity economy circuits (Kane, 2000).

Acknowledging potential counterarguments, I see downshifting through material self-help projects as a significant factor when discussing the antisystemic capacity of new middle class mobilizations. This is because at least in the short term, it makes it possible to reinvest middle class ambitions into livelihoods that allow a detachment from white-collar jobs and turn entrepreneurial capacities toward political innovation directed at material structures of livelihood that resist the capitalist logic. This capacity seems to be especially relevant in a situation where the global crisis of capitalist expansion narrows down the potential of systemic solutions to middle class claims to increasingly exclusionary and authoritarian models, where the imminent threat of climate crisis places emancipative politics against the challenge of renouncing previous gains from systemic integration, and where the window for significant action against the climate crisis lays in the short term. In Eastern Europe, just like in other noncore regions, the long tradition and recent surge in widespread popular practices of informal solidarity and reproductive solutions is another condition that makes new left middle class actors' capacity for organization potentially relevant for creating broader antisystemic coalitions (Gagyi, 2019b). Grounding middle class activists' positions in material livelihoods tied to widening solidarity economy circuits integrated with labor struggles seems to provide a slight but realistic chance to avoid limiting new left politics to the recurrent patterns of middle class mobilizations described in this book.

CONCLUSION

This chapter looked at new left segments within post-2008 mobilizations in Hungary and Romania. In contrast to interpretations which treat the appearance of new left thought as an awakening to a class consciousness that transparently links structural analysis to actors' own political orientation, the chapter claimed that the connection between postsocialist experience and new left politics has been construed in different ways throughout an embedded process of politicization. It pointed out three aspects that illustrate how these connections reflect postsocialist and long-term conditions of present mobilizations, as well as how the cumulative effect of activist work becomes a factor within those conditions.

The first aspect the chapter pointed out regarded specificities of Hungarian and Romanian new left fields linked to different conditions of national political constellations. In Romania, post-2008 middle class demonstrations largely allied with liberal-technocratic elites and intellectual anticommunism rooted in late socialist repression. In this context, new left stances developed in an explicit opposition to dominant forms of anti-communist neoliberalism, as well as to conventional intellectual roles and frameworks integrated into the anti-communist neoliberal coalition. In Hungary, anti-austerity movements after 2010 appeared in the form of anti-government demonstrations, dominated by middle class segments formerly allied with socialist-liberal coalitions' politics. In face of the Orbán regime's explicit anti-poor stances, anti-government mobilizations became open to social messages. In this context, a closer alliance between liberal and new left segments of anti-government protests developed, favoring less conflictual formulations of left stances within oppositional coalitions.

The second aspect the chapter discussed regarded the way the experience of middle class crisis and reorientation appears in political expressions. Looking at connections between biographical experience and political convictions, the chapter claimed that while activists generally linked present political stances to personal experience of postsocialist transformation, this link cannot be interpreted as reflecting a direct, unilinear connection between experience and political consciousness, due to the large variation in the ways actors inferred political meaning to moments of life experience. Instead, I saw this connection as being constructed through a complex process of meaning-making embedded into local and transnational dialogues and activist work.

Regarding how middle class political reorientation informs the dynamics of new left fields, the chapter discussed the characteristics of a relatively early stage of field formation, where middle class actors already turn toward political investments, but their efforts are not yet embedded into real forms of organization that could bind new left political programs into concrete alliances and corresponding political paradigms. Such characteristics included intensive symbolic competition, the extension of symbolic chains of reference to small examples of actual fieldwork, and a rhetorical structure which translates actors' experience of their own political reorientation into images of a broader historical change.

The third aspect the chapter discussed was the development of political substance. By this I referred to the various ways new left initiatives built out alignments between personal experience, political-theoretical frameworks, local and transnational alliances, movement practice, and corresponding forms of organization. Throughout the 2010s, in both countries new left scenes moved from a stage of search and experimentation where left programs were announced in incipient, general forms, to a stage where various initiatives have established concrete forms of theoretical frameworks, empirical data, activist practice, organization, and social alliances, which constitute a substantial grounding of political work, enabling it in certain directions and limiting it in others. The chapter pointed out three main tendencies as illustrative to this shift: the accumulation of new expertise, linkages between political programs and social alliances built out by activist practice, and practices of voluntary downshifting through material self-organization. The chapter highlighted the latter as particularly significant, due to its potential to delink middle class politics from material needs tied to white-collar positions. In terms of party politics' relation to the issue of political substance, the chapter maintained that building on politicized middle class constituencies facilitated the formalization of party initiatives, but also tied them to existing political infrastructures and middle class expert ambitions, generally resulting in expressions of social claims through developmentalist programs.

References

Abăseacă, R. (2018). Between continuities and social change: Extra-parliamentary radical left in post-communist Romania. *East European Politics, 34*(1), 39–56.

Adăscăliţei, D., & Guga, Ş. (2017). Negotiating agency and structure: Trade union organizing strategies in a hostile environment. *Economic and Industrial Democracy, 38*(3), 473–494.

Arnoldus, M. (2004). A discovery of creative talent in the margins of urban development. *Built Environment (1978-), 30*, 204–212.

Azzellini, D. (2013). The communal state: Communal councils, communes, and workplace democracy. *NACLA Report on the Americas, 46*(2), 25–30.

B. P. (2015). Personal interview, Bucharest.

Bagi, Zs. (2015, October 27). Felszabadulni a polgárháborús képzelet alól. *Kettős Mérce*. https://merce.hu/2015/10/27/felszabadulni_a_polgarhaborus_kepz elet_alol_wtf_baloldal/. Accessed 3 February 2021.

Ban, C. (2015). Beyond Anticommunism: The fragility of class analysis in Romania. *East European Politics and Societies, 29*(3), 640–650.

Bartha, E. (2011). 'It can't make me happy that audi is prospering': Working-class nationalism in Hungary after 1989. In G. Halmai & D. Kalb (Eds.), *Headlines of nation, subtexts of class: Working-class populism and the return of the repressed in neoliberal Europe* (pp. 92–112). Berghahn.

Boatcă, M. (2006). Semiperipheries in the world-system: Reflecting Eastern European and Latin American experiences. *Journal of World-Systems Research, 12*(2), 321–346.

Bourdieu, P. (1984). *Distinction*. Harvard University Press.

Böcskei, B. (Ed.). (2017). *A forradalom végtelensége. Lukács György politika- és társadalomelmélete*. L'Harmattan.

C. G. (2016). Personal interview, Bucharest.

C. Z. (2015). Personal interview, Budapest.

C. P. (2016). Personal interview, Bucharest.

Cistelecan, A., & State, A. (Eds.). (2015). Plante exotice: Teoria şi practica marxiştilor români. Tact.

Collins, R. (2001). Social movements and the focus of emotional attention. In Goodwin, J. M. Jasper, & F. Polletta (Eds.), *Passionate politics: Emotions and social movements* (pp. 27–44). University of Chicago Press.

Cserháti, É. (2015, October 25). A baloldaliságom a mentálhigiéném alapja. *Kettős Mérce*. https://merce.hu/2015/10/21/a_baloldalisagom_a_mental higienem_alapja/. Accessed 3 February 2021.

Cucu, A. S. (2019). *Planning labour: Time and the foundations of industrial socialism in Romania*. Berghahn.

D. G. (2016). Personal interview, Budapest.

Demos. (2018). Program. http://demos.org.ro/wp-content/uploads/2018/05/DEMOS_PROGRAM%20FINAL_web.pdf. Accessed 3 February 2021.

Dialoguing Posts. (2019). *Dialoguing Posts network*. https://dialoguingposts. wordpress.com/idea/. Accessed 3 February 2021.

Diycraiova. (2014). *Salvaţi Roşia Montană fără fascişti*. https://diycraiova.nob logs.org/?page_id=624. Accessed 3 February 2021.

Éber, M. Á., Gagyi, Á., Gerőcs, T., Jelinek, C., & Pinkasz, A. (2014). 1989: Szempontok a rendszerváltás globális politikai gazdaságtanához. *Fordulat, 21*, 10–63.

Ehrenreich, B., & Ehrenreich, J. (1977). The new left. *Radical America, 2*(3), 7–22.

Eperjesi, Á. (2015, November 13). Civilek dicséretére. *Kettős Mérce.* https://merce.hu/2015/11/13/civilek_dicseretere/. Accessed 3 February 2021.

Ernu, V., Rogozanu, C., Şiulea, C., & Ţichindeleanu, O. (2008). *Iluzia anticomunismului: lecturi critice ale Raportului Tismăneanu.* Cartier.

F. A. (2016). Personal interview, Budapest.

Fisher, M. (2013, November 22). Exiting the vampire castle. *The North Star.*

Florea, I., & Popovici, V. (2020). Personal communication, January 30, 2021.

G. L. (2018). Personal interview, Budapest.

Gagyi, A. (2011). *A civil globalizáció univerzális eszméje a 'periférián': Globalizációkritikus csoportok Romániában és Magyarországon.* Doctoral dissertation, University of Pécs.

Gagyi, A. (2013). The shifting meaning of 'Autonomy' in the East European diffusion of the Alterglobalization movement. In L. Cox & C. F. Fominaya (Eds.), *Understanding European movements: New social movements, global justice struggles, anti-austerity protest* (pp. 143–157). Routledge.

Gagyi, A. (2019a, May 13). New politics in post-socialist Eastern Europe and the former USSR: A workshop for sharing knowledge and experience. *LeftEast.* http://www.criticatac.ro/lefteast/new-politics-conference-tbilisi/. Accessed 3 February 2021.

Gagyi, A. (2019b, April 10). Solidarity economy and the commons in Central and Eastern Europe. *Green European Journal.* https://www.greeneuropeanjournal.eu/solidarity-economy-and-the-commons-implications-for-central-and-eastern-europe/. Accessed 2 February 2021.

Gagyi, A., & Éber, M. Á. (2015). Class and social structure in Hungarian sociology. *East European Politics and Societies, 29*(3), 598–609.

Gagyi, A., & Gerőcs, T. (2019). The political economy of Hungary's new "Slave Law". LeftEast, January 1, 2018. http://www.criticatac.ro/lefteast/the-political-economy-of-hungarys-new-slave-law/. Accessed 4 February 2021.

GAP. (2015). *Ce-am fi dac-am şti. Feerie politică protestatară.* http://artapolitica.ro/2015/10/08/comunicat-ce-am-fi-dac-am-sti-feerie-politica-protestatara/. Accessed 4 February 2021.

GAP. (2017, March 25). Marş, B.O.R.! *Gazeta de Artă Politică.* http://artapolitica.ro/2017/03/25/mars-b-o-r/. Accessed 4 February 2021.

Gille, Z. (2010). Is there a global postsocialist condition? *Global Society, 24*(1), 9–30.

Ginelli, Z. (2018, July 19). Decolonization and semiperipheral postcoloniality in socialist Hungary: Hungarian experts in Nkrumah's Ghana. *LeftEast.*

https://www.criticatac.ro/lefteast/decolonization-and-semiperipheral-pos
tcoloniality-in-socialist-hungary-hungarian-experts-in-nkrumahs-ghana/.
Accessed 4 February 2021.

Ginelli, Z., & Mark, J. (2021). *Decolonizing the non-colonizers? Historicizing
Eastern Europe in global colonialism.* Amsterdam Centre for European Studies
online series nr. 12. https://aces.uva.nl/content/events/events/2021/02/
decolonising-europe-12.html?origin=MjeRQ4faQcWbraDTU9dsnw&cb&cb.
Accessed 17 February 2021.

Gotev, G. (2018, February 21). *Dan Barna: Save Romania Union similar
to Macron's En Marche.* Euroactiv. https://www.euractiv.com/section/ele
ctions/interview/dan-barna-save-romania-union-similar-to-macrons-en-mar
che/. Accessed 4 February 2021.

Gramsci, A. (1971). The intellectuals. In Q. Hoare & G. N. Smith (Eds.),
Selections from the prison notebooks (pp. 3–43). International Publishers.

Guga, Ş. (2015). *Sociologia istorică a lui Henri H. Stahl.* Tact.

Gyenge, Z. (2015, September 29). Öt ballaszt húzza mélybe a baloldalt.
Kettős Mérce. https://merce.hu/2015/09/29/ot_ballaszt_huzza_melybe_
a_baloldalt/. Accessed 4 February 2021.

h.arta (2013). Arta, politica, educatie si esec. *Gazeta de arta politica 3,* 37–64.

Hagbert, P., Larsen, H. G., Thörn, H., & Wasshede, C. (Eds.). (2019).
Contemporary co-housing in Europe: Towards sustainable cities? Routledge.

Halmai, G. (2011). (Dis)possessed by the spectre of socialism: Nationalist mobilization in 'transitional' Hungary. In G. Halmai & D. Kalb (Eds.), *Headlines
of nation, subtexts of class: Working-class populism and the return of the repressed
in neoliberal Europe* (pp. 113–141). Berghahn.

Horvat, S., & Štiks, I. (Eds.). (2015). *Welcome to the desert of post-socialism:
Radical politics after Yugoslavia.* Verso.

ISS. (2019). Institute for Social Solidarity: Call for abstracts and panels for the
international conference "Thirty years of capitalist transformations in Central
and Eastern Europe". https://socasis.ubbcluj.ro/iss2020-international-confer
ence/. Accessed 11 February 2021.

Kalb, D. (2009). Conversations with a Polish populist: Tracing hidden histories of globalization, class, and dispossession in postsocialism (and beyond).
American Ethnologist, 36(2), 207–223.

Kane, L. (2000). Popular education and the Landless People's Movement in
Brazil (MST). *Studies in the Education of Adults, 32*(1), 36–50.

Kósa, E. (2015, October 5). Baloldalinak lenni cool. *Kettős Mérce.* https://
merce.hu/2015/10/05/baloldalinak_lenni_cool_wtf_baloldal/. Accessed 11
February 2021.

Kováts, E. (2018). *Nőügyek 2018. Társadalmi problémák és megoldási stratégiák.*
Friedrich Ebert Stiftung.

Krasztev, P. (2015). Kez'csókolom, megjött a bal!. *Kettős Mérce,* November 16, 2016. https://merce.hu/2015/11/16/kez_csokolom_megjott_a_bal_wtf_baloldal/. Accessed 11 February 2021.

Michailov, M. (2014, January 6). Teatrul spectatorului indecent. *Gazeta de artă politică.* https://artapolitica.ro/2014/01/06/teatrul-spectatorului-ind ecent/. Accessed 11 February 2021.

Michailov, M., & Schwartz, D. (2017). *Teatru politic.* Tact.

Misetics, B. (2017). Homelessness, citizenship and need interpretation: reflections on organizing with homeless people in Hungary. *Interface: A Journal on Social Movements, 9*(1), 389–423.

N+1. (2014). *What was the hipster?: A sociological investigation.* HarperCollins e-Books.

Nagle, A. (2017). *Kill all normies: Online culture wars from 4chan and Tumblr to Trump and the alt-right.* John Hunt Publishing.

Nemes, C. (2015, August 23). A dermedtség és reménytelenség ellenszere. *Kettős Mérce.* https://kettosmerce.blog.hu/2015/08/23/a_dermedtseg_es_remeny telenseg_ellenszere_wtf_baloldal. Accessed 11 February 2021.

Ozarow, D. (2019). *The mobilization and demobilization of middle-class revolt: Comparative insights from Argentina.* Routledge.

Pascariu, K. (2016). Teatru pentru cei exclusi. http://viitorulromaniei.ro/katia-pascariu-teatru-pentru-cei-exclusi/. Accessed 25 May 2021.

Patti, D., & Polyák, L. (2017). *Funding the cooperative city: Community finance and the economy of civic spaces.* Cooperative City Books.

Petrovici, N. (2018). *Zona urbana. O economie politica a socialismului romanesc.* Tact.

Poenaru, F. (2013). *Contesting illusions: History and intellectual class struggle in post-communist Romania.* PhD dissertation, Central European University.

Poenaru, F. (2017). *Locuri Comune: clasă, anticomunism, stânga.* Tact.

Pogátsa, Z. (2015, October 19). Az északi modell esélyei Magyarországon. *Kettős Mérce.* https://merce.hu/2015/10/19/az_eszaki_modell_eselyei_m agyarorszagon_wtf_baloldal/. Accessed 11 February 2021.

Popovici, V. (2020). Residences, restitutions and resistance: A radical housing movement's understanding of post-socialist property redistribution. *City.* https://doi.org/10.1080/13604813.2020.1739913.

Popovici, V., & Pop, O. (2016, February 11). From over here, in the periphery: A decolonial method for Romanian cultural and political discourses. *LeftEast.* http://www.criticatac.ro/lefteast/from-over-here-in-the-periphery-a-decolonial-method-for-romania/. Accessed 11 February 2021.

Popovici, V., & Schwartz, D. (2015, February 27). Națiune, subalternitate și dorința de Europa. O discuție despre identitate națională și nevoia apartenenței europene. *Gazeta de Artă Politică.* http://artapolitica.ro/2015/02/27/natiune-subalternitate-si-dorinta-de-europa-o-discutie-despre-identitate-nationala-si-nevoia-apartenentei-europene/. Accessed 11 February 2021.

R. G. (2008). Personal interview, Budapest.

Ritók, N. (2015, October 29). Az emberi értékeket szeretném kihangosítani. *Kettős Mérce*. https://merce.hu/2015/10/29/az_emberi_ertekeket_sze retnem_kihangositani_wtf_baloldal/. Accessed 2 February 2021.

Rogozanu, C. (2006). *Agresiuni, digresiuni*. Polirom.

Sacks, J. (2019). Rethinking surplus-value: Recentring struggle at the sphere of reproduction. *Interface: A Journal on Social Movements, 11*(1), 147–177.

Schein, G. (2015, December 27). Két évvel később. *Kettős Mérce*. https://merce. hu/2015/12/27/ket_evvel_kesobb_407/. Accessed 2 February 2021.

Scheiring, G. (2020). *The retreat of liberal democracy: Authoritarian capitalism and the accumulative state in Hungary*. Springer Nature.

Schwartz, D. (2019). Genealogy of political theatre in post-socialism. From the anti-"system" nihilism to the anti-capitalist left. *Studia Universitatis Babes-Bolyai Sociologia, 64*(2), 13–40.

Scott, M. (2017). 'Hipster capitalism'in the age of austerity? Polanyi meets Bourdieu's new petite bourgeoisie. *Cultural Sociology, 11*(1), 60–76.

Selyem, Z. (2015, September 16). Az állatkertbe zárt oroszlán. *Kettős Mérce*. https://merce.hu/2015/09/16/az_allatkertbe_zart_oroszlan_wtf_ baloldal/. Accessed 11 February 2021.

Simionca, A. (2012). Neoliberal managerialism, anti-communist dogma and the critical employee in contemporary Romania. *Studia Sociologia, 57*(1), 125–149.

Sipos, B. (2016, April 24). A Fidesszel feleselés helyett újra kell tanulnunk gondolkodni a bajainkról. *Kettős Mérce*. https://merce.hu/2016/04/24/ a_fidesszel_feleseles_helyett_ujra_kell_tanulnunk_gondolkodni_bajainkrol/. Accessed 11 February 2021.

Szalai, E. (2017, February 5). A WTF baloldal – egy év után. *Kettős Mérce*. https://merce.hu/2017/02/05/szalai_erzsebet_a_wtf_baloldal_egy_ ev_utan/. Accessed 3 February 2021.

Szombati, K. (2018). *The revolt of the provinces: Anti-gypsyism and right-wing politics in Hungary* (Vol. 23). Berghahn Books.

T. A. (2016). Personal interview, Budapest.

Țichindeleanu, O. (2018). Does Eastern Europe have the power to de-link itself from the mechanisms of dependence? *Baricada*, August 5, 2021. https://en. baricada.org/ovidiu-Țichindeleanu-interview/. Accessed 3 February 2021.

Udvarhelyi, É. T. (2015, August 21). Homokszemről homokszemre. Egy optimista baloldali jövőképe. *Kettős Mérce*. https://kettosmerce.blog.hu/ 2015/08/21/_homokszemrol_homokszemre_egy_optimista_baloldali_jov okepe. Accessed 3 February 2021.

Unkovski-Korica, V. (2016, August 2). Where next after Syriza: A view from the left in South-Eastern Europe. *Counterfire*. http://www.counterfire.org/articles/analysis/18164-where-next-after-syriza-a-view-from-the-left-in-south-eastern-europe. Accessed 3 February 2021.

Vincze, E., Petrovici, N., Raț, C., & Picker, G. (Eds.). (2018). *Racialized Labour in Romania: Spaces of marginality at the periphery of global capitalism*. Springer.

Walker, Sh. (2018). We won't keep quiet again: The women taking on Viktor Orbán. https://www.theguardian.com/world/2018/dec/21/hungary-female-politicians-viktor-orban?fbclid=IwAR1CLceY50TRW4b3ejA1yzlZO eUsM-_SD708a9mzb_KNUsxYSr-y98h-NwM. Accessed 24 May 2021.

Z. A. (2016). Personal interview, Budapest.

CONCLUSION

This book addressed interlinkages between two problematics: an East European perspective on the historical significance of post-2008 movements, and the question of middle class politics from a left perspective. A dominant approach in interpreting post-2008 movements, which the book summarized as the narrative of "the crisis of democratic capitalism", has connected post-2008 mobilizations and middle class politics in the following way. The expansion of welfare and democracy which characterized the post-WWII period was rolled back by neoliberal reforms and post-2008 crisis measures. This brought a wave of movements that reacted simultaneously to economic injustice and the emptying out of democratic representation. Anti-austerity pro-democracy movements brought a new promise of emancipative politics, which crystallized in various forms of political institutionalization during the 2010s, and today represent the progressive alternative to the rise of right-wing populism in the face of the crisis. In this narrative, the strong visibility of middle class actors in these mobilizations appears as a proof that the promises of post-1945 development have recently failed; but it is also pictured as a new promise for a politics that can combine expanding welfare with democracy. This book argued that this narrative misunderstands the situation of Western movements, and obscures the conditions of non-Western ones, because it invisibilizes the global conditions of Western "democratic capitalism". It proposed to add to the debate a comparative analysis of

A. Gagyi, *The Political Economy of Middle Class Politics and the Global Crisis in Eastern Europe*, International Political Economy Series, https://doi.org/10.1007/978-3-030-76943-7

two East European cases, in an approach that considers post-2008 movements, and middle class participation in them, from the perspective of capitalist crisis as a global process.

Chapter 1 criticized social movement studies' understanding of social movements as one that abstracts the question of short-term movement formation from its broader context, and universalizes characteristics of paradigmatic postwar Western examples across space and time. In face of post-2008 mobilizations, economic conditions, global relations, and movement knowledges outside normative paradigms were increasingly brought into the horizon of social movement studies. However, the chapter argues that in the narrative of the "crisis of democratic capitalism", biases ingrained in dominant postwar paradigms of understanding movements have been reactualized. If pre-2008 paradigms presupposed the expansion of welfare and democracy in line with the modernizationist ideology of postwar Western capitalism, the "crisis of democratic capitalism" announces the failure of that program—and, with the same move, reenacts it as the base concept of new emancipative programs.

Looking at Eastern Europe, the limitations of this new type of universalized narrative become clearly visible. While the region also saw a series of mobilizations after 2008, these do not fit into a story where postwar welfare democracy would have been destroyed by recent neoliberal reforms. From its birth, the promise of postsocialist democratization was tied to neoliberal measures as harsh as those that mobilized masses in Western or Southern Europe after 2008. The idea of civil society, a dominant paradigm of understanding social movements in the region, was shaped by underlying contradictions between democratization and economic subordination. Academic and movement debates have addressed these contradictions in critiques of the paradigm of civil society since the 1990s. Yet after 2008, the new wave of mobilizations was reinscribed into the normative civil society paradigm, presenting local movements as a reactualization of the project of democratic transition. Movements' claims about the failure of the postsocialist transition project went hand in hand with new claims for its fulfillment. In a double loop of historical projections, this reactualization of the transition project was linked to Western movements' claims on "the crisis of democratic capitalism"—with the difference that while Western movements could refer to former welfare levels, East Europeans saw that "past" as a desirable future.

In order to be able to interpret how East European movements relate to other instances of global mobilizations, the chapter proposed an approach inspired by the world-systems tradition, which sees movements as embedded within integrated but differentiated processes of global capitalist development. For the interpretation of post-2008 movements, the main point emphasized from this perspective was that contrary to the claims of modernization ideology, welfare democracy did not constitute a model that could be generalized over other regions with time. Instead, it was a core characteristic of the boom phase of the postwar hegemonic cycle, which was conditioned by global hierarchies of extraction, and which necessarily built up its own crisis after the 1970s. The shift from welfare to neoliberal systems in the West was not only a shift on the political level, but was based in the structural conditions established by the same hegemonic cycle reaching its crisis phase, and was preceded and complemented by global neoliberalism that used semi-peripheral and peripheral crises to compensate for the crisis of core capital. Reclaiming this model of capitalist growth, and trying to increase workers' share of income based on the expansion of capital's profitability cannot provide a base for contemporary emancipative politics.

Chapter 2 turned to the issue of middle class mobilizations. In East European contexts, it conceptualized middle class politics as an element of recurrent developmentalist coalitions which promise upward mobility within global capitalist hierarchies, yet in effect contribute to maintaining uneven development. As developmentalist coalitions struggle for better integration conditions for limited local groups, they can only create short-lived local hegemonies of specific integration models, threatened by both the internal exhaustion of accumulation conditions and changes in its external circumstances. Within this volatile context of political alliances, described in the book by Andrew C. Janos's term "politics of backwardness", middle classes are not the strongest actor, but constitute a politically significant element. In order to achieve Western middle class standards beyond the potential of local economies, middle class actors regularly mobilize to secure favorable treatment by the state. While their success to realize middle class lifestyles is broadly represented as a sign of social progress, in fact the maintenance of such lifestyles presupposes disproportionate redistribution toward middle strata, and corresponding forms of undemocratic politics.

The chapter differentiated two tendencies in the politics of maintaining and expanding middle class status takes different forms, across boom

and bust phases of developmental dynamics: revolutionary mobilizations during crisis, and systemic integration during conjuncture periods.
In times of crisis, disillusioned middle classes tend to turn away from
previous developmentalist coalitions, but in following conjure periods,
they recapture positions by joining new ones. In this sense, the intense
political conflicts and ideological turnabouts in middle class politics in the
region reflect a long-term strategy to stabilize class position. In what Iván
Szelényi and his colleagues called the ideological "cycles" of middle class
politics in Eastern Europe, the current turn toward new left perspectives
in some segments of contemporary middle class mobilizations can be seen
as part of a new revolutionary phase. But what does this tell us about the
emancipative potential of new left stances in a global perspective, and how
does it relate to other global cases?

The chapter claimed that in order to conceive the relationship between
middle class politics in different global positions, the postwar expansion
of middle class lifestyles in Western countries, as the paradigmatic and
normative referent of middle class development (and associated democratization), needs to be revised. The idea of a continuous expansion of
the middle class, which would annihilate class tensions in the West and
globally, constituted an important element of postwar global hegemony.
Yet even in Western contexts, it has been challenged by tensions resulting
from the actual limitations of middle class expansion. Throughout the
postwar cycle, in Western contexts, too, research and political thought
pointed out the volatility of middle class politics, as well as its segmenta-
tion and changes of alliances according to changing systemic contexts of
mobility potential. In these debates, middle classness as a project of favorable systemic integration has been characterised as a source of renewing
tensions and politicization, changing together with the structural conditions of middle class development. In terms of newly rising global middle
classes, similar limitations, tensions, and political volatility resulting from
the project nature of middle classness have been described by newer literature. In debates about post-2008 mobilizations, these dynamics have been
pointed out as significant factor in the politicization of the present crisis.
Therefore, instead of an organic global coming together of critical and
democratic middle class voices who lament the loss of postwar promises of
development, the chapter proposed to look at relations between new
middle class movements in different locations in terms of interlinkages
between instances of middle class politicization that articulate the same

crisis from the standpoint of middle class ambitions voiced from different and often contradictory interest positions on a systemic level.

Regarding the emancipatory potential of new mobilizations, the book asked how dynamics of middle class politics play into the articulation of systemic tensions within the crisis. Left traditions have long emphasized the volatility of middle class politics, often deeming it untrustworthy from labor's perspective. Looking into the sociological conditions of postwar middle class politics, these traditions have emphasized middle class politics' organic ties to the maintenance of salaried positions, which they saw as a major structural barrier in terms of antisystemic politics. They claimed that coming from positions that rest on the extraction and monopolization of social functions of knowledge-making and organizing, even emancipative segments of middle class politics tend to be limited to the aim of maintaining and expanding those positions. Due to the same positions' dependence on the valorization of knowledge monopolies, this interest remains hidden in the ideological forms of middle class politics, which instead are expressed in the name of others.

Against this political volatility and ideological blindness in middle class politics, left traditions have recurrently proposed that middle class left actors maintain an antisystemic direction by getting rid of middle class determinations—through ideological discipline, worker alliances, or by applying their analytical capacities to destroy middle class illusions. The book argued that calls that expect middle class politics to take an antisystemic direction through a shift of consciousness overestimate the extent to which projections of universal aims can be split from the underlying conditions of knowledge-based positions. Such claims of knowledge-based emancipative politics devoid of selfish interest have been at the core of the long-term politics of middle class self-preservation. Instead of attributing an exceptional potential to the element of consciousness, the book emphasized the significance of organizational links that tie middle class political ambitions into broader coalitions, and the practical possibilities to link structural characteristics of middle class politics into antisystemic coalitions. From this perspective, the question whether middle class politics can exit the range of crisis politics that answers fears of proletarization by a promise to stabilize white-collar positions, appeared as a key issue.

Chapter 3 presented a comparative study of crisis processes and middle class politics in Hungary and Romania, applying the analytical insights presented in the previous chapters. The chapter traced the connection between global crisis processes, local integration regimes, and their contestations, from the transformations of the two state socialist systems engendered by the global crisis of the 1970s, through the phases of regime change and postsocialist integration, to the aftermath of the 2008 crisis. During this time, Hungary's and Romania's politics differed significantly, with their successive regimes often promoting seemingly contradictory development paths. In Hungary, alliances favoring liberalization were strengthened after 1973, and dominated the process of socialist crisis, transformation, and postsocialist integration. The Romanian regime reacted to the pressures of the 1970s crisis with a strengthening of orthodox industrialization policies, and applied extreme austerity to avoid the influence of international lending organizations. Here, after 1989, the priority of protectionism was maintained by ex-socialist elites, and liberal-technocratic elites only strengthened in the 2000s, through international alliances provided by EU integration. In contrast, in Hungary, the 2000s brought an exhaustion of the liberal development model, and cumulating anti-neoliberal sentiments expressed in vocabularies promoted by right-wing elites. The aftermath of 2008 brought the fortification of neoliberal coalitions in Romania, and a nationalist regime in Hungary, which combined the support of domestic capital with tactical coalitions with foreign capital. These circumstances set different conditions for late socialist and post-2008 movements.

While they addressed issues that followed from similar systemic factors like public debt and hard currency pressure, the largest late socialist mobilizations took different forms in the two cases. Relying on a larger base of intellectuals and experts, strengthened through liberal reforms, Hungary's environmental movement promoted a broader political critique of socialism, which came to be integrated later into the narrative of the regime change. Romania's labor strikes formulated their claims in strategic forms rooted in workers' material and political position within the Ceauşescu regime. Due to the repression of intellectuals and the regime's enmity to Western lenders, these movements could not rely on intellectual alliances or Western support that would integrate their struggles in later narratives of transition. Instead, ex-socialist elites' use of miners to attack oppositional demonstrators in 1990 consolidated anti-communist intellectuals' idea of a political coalition between workers and communists which hinders democratic development.

Throughout the second half of the 2000s, in Romania the liberal-technocratic elite bloc that gained power in the context of EU integration formed an alliance with intellectual anti-communism. In the 2010s, demonstrations that expressed frustrations with postsocialist politics came to be aligned with liberals' struggle against socialists' political power, combining a neoliberal program with anti-poor stances—and, in a smaller degree, contributed to the political development of a new strain of the extreme right. In contrast, in Hungary, protest waves after 2010 criticized Orbán's regime mainly from the perspective of middle class segments formerly allied with the socialist-liberal coalition, and combined liberal traditions of the political "left" with an increasing social sensitivity that contrasted with the regime's anti-poor measures. In both cases, the chapter showed that protests combined expressions of middle class grievances with developmental claims voiced in the normative vocabulary of earlier transitional discourses. This analysis did not imply that middle class protests in Hungary and Romania are outliers compared to a general paradigm of anti-austerity pro-democracy movements after 2008. Instead, it aimed to show that during the long crisis of the postwar global capitalist cycle, the same elements of neoliberalization, democracy and middle class politics were present, but fit into constellations different from those presupposed by either the "crisis of democratic capitalism" narrative, or its versions of a transitional delay applied to contemporary East European movements.

The last chapter discussed new left politics within new middle class mobilizations, with regard to the relation between new left politics and middle class positions. It looked at new left stances as a new moment of middle class political thought in the region, which articulates long-term patterns of middle class politics in various forms of critique specific to local contexts of the present crisis. The chapter highlighted three aspects of how various forms of new left politics relate to their contextual conditions: connections with meso-level characteristics of local integration regimes, the relationship between new left politics and middle class activists' own experience, and the construction of political substance through alignments between various types of political theory, organizational practice, and the social alliances that various groups develop throughout their work.

In terms of the structural conditions of the integration of middle class politics into the broader politicization of the present crisis, the book's main conclusion emphasized the material basis of middle class positions as especially significant for the relatively short term, but high stake period of climate politics. The book maintained that the trend toward downshifting through material self-help projects may constitute a significant development in this respect, as it allows middle class politicization to delink from the need to reproduce white-collar positions, and instead invest capacities built by previous structural integration into broadening alternative circuits of reproduction. Building such circuits is only one element in the struggle for systemic transformation. Yet in terms of middle class politics, this reorientation of investment on the level of material positions seems to be a necessary condition of a transformation that requires the abandonment of systemic gains made possible by capitalist extraction.

On the whole, the book's argument developed on how middle class politics works as an element of systemic reorganizations. Speaking to recent debates on different global instances of middle class protest, it approached the question of global comparison in terms of how local middle class politics are embedded in local reconfigurations of the global crisis. It maintained that communication between global instances of protest represents less of a global coming together of anti-austerity pro-democracy agendas, but rather mutual references across struggles fought from different and often contradictory interest positions within the global crisis. The book argued that the "crisis of democratic capitalism" narrative, as a paradigm of interpreting post-2008 protests, reactualizes an ideological bias inherent in postwar Western ideologies of global progress. As it denies the systemic contradictions of middle class development, it consequently obscures that in the present state of crisis, progressive aims expressed in terms of middle class expansion necessarily propel alliances that create security for limited circles by excluding and exploiting others. In the global negative-sum environment of capitalist climate adaptation, further frustrations of such projects will probably sustain the waves of middle class discontent. Regarding whether these can become a resource for antisystemic struggle, the book emphasized the significance of the link between middle class politicization and the systemic promise of middle class development. It argued that without severing this link in a practical, and not merely ideological way, middle class politics remains an unlikely ally of an emancipative response to the climate crisis.

INDEX

A

accumulation, cycles of, 30, 38, 39, 46, 57, 61, 63

activism, viii, 23, 160, 225, 234, 235, 241, 242, 245, 262, 263, 265, 268

Alliance for the Union of Romanians (AUR), 177, 178, 234

Alliance of Free Democrats, 185–187, 192

alterglobalization movement, 11, 15, 52, 54, 64

anticommunism, 188, 233, 236, 273, 287

austerity, 8, 11, 12, 16, 18, 24, 25, 51, 55, 135, 146, 153, 158, 159, 164, 173, 174, 178, 180, 189–191, 198, 206, 208, 270, 286

B

backwardness, politics of, 81, 82, 88, 93, 99, 124, 283

beautiful youngsters/people, 182, 183

biography, activists, 229, 262

bureaucratic power, 14, 119, 122, 160

C

capitalism, 5, 8–12, 20, 25, 28–32, 34, 42, 43, 45, 46, 53, 55, 56, 64, 89, 90, 100, 115–117, 138, 143, 147, 231, 238, 256, 282

catching-up, 18, 48, 190

Ceaușescu, Nicolae, 155–159, 163–167, 206, 236, 263, 286

Central European University (CEU), 198, 203, 239

civil society, 13–24, 27, 52, 63, 89, 198, 200, 201, 242, 282

class suicide, 104, 107

Cold War, 14–16, 26, 138, 143, 150, 202

Colectiv, 175, 176, 182, 183

commons, commoning, 53, 111

communism, 45, 169, 170, 173, 207, 233, 236, 240

CPSIA information can be obtained
at www.ICGtesting.com
Printed in the USA
LVHW010930170821
695490LV00003B/510